NAVIGATING
WORLDS

NAVIGATING WORLDS

COLLECTED ESSAYS
VOL. II
(2006-2020)

BEZALEL NAOR

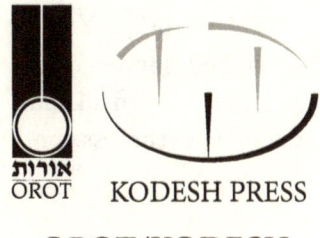

OROT/KODESH

2021/5781

NAVIGATING WORLDS
Collected Essays
(2006-2020)

© Bezalel Naor 2021
978-1-947857-59-9

Hardcover edition
Volume 2

All rights reserved.
Except for brief quotations in printed reviews,
no part of this publication may be reproduced,
stored in a retrieval system, or transmitted in any form or by any means
(printed, written, photocopied, visual electronic, audio, or otherwise)
without the prior permission of the publisher.

For permission requests, write to the Publisher:
Kodesh Press LLC
New York, NY
www.kodeshpress.com
kodeshpress@gmail.com
sales@kodeshpress.com

Layout, design, and typesetting by
Dynagrafik Design Studio, Monsey, NY
Printed in the United States of America

TABLE OF CONTENTS

VII. THE THOUGHT OF RAV KOOK

Reflections on *Yom ha-'Atsma'ut*	299
Searching for the Lost Dimensions of Judaism	307
The Scribal Art of Rabbi Meir: A Study in Metanomianism	311
The Hasidism of Rav Kook	327
The Universalism of Rav Kook	341
Rav Kook's Space Odyssey	351
Rav Kook on Teaching Torah to Girls	365
Rav Kook and Rav Harlap— Truth and the Pursuit of Truth	377
Zion and Jerusalem: The Secular and the Sacred	393
Rav Kook's Shattered Vessels and Their Repair	411

VIII. RAV KOOK: HISTORICAL STUDIES

Rav Kook's Missing Student	431
When Rav Kook Was the Zealot (*Kana'i*) and His Opponent the Advocate (*Melits Yosher*)	445

IX. MESSIAH

The Two Faces of Messianism	463
"My Beloved is Like a Gazelle" (*Domeh Dodi li-Tsevi*): The Esthetic Messiah	485
The Philosopher King and the Poet Messiah: Hellenic and Hebrew Republics Compared	503
Messiah's Donkey of a Thousand Colors	513

X: Book Reviews

The Maggid of Kozhnits,
　　Rabbi Israel ben Shabtai Hopstein. *'Avodat Yisrael*　　521

The Jackals and the Lion:
　　Animal Fables of Kafka and Rav Kook　　531

Bridging the Kabbalistic Gap:
　　Nefesh HaTzimtzum by Avinoam Fraenkel　　537

Maimonides Between Philosophy and Halakhah
Rabbi Joseph B. Soloveitchik's Lectures
on the Guide of the Perplexed
　　Edited with an Introduction by Lawrence J. Kaplan　　551

Hallel from Heaven and *Hallel* from Hell:
　　The Post-Holocaust Responses of Paul Celan,
　　Aharon Appelfeld and Meshulam Rath　　561

When Elijah's Mantle Fell:
　　The Judaism of Leonard Cohen　　567

The Religious-Zionist Manifesto
　　of Rabbi Yehudah Leib Don Yahya　　573

Of Priests and Prophets: The Way of Knowing
　　and the Way of Not Knowing
　　Shnayor Z. Burton. *Mishnat Ya'akov*　　591

The Two Luminaries: Rabbi Nahman of Breslov
　　and Rav Kook
　　Moshe Nahmani. *Shnei ha-Me'orot*　　599

Etatism and Halakhah: Family Feud and Political Theory
　　Rabbi Yitzhak Goldstoff. *Mikdash ha-Kodesh*　　609

Rav Yosef Dov Soloveitchik on the *Seder ha-'Avodah*
　　of *Yom ha-Kippurim:* A Synopsis of the Rav's
　　Yiddish *Teshuvah Derashah* 5736 (1975)　　615

A King's Palace
　　Aharon Hayyim Zimmerman. *Agra la-Yesharim*　　625

Bibliography　　631

VII

THE THOUGHT OF RAV KOOK

Reflections on *Yom ha-'Atsma'ut*
Based on the Works of Rav Kook
5 Iyyar, 5773

The fifth of Iyyar commemorates the establishment of the State of Israel in 1948. When it came to the State of Israel, the Orthodox community adopted three different stances. At one extreme was Rabbi Abraham Isaac Hakohen Kook who viewed the rebirth of Israel in its ancestral land as an *event* of major, even Messianic proportions.[1] At the opposite extreme was Rabbi Joel Teitelbaum, the Rebbe of Satu Mare, who saw in the Zionist entity an *anti-event*, once again of mythic proportions, evoking images of the anti-Messiah, Shabbetai Tsevi.[2] The middle ground was the position adopted by Rabbi Abraham Isaiah Karelitz (*"Hazon Ish"*) and Rabbi Isaac Ze'ev Halevi Soloveitchik ("Brisker Rav"), which was basically to treat the establishment of the State as a *non-event*.[3]

Let us leave aside for the moment the rhetoric of redemption and think in less romantic, more pragmatic terms of *transvaluation*. What is undeniable by all camps is that the State represents a transvaluation, an introduction of new values to Jewish life. What are these values, what is their import, and how are they to be contextualized within the ongoing history of the Jewish People?

It is to Rav Kook's credit that in several important essays he undertook the herculean task of identifying these elements that surfaced with twentieth-century Zionism and grappled with their larger significance. To the table he brought prodigious erudition in both the exoteric and esoteric traditions of Judaism, coupled with a talent for engaging in historiosophy.[4] Three major essays were devoted to this task:

- *The Lamentation in Jerusalem* (1904)
- *The Way of Renascence* (1906)
- *To the Process of Ideas in Israel* (1912)[5]

Different elements and emphases come to the fore in each essay.

In *The Lamentation in Jerusalem*, Rav Kook examines the rabbinic and kabbalistic notion that there are two Messiahs, Messiah Son of Joseph and Messiah Son of David. In Rav Kook's analysis, Messiah Son of Joseph symbolizes the physical as well as universal aspect of the Jewish People, while Messiah Son of David represents the spiritual as well as particularist or Torahitic aspect of the nation. Rav Kook boldly situated political Zionism, brainchild of Herzl, within the tradition of Messiah Son of Joseph.[6] Recalling the prophecy of Ezekiel 37, Rav Kook appealed for a unity of the "Tree of Joseph" and the "Tree of Judah," expressing at the same time the fervent hope that the secular leaders of the Jewish People would recognize the authority of the great Torah sages.

In *The Way of Renascence,* Rav Kook views Jewish history as a pendulum swinging back and forth between the two poles of "charisma" (Rav Kook actually employs this term), raw, unmediated experience, and book-learning with all of the discipline and rigor that it demands. Rav Kook recognizes in the Zionist romance of return to the Land yet another outburst in a series of spiritual eruptions, some ignoble, such as early Nazarene Christianity, Sabbatianism, and Frankism, while others noble, such as Beshtian Hasidism. These are instances of the spirit bursting the envelope of Torah learning. Whereas Rav Kook views Rabbi Akiva with his emphasis on Torah study as the corrective to the wild, unbridled charisma of Jesus; and the Gaon of Vilna with his call for devotion to Torah learning as the foil to the Hasidism of the Ba'al Shem Tov—in the case of the People's meeting up once again with its land, Rav Kook feels a different kind of solution is called for. The People are in need, not of rabbis who will dispense a dry, legalistic teaching, but exactly charismatic leaders who will be capable of channeling revelatory experience through the inwardness of Torah!

In any case, Rav Kook has identified in the new Israel the element of charisma, of untutored, direct apperception of God.[7] Coming from his background in the Volozhin Yeshivah,[8] which continued the tradition of the Vilna Gaon, whereby Torah learning is the bedrock of Jewish existence, there is a remarkable openness here to alternative models. (One might counter that Rav Kook's view was never as monastic as that of the true Volozhiner, for in his youth Abraham Isaac was exposed by his maternal grandfather Rabbi Raphael to HaBaD Hasidism.)

In *To The Process of Ideas in Israel*, Rav Kook embarks upon exploration of the three "Houses," or Temples (or Commonwealths) of Israel—*Bayit Rishon* (the First Temple Period), *Bayit Sheini* (the

Second Temple Period), and *Bayit Shelishi* (the Third Temple Period)—the last period (our own) to be, according to Rav Kook, a synthesis of the more salient features of the first and second.

This is a lengthy essay which deserves much study. In a nutshell, the "idea" (Rav Kook employs this exact term, Greek in origin, in the Hebrew essay) of the First Temple was nation; the idea of the Second Temple was religion. Conveniently, by the insertion of a hyphen, this yields in the Third Temple the national-religious idea. Rav Kook is acknowledging that whereas in Exile, Judaism was restricted to a strictly religious phenomenon, in the modern era of the Return to Zion, Judaism once again (as in the First Temple Period) assumes the role of a nation. And whereas Second Temple religion focuses on personal salvation and afterlife, the earlier edition of Judaism—brought back to life by Zionism—trains its sights on the eternity of the People.

Yet this is an extremely superficial reading of the essay. If one reads with proper concentration, one discovers that Rav Kook is saying that in the Third Temple period—our very own era—we shall discover the higher idea which subsumes and unites these two ideas of nation and religion, and that is: *"ha-idea ha-Elohit"* (the divine idea, or the idea of God).[9]

CONCLUSION

During his tenure as Rabbi of Jaffa (1904-1914), considered by many his most fruitful years in terms of Jewish Thought, Rav Kook penned three essays designed to place the modern Return to Zion in historic perspective. Taken together as a unit, they identify in the Zionist enterprise the following elements:

- Physicality and universalism, as opposed to disembodied spirituality and particularism rooted in Torah perspective
- Charismatic or experiential spirituality, as opposed to didactic book-learning
- National, collective consciousness, as opposed to personal, religious consciousness

---

[1] Though Rabbi Abraham Isaac Hakohen Kook died in 1935, thirteen years before the proclamation of the State, he could clearly see the "handwriting on the wall," and in his writings (perhaps prophetically) enunciated the name *"Medinat Yisrael."* See *Orot ha-Kodesh*, vol. 3, p. 191 = *Shemonah Kevatsim* 1:186. His legacy and viewpoint were continued by his biological and/or spiritual heirs, Rabbi Tsevi Yehudah Hakohen Kook and Rabbi Ya'akov Moshe Harlap, who lived to see the establishment of the State.

[2] Shabbetai Tsevi (1626-1676), Turkish pseudo-Messiah.

[3] Rabbi Dr. Zvi A. Yehuda, a student of the *"Hazon Ish,"* shared with this writer (BN) that the *"Hazon Ish"* would poke fun at the term *"athalta di-ge'ulah"* ("beginning of redemption") popular in Religious Zionist circles. He would say that with each day gone by, we inch ever closer to the redemption, but who is to determine whether we are in the beginning, the middle or the end?

Rabbi Dr. Joseph B. Soloveitchik, nephew of the Brisker Rav, in his eulogy for his uncle, *"Mah Dodekh mi-Dod,"* observed stoically that from his uncle's perspective, the *Medinah* (State) had no halakhic relevance because it did not occur in Maimonides' code *Mishneh Torah*. Thus the eulogist explained the fact that unlike the *"Hazon Ish"* who received Prime Minister David Ben-Gurion in his home in B'nei Berak, the Brisker Rav refused to countenance Ben-Gurion.

[4] A brilliant student of Rav Kook, Rabbi Shim'on Starelitz referred to his mentor's work as a *"historiosophia di-mehemnuta"* ("historiosophy of faith").

[5] All three essays were translated by this writer and included in his collection *When God Becomes History: Historical Essays of Rabbi Abraham Isaac Hakohen Kook* (New York, NY: Kodesh, 2016).

[6] Perhaps in the recesses of Rav Kook's mind was the saying of the *Midrash Tanhuma, Vayyigash* (10): "Whatever happened to Joseph, happened to Zion." The commentators elucidate that "Zion" has the same numerical value as "Joseph" (156). By an extension, Zionism becomes Josephism.

[7] Compare the opening salvo of *Reish Millin* (London, 1917), Rav Kook's mystical meditation on the letters of the Hebrew alphabet:

"יודעת היא הנשמה שכל הבא בלימוד—איננו מקורי".

"The soul knows that whatever comes through learning—is not of the source."

In his lectures on the *Book of Kuzari*, Rav Kook railed against "learning in translation" (*"limmud targumi"*) as opposed to "learning from the source" (*"limmud mekori"*). These lectures were preserved in the notes of Rabbi Mordechai Gimpel Barg and published in *Ma'amrei ha-RAYaH*, vol. 2, ed. Rabbi Elisha Aviner (Langenauer) (Jerusalem, 1984), pp. 485-495. See ibid., p. 490, beginning chap. 5, and p. 488, end chap. 3.

See too Rav Kook's paraphrase of the Midrash: "In the past, I gave you Torah; in the future, I shall give you life" (*Shemonah Kevatsim* 6:198). The original wording of the *Midrash Exodus Rabbah* (48:4) reads: "Said the Holy One, blessed be He: 'In this world My spirit gives you wisdom, but in the future, My spirit will enliven you, as it says, *I will put My spirit in you, and you shall live* [Ezekiel 37:14].'"

[8] Himself a product of the Volozhin Yeshivah, Rav Kook prided himself that his paternal ancestor Rabbi Dov Baer Jaffe of Turetz and Utian had been one of Rabbi Hayyim Volozhiner's original ten students.

On the title page of *Elef ha-Magen* (Warsaw, 1912), co-authored by Rabbi Mordechai Gimpel Jaffe and his brother-in-law Rabbi Nathan Nota Luria, we read that Rabbi Mordechai Gimpel was "the son of the famous *maggid* (preacher) Rabbi Dovid Baer, of blessed memory, who served as rabbi in Utian, Karelitz and Turetz; who was called 'Rabbi Baer Maggid of Utian,' a *talmid-haver* (disciple-companion) of the Gaon Rabbi Hayyim of Volozhin, of blessed memory, and a companion of the Gaon Rabbi David Tevel of Stoiptz, of blessed memory, *mara de-'atra* (rabbi) of Minsk."

[9] While at a glance one might think that MK Ruth Calderon in her recent inaugural speech before the Knesset, or Israeli Parliament, on February 2, 2013, essentially captured Rav Kook's picture of the Third Temple, with a little probing we see that this is not so.

Calderon recounted that she grew up in a household imbued with Zionism, for which the study of *Tanakh* (Bible) was of paramount importance. After pronouncing a personal and collective *mea culpa* on behalf of secular Israelis for jettisoning the study of Talmud, Calderon held up a tome of Talmud, which, in her words, "transformed her life." She then proceeded to teach a homily from the Talmud, Tractate *Ketubot* 62b, concerning Rav Rehumai, whose extreme devotion to his study of Torah was at the expense of his conjugal duties to his poor wife, for which Rav Rehumai was punished by accidentally falling to his death when the roof of the study house collapsed. Calderon's point was that it is inhumane and unconscionable for Torah students not to fulfill their responsibility toward their partners in society, in this case the military service incumbent upon Israeli citizens.

With all due respects to MK Calderon, I believe that her presentation is flawed for two reasons. First, it fails to grasp that just as the study of Bible is not value-neutral but carries with it responsibility (in her words, *"mi-Tanakh le-Palmah,"* "from Bible to military service"), so the study of Talmud cannot be reduced to an academic exercise, to an appreciation of the humor and linguistic subtleties of the Talmud as she has demonstrated, but rather carries with it the *"'ol mitsvot"* ("yoke of commandments") and *"shi'buda de-'oraita"* ("obligation of the Torah").

But beyond that criticism, even if we should arrive at a hyphenation of the two Judaisms, Biblical Judaism and Rabbinic Judaism, à la *dati-le'umi* (national-religious), or more recently *HaRDaL* (acronym of *haredi-le'umi*, or national-Orthodox), we would come up short, for we would not have realized the unifying principle, the supernal root of these two ideas, nation and religion, and that is the God idea, or as Judah Halevi termed it in Arabic, *al-'amr al-ilahi* (translated by Ibn Tibbon into Hebrew as *"ha-'inyan ha-elohi"*).

Searching for the Lost Dimensions of Judaism
Thoughts on Rav Kook's 80th *Yahrzeit*
3 Ellul, 5775

Abraham Isaac Hakohen Kook (1865-1935) served as the first Ashkenazic Chief Rabbi of Erets Israel. He was a preeminent Talmudist and Halakhist, as well as mystic and poet. Revered as the seer of the rebirth of Israel in its land, Rav Kook had a rare gift for reaching out to even the most alienated sectors of the nation.

I ask myself: How would Rav Kook wish to be remembered today?

Certainly he would not want us to dredge up old animosities surrounding his person. It was he who taught that the *tikkun* or remedy for the abominable sin of *sin'at hinam* (senseless hatred) is *ahavat hinam* (senseless love).

Rather, I imagine that the Rav would want us to learn and practice the most salient features of his teaching. Rav Kook was a man who in the course of a lifetime grew spiritually by quantum leaps, and he would demand of us our own spiritual growth and development.

By nature, he was a *homo mysticus* drawn inexorably to the mysteries of the Torah. His core learning was obtained in the bastion of Lithuanian scholarship, the famed Volozhin Yeshiva. To his dying day, he would remain faithful to the legacy of the Vilna Gaon as embodied in that great Torah institution. But as time went on, this *Litvak* broadened his being. A sea change occurred in Rav

Kook's consciousness at the time of his *'aliyah* to Erets Israel in 1904, when he assumed the rabbinate of Jaffa (precursor to Tel-Aviv) and the outlying communities. This spiritual *'aliyah* (ascent) is reflected in the abrupt shift in style. In Lithuania, Rav Kook wrote prose. In Erets Israel, Rav Kook's writing assumed the flowing stream of consciousness that has become his hallmark. Rav Kook is first and foremost a poet, and admission to his inner sanctum hinges on ability to tune in to the wavelength of his poetry. The shift in style is symbolic of a much deeper phenomenon: the search for the lost dimensions of Judaism.

(It is no mere coincidence that during that same Jaffa period, the works of Rabbi Nahman of Breslov became a staple of Rav Kook's spiritual diet. Rabbi Nahman of Breslov was experimenting with new forms of expression, whether it be converting the *torot*, or teachings, in *Likkutei MOHaRaN* into *tefillot*, or prayers; or his foray into the enchanted world of storytelling, an activity that he described as *"dertzehlen ma'asiyos."*)

Rav Kook was thirsty for the *nishmata de-'oraita* (the soul of the Torah). His spiritual quest took him beyond the "dry" Halakhah to the "moist" environment of the *Aggadah*. Beyond that, he expressed a longing for the resumption of *nevu'ah*, outright prophecy. All those who had substantive exposure to the Rav; all those who warmed to this great luminary, experienced this *"hitpashtut kedushah,"* this expansion of holiness. To Rabbi Ya'akov Moshe Harlap, suffocating within the confines of the Old Yishuv of Yerushalayim, the *"Yaffo'er Rov"* ("Jaffa Rabbi") appeared as a breath of fresh air. Under Rav Kook's guidance, Lithuanian Yeshiva students such as Rabbi Yehudah Gershuni ("Yudel Grodner" of the Kamenets Yeshiva) and Rabbi Isaac Hutner ("Itche Varshaver" of the Slabodka Yeshiva) were turned on to works of Jewish Thought generally beyond the purview of the average yeshiva man. And an unusual seeker such as Rabbi David Cohen (the "Nazirite"), who had studied in both *yeshivot* and universities, and was yet thirsting for the Living God, received validation from the Rav for his "vision quest," a trek in the inhospitable Judean wilderness with a select group of students of Merkaz Harav. If you allowed him to touch your soul, Rav Kook would broaden your horizon so that you too might experience a quantum leap.

Rav Kook's spiritual journey encompassed all these dimensions and more: ecstatic song and dance (à la Hasidism), body work, a love for the green vegetation of the Earth, animal welfare, etc. Rav Kook stretched the limits of "book learning," but furthermore, impressed upon his listeners the importance of recapturing dimensions of Judaism that go beyond the book, to the body and the soul, and ultimately "to the wellspring of prophecy" (*"el ma'ayan ha-nevu'ah"*).

Lest anyone surmise that Rav Kook was out to create an elite cadre of *hasidim* who would be clones of the master, let it be stated in no uncertain terms that this clearly was not his goal. On more than one occasion, the Rav said outright that he had no interest in producing "Kookists." When the Rebbe of Gur, Rabbi Abraham Mordechai Alter (*"Imrei Emet"*), duly impressed by Rav Kook's many talents, remarked that Rav Kook could have 100,000 *hasidim* (perhaps the number of Gerrer Hasidim in pre-Holocaust

Poland), Rav Kook was quick to reply: "I think only about *Kelal Yisrael*, the Jewish People as a whole!"

If we had to sum up Rav Kook's teaching in a single word (which became the *bon mot* of his son Rabbi Tsevi Yehudah), it would be: *"Kelaliyut"* (Universality). It was that unitive vision that enabled Rav Kook to open the conversation between the disciples of the Vilna Gaon and the disciples of the Ba'al Shem Tov; between pietists and secularists; between Russian Jews and Yemenite Jews; and between Jews and Arabs.

Does Rav Kook have all the answers? No! But he can certainly point us in the right direction.

Rabbi Isaac Hutner wrote in a by now famous letter that it took him forty years to properly grasp Rav Kook's *de'ah* or opinion.[1] And now, on the eightieth *yahrzeit* of Rav Kook, we collectively respond: Ditto.

---

[1] See *b. 'Avodah Zarah* 5b.
 Rabbi Hutner's letter to Rabbi Tsevi Yehudah Hakohen Kook was published in *Iggerot la-RAYaH*, ed. Ben-Zion Shapira (2nd edition, Jerusalem, 1990), Appendix, Letter 47 (p. 585).

THE SCRIBAL ART OF RABBI MEIR:
A STUDY IN METANOMIANISM

(RAV KOOK'S PRE-PURIM TALK 5677/1917)

INTRODUCTION

In a personal letter to his son Tsevi Yehudah, dated "11 Adar, 5677," Rav Abraham Isaac Hakohen Kook shared a talk he delivered the previous Sabbath (*Parashat Zakhor*) before a London audience, concerning the commandment to erase or obliterate Amalek.[1] The hero of this discourse is the second-century sage Rabbi Meir. By cobbling together various references to Rabbi Meir in *Talmud Bavli, Talmud Yerushalmi* and *Midrash Rabbah*, Rav Kook is able to deftly paint a vivid portrait of the *tanna* (sage of the *Mishnah*) Rabbi Meir.[2] It is possible that some of what Rav Kook arrived at concerning writing and erasing, will jibe with postmodern deconstructionist literary theory.[3]

Before we launch into study of the actual discourse, we should point out that which, though unstated, may be obvious to some readers, namely that Rav Kook identifies with the protagonist. This is of extreme interest because just four years later, the Hasidic Rebbe of Gur (Gora Kalwaria, Poland), Abraham Mordechai Alter, in a letter to his family, published in the Jewish press of the day, would compare Rav Kook to—Rabbi Meir. It is highly unlikely that the Rebbe read our epistle of Rav Kook to his son. How did the

Rebbe so uncannily size up the situation? Was it something that Rav Kook let drop in conversation? Did the *tsaddik* (righteous man) read the "root" of Rav Kook's soul? (In Kabbalah, the term would be *"shoresh ha-neshamah."*) Whatever the answer, the Gerrer Rebbe took it with him to his eternal reward.

I quote the Rebbe of Gur's impression of Rav Kook, whom he had just met for the first time in Jerusalem in Nissan of 1921:

> The Rav, the Gaon, R. Avraham Kook, may he live, is a man of many-sided talents in Torah, and noble traits. However, his love of Zion surpasses all limit and he "declares the impure pure and adduces proof to it,"[4] reminiscent of the one [=Rabbi Meir] who the rabbis said in the first chapter of *'Eruvin* (13b) "had no equal in his generation," and therefore, "the final *halakhah* did not follow his opinion."[5]

TRANSLATION OF TEXT OF *IGGEROT HA-RAYAH*

> I spoke this holy Sabbath before an attentive audience concerning the erasing of Amalek, as a means of purifying all the values of existence; all the systems laden with the burden of the impurities, the pollution of wickedness, that extends from the "first of nations" [i.e., Amalek][6] even into the contents of the holy—which are corrupted by the evil influence of the wicked of the world.

This is the reason[7] for the prohibition of putting *kankantum*[8] into the ink.[9] The law requires "'And he shall write....and he shall erase'—a writing that is able to be erased."[10] [This is] on account of the particles of wickedness that infect the values of holiness. If the hand of wickedness would pollute the entire foundation [of holiness] with its actions, then we would burn it [i.e., the Torah scroll] and the names of God contained therein, so as not to preserve the memory[11] of the sectarians and their deeds.[12] [But] the totality of the holy is merely *touched* by wickedness, as Jacob was touched by the man who wrestled him,[13] and for the purpose of this erasure there suffices a *potential* erasing (*mehiyah kohanit*), "a writing that is able to be erased."[14]

In the Torah scroll written by Rabbi Meir, "whose contemporaries were not able to fathom his thinking,"[15] instead of *"kotenot 'or"* (with an *'ayin*), "tunics of skin," it was written *"kotenot 'or"* (with an *aleph*), "tunics of light."[16] And in the Jerusalem Talmud, he referred to himself by saying: "Here is your Messiah."[17] In other words, the illumination of his soul was from the [future] state that the world will ascend to after the light of Messiah will shine "and the wickedness will be consumed as smoke."[18]

In the case of Rabbi Meir, there was no need to prevent the placing of *kankantum* [in the ink]. (We could even go so far as to say that without *kankantum*, something would have been missing.) The very possibility and capability of erasing stands in opposition to the pure light, the supernal light,[19] "that illumines and lights up the eyes of the sages in *Halakhah*."[20] So, true to his character, Rabbi Meir used to put *kankantum* into the ink.

But Rabbi Akiva[21] said to him that the [present] state of the world still requires—even in the values of holiness—the potential of erasure, so that there might ramify from it the absolute erasure: the erasure of the memory of Amalek in all its branchings, and the existence of the darkness of Amalek. [This darkness consists of] the spread of all the evil characteristics (*ha-middot ha-ra'ot*) in the national soul of every people,[22] which brings about all the tragedies, individual and collective.[23] In the words of the *Pesikta*: "As long as there is Amalek in the world, a wing (*kanaf*) covers the face [of God]. Only with its erasing, will it be said, 'No longer shall your Teacher be hidden (*yikanef*).'"[24]

At that time, the light of the Oral Torah shall unite with [the light of] the Written Torah; the lights shall interpenetrate.

"Write this a remembrance in the book"—Written Torah. "And place in the ears of Joshua"—Oral Torah.[25]

We are not allowed to write any of the Written Torah [from memory] without having an exemplar of the Scripture before us[26]—so as not to confuse [the realms of] scripture and orality. This concept [of not confusing the written with the oral] is explained in the *Yerushalmi*, [Tractate] *Megillah*.[27]

But none of this applies to the great of stature, "who see their eternity in their lifetime."[28] "Whoever possesses knowledge, it is as if the Holy Temple were rebuilt in his days."[29] And the light of Messiah shines upon him. And [thus] Rabbi Meir, concerning whom it is said, "And your eyelids [look] straight before you,"[30] wrote [by heart] without consulting Scripture[31]—just as he placed *kankantum* into the ink.

And in the days of Purim, when the erasing of Amalek intensified, the foundation of the Oral Torah was united with the Written Torah. The Torah that had been accepted under duress on Mount Sinai, was once again accepted *willingly* in the days of Ahashverosh.[32] In the well-known words of the [Midrash] *Tanhuma*, the coercion on Mount Sinai was directed at the Oral Torah.[33]

(*Iggerot ha-RAYaH*, Vol. III [Jerusalem, 1965], Letter 808 [pp. 86-87])

COMMENTARY

Rabbi Meir was a *lavlar* or scribe by profession.[34] Rav Kook, by marrying two *sugyot* of the Talmud ('*Eruvin* 13a and *Megillah* 18b) drew a composite sketch of Rabbi Meir, whereby he deviated from the norms prescribed by the sages in two respects: He added *kankantum* to his ink rendering it indelible; and wrote scripture from memory. The simple explanation for these deviations was his exceptional, flawless recall of the text of the Scripture. But Rav Kook chalks up Rabbi Meir's unusual behavior to the fact that his soul was from a future, Messianic time. (Thus, on one occasion Rabbi Meir referred to himself as the Messiah.) For that reason, in the verse in Genesis which narrates how after the Primordial Sin, the LORD fashioned for Adam and Eve tunics of animal skins, Rabbi Meir substituted in his Torah scroll "light" (*'or*) for "skin" (*'or*).[35] In Rabbi Meir's reality, the outer *"levushim"* or garments have shed their opacity; they have become translucent.[36]

Our world is tainted by the wickedness of Amalek. So insidious is this influence of Amalek that it penetrates even into the inner precincts of holiness. Even our Torah has been infected by the corrupting influence of Amalek. *Horribile dictum.*

(Some years ago, there appeared a popular film, *The Matrix* [1999], which envisioned a dystopia whose reality had been thoroughly subverted by aliens.)

In this vein, Rav Kook interprets the prohibition of adding *kankantum* to the ink. In our present reality, the Torah is subject to corruption; therefore, the Torah must carry within itself the capability of being erased.

But Rabbi Meir's Torah is a scroll from the future, the Messianic future which basks in the light of the Face of God, no longer obscured by the wing of Amalek. That scroll is not subject to corruption and is in no need of erasure. Rabbi Meir adds *kankantum* to the ink, rendering it permanent.

Collateral damage resulting from the "wing of Amalek" is the wedge that it drives between Written and Oral Torah. Here it would be almost impossible to glean Rav Kook's meaning, were it not for a passage in the writings of his beloved disciple, Rabbi Ya'akov Moshe Harlap, which serves as a "Rosetta Stone" to decipher the master's allusion.

Employing Kabbalistic terminology, Rabbi Harlap informs us that the Written Torah is code for the *"kelim"* ("vessels"), while the Oral Torah is code for the *"'orot"* ("lights").[37] In other words, the Written Torah represents the outer manifestation, the material side of existence; the Oral Torah is evocative of the inner content, the spiritual aspect of existence.

Amalek drives a wedge between those two. And in an era in which the Face of God is eclipsed by the Wing of Amalek, we are told to maintain the separation of the two realms of Written Law and Oral Law. In the words of the Babylonian Talmud: "Words that are in writing, you are not permitted to recite orally; words that are oral, you are not permitted to commit to writing.[38] Once again, Rabbi Meir, who lives already in the Messianic Era, recognizes no such opacity. In his reality, the Written Torah and the Oral Torah collapse into one. In Rabbi Meir's world there is total transparency. The "tunics of skin" have been transcribed into "tunics of light."

On Mount Sinai, there yet existed separation of Torah into two distinct realms: the Written and the Oral. On Purim, with the erasing of Amalek, this gap between the Written Law and the Oral Law is bridged; the two dimensions dissolve into one.

CONCLUSION

Contained in this pre-Purim talk of Rav Kook is radical theology, the assertion that the Torah of our age—as opposed to the Torah of the eschatological future[39]—has been tainted by the evil of Amalek, and therefore requires by halakhic mandate (no less!) the potential of erasure. Rav Kook makes very clear that he is not referring to a Torah scroll written by a sectarian with improper intention (which the *halakhah* would have us consign to flames), but rather a "kosher" Torah scroll written with the most holy of intentions. The thought that the quintessence of holiness, the Torah, is subject to corruption, is a prospect so frightening as to cause us to shudder. But that very outlook may also be a source of hope, reminding us that "hardwired" into the script of the Torah is the capability of catharsis.

---

[1] See Exodus 17:14; Deuteronomy 25:19; Maimonides, *Sefer ha-Mitsvot*, positive commandment 188; idem, *MT, Hil. Melakhim* 5:5; and the anonymous *Sefer ha-Hinnukh*, commandment 604.
    Rabbi Hadari included this talk on *Parashat Zakhor* in *Shemu'ot RAYaH*. See *Shemu'ot RAYaH: Bereshit/Shemot*, ed. Kalman Eliezer Frankel and Hayyim Yeshayahu Hadari (Jerusalem: WZO, 2015), *Parashat Zakhor*, pp. 334-338.

[2] Cf. Rav Kook's spiritual sketch of Rabbi Meir, written a decade earlier, in a letter to fellow Lithuanian kabbalist, Rabbi Pinhas Hakohen Lintop. Datelined "Jaffa, 11 Adar Rishon 5668 [i.e., 1908]," the letter was published in *Iggerot ha-RAYaH*, vol. 1 (Jerusalem: Mossad Harav Kook, 1962), Letter 111 (pp. 140-141).

[3] See Marc-Alain Ouaknin, *The Burnt Book: Reading the Talmud*, transl. Llewelyn Brown (Princeton, 1995).

[4] For Rabbi Zadok Hakohen's thoughts regarding this passage in *'Eruvin* 13, see *Dover Tsedek* (Piotrków, 1911), 4a-c. In brief, Rabbi Meir had the power to reveal the underlying unity of all existence, and from that perspective of the divine unity, the duality of pure versus impure is transcended.

[5] The letter was published in serial form in three successive issues of *Der Jud*,

the Warsaw newspaper of the Agudat Yisrael movement (27 May, 3 June and 10 June, 1921). (The English translation is from my introduction to Rav Kook's *Orot*.) To this day, in at least some Agudist circles, the Rebbe of Gur's assessment of, and pronouncement upon Rav Kook is considered well-nigh authoritative.

6 Numbers 24:20.

Cf. Rabbi Michael Eliezer Hakohen Forshlager, *Torat Michael* (Jerusalem, 1967), *"Derush be-'inyan mehiyat zikhro shel 'Amalek,"* 250a: "'The first of nations is Amalek,' for he is the first of, and includes all the evil." (Rabbi Forshlager was a disciple of Rabbi Abraham Bornstein of Sochatchov, author of Responsa *Avnei Nezer*. Cf. below note 22.)

7 The Hebrew word is *"ta'am."* Rav Kook contributed much in the area of *"Ta'amei ha-Mitsvot"* (rationales of the commandments), beginning with his essay *"Afikim ba-Negev,"* published in the Berlin journal *Ha-Peless* in 1903-1904 (reprinted in Rabbi Moshe Zuriel, *Otserot ha-RAYaH*, vol. 2 [Tel-Aviv, 1988], pp. 733-779), and continuing with his essay *"Talelei Orot,"* published in the Bern journal *Tahkemoni* in 1910 (reprinted in *Ma'amrei ha-RAYaH*, vol. 1 [Jerusalem, 1980], pp. 18-28). See also the collection entitled *Orot ha-Mitsvot* in Rabbi Moshe Zuriel, *Otserot ha-RAYaH*, vol. 4 (Ashdod, 1992), pp. 31-47. And see now Don Seeman, "Evolutionary Ethics: The *Taamei Hamitzvot* of Rav Kook," *Hakirah* 26 (Spring 2019), pp. 13-55.

For a survey of the earlier literature, see Isaak Heinemann, *Ta'amei ha-Mitsvot be-Sifrut Yisrael* (Jerusalem, 1966).

In this particular instance, I do not believe that Rav Kook intended to supplant the practical reason for the law forbidding adding *kankantum* to the ink, which is simply to allow erasure in the case of scribal error. Rather, it appears that Rav Kook wrote in a homiletic vein.

8 Medieval opinions were divided as to the identity of *kankantum*. Rabbi Nathan of Rome, *'Arukh*, s.v. *kalkantum*, and Rashbam opined that the substance is vitriol. See the various opinions in *Tosafot*, *'Eruvin* 13a; idem, *Megillah* 18b; Rashi, *Shabbat* 104b; idem, *Sotah* 17b; Maimonides, *Commentary to the Mishnah*, *Shabbat* 12:4 (Kafah ed., p. 41); *Megillah* 2:1 (Kafah ed., p. 231); *Gittin* 2:3 (Kafah ed., p. 141); *Teshuvot ha-Rambam*, ed. Freimann (Jerusalem, 1934), no. 126.

For our purposes, we need not concern ourselves with the *realia*. However one identifies *kankantum*, the upshot is that it renders the ink indelible.

9 b. *'Eruvin* 13a; *Sotah* 20a.

10 Numbers 5:23; m. *Sotah* 2:4; b. *'Eruvin* 13a; *Sotah* 17b, 20a; Maimonides, *MT, Hil. Sotah* 3:8; 4:9.

Originally stated in regard to the *Megillat Sotah* (the Scroll of the Suspected Adulteress), Rabbi Yishmael extended this requirement to the entire Torah scroll. *Tosafot* speculate by what Biblical exegesis Rabbi Yishmael accomplished this extrapolation. The alternative is that Rabbi Yishmael merely stated a matter of rabbinic law. See *Tosafot, 'Eruvin* 13a, s.v. *huts mi-parashat sotah*.

Maimonides ruled that as a *mitsvah min ha-muvhar*, *kankantum* (or in his reading, *kalkantum*) should not be added to the ink of the Torah scroll; however, those who would invalidate a Torah scroll written with indelible ink, err in their judgment. In both his *Commentary to the Mishnah* and in a responsum

to Rabbeinu Ephraim of Tyre, Maimonides fleshed out his decision by explaining that the *halakhah* follows the *lishna batra* (later statement) of the Talmud:
> Rabbi Judah says, "Rabbi Meir used to say: 'For all [Scripture] we may place *kankantum* into the ink, except for the portion of the suspected adulteress (*parashat sotah*).'"

See Maimonides, *Commentary to the Mishnah*, Sotah 2:4 (Kafah ed., pp. 171-172); *MT, Hil. Tefillin* 1:4; *Teshuvot ha-Rambam*, ed. Freimann (Jerusalem, 1934), no. 126.

Par contre, the admixture of *kankantum* to the ink of the *Megillat Sotah* (Scroll of the Suspected Adulteress) does invalidate the scroll. See Maimonides, *Hil. Sotah* 4:9.

[11] Rav Kook wrote literally: "so as not to leave room" (*"kedei she-lo lehani'ah makom"*). However, the wording of Maimonides, *Hil. Yesodei ha-Torah* 6:8 (which is the source for Rav Kook's statement) is: "so as not to leave a name" (*"kedei she-lo lehani'ah shem"*).

[12] b. Shabbat 116a; Gittin 45b; Maimonides, *MT, Hil. Yesodei ha-Torah* 6:8; *Hil. Tefillin* 1:13.

Rabbi Aharon Soloveichik wrote that in our contemporary society, burning a Torah scroll written by a heretic would be counterproductive. In so many words, Maimonides wrote that the reason for doing so would be to prevent Jews from being drawn to heresy. But today we have the opposite scenario. Burning the Torah scroll would make heresy that much more attractive!

> All this applies only in a situation where by burning the Torah scroll written by the heretic, Jews will be prevented from being drawn to heresy. But if there should arise a situation (such as ours today) that by burning the Torah written by the heretic, Jews with limited commitment to the commandments will be drawn to heresy, as a result of the influence of the Reform and Conservative rabbis, who will say that the *"gedolim"* (great men) are intolerant and wish to coerce everyone into performing the commandments against their will—not only is it not a *mitsvah* (commandment) to burn the Torah scroll written by the heretic, but this would be a great desecration of the Name (*hillul hashem*).
> (Rabbi Aharon Soloveichik, *Perah Mateh Aharon*, novellae to Maimonides, *Sefer Madda'* [Jerusalem, 1997], *Hil. Yesodei ha-Torah* 6:8 [pp. 49-50])

Rabbi Soloveichik cites as his source the by-now famous ruling of the sage of B'nei Berak, Rabbi Abraham Isaiah Karelitz (*Hazon Ish*) regarding the inapplicability of the law of *"moridin ve-lo ma'alin"* in modern society:

> ....But in the time of the concealment, when belief has been cut off from the feeble of the people, the act of *horadah* [elimination of heretics] does not constitute a fence against the breach, but rather an addition to the breach, for in their eyes it will appear as a wanton act of violence, God forbid. Since our whole striving is to remedy, the law does not apply at a time when this is no remedy. [Rather,] we must return them with cords of love and stand them in the light (*leha'amidem be-keren 'orah*), to the extent of our ability.
> (*Hazon Ish, Yoreh De'ah* 2:16; cited in *Perah Mateh Aharon*, p. 5)

See further Benjamin Brown, *The Hazon Ish: Halakhist, Believer and Leader of the Haredi Revolution* (Hebrew) (Jerusalem, 2011), pp. 708-719. (The phrase *"leha'amidem be-keren 'orah"* derives from *b. Berakhot* 17a.)

In the Table of Contents, this chapter of *Perah Mateh Aharon* is summarized: If the burning of Torah scrolls of heretics will alienate Jews because of the impression of extremism, it is forbidden to burn them.

[13] Genesis 32:25.

[14] Although Rav Kook discusses the Torah scroll rather than the *"Megillat Sotah"* (Scroll of the Suspected Adulteress), it may interest the reader to learn that even in the latter regard (which is the source of our law), the verse "And he shall write....and he shall erase" (Numbers 5:23) is interpreted strictly *in potentia* ("that the ink is *capable* of being erased"), but the actual total erasure is derived from another verse: "'And after he shall give drink' [Numbers 5:26]—provided that no imprint [of the writing] be discernible" (*b. Sotah* 19b). See the clarification in *Tosafot Sens* (ibid.)—which differs with our *Tosafot, Sotah* 19a, s.v. *ve-ahar yashkeh*; Rabbi Hayyim Joseph David Azulai, *Hayyim Sha'al*, vol. 2 (Livorno, 1795), no. 5(3) (to Maimonides, *MT, Hil. Sotah* 4:14); Rabbi Pinhas Epstein, *Minhah Hareivah* (Jerusalem, 1923), *Sotah* 19a (93a).

Concerning the two *Tosafot* to Tractate *Sotah* ("our" *Tosafot* versus *Tosafot Sens*), see *Hayyim Sha'al*, vol. 2, no. 41. (Azulai's father possessed a manuscript of *Tosafot Sens* and remarked to his son that *Piskei Tosafot, Sotah* are based on *Tosafot Sens*.)

[15] *b. 'Eruvin* 13b.

[16] Genesis 3:21; *Genesis Rabbah* 20:12. Cf. *Genesis Rabbah* 9:5: "In the Torah of Rabbi Meir they found written [for] *'Ve-hinneh tov me'od'* ('And behold it was very good')—*'Ve-hinneh tov mot'* ('And behold it is good to die').

Saul Lieberman discussed at length "the book of Rabbi Meir." See his study, "The Texts of Scripture in the Early Rabbinic Period," in Saul Lieberman, *Hellenism in Jewish Palestine* (New York, 1994), pp. 24-26.

[17] *y. Kil'ayim* 9:3. The context was that Rabbi Meir, who had traveled to Asya, was about to die. He sent a message to his disciples in *Erets Yisrael* to bury him in the Land. The sense of his statement was: "Here is your rabbi." (See *P'nei Moshe* ad locum.) Rav Kook seizes upon Rabbi Meir's peculiar use of the word "Messiah."

[18] From the prayer of Rosh Hashanah and Yom Kippur.

[19] Aramaic, *"nehora 'ila'ah."*

[20] *b. Shabbat* 147b; *'Eruvin* 13b.

[21] It seems that Rav Kook's prodigious memory deceived him. It was not Rabbi Akiva but Rabbi Yishmael who had the exchange with Rabbi Meir. See *b. 'Eruvin 13a* and *Sotah 20a*.

In the very different *Yerushalmi* account, "Said Rabbi Meir, 'All the days that I studied under Rabbi Yishmael, I did not place *kankantum* into the ink.'" See *y. Sotah* 2:4; quoted in *Tosafot, Sotah* 17b, s.v. *she-ne'emar*. Maimonides explained in a responsum to Rabbeinu Ephraim of Tyre that the *Yerushalmi* refers to the practice of the student Rabbi Meir; later, the mature Rabbi Meir did add *kankantum* to the ink. See *Teshuvot ha-Rambam*, ed. Freimann (Jerusalem, 1934), no. 126.

[22] Cf. Rabbi Abraham Bornstein of Sochatchov: "This is Amalek, 'the first of

nations,' head of the seven evil characteristics" (*Ne'ot ha-Deshe*, vol. I [Tel-Aviv, 1983], *Parashat Zakhor*, p. 179, par. 6). The editor, Rabbi Aharon Israel Bornstein, clarifies that the seven Canaanite nations symbolize the seven evil characteristics and Amalek is the head of these nations. Ibid., n. 45.

23 Rav Kook penned these lines at the height of World War One. He witnessed how the phenomenon of nationalism decimated Europe. Cf. *Orot*, "Ha-Milhamah" ("The War").

24 Isaiah 30:20; *Pesikta Rabbati* 12:9. Rav Kook paraphrased. The exact wording of the *Pesikta* reads: "As long as the seed of Amalek exists, the Face is covered, as it were; once his seed is removed from the world, the Face that was covered, is revealed. 'No longer shall your Teacher be hidden (*yikanef*), but your eyes shall see your Teacher' [Isaiah 30:20]." See *Pesikta Rabbati*, ed. Meir Ish-Shalom (Vienna, 1880), chap. 12, "*Zakhor*" (51a).

25 Exodus 17:14.

Cf. Rabbi Isaac Ze'ev Halevi Soloveitchik, *Hiddushei Maran RIZ Halevi 'al ha-Torah, Beshallah*, s.v. *Ketov zot zikaron ba-sefer ve-sim be-'oznei Yehoshua* (I). The author juxtaposes the comment of the *Sifré, Pinhas*: "'*Ve-Tsav et Yehoshua*' ('And charge Joshua') [Deuteronomy 3:28]—*Tsavehu 'al divrei Talmud* (Charge him concerning the Oral Law)." See *'Emek ha-Netsiv* ad loc. Rabbi Soloveitchik (the "Brisker Rav") supposed that the *Sifré* is the source of Maimonides' statement in the Introduction to *Mishneh Torah*: "To Joshua, his disciple, Moses, our teacher, delivered the Oral Law and charged him concerning it."

The verse in Exodus 17:14 follows upon Joshua's armed conflict with Amalek. Rav Kook suggests that the separation and bifurcation into two distinct entities of Written Law versus Oral Law, came about under the spell of Amalek's influence.

26 b. *Megillah* 18b; *Menahot* 32b; Maimonides, *MT, Hil. Tefillin* 1:12.

27 y. *Megillah* 4:1:

> Rabbi Haggai said: "Rabbi Samuel bar Rav Yitzhak entered the synagogue. He saw a scribe reading the *Targum* [the Aramaic translation of Scripture] from a book. He said to him: 'It is forbidden for you [to read the *Targum*—an oral transmission—from a book]. Words that were said orally, [must be transmitted] orally; words that were said in writing, [must be transmitted] from writing.'"

Cf. b. *Gittin* 60; *Temurah* 14b. Rav Kook might as well have made his point from the *Talmud Bavli*. Perhaps the *Yerushalmi Megillah* was uppermost in his mind, because his talk preceded Purim (and the incident concerning Rabbi Meir writing a Scroll of Esther by heart in Asya, occurs later in that passage of *Yerushalmi*).

But there is another possibility. Alfasi transcribed the *Yerushalmi* in his *Halakhot, Megillah*, chap. 4 (14a). (See Rabbi Solomon ben Simon Duran, *She'elot u-Teshuvot ha-RaShBaSh* [Livorno, 1742], no. 277.) Perhaps Rav Kook, like his mentor Rabbi Naphtali Tsevi Yehudah Berlin (NeTsIV) of Volozhin, was especially conversant with Alfasi. (According to anecdote, one Friday night in the Volozhin Yeshiva, the lights went out, yet Netsiv was able to continue studying, having committed Alfasi to memory.)

Confirmation of this theory comes from Rabbi Shim'on Glitzenstein, who acted as Rav Kook's secretary during the latter's stay in London. Glitzenstein attests that an Alfasi in small format never left the Rav's hands during his medically prescribed walks. The custom of daily study of Alfasi goes back to the Vilna Gaon. See Rabbi Moshe Tsevi Neriyah, *Sihot ha-RAYaH* (Jerusalem, 5755/2015), pp. 184-185.

And then the question arises why Rabbi Isaac Alfasi (RIF) quoted the *Yerushalmi* and not the *Bavli*. This question of Alfasi was asked by Rabbi Chaim Zimmerman, *Binyan Halakhah* (New York, 1942), *Hakdamat ha-Rambam* (p. 2).

Here too (as above note 7) it is unwarranted to assume that Rav Kook rode roughshod over the simple reason for the sages' prohibition of writing Scripture from memory, namely to prevent scribal error. (See Rabbeinu Menahem ha-Me'iri, *Beit ha-Behirah, Megillah*, ed. Rabbi Moshe Hershler [Jerusalem: Makhon ha-Talmud ha-Yisraeli, 1968], *Megillah* 18b.) Rather, Rav Kook wrote in a homiletic vein.

[28] *b. Berakhot* 17a.
[29] *b. Berakhot* 33a.
[30] Proverbs 4:25; *b. Megillah* 18b.
[31] *b. Megillah* 18b.

Rav Kook stopped short of the *sugya*'s conclusion, which is that "an exigency is different" (*"she'at ha-dehak shanei"*). Provisionally, the Talmud assumed that Rabbi Meir, because of his phenomenal recall of Torah, was *sui generis* (as correctly quoted by Rav Kook). However, when challenged by the example of Rav Hananel, whose total command of Torah was certainly comparable to that of Rabbi Meir, the Talmud was forced to retract, attributing Rabbi Meir's writing of Scripture (in the case in question, the Scroll of Esther) from memory to the extraordinary circumstances in which he found himself. In 'Asya, there simply was no preexisting *Megillah* to refer to.

In the final analysis, we may say that that there were two factors that contributed to Rabbi Meir's writing Scripture by heart: 1) *"she'at ha-dehak"* (exigency); and 2) the fact that Rabbi Meir was *"shalem she-bi-shelemim"* ("perfect among perfect"), in the words of Me'iri. See *Rabbeinu Menahem ha-Me'iri, Beit ha-Behirah, Megillah* 18b (p. 51, right column).

Rabbi Ya'ir Hayyim Bachrach equated the waiving of the prohibition of writing scripture by heart in the case of *she'at ha-dehak* (*b. Megillah* 18b), to the waiving of the prohibition of writing down the *Aggadeta* in an *"'et la'asot la-Adonai—heferu toratekha,"* "A time to do for the [sake of] the LORD—they annulled your Torah" (Psalms 119:126; *Temurah* 14b). The same permission that makes allowances for turning the oral into the written, allows turning the written into the oral in extenuating circumstances. They are but two sides of the same coin. See *Havot Ya'ir*, no. 175.

The parallel *sugya* in *Yerushalmi, Megillah* 4:1 offers an alternative solution to the problem of how Rabbi Meir in 'Asya could write the Scroll of Esther by heart. Besides *"Ein lemedin mi-she'at ha-dehak"* ("We do not learn from an exigency"), as in *Bavli*, there is proffered the following ingenious solution: "And some say that [Rabbi Meir] wrote two [*megillot*]; the first, he wrote by heart, and the second from the first, and archived (*ganaz*) the first."

Rabbeinu Nissim (in pagination of Alfasi, *Megillah*, 5b, s.v. *heikhi damei mitnamnem*) ruled that other than a *she'at ha-dehak*, it is forbidden to read from Scripture that had been written by heart. Rabbeinu Manoah, on the other hand, wrote that the law of not writing by heart is strictly at the outset (*lekhatehillah*), but the Scripture is not invalidated thereby. The two opinions are brought in Rabbi Joseph Karo, *Beit Yosef* on *Tur, Yoreh De'ah* 274.

32 *b. Shabbat* 88a.

33 *Midrash Tanhuma*, Noah, 3.

According to the Talmud *(Shabbat* 88a), at Mount Sinai, God held the mountain over the heads of the people "as a vat" and threatened that if they did not accept the Torah, that would be their burial place. *Tosafot* (ibid.) raise the question that the Children of Israel had already willingly accepted the Torah by saying, "We shall do and we shall hearken" (Exodus 24:7). The *Midrash Tanhuma* resolves this difficulty by differentiating between Written and Oral Law. The Israelites' voluntary acceptance extended only to the Written Law; the heavy-handed tactic was required to force their submission to the Oral Law as well. On Purim, this situation was remedied, when the Jews lovingly committed to the Oral Law.

34 *b.'Eruvin* 13a; *Sotah* 20a. See also *Ecclesiastes Rabbah* 2:17: "Rabbi Meir was an excellent scribe" (*"Rabbi Meir havah katvan tav muvhar"*). Quoted in Lieberman, op. cit., p. 25.

35 Genesis 3:21; *Genesis Rabbah* 20:12.

Perhaps this Midrash was the inspiration for the phrase "rags of light" in Leonard Cohen's song "If It Be Your Will."

36 See Rabbi Zadok Hakohen Rabinowitz of Lublin, *Dover Tsedek* (Piotrków, 1911), 4b.

37 Rabbi Jacob Moses Harlap, *Mei Marom*, Vol. 10 (Leviticus) (Jerusalem, 1997), *ma'amar* 41, "*Ihud Torah she-bi-khetav 'im Torah she-be-'al peh*" (p. 131, para. 2). Earlier in that discourse, Rabbi Harlap writes: "The Written Torah is the essence of the worlds, the essence of all existence; and the Oral Torah, the light of existence....In the hands of Israel is the power to unify the essence of existence with the light within, and combine them into one unit, with the result that existence itself will be synonymous with the light, the Oral Torah...." (p. 128).

38 *b. Gittin* 60; *Temurah* 14b; Maimonides, *MT, Hil. Tefillah* 12:8; idem, *Guide of the Perplexed*, transl. Schwarz (Jerusalem, 2002), I, 71 (pp. 185-186).

Rav Kook demonstrated an abiding interest in the problematic of committing the Oral Law to writing, revisiting this theme on more than one occasion in his halakhic *oeuvre*. On the issue of whether the prohibition of writing down the Oral Law is biblical or rabbinic in origin, he wavered. See Rav Kook's earliest halakhic work, *'Ittur Soferim*, vol. 1 (Vilna, 1888; photo offset Jerusalem, 1974), 7a (*"Lishkat ha-Sha'ar"*) and 20a (*"Lishkat ha-Sofer"*). See the earlier literature: Rabbi Eliezer of Metz, *Yere'im*, chap. 128; Rabbi Ya'ir Hayyim Bachrach, *Havot Ya'ir* (Frankfurt am Main, 1699), no. 175; Rabbi Hayyim Joseph David Azulai, *Birkei Yosef*, vol. I (Livorno, 1774), *Orah Hayyim*, chap. 49, para. 2; idem, *Mahazik Berakhah* (Livorno, 1785), *Orah Hayyim*, chap. 49, para. 1.

And then there is Rav Kook's scintillating explanation of the passage in Maimonides' Introduction to *Mishneh Torah*:

> From the time of Moses to that of *Rabbeinu ha-Kadosh* [i.e., Rabbi Judah the Prince], no work had been composed from which the Oral

Law was publicly taught. But in each generation, the head of the court or the prophet of that generation wrote down for his private use a memorandum of the traditions which he had heard from his teachers, while teaching orally in public.

Rav Kook's commentary thereto was transcribed by Rabbi Ya'akov Filber in his work *Le-'Oro* (Jerusalem, 1995), pp. 164-167; reprinted (in a truncated version) in Rabbi Moshe Zuriel, *Otserot ha-RAYaH*, old series, vol. 2 (Tel-Aviv, 1988), pp. 849-850, and (in a lengthier version) in idem, *Otserot ha-RAYaH*, new series, vol. 3 (Rishon le-Zion, 2002), pp. 11-13. In both *'Ittur Soferim* (loc. cit.) and the commentary to Maimonides, Rav Kook probed whether the prohibition consists in the initial act of writing the Oral Law or in the subsequent act of teaching it in public from a written text, or both.

For a scholarly treatment of the subject, see Saul Lieberman, "The Publication of the *Mishnah*," in idem, *Hellenism in Jewish Palestine* (New York, 1994), pp. 83-89.

Inter alia, in Jerusalem, in the 1930s, Rav Kook and the young, budding scholar Saul Lieberman studied together *be-havruta* on a regular basis *Tur* with the commentary of *Beit Yosef*. The precondition for this arrangement was that neither would prepare the text beforehand. (Heard from Dov Zlotnick, disciple of Lieberman and executor of his will—BN.)

[39] Cf. the work ascribed to Rabbi Moses Hayyim Luzzatto, *KaLaH Pit̲hei Hokhmah*, ed. Spinner (Jerusalem, 1987), *petah* 30 (pp. 93-94), referencing Isaiah 51:4 and *Leviticus Rabbah* 13:3.

The Hasidism of Rav Kook

We usually associate the term "Neo-Hasidism" with thinkers such as Martin Buber, Hillel Zeitlin, and Abraham Joshua Heschel. It may come to many of us as a surprise that Rabbi Abraham Isaac Hakohen Kook also proposed a new Hasidism, but it should not.[1] During Rav Kook's lifetime, there were those who perceived him as the founder of a new Hasidic movement. Both admirers and detractors understood that this charismatic teacher embodied a renewed spirituality.

Rabbi Ya'akov Moshe Harlap, eminent disciple of Rav Kook, wrote a letter intended for the Gerrer Rebbe, in which he portrayed his mentor as a modern-day Hasidic master reaching out to alienated Jews in an attempt to bring them back to the fold.[2] A cynical writer of the Agudah camp, critiquing Rav Kook's seminal work *Orot* (1920), segued to the secular *"tsaddik"* Martin Buber and expressed fear lest there develop around Rav Kook yet another mystery religion.[3]

What are the facts? How did Rav Kook himself envision the new Hasidism? Was it to be a reincarnation of the East European variety attributed to Rabbi Israel Ba'al Shem Tov?

Untrained observers have the answer ready. One need merely point to the *spodik*, the tall fur hat perched on his head, to determine that Rav Kook viewed himself as a Hasidic rebbe. However there is an historical context to the headwear. Rav Kook's predecessors in the Ashkenazic Jerusalem rabbinate—his father-in-law, Rabbi Elijah David Rabinowitz-Te'omim (ADeReT), and Rabbi Samuel Salant, staunch Lithuanian *Mitnagdim*—wore the identical fur hat. Excuse the cultural confusion and move on to Rav Kook's own words.

In his much calumniated *Orot*, Rav Kook threw down the gauntlet, calling for a "great Hasidism," "very superior Hasidim" and "great Hasidim, unique in greatness of knowledge."[4] He even pushed the term to its extreme limits, signing off: "Give strength to the higher knowledge; to the exalted, radical, godly Hasidism (*Hasidut ha-elohit ha-radikalit ha-romemah*)!"[5] And with that, the reader is left wondering where exactly Rav Kook's *poignard* is pointing.

This year, yet another heretofore unknown journal of Rav Kook was released in Jerusalem.[6] An entry in the journal fleshes out Rav Kook's vision of a new Hasidism.

We should pay careful attention to this recently released passage. It should disabuse us of many well-intentioned but ill-conceived attempts to reduce Rav Kook to the status of one more Hasidic rebbe with a fur hat on his head. The entry, which is easily an essay in its own right, contains several subtle nuances which might be missed in our contemporary popular culture. Evidently, Rav Kook anticipated our ability to manufacture facile acronyms such as *HaBaKUK* (HaBaD, Breslov, Kook). In a "preemptive strike," he unleashes his own byword, *KeMaH*, the initials of *Kabbalah, Madda', Hasidut* (Kabbalah, Science, Hasidism).

The Hasidism of Rav Kook

Early on in the piece, Rav Kook holds up as a lodestar the book *Sha'ar ha-Shamayim* by Abraham Cohen de Herrera (a.k.a. Alonso Nunez de Herrera).

Herrera (d. 1635) studied in Ragusa (today Dubrovnik, Croatia) under Rabbi Israel Sarug, a peripatetic teacher who transmitted a form of Lurianic Kabbalah to several distinguished students in Italy, the greatest being Rabbi Menahem Azariah of Fano.[7]

Herrera's Spanish work of Kabbalah, *Puerta del Cielo* (*Gate of Heaven*), remained until recently an unpublished manuscript. Luckily, Rabbi Isaac Aboab da Fonseca (1605-1693), eventual *Hakham* of the Spanish-Portuguese community of Amsterdam, translated the work (which is to say, portions thereof) into Hebrew at Herrera's behest. The book was printed in Amsterdam in 1655 under the title *Sha'ar ha-Shamayim*.

What strikes the reader of *Sha'ar ha-Shamayim* is the ease with which Herrera juxtaposes arcane Lurianic Kabbalah and Neo-Platonic philosophy, prompting Alexander Altmann to title his 1982 study of *Puerta del Cielo*, "Lurianic Kabbalah in a Platonic Key." Herrera shuttles between Israel Sarug and Marsilio Ficino without batting an eyelash.

The reader may find curious the fact that Rav Kook, rather than viewing this Spanish work of Kabbalah, chock-full of Western philosophy, as an aberration or serious departure from tradition, regards it as mainstream. Furthermore, Rav Kook holds it up as a role model for the direction in which he wishes to lead us. As he writes regarding *Sha'ar ha-Shamayim*, "So did the great throughout the ages."

Rav Kook's perception of *Sha'ar ha-Shamayim* may have been influenced by the publisher's introduction to the Warsaw 1865 edition. Israel Jaffe of Kalisz wrote: "All that was investigated by the great godly geniuses—Rabbi Moshe Hayyim Luzzatto; the Vilna Gaon; his disciple Rabbi Hayyim of Volozhin; Rabbi Shneur Zalman of Liadi; his son Rabbi Dov; and his disciple Rabbi Aaron, all of blessed memory—all their systems are gathered together in this book." Jaffe certainly engaged in hyperbole, but his point was well taken. Herrera's book did in fact set the tone for an entire approach to Lurianic Kabbalah that came to be known as *"hasbarah,"* or conceptualization. In Padua, Vilna, Volozhin, Liadi, Lubavitch, and Staroshelye, Kabbalah was demythologized and translated to the language of reason and discourse.

But that is not exactly what Rav Kook is saying. Rav Kook asserts that *Sha'ar ha-Shamayim* represents a rapprochement between Kabbalah and the science of the day. In this respect, Rav Kook may be barking up the wrong tree. In the seventeenth century, in Holland as well as in Italy, there was a demarcation (however blurred) between philosophy and science. Rather than choosing Herrera as his role model, Rav Kook might have done better opting for Herrera's contemporary, Joseph Solomon Delmedigo (or as he is known in Hebrew, *"YaShaR mi-Candia"*) as an exemplary amalgam of Kabbalah and science. (By the way, Delmedigo's Kabbalah too is of Sarugian lineage.)

The Hasidism of Rav Kook

Be that as it may, Rav Kook advocates the marriage of Kabbalah and science. Where does Hasidism enter into the discussion?

Midway through the essay, Rav Kook rather abruptly quotes the rabbinic maxim, "The greater the man, the greater his inclination (*yetser*)."[8] *Yetser* is usually understood as *yetser ha-ra'*, the evil inclination. In truth, *yetser* derives from the root *yatsar*, "create." Rav Kook seems to be saying that the new creativity unleashed by the fresh synthesis of Kabbalah and *madda'* (science) demands a new ethic.[9]

Rather than the mediocre *Mussar* of the masses, Rav Kook writes, a new Hasidism is called for. Here, both the terms *Mussar* and Hasidism beg definition. What *Mussar*? What Hasidism?

By "*Mussar*," Rav Kook undoubtedly refers to the *Mussar* movement founded in Lithuania by Rabbi Israel Salanter. Rav Kook was a product of the Volozhin Yeshiva, whose heads (Rabbi Naftali Tsevi Yehudah Berlin and Rabbi Hayyim Soloveitchik) rejected the *Mussar* movement. Rav Kook finds *Mussar* enervating. The new Hasidism he proposes is empowering. "It takes them out from fear and darkness to confidence and light; from servitude and weakness to sovereignty and strength of spirit."[10]

To put his new Hasidism into clearer perspective, Rav Kook juxtaposes it to the previous Hasidism. "Such a Hasidism will certainly not be lacking all the (spiritual) wealth of the latter-day Hasidism." "The latter-day Hasidism" (*ha-hasidut ha-me'uharah*) is code for the Hasidism that originated with the Ba'al Shem Tov (BESHT). In *Orot*, Rav Kook refers to Beshtian Hasidism as "the latest Hasidism" (*ha-hasidut ha-aharonah*).[11] This is done to distinguish between East European Hasidism and earlier pietist movements, such as *Hasidei Ashkenaz*, the medieval Pietists of the Rhineland.

So what would Rav Kook's Hasidism look like? Perhaps the Hasidism advocated in Rabbi Moshe Hayyim Luzzatto's classic, *Mesillat Yesharim* (*Path of the Just*) could serve as an analog. In its original form, *Mesillat Yesharim* consisted of a dialog between a *hakham*, a wise man, and a *hasid*, a pious man.[12] Luzzatto, a Renaissance man in the tradition of Italian Jewry, combined Kabbalah and the science of his day. In Padua, a university town renowned for its medical school, Luzzatto's immediate circle included physicians Moshe David Valle and Yekutiel Gordon. In *Mesillat Yesharim*, Luzzatto included an entire section on *Hasidut* (chaps. 18-21). So enamored was Rav Kook of Luzzatto's work, that he penned a digest, *Kitsur Mesillat Yesharim*.[13]

Many years ago, a famous Rosh Yeshivah by the name of Rabbi Abba Berman (quoting his father who led a *metivta* in Lodz, Poland before World War Two), told this writer (BN) in private conversation: "The only Hasidism is that of the *Mesillat Yesharim*."

Speaking of his new Hasidism, Rav Kook writes:

> It must be expansive. It must reach to the depth of its source in the nation and the individual, and it must reach to the heights of God's loving-kindness (*hesed*).

This is Rav Kook's way of reminding us subtly (or not so subtly)—as did Luzzatto in *Mesillat Yesharim*—that the word *"hasidut"* (piety) derives from *"hesed"* (loving-kindness).[14]

The Hasidism of Rav Kook

In his *modus vivendi*, Rav Kook certainly internalized the words of the *"Hasid* Rabbi Moshe Hayyim Luzzatto"[15]:

> It is worthy for every *hasid* to intend with his actions for the good of his entire generation, to acquit them and protect them...for the Holy One, blessed be He, loves only the one who loves Israel; and the more a person loves Israel, the more the Holy One, blessed be He, loves that person.[16]

※※※

TRANSLATION OF THE TEXT OF *PINKESEI HA-RAYAH*

Kabbalah must bond with all the sciences; to live with them and through them. So did the great [sages] throughout the ages; and more than they achieved—it is obligatory upon us to achieve. The spiritual world that bestows its spirit upon the thinking man, was enhanced by constant appearances of the light of intellect. This enhancement dulls the oppositions between one science and another, and once the barriers have come down—the different sciences actually come to one another's aid.

Science in all of its breadth, in all of its various aspects—spiritual and practical, societal and global—must find its place alongside the supernal wisdom [i.e., Kabbalah].

A shining example of this would be the book *Sha'ar ha-Shamayim* by Rabbi Abraham Cohen Errera (!), who was the second in a line extending from the ARI [i.e., Rabbi Isaac Luria] through Rabbi Israel Sarug, disciple of the ARI.[17] [Herrera] was inspired to write his book in Spanish, in full view of the cultured world of the day. With a breadth of intellect and feelings of respect and affection, the author toured all the philosophical studies that represented the finest literature of his time. Rabbi Isaac Aboab [da Fonseca] who admired him [i.e., Herrera]—translating the work into Hebrew for the benefit of Hebrews—followed in his spirit, which is the spirit of true culture worthy of Torah scholars who are truly "men of holiness."

It is understood that according to the changes of the *Zeitgeist*, so must the synthesis (between the supernal, divine wisdom and all the human thoughts that proceed from the sciences) shift, but the principle remains the same. The preparedness of the thinker—pure of knowledge and holy of thought—to absorb into his midst the best thoughts of the finest writers, the thinkers, the sages of every people and language, of every subject of science; and to shine upon them, from them and through them, the divine light—this is the unchanging way of the world, upon which we are obligated to travel.

Only "if you have heard the old, will you hear the new."[18] The old must be studied and researched, and it will bring the new, good and fundamental.

[This synthesis of] science and the supernal illumination that expands the soul, produces a strong character in our entire organic unity, spiritual and material.

Through the supernal splendor and the fullness of life that beats in its midst, the natural inclinations of the soul and the body, and all its senses and faculties, are invigorated, strengthened and expanded. "The greater the man, the greater his inclination (*yetser*)."[19]

In order to purify great powers; to refine powerful, luminous, lofty ambitions, much preparation is required. So the synthesis of Kabbalah and science immediately beckons us to—Hasidism (Pietism).

We need now a rich, broad, luminous Hasidism to illumine us!

Such a Hasidism will certainly not be lacking all the [spiritual] wealth of the latter-day Hasidism [i.e., of Rabbi Israel Ba'al Shem Tov], but it must be expansive. It must reach to the depth of its source in the nation and the individual, and it must reach to the heights of God's lovingkindness (*hesed*).

[We need] a Hasidism that negates no good; no science, peace, Torah or talent, but rather crystallizes and purifies all. When understood as such, people with heart will not oppose it.

This Hasidism is needed by men of powerful spirit, just as the average *Mussar* (Ethics) is necessary for the masses. This Hasidism contains all the ways of *Mussar*, but it surpasses them; it takes them out from fear and darkness to confidence and light; from servitude and weakness to sovereignty and strength of spirit. This Hasidism must be combined with Kabbalah and science, so that greatness of spirit not grow inimical to routine ethics (which the average acquire through revulsion brought on by fear).

When we will have this order in hand—first in theory, and later in action—we will have the basis for all the light of Torah; for the theory of *Halakhah* and for all the parameters of action, education and true *hiddush* (creation). A *hiddush* that is at once sharp and esthetic, straight and clever.

And the more enhanced the knowledge and understanding of Torah—real Torah, permeated with the everlasting Holy Covenant—the more the ideal soul will expand, as it fills with the splendor of Kabbalah, the sciences and Hasidism.

In this regard I invoke the adage: "If there be no *KeMaH* (Flour), there be no Torah; if there be no Torah, there be no *KeMaH* (Flour)."[20] [*KeMaH* being an acronym for *Kabbalah, Madda', Hasidut*, or Kabbalah, Science, Hasidism.]

This is the straight way of the LORD that the new life and the feelings of freedom ringing throughout the sacred soil at this time require us to embark upon.

And a highway shall be there, and a way, and it shall be called the way of holiness….the redeemed shall walk there. (Isaiah 35:8-9)[21]

---

[1] Incidentally, both Buber and Zeitlin met with Rav Kook in Jerusalem and were favorably impressed.

[2] See my introduction to *Orot* (Maggid, 2015), p. 33.

The letter was addressed directly to the Rav of Bendin, Rabbi Hanokh Tsevi Hakohen Levin, brother-in-law of the Gerrer Rebbe, Rabbi Abraham Mordechai Alter (author of *Imrei Emet*).

[3] Ibid., p. 53.

[4] *Orot ha-Tehiyah*, beginning chap. 4.

[5] Ibid. end chap. 4.

[6] *Pinkesei ha-RAYaH* 4, ed. Tsevi Mikhel Levin and Benzion Kahana-Shapira (Jerusalem, 5777/2017).

[7] Gershom Scholem lavished much scholarly attention on both Herrera and his teacher Sarug. In the first case, Scholem published a small biography, *Abraham Cohen Herrera: Leben, Werk und Wirkung* (1978). As for Sarug, in an early essay, caustically entitled, "Israel Sarug: Student of the Ari?" (1940), Scholem attempted to expose this sketchy figure as a fraud. Scholem presumed that Sarug was an impostor who passed himself off to unsuspecting Europeans as an erstwhile disciple of Rabbi Isaac Luria in either Egypt or Erets Israel. Lately, researchers such as Ronit Meroz and Yosef Avivi have made some headway in rehabilitating Sarug's image as a genuine conduit of Lurianic teaching.

[8] b. *Sukkah* 52a.

[9] Rav Kook revisits this theme later in that volume:

> One who feels in his soul that he needs much divine illumination, many ethical studies, and much contemplation, let him not delude himself by saying that he can throw off this burden and be like everyone else and like the masses of *"b'nei Torah"* (Torah students); that he can engage totally or for the most part in practical affairs, and that will suffice for him. *"The greater the man, the greater his inclination."* In direct proportion to the potential that one has for spiritual ascent, are the deficiencies, the strange desires and the pull to gross corporeality—that have no comparison among the average. The only way that one can be spared them (and even profit from them, inasmuch as their mighty power can be harnessed to pull one to a supernal loftiness) is if one fortifies one's character, raising thereby one's essence to its proper place: to "stroll in the Garden of Eden" of lofty matters, and the splendor (*Zohar*) of the joy of the LORD shall be his strength. But if one should wish to be like the masses of *"b'nei Torah,"* one will actually end up much lower than them, descending to the depth of bad traits. He shall find himself extremely corrupted—

until he reassumes the spiritual quality that is unique to him.
(*Pinkesei ha-RAYaH* 4 [Jerusalem, 5777/2017], *Pinkas ha-Dapim* 2:14 [p. 232])

10 Rav Kook's critique of Rabbi Israel Salanter's Mussar movement deserves a separate study. I hope one day to treat that subject at length. For now, one would do well to consult Rabbi Moshe Zuriel's collection, *Otserot ha-RAYaH* (Rishon le-Zion, 2002), vol. 2, pp. 311-312, 314, 329-330.

(See now Rabbi Abraham Isaac Hakohen Kook's commentary to *The Legends of Rabbah bar Bar Hannah*, ed. Bezalel Naor [New York, NY: Orot/Kodesh, 2019], Appendix 6, "Rav Kook's Critique of the Mussar Movement," pp. 214-221. Add now to the references cited in that appendix, Rav Kook's Introduction to *'Eyn Ayah*, ed. Rabbi Ya'akov Filber, vol. 1 [Jerusalem: Makhon RZYH, 1987], p. 23.)

11 *Orot ha-Tehiyah*, chapter 35.

12 See Rabbi Moshe Hayyim Luzzatto, *Mesillat Yesharim* (Dialogue Version from Ms. Günzburg 1206, Russian State Library, Moscow; and Thematic Version from first edition, Amsterdam, 1740), ed. Avraham Shoshana (Jerusalem: Ofeq, 1994).

13 First published as an appendix to Rabbi Tsevi Yehudah Kook's *Li-Sheloshah be-Elul*, vol. 2 (5707/1947), pp. 23-31, *Kitsur Mesillat Yesharim* has since been reprinted in *Ma'amrei ha-RAYaH*, vol. 2 (Jerusalem, 5744/1984), pp. 273-276; and Rabbi Moshe Zuriel, *Otserot ha-RAYaH*, new series, vol. 2, pp. 297-300.

14 Rabbi Moshe Hayyim Luzzatto, *Mesillat Yesharim*, ed. Avraham Shoshana (Jerusalem, 1994), chap. 19 (p. 282).

15 Thus did Rav Kook refer to the author of *Mesillat Yesharim*. See Rav Kook's eulogy for Rabbi Israel Salanter in *Ma'amrei ha-RAYaH*, vol. 1 (Jerusalem, 1980), p. 121; and Rabbi Moshe Zuriel, *Otserot ha-RAYaH*, vol. 2, p. 311.

16 Rabbi Moshe Hayyim Luzzatto, *Mesillat Yesharim*, end chap. 19 (p. 296).

17 In a letter to Rabbi Shemariah Menashe Hakohen Adler, who penned a commentary to Rav Kook's mystical tract *Reish Millin*, Rav Kook quoted from the "book *Beit Elohim* by the kabbalist, the philosopher, Rabbi Abraham Errera (!), disciple of Rabbi Israel Sarug, disciple of the ARI [i.e., Rabbi Isaac Luria], of blessed memory." See *Iggerot ha-RAYaH*, vol. 3 (Jerusalem: Mossad Harav Kook, 1965), Letter 896 (p. 208).

Like *Sha'ar ha-Shamayim*, *Beit Elohim* was written by Herrera in Spanish. The author titled his work, *Casa de la Divinidad* (House of Divinity). It was titled *Beit Elohim* by Rabbi Isaac Aboab da Fonseca in his Hebrew translation, published in Amsterdam in 1655 (after Herrera's death). Concerning the significance of the original Spanish title, see Nissim Yosha, *Myth and Metaphor: Abraham Cohen Herrera's Philosophic Interpretation of Lurianic Kabbalah* (Hebrew) (Jerusalem: Magnes, 1994), pp. 51-54.

Obviously, Rav Kook accepted at face value Rabbi Israel Sarug's claim that he was a bona fide disciple of Rabbi Isaac Luria. See too Rabbi Isaac Hutner's *haskamah* (encomium) to Rabbi Menahem Azariah of Fano's work, *Alfasi Zuta*; reprinted in Rabbi Isaac Hutner, *Pahad Yitzhak: Iggerot u-Ketavim*, ed. Rabbi Yonatan David (Brooklyn, NY, 2016), no. 80 (pp. 147-148). Rabbi Hutner accepted the theory of Rabbi Zadok Hakohen (Rabinowitz) of Lublin that Rabbi Israel Sarug studied under Rabbi Isaac Luria before Rabbi Hayyim Vital was apprenticed to the master. (See Rabbi Zadok Hakohen of Lublin, *Sefer ha-Zikhronot*, appended to idem, *Divrei Soferim* [Lublin, 1913; photo-offset B'nei Berak, 1967], 31a.) In order to determine that Sarugian Kabbalah was embraced in the "study-house of the Gaon Rabbi Elijah [of Vilna]," Rabbi Hutner referred to the work of the *Leshem* (i.e., Rabbi Solomon Eliashov), who demonstrated that *Nefesh ha-Hayyim* by Rabbi Hayyim of Volozhin, the Gaon's premier disciple, incorporates elements of Sarugian Kabbalah ("'*Olam ha-Malbush*," etc.). See Rabbi Solomon Eliashov, *Sefer Hakdamot u-She'arim* (Piotrków, 1909), Introduction to *Sha'ar ha-Poneh Kadim* (f.59).

Perhaps it should be pointed out that Rabbi Zadok Hakohen advised maintaining distance from works that mix Kabbalah with gentile philosophy. After censuring Delmedigo's *Novelot Hokhmah*, Rabbi Zadok continues: "And so, in my opinion, it is advisable to stay far away from the book *Beit Elohim* and the book *Sha'ar ha-Shamayim*, composed by Rabbi Abraham Cohen Errera (!), who invented theories on his own and from what he derived from the early philosophers of the nations, and wished to unite them with the wisdom of Kabbalah, attained through prophecy and the divine spirit" *(Sefer ha-Zikhronot*, 36b).

For the positive reception of Sarugian Kabbalah by the masters of HaBaD Hasidism, see the exchange between Rabbi Dan Tumarkin of Rogatchov (a Lubavitcher Hasid) and the Kopyster Rebbe, Rabbi Shelomo Zalman Schneerson (author of *Magen Avot*), in Rabbi Mordechai Menashe Laufer, *Ha-Melekh bi-Mesibo*, vol. 2 (Kefar Habad, 1993), pp. 273 (*Magen Avot* quoting Rabbi Naftali Bacharach's *'Emek ha-Melekh*), 287 (i.e., 286, Rabbi Shelomo Zalman of Kopyst discussing the controversy surrounding Sarugian Kabbalah and its endorsement in Mezritch), 290 (Rabbi Shelomo Zalman of Kopyst quoting Sarug's teaching of a second *Tsimtsum*, and the *Alter Rebbe*'s excited quotation from *'Emek ha-Melekh*), 291 (Rabbi Shelomo Zalman of Kopyst referring to Sarugian Kabbalah), 292 (Rabbi Menahem Mendel Schneerson of Lubavitch-Brooklyn noting that the references to *'Emek ha-Melekh* emanate from the *Tsemah Tsedek*), 293 (*Tsemah Tsedek* quoting from *'Emek ha-Melekh* and from Rabbi Meir Poppers in *Zohar ha-Raki'a*).

The last reference is of special interest. Contained in the Korets 1785 edition of Rabbi Jacob Tsemah's *Zohar ha-Raki'a* is a section of commentaries to *Zohar* by his student Rabbi Meir Hakohen Poppers (starting on 19b). The passage that *Tsemah Tsedek* cites is found there at 20a. After briefly alluding to the *'Olam ha-Malbush* of Rabbi Israel Sarug, Rabbi Meir Poppers distances himself by saying:

> But I do not study these discourses [i.e., of Sarug] for so commanded Rabbi Hayyim Vital in the introduction to *'Ets Hayyim* that we not study the works of any other man. And it is a *mitsvah* to fulfill his words. Therefore, you will not find in any of my compositions a discourse outside of the holy words of Rabbi Hayyim Vital, of blessed memory. I just came to show you that I did not say anything of my own theorizing, for it is true and correct.

[18] *b. Berakhot* 40a.
[19] *b. Sukkah* 52a.

[20] *m. Avot* 3:17.
[21] *Pinkesei ha-RAYaH*, vol. 4, ed. Z.M. Levin and B.Z. Kahana-Shapira (Jerusalem, 5777/2017), *Pinkas ha-Dapim* 1:34 (pp. 88-92).

THE UNIVERSALISM OF RAV KOOK

Stereotypes are difficult to overcome. Until recently, the stereotype of Rav Avraham Yitzhak Hakohen Kook (1865-1935) was of a nationalist (perhaps even ultranationalist) who lent his rabbinic aegis to the Zionist enterprise in the first third of the twentieth century.

In his seminal work *Orot* [*Lights*] (Jerusalem, 1920), the very first section of the book is entitled *"Erets Yisrael."* The punchline of the first chapter reads:

> The expectation of salvation (*tsefiyat ha-yeshu'ah*) is the force that preserves exilic Judaism; the Judaism of the Land of Israel is salvation itself (*ha-yeshu'ah 'atsmah*).

Thus, Rav Kook placed Israel's return to its ancestral homeland front and center, and provided it with theological underpinnings sorely lacking in the secular Zionist movement.

In this respect, Rav Kook's bold initiative, courageous and outspoken, at times alienated him from his more conservative-minded rabbinic peers. The Gerrer Rebbe, Avraham Mordechai Alter (1866-1948), wrote in a much publicized letter:

> The Rav, the Gaon R. Avraham Kook, may he live, is a man of many-sided talents in Torah, and noble traits. Also, it is

public knowledge that he loathes money. However, his love for Zion surpasses all limit and he "declares the impure pure and adduces proof to it."… From this, came the strange things in his books.

With the passage of time and the publication of many hitherto suppressed manuscripts, we become increasingly aware of another facet to the extremely complex personality of Rav Kook: the cosmopolitan or universalist.[1] Rav Kook's passionate love for his land and his nation of Israel in no way vitiated the larger scope of his Messianic or utopian vision. Such an illuminating manuscript is that designated *Pinkas 5*, published this year of 2018 by Boaz Ofen in volume 3 of his ongoing series *Kevatsim mi-Ketav Yad Kodsho (Journals from Manuscript)*. The *Pinkas* has been dated by the editor to the years 1907-1913, during which time Rav Kook served as Rabbi of Jaffa.

In the following *pensée* (perhaps "essay" is the better word), Rav Kook argues that just as the "seventy nations" of the world form an organic unity, the proverbial "family of man," so too the various faith communities or religions complement one another in a parallel organic unity.

Though Rav Kook probably never heard of the mythic bird Simorgh—which figures prominently in the twelfth-century work *The Conference of the Birds* by the Persian poet Farid ud-Din Attar—Rav Kook's imagery is roughly reminiscent. In that allegorical tale, the birds of the world set out to find a leader. It has been suggested to them that they appoint as their king the legendary

Simorgh. To reach the remote mountain abode of the Simorgh, the birds must embark on a perilous journey. Most of the birds succumb to the elements along the way. At journey's end, there remain but thirty birds. They discover that they themselves, together, form the sought Simorgh. In Farsi, *"Simorgh"* means "thirty birds" (*si-morgh*).

Lest the reader mistakenly surmise that Rav Kook suggests that the faith of Israel will in some way be subordinated to a higher unity, Rav Kook writes at the intermezzo:

> And with this, automatically the horn of Israel must be uplifted.
> *"Bow down to Him, all gods"* [Psalms 97:7].

Rav Kook sees no contradiction between the aspiration of Israel to settle their land and the blessing of peace for all mankind. On the contrary, he believes that precisely from its ancestral homeland the Nation of Israel will broadcast this prophetic message of global reconciliation to all the inhabitants of the planet. As he writes: "So the turn of Israel to shine has come—together with the demand of its independence, the desire of its renascence upon the holy soil, the source of the opinions and beliefs most worthy of spreading in space, and of taking up time and epochs in the life of all mankind."

The Thought of Rav Kook

TRANSLATION OF THE TEXT OF
KEVATSIM MI-KETAV YAD KODSHO

The aspiration to bring peace to the world, has forever been the aspiration of Israel. This is the interior of the soul of *Knesset Israel* (*Ecclesia Israel*), which was given full expression by the chosen of her children, the Prophets who foresaw at the End of Days humanity's happiness and world peace.

However, light advances slowly. The strides made are not discernible because divine patience is great, and that which appears in the eyes of flesh insignificant—is truly exalted from the vantage of the supernal eye. "In the place of its greatness, there you find its humility."[2] Even in the worst life; the hardest, lowest, most sinful life—there is abundant light and sufficient place for the divine love to appear. That life need not be erased from existence, but rather uplifted to a higher niveau. There is no vacuum,[3] no empty space; every level needs to be filled.

Truly, world peace, in the material sense, comes into our vision. The nationalism that ruled supreme during the days of "barbarism," when each nation perceived a foreign nation as uncivilized,[4] [and held] that all man's obligations to man are cancelled in regard to the "barbarians"—this evil notion is being erased. On the other hand, with the passing of generations, the intellect, the light of fairness, and the necessity of life—which together comprise the windows through which the divine light wends its way—all together impress the stamp of universal peace upon the national character. Gradually, there arrives the recognition that humanity's division into nations does not pit them against one another, such that nations cannot dwell together on the planet Earth. Rather, their relation is organic—just as individuals relate to the nation, and the limbs to the body. This notion, when completely manifest, shall renew the face of the world, purifying hearts of their wickedness and uplifting souls.

However, the relation of nations—their pacification—must correspond to the relation of religions. A complete nationalism is not possible without correlate feelings of holiness. Those sentiments—whether few or many—change opinions; those sentiments are sensitive to the variables of geography and genetics.[5]

Peace between nations cannot come about by minimizing the value of nationalism. On the contrary, people of good will recognize that just as the feeling for family is respectable and pleasant, holy and pure, and were it to be lost from the world, humanity would lose with it a great treasure of happiness and holiness—so the loss of the "national family" [i.e., nationalism] and all the sentiments and delicate ideas bound to it, would leave in its place a destruction that would bring to the collective soul a frustration much more painful than all the pains that it suffered on account of the demarcation of nationalism.

Humanity must receive the good and reject the evil. The force of repulsion and the force of attraction together build the material world; and the cosmopolitan[6] and national forces together build the palace of humanity and its world of good fortune.[7]

As it is in regard to nationalism, so it is in regard to religions. It is not the removal of religion that will bring bliss, but the religious perceptions eventually relating to one another in a bond of friendship. (With the removal of religion there would pass from the world a great treasure of strength and life; inestimable treasures of good.) Every thought of enmity, of opposition, of destruction, will dissipate and disappear. There will remain in the religions only the higher, inner, universal purpose, full of holy light and true peace, a treasure of light and eternal life. The religions will recognize each other as brothers; [will recognize] how each serves its purpose within its boundary, and does what it must do in its circle. The relation of one religion to another will be organic.[8] This realization automatically brings about (and is brought about by) the higher realization of the unity of the light of *Ein Sof* [the Infinite], that manifests upon and through all. And with this, automatically the horn of Israel must be uplifted.

"*Bow down to Him, all gods*" [Psalms 97:7].

This teaching of peace, which broadens the heart and refines the soul; which brings life and light to all the nations of the earth and to the "chambers of the heart" of each individual; which shines light on every home and family, every society and association—requires much study from the source of light. Humanity has hardly opened the first page of this teaching of peace; has yet to invoke the name of the Holy One, blessed be He, *"Shalom"* ("Peace").[9]

There was no opportunity for this as long as the blossom of national peace had not appeared. Now it has appeared, brought about by the humanistic[10] notions that grew stronger in the world for the past century and more. Yet they could not maintain their stand because they did not reach the pinnacle; they could not find firm footing in the peace of religions, that which would bring life and light, the blessing of heaven to individuals and to collectives, increasing true faith, love of God and the creations, the strength of life and joy of souls.

So the turn of Israel to shine has come—together with the demand of its independence, the desire of its renascence upon the holy soil, the source of the opinions and beliefs most worthy of spreading in space, and of taking up time and epochs in the life of all mankind. Once this encompassing light,[11] full of holiness and strength, appears upon them, the entire world of man, from one end to the other end, must be moved thereby, for light and for good, for the blessing of life and peace.

"Like the dew of Hermon descending upon the mountains of Zion, for there the LORD commanded the blessing, life eternal."[12]

(*Kevatsim mi-Ketav Yad Kodsho*, ed. Boaz Ofen, vol. 3 [Jerusalem, 2018], *Pinkas* 5, par. 43 [pp. 96-98])

---

[1] In Rav Kook's seminal work, *Orot* (1920), there was a chapter which I entitled in my edition, "The Three Wrestlers—Orthodoxy, Nationalism, and Liberalism—and the Referee." See Rabbi Abraham Isaac Hakohen Kook, ed. Bezalel Naor (Maggid, 2015), *Orot ha-Tehiyah* (Lights of Renascence), chap. 18 (pp. 320-327). A key sentence reads: "The Holy, the Nation, and Humanity—these are three major demands of which all life, our own and every man's, is composed" (ibid, p. 321).

[2] A play upon the saying of Rabbi Yohanan in *b. Megillah* 31a: "Wherever you find the strength of the Holy One, blessed be He, you find His humility."

[3] Based on the saying attributed to Aristotle: "Nature abhors a vacuum."

[4] Rav Kook explains the meaning of the original Greek word "*barbaros*" (βάρβαρος).

[5] Cf. this passage in *'Arpilei Tohar*:

> Messiah will interpret the Torah of Moses, by revealing in the world the vision how all the peoples and divisions of mankind derive their spiritual nourishment from the one fundamental source, while the content conforms to the spirit of each nation according to its history and all its distinctive features, be they temperamental or climatological; [according to] all the economic vagaries and the variables of psychology—so that the wealth of specificity lacks for nothing. Nevertheless, all will bond together and derive nourishment from one source, with a supernal friendship and a strong inner assurance. "'The LORD will give a saying; the heralds are a great host' [Psalms 68:12]—Every word that emitted from the divine mouth divided into seventy languages" [*b. Shabbat* 88b].
>
> And the absolute reconciliation of the spiritual unity of the entire human world—in a fashion that affirms the good of individual and collective freedom—is the beginning of that which is more exalted: the grand conception that flows from the revelation of the rich unity of the entirety of existence....
>
> (*'Arpilei Tohar* [Jerusalem, 1983], pp. 62-63)

'Arpilei Tohar was first printed in Jerusalem in 1914, before the outbreak of World War One. For various reasons that we need not go into, that edition remained unbound and uncirculated. Random copies found their way into private collections. In 1983, *'Arpilei Tohar* was reprinted in a slightly censored fashion. The complete contents of *'Arpilei Tohar* are now available in the unexpurgated collection, *Shemonah Kevatsim*, where it is designated "*Kovets 2.*"

This particular passage occurs in *Shemonah Kevatsim* (Jerusalem, 2004), 2:177.

Parenthetically, it seems to this writer that Rav Kook's vision of the Messiah differs significantly from that of Rabbi Nahman of Breslov, as becomes apparent from the latter's recently revealed *Megillat Setarim*. In Rav Kook's scheme, the Messiah reveals *retroactively* how the various peoples' spiritual paths are appropriate, given their national psychology; in Rabbi Nahman's scheme, the Messiah will act *proactively* to produce for the various peoples prayers befitting their respective mentalities:

> Afterwards he will travel to all the kings...and he will make for them customs similar to Israel's religion. Also there will be prayers that the nations will pray. (*Ahar kakh yisa' le-khol ha-melakhim...ve-ya'aseh lahem nimus samukh le-dat Yisrael. Gam yiheyu tefillot she-yitpallelu ha-'ummot.*)
>
> (Zvi Mark, *The Scroll of Secrets: The Hidden Messianic Vision of R. Nachman of Breslav* [Brighton, Mass.: Academic Studies Press, 2010], pp. 52-53)

Later, during World War One, in his place of exile, St. Gallen (Switzerland), Rav Kook would revisit this theme of spiritual diversity:

> [The] foundation was established in Israel, a holy nation, and from its ramifications, many peoples can receive nourishment, each nation according to its content, its ethics, and its natural, historic and racial disposition; according to its education and geographic and economic situation, and all the social and personal factors that combine with this.
>
> (*Shemonah Kevatsim* 7:45; *Orot, Yisrael u-Tehiyato* (Israel and Its Renascence), chap. 15 [Maggid edition, pp. 194-195])

[6] The loanword *"kosmopoliti"* occurs in Rav Kook's manuscript.
[7] Rav Kook likens nationalism and cosmopolitanism to the repulsive and attractive forces of a magnet.
[8] Rav Kook employs the loanword *"organi."*
[9] Rav Kook quotes Gideon in Judges 6:24: "[Gideon] called it [i.e., the altar] *'YHVH Shalom.'*"

The Talmud (*b. Shabbat* 10b) adduces this verse to establish that *"Shalom"* is a name of God of sufficient sanctity that it is forbidden to mention it in the bathroom. Maimonides' omission of this *halakhah* is curious; see Rabbi Joseph Karo, *Kesef Mishneh* to MT, Hil. *Keri'at Shema'* 3:5, and Maimonides' commentary to the *Mishnah, Berakhot* 9:7 (Kafah ed., p. 52, n. 27).

See further *Leviticus Rabbah* 9:9; *Numbers Rabbah* 11:7; Rabbi Nathan of Rome, *'Arukh*, s.v. *'et*; and Rashi, *Makkot* 23b, s.v. *u-she'elat shalom be-shem*.

Tosafot (*Sotah* 10a, s.v. *ela me-'atah lo yimaheh*) were of the opinion that the name *"Shalom"* must not be erased. For this reason, some have the custom of not writing the full name, substituting a slash for the final letter *mem*; see the gloss of Rabbi Moses Isserles to *Shulhan 'Arukh, Yoreh De'ah* 276:13.

[10] *Humaniyot* occurs in the Hebrew original.
[11] The Hebrew *"'or makif"* ("encompassing light") is a term borrowed from Lurianic Kabbalah.
[12] Psalms 133:3.

Rav Kook's Space Odyssey

"I am certain that one day men will fly from one planet to another, for this is something good and beautiful, and everything which is good and beautiful—will be!"
(Rav Kook)[1]

This year marks the fiftieth anniversary of the appearance of the classic film *2001: Space Odyssey* (1968), a collaborative work by science fiction writer Arthur C. Clarke and filmmaker Stanley Kubrick. The film traces the evolution of mankind "from ape to angel," starting with prehistoric hominids and ending with the Star Child, while much attention is lavished on the intervening species we call *Homo sapiens*. The development of man is carefully monitored from outer space by vastly superior unseen aliens who from eon to eon accelerate the process of evolution through the intervention of a mysterious monolith. Indeed, the iconic black monolith is the motif that remains with most viewers of this cinematic wonder.

To this day, interpreters are divided as to whether *Space Odyssey* is optimistic or pessimistic in outlook. According to the latest filmography by Michael Benson, *Space Odyssey: Stanley Kubrick, Arthur C. Clarke, and the Making of a Masterpiece* (New York: Simon and Schuster, 2018), the two collaborators brought to the project diametrically opposed perspectives. Kubrick, hot on the heels of his 1964 satire, *Dr. Strangelove* (a noir comedy concerning the nuclear arms race), had a rather dark vision of humanity. Clarke on the other hand, was the eternal optimist. In Benson's words: "It was an idea both could get behind, Clarke with his innate optimism about human possibilities, and Kubrick with his deeply ingrained skepticism" (p. 3). The unlikely alliance between a Jewish boy from the Bronx and an English gentleman (later knighted by Queen Elizabeth II as Sir Arthur C. Clarke), "was the most consequential collaboration in either of their lives" (p. 13). The savage brutality of prehistoric man on the African savanna may be credited to Kubrick; the beatific, almost messianic, image of the Star Child at the film's conclusion was Clarke's contribution. "The single most optimistic vision in [Kubrick's] entire body of work—2001's Star Child—was Clarke's idea" (ibid.).

※

By all accounts, Abraham Isaac Hakohen Kook (1865-1935) was a child of the cosmos. This is apparent to any student of his works. His famous *pensée*, *Shir Meruba'* or *Fourfold Song* (the title was provided by his disciple, the Nazirite), bespeaks the evolution of human consciousness in ever-widening circles from individualism to nationalism to humanism to a loving embrace of the universe as a whole. The *pensée* ends on this note:

> The Song of the Soul,
> the Song of the Nation,
> the Song of Man,
> and the Song of the World –
> all combine....[2]

(*Space Odyssey* has its own four movements marked by the appearance of the monolith at four crucial junctures in the film.)

What is certainly less known is that as a young man, Rav Kook actually composed a poem (in free verse), "*Sihat Mal'akhei ha-Sharet*" ("The Conversation of the Angels"), which well before Kubrick, traces the trajectory of man from earthbound existence to future space travel. In 1968, when *Space Odyssey* took the "silver screen" by storm, travel beyond the earth's atmosphere was already a reality. NASA's Apollo program was well under way and, just a year later, on July 20, 1969, Neil Armstrong and Buzz Aldrin would be the first men to walk on the surface of the moon. But when Rav Kook composed his poem, space travel was truly visionary.

The recurring image of Rav Kook's overview of human history—written from the perspective of the angels above—is the dyad of "speck of dust" (*garger avak*) and "shining disk" (*'adashah notsetset*), i.e., earth and sun. It will take many "revolutions" (*sibbuvim*) of the speck of dust around the shining disk; many "changings of creatures" (*halifot yitsurim*), which is to say generations of man, in order to break free of the hold the dyad clamps on human consciousness. Progressing from the primitive state, "the creature" is subjected to a rude awakening when the Copernican Revolution reveals that its "home" (*ma'on*) is in motion around the sun. However, the supposed "lesson in humility" fails to unify mankind. Instead, as Rav Kook points out, in the several centuries that have passed since Copernicus published *De Revolutionibus orbium coelestium* (*On the Revolutions of the Celestial Spheres*) in 1543, territorial disputes, fratricide and warfare have been the order of the day.

Coming from Rav Kook, this stark realism is refreshing. Too often, his presentations have been stereotyped as Pollyannish. While yet he lived, he was on occasion ridiculed by his rabbinic contemporaries for being overly optimistic. The Ashkenazic Rabbi of Tiberias, Moshe Kliers, quipped: "Dots appear to him as lights." (The reference was to the title of Rav Kook's seminal work, *Orot*, or *Lights*, his messianic vision of the renascence of Israel.) Surprisingly, Rav Kook's narrative of the human race seems spot-on.

Though the road to intellectual maturity may be bumpy, eventually man will make it to the stars. Rav Kook is confident that the humbling discovery of how infinitesimally small we truly are will register with an unbelieving humanity. In the final stanza, the angels acknowledge, perhaps begrudgingly, that the "mighty among midgets," by dint of its intellect and imagination, and above all, its sheer willpower, shall one day overtake them.

Postscript: When I read Rav Kook's coinage, "mighty among midgets" (*abbir nanasim*), I was reminded of Rabbi Isaac Hutner's response to someone who argued that those who bitterly opposed his mentor Rav Kook in Jerusalem were *gedolim* (greats): *"Velkher gedolim? Zei zennen alle geven Lilliputen!"* "Which greats? They were all Lilliputians!" (The *Rosh Yeshivah* was well acquainted with Jonathan Swift's satire, *Gulliver's Travels*.)

Sihat Mal'akhei ha-Sharet
The Conversation of the Angels
Abraham Isaac Hakohen Kook

Translated and Adapted by Bezalel Naor

A speck of dust
orbits a shining disk.
Some fragile creatures call it "Earth."
The disk they revere as "Sun."

As tiny as the speck is,
it is great
compared to its neighbor
circling it about.

Of the creatures there is one
possessing language and logic.
It named itself "Man,"
mighty among midgets.

It stands erect.
So does it walk,
moving parts of its body.
It calls them "legs."

The Thought of Rav Kook

From the rays of the disk
enveloping the speck
there is light,
perceptible by a small circle,
aqueous and fleshly.
The creature calls it the "eye."

This tiny creature
is full of powerful imagination,
as it rises up on its speck of dust
facing the shining disk.

The speck is great in its eyes
and to the disk it accords the glory of a god.
The creature is filled with
feelings of pride.

It measures the speck's orbit around the disk
to mark "Time"
sufficient to gauge
its habitation upon its speck.

The rays of the disk
also stream heat
that the creature and its neighbors on the speck
might live.

Space Odyssey

The duration of its life
amounts to so many orbits
of the speck
around the shining disk.

Life is in flux.
A creature dies.
And others replace it.
Wondrously, they are all of a single image.

This wonderful creature,
mighty among midgets,
has a conception, a thought
and a very mighty will.

Among the flock of this creature
the will differs much.
And so the conception.
What a wonder!

And in the fluctuation of these wondrous creatures
a conception settles in.
It continues to grow
and to expand its horizon.

The Thought of Rav Kook

After many orbits of
the speck around the disk,
the secret is known:
Man's manor is in motion!

The discovery is great.
A mystery has been divulged:
The entire speck
revolves around the shining disk.

The creature is so proud
of its wonderful discovery.
As if it created
worlds for eternity.

When these creatures meet
upon parts of the speck,
sometimes there breaks out an altercation,
a mighty disagreement.

They all come up with
the novel idea of fratricide.
They meet to plan
terminating life.

Space Odyssey

They quarrel over a piece of the speck.
Who should rule?
"Sovereignty" they call it.

After many orbits
and many changings of the creatures,
the conception grows,
the thought takes wing.

It appears from their movements
that they've begun to appreciate their petty value
and their pride in the speck-and-the-disk
has been reduced.
It's but a few more orbits until their intelligence
is sharpened.

When these puny creatures
will inherit the earth of "Truth,"
their spirit will soar
despite their humble abode.

They will recognize their true measure,
these tiny creatures.
Then they will truly grow in spirit.
When they will search for habitation
upon the terrain of "Truth."

"Truth is the living spring
to which we angels
accord honor."

With intelligence they will ascend
beyond the orbit of the speck,
beyond the compass of the disk.
In infinite expanses they will dwell.

Love will nestle in their midst,
strength of spirit from the Life of Worlds.
When they fully comprehend
how miniscule they are.

"These diminutive creatures
surpass us in knowledge and *élan*;
in mighty will,
full of unbounded expanses."

Eternal life shall start flowing in them.
Mighty horizons shall open for them.
From world to world they'll garner strength
and the spirit of the Living God will pulsate in them.[3]

[1] Quoted by his disciple in Boisk (Bauskas, Latvia), Dr. Moshe Seidel; see Hayyim Lifschitz, *Shivhei ha-RAYaH* (Jerusalem, 1995), p. 70.
[2] *Orot ha-Kodesh*, ed. Rabbi David Cohen, vol. 2 (Jerusalem: Mossad Harav Kook, 1971), p. 445.
[3] *Otserot ha-RAYaH*, ed. Rabbi Moshe Zuriel, vol. 2 (Rishon le-Zion, 2002), pp. 575-577.

Rav Kook
on Teaching Torah to Girls

The following letter of Rav Kook, addressed to his son, Tsevi Yehuda, and daughter, Freida Hannah, then residing with Rav Kook's in-laws in Jerusalem, discusses the Rav's educational philosophy. It touches upon the subject of teaching Torah to girls in particular, and on the goals of education in general.

Rav Kook maintains that in an ideal state—past and future—mankind would have no need of external learning; the individual would find all the necessary spiritual nourishment within the soul. Only with the "downfall" (*"nefilah"*) of mankind and distancing from its soulful resources does an artificial form of education become a necessity.

The Rav makes some very bold statements, referring to books as "medicaments," and schools as "prisons" and "hospital rooms."

From this perspective, the women of Israel, who traditionally were not subjected to the artifices of book-learning, were more fortunate. They continued to be taught by their own innate spiritual gifts, while their brothers were put through the contortions of formal education.

Though Rav Kook's epistle strikes the modern reader as antifeminist, Rabbi Ari Shvat rightfully defends Rav Kook as neither a misogynist nor an apologist for rabbinic law, which discouraged a father from teaching Torah to his daughter.

The ideas conveyed in this letter must be viewed against the backdrop of other such statements spread throughout the vast literary *oeuvre* of Rav Kook. A decade later, in his petite mystical work, *Reish Millin*, Rav Kook fires this opening salvo:

> The soul knows that whatever comes through learning is not from the source. Sourceful is the inner idea that is not expressed, that will be the world's inheritance on the great day that no more shall a man teach his brother and a man his neighbor to know the LORD, for all shall know Him from the least of them to the greatest of them.[1]

Another passage in *Shemonah Kevatsim* (*Eight Journals*) resounds with this same sentiment:

> The truly great men find within them an inner opposition to being taught (*hitlamdut*), for all is alive in their midst and flows from their spirit. They must constantly delve deeper into their inner spirit. In their case, the aspect of learning is but an aid and ancillary; the main thing that brings about their perfection is their very own Torah (*Torah didehu*). "And in *his* Torah he shall meditate day and night."[2] Sometimes a man does not realize his worth and turns his back on his very own Torah (*Torah dileh*), and desires specifically to be taught (*melummad*), either because of habit or a learned theory, such as, "Inquire and

receive reward."³ Then the angst of the descent begins to darken the world of these weak greats (*gedolim halashim*).⁴

Though one cannot say with any certainty that Rav Kook was aware of the writings of Jean-Jacques Rousseau, some of the ideas expressed in our letter are definitely reminiscent of Rousseau's theory of the "noble savage."⁵ But then again, a strong case could be made that Rav Kook developed his ideas from the prophetic tradition of Judaism.

This call for direct apperception of divinity without recourse to sacred literature will become even more pronounced in the intimate diaries of Rav Kook's disciple, Rabbi David Cohen ("the Nazirite"):

> The prophets and the disciples of the prophets went into isolation in the mountains and valleys, taking in the view of fields and pure skies. A fresh breeze blows, reviving the soul, to pay attention, to hear the holy word of the LORD. For shelter from rain and the cold of night, they would gather in caves.
>
> They did not have with them many books. They did not require libraries of works such as Talmud, codes and commentaries. This burden of books that stuff the soul with paper, and that divert attention from the uplifted and exalted, the purity of the heavens of the LORD—not by this will be revealed and revived the spirit of prophecy, rather by oral Torah, by studies in the mountains and the

valleys, upon fields of holiness, in full view of the heavens of the LORD.[6]

Before the Nazirite, similar sentiments were expressed by the medieval mystic Abraham Abulafia, an elusive figure whom Rabbi David Cohen would come to greatly appreciate.[7] (He was treated to Abulafian manuscripts by Gershom Scholem, librarian of Hebrew University in Jerusalem.)[8] Abulafia, famous as the founder of the school of "Prophetic Kabbalah," evidently prized more knowledge transmitted from Above (*"bat kol"*) than that obtained from books of Kabbalah (*sifrei ha-kabbalah*).[9]

※

In what is perhaps the most surprising statement of the entire letter, Rav Kook confides that on rare occasions he is able to get in touch with "the Torah of your mother" within him. Rav Kook is alluding to the verse in Proverbs: "Hear, my son, the reproof (*mussar*) of your father and forsake not the teaching (*torah*) of your mother."[10] If we follow through, Rav Kook believes that a human walks around with both of these introjected voices; the voice of the father and the voice of the mother. In the male, while it is the voice of the father, which represents book-learning, that predominates, nevertheless, the maternal voice, of a more soulful nature, remains intact, though its influence is more subtle and thus more difficult to tap into.

The confession sounds somewhat Jungian. Carl Gustav Jung theorized that every human possesses an animus and an anima, a male and female aspect. In the male, the animus is dominant and the anima recessive; in the female, the anima presides and the animus becomes the shadow side of the personality.

Finally, one detects that there runs through the letter an aversion to orthodox medicine ("textbook medicine") and perhaps an attraction to alternative medicine. (Once again, it seems that this outlook on the *ars medica* was amplified in Rav Kook's disciple, the "Nazirite," who famously said: *"Rofé hinam* [free physician] is the numerical value of *Shekhinah* [divine presence].")[11]

The letter was published for the first time in its entirety by Rabbi Ari Shvat, a researcher at Beit Harav in Jerusalem.[12]

Jaffa, 2 Shevat 5667 [i.e., 1907]

With the help of God

My son and daughter, the apples of my eye, may you live well,

My parsimony of letters—brought about by various botherances ill-suited to my disposition and inner desire, that forcefully invade my domain and seek action of a man who neither knows them nor desires to know them—has affected you too, my beloved children, causing you aggravation because of the paucity of my writing. Beloved children, you must forgive. I imagine that you recognize how much my heart desires to fulfill your wishes in general, and specifically your ideal wish to enjoy my words, to reflect upon them, and perhaps even to learn from them. But the surrounding situation oftentimes drives me from my "house of pleasure." My soul hopes for the salvation of the LORD to restore to me the joy of my salvation and to avail me a mood fitting my soul's yearning.

Beloved of my soul, I do not want to write to you separately, for the spiritual things which are the main foundation, should always apply in some aspect to both of you. Knowledge is universal; it knows no differences of gender, except for the specific ramifications; it is in those ramifications that there arise divisions based upon the individual's value, and upon the character of each gender. And I generally elude the specifics and seek to latch on to the universals of the ideas, which are dimly present in the soul of each of us, except that most people are too lazy to roll away the curtain in their midst in order to know how great is the treasure that lives in their soul. I, and those who are like-minded, try our utmost—in every time and place—to drive away this lassitude that prevents thousands upon thousands of humans from illuminating the splendor of their lives, the wealth and goodness that is in their very midst. [This lassitude] causes them to go in ways of darkness—pettiness, hatred, envy and competitiveness—which suffocate even more the light of clear, pure life. Therefore, the difference [of gender] is not taken into account by me; thank God that both of you are—each in his/her own way—intelligent and sensitive, whether more or less, but thank God, at least [you] are accustomed to see and to hear the inner desire of straight living, of purity, justice and universal love. One in whose soul these good plants are absorbed, is ready to hear things much higher and more exalted than the convention of the marketplace. The inner understanding is not measured by the pages or the books but by the dimension of goodwill that lives inwardly within the soul. Certainly, there will be found things that are specific to one gender or the other of you, but the benefit derives from the knowledge that encompasses both worlds, that of the brother and that of the sister; and this unifies the form of the letters.

The main difference, my dear daughter, between the souls of man and woman, is only in regard to the necessity of studies. On their own, books are not the natural nourishment of the human spirit. They are, at best, medicines for a humanity already sickened long ago. "I am the LORD your healer."[13] The healthy inner feeling that emerges in its pure nature through uncorrupted education, should teach man what there is within him sufficiently. Not for one moment in life do the brain and the heart cease to work; if they are straight, their entire natural, perpetual work is learning and Torah. However, we have descended much, the deeds have become crooked, the life impoverished; the disease of materialism has attacked all of humanity, so that they cannot conduct their physiological affairs without doctors and medicines learned from textbooks and uncertain theories. The spirituality in us has generally arrived at this unfortunate state. We are forced to imprison our beloved children from the "morning dew of their youth"[14] for several hours each day in schoolrooms; to tie them to books and letters—just as we are forced to place the sick in hospital rooms and harsh confinement chambers (of textbook medicine).

The Holy One, blessed be He, acted charitably with His world by bestowing upon woman more understanding than man.[15] [This added understanding is expressed] through her domestic sense being deeper, though by the same token it does not extend outward as much. There is no advantage to a "woman of valor"[16] observing worldly affairs of princes and kings, and their cruel wars, which add several chapters to books[17] and increase the work of tender children, chaining them ever more to prison, and in no small measure injecting in their spirit the pollution of murder and misanthropy that darkens the splendor of life. A "woman of valor" is exempted from all this catastrophe. She was created to oversee the affairs of her house; to extend her palm to the poor and needy; to clothe her household. These deeds are beautiful; they are pleasant, and a "fragrance of Lebanon"[18] and natural holy idealism encompasses them all about. If life were healthy and whole, there would be no need for any learning to supplement the beautiful, delicate domestic character.

But life has become so deficient, the human heart has so lost its feeling that it does not know how to find peace in the tranquil tent that is entirely love and generosity. In proportion to the fall (*nefilah*), we need to strengthen the hands of our daughters too by broadening the education. Yet Heaven forefend that a delicate daughter destined to be a true "woman of valor"—especially a daughter of Israel whose inner tent is destined to be a holy sanctuary—exchange her living world for books; nourishment for medicaments.

The wide circle of human society—in which a man is called to work based on his physiological and psychological makeup—is already so dark, that were it not for luminaries from on high, and generally, from outside of life, not a single ray of light would penetrate its midst. [Mankind] is so sick that its diet consists of drugs and its raiment is the bandages to bind broken bones. [Mankind] must teach and learn. And the more devoted it is to its healing, the more it shall advance, until with time, its health will be restored and it shall live an Edenic life as of yore, "a world that is entirely Sabbath and eternal rest."[19]

But the inner world—which is also great and wide if one be but capable of beholding its myriad details that gladden and pleasure every straight soul—especially in Israel, is yet close to its purity and natural happiness. And the European confusion that imprisons daughters as well in the prime of their youth in a prison called "school," produces generations weak in spirit and in body. From both aspects [i.e., spirit and body] there is extinguished in their midst the last spark of straight and holy naturalness. Thus, when the honored daughter—whose honor is inward, inward within her tent, inward in the chambers of her heart,[20] where there is an entire living world, yet perfect, "a semblance of the World to Come"[21]—forgets her worth; or a foolish cruelty, a false pride of her parents, causes her to forget her worth, and insists upon teaching her on a permanent basis, by tying her to the school, to the "hospital," to the book, then "it is as if [the father] teaches her folly."[22]

I desired to write and write, my dear ones, but what shall I do? Here they come, my cruel overseers, my nuisances, and interrupt me, dragging me from my peaceful inner tent—where fortunately, I sometimes find the maternal side in me, "the Torah of your mother"[23]—and bring me to the harsh atmosphere of the outer, corrupt life, compounded with troubles and woes, stress and strain, plaints and complaints.[24] I must go; they push me with force.

I pray to the LORD that He show me His broad salvation.

My dear daughter and son, please inform me of all the good and blessing that come your way. Gladden my soul with your dear words. Write and write as much as you are able. Every letter, every word of yours, showers upon me the "dew of lights"[25] and gladdens my soul.

Blessed is the LORD for the life and peace which is ours. Were it not [for the fact] that I must be brief because I must stop, I would certainly [write] at more length regarding sacred and secular matters. But for the time being, this is not possible. May the Master of Peace bless you with all manner of goodness, and may we merit to see from you much satisfaction, blessing and peace. As is your dear wish and the wish of your father who looks forward to your happiness and good all the days.

Avraham Yitzhak Ha[Kohen] K[ook]

---

[1] Rav Kook paraphrases the verse in Jeremiah 31:33: "And they shall teach no more every man his neighbor, and every man his brother, saying, 'Know the LORD,' for all shall know Me, from the least of them to the greatest of them, says the LORD."
   Rabbi Abraham Isaac Hakohen Kook, *Reish Millin* (London, 1917), *"Aleph"* (p. 2). The occasion for this striking remark is the fact that the first letter of the Hebrew alphabet, *Aleph*, means "teach" in Aramaic, which traditionally is the language of translation (*Targum*) from the original language of Hebrew. (In Hebrew, the word for "teach" is *lamed*.)

[2] Psalms 1:2; *b. Kiddushin* 32b; *b. 'Avodah Zarah* 19a.

[3] *b. Sanhedrin* 71a; *Zevahim* 45a.

[4] Rabbi Abraham Isaac Hakohen Kook, *Shemonah Kevatsim* 2:172.

[5] See now Emanuel Haronian, *The Attitude to Human Self in the Teaching of Rav Kook and Rav Harlap* (Hebrew), M.A. Thesis, Ben-Gurion University, February 2020, p. 23, note 179. Available at: academia.edu

[6] Rabbi David Cohen, *Mishnat ha-Nazir*, ed. Harel Cohen and Yedidyah Cohen (Jerusalem: Nezer David, 2005), pp. 52-53.

[7] See the section on *"Kabbalah Nevu'it"* (Prophetic Kabbalah) in Rabbi David Cohen, *Kol ha-Nevu'ah* (Jerusalem: Mossad Harav Kook, 1979), pp. 158-160.

[8] *Mishnat ha-Nazir*, p. 75.

[9] Abraham Abulafia, *Sefer ha-Heshek*, ed. Matithyahu Safrin (Jerusalem, 1999), p. 7; quoted in Moshe Idel, "Maimonides' *Guide of the Perplexed* and the Kabbalah," *Jewish History* 18 (2004), p. 213.

[10] Proverbs 1:8.
   Cf. Rabbi J.B. Soloveitchik, "A Tribute to the Rebbetzin of Talne," *Tradition* 17:2 (Spring 1978), pp. 73-83.

[11] They share the numerical value of 385. See Hilah Wolberstein, *Harav ha-Nazir: Ish ki yafli'* (Jerusalem: Makhon Nezer David, 2017), p. 286. The source of the *gematria* is Rabbi Aaron Berechiah of Modena's *Ma'avar Yabok* (Mantua, 1626), *ma'amar* 1 (*Siftei Tsedek*), chap. 21 (19b): "But the true physician is the *Shekhinah* (divine presence) for numerically it is *rofé hinam*."
   Apparently, the Nazirite expressed his thoughts on psychosomatic or alternative medicine in an essay entitled *"Megillat ha-Rof'im ve-ha-Refu'ot"* ("Treatise on Doctors and Medicines"). See Wolberstein, p. 285. Dr. Joshua Ritchie told this writer (BN) that when he paid a visit to the Nazirite, the latter began to expound to him his original theory of medicine.

[12] Ari Yitzhak Shvat, *"Iggeret Harav Kook be-Nose' Talmud Torah le-Nashim,"*

in *Me'orot li-Yehudah* (Rabbi Yehudah Feliks Festschrift), ed. M. Rehimi (Elkanah, 2012), pp. 343-362.
[13] Exodus 15:26.
[14] Cf. Psalms 110:3. In other words, from early childhood.
[15] *b. Niddah* 45b.
[16] Proverbs 31:10.
[17] Rav Kook's caustic remarks in this regard may have been influenced by Maimonides' earlier disparagement of the Arabic chronicles of kings. Maimonides thought reading such literature a complete waste of time. See Maimonides, *Commentary to the Mishnah, Sanhedrin* 10:1 (Kafah ed., pp. 140-141), and *Avot* 1:16 (Kafah ed., p. 273, "the third division").
[18] I.e., the fragrance of the legendary cedars of Lebanon. Cf. Hosea 14:7; Rabbi Abraham Isaac Hakohen Kook, *Orot, Orot ha-Tehiyah* (Lights of Renascence), chap. 38 (Naor ed., p. 363).
[19] *m. Tamid* 7:4 in version of Maimonides.
[20] Rav Kook paraphrases Psalms 45:14. See the rabbinic interpretation of the verse in *b. Gittin* 12a; *Yevamot* 77a; *Shavu'ot* 30a.
[21] The phrase "*me-'eyn 'olam ha-ba*" occurs in various hymns for the Sabbath. See *b. Berakhot* 57b: "The Sabbath is one sixtieth of the World to Come."
[22] *m. Sotah* 3:4; *b. Sotah* 21b; Maimonides, *MT, Hil. Talmud Torah* 1:13.
[23] Proverbs 1:8.
[24] Hebrew, *tevi'ot ve-kublanot*. Possibly an allusion to Rav Kook's position as *Av Beit Din*, or Chief Justice, of the Jaffa rabbinical court.
[25] Cf. Isaiah 26:19.

Rav Kook and Rav Harlap:
Truth and the Pursuit of Truth

In a poetic flourish—even more poetic than most of his personal *pensées*—Rav Kook let out this *cri de coeur*:

I thirst for truth (emet), *not for the attainment of truth* (hasagat ha-emet).[1]

The syntactical combination *"hasagat ha-emet"* is difficult to define. Prominent use of it is made by Maimonides in the first chapter of *Misneh Torah* in regard to comprehending the truth of God's existence.

First, there is Maimonides' categorical pronouncement: "And the truth of (*'amitat*) the thing, man's mind cannot comprehend (*le-hasig*) and investigate."[2]

Having posited that this is an impossible goal to achieve, Maimonides then probes what exactly Moses sought when he asked of God, "Show me please Your glory."[3] In Maimonides' paraphrase of Exodus 33:20 ("You cannot see My face, for man cannot see Me and live"), God's definitive response was: "It is not within the power of the intellect of a living man, composed of body and soul, to comprehend the truth of (*le-hasig amitat*) this thing with clarity."[4]

Finally, Maimonides attempts to explicate the enigmatic concession granted Moses by God, "You shall see My back, but My face shall not be seen."[5] "[The Holy One], blessed be He, let

[Moses] know that which no man before or after knew, until he comprehended of the truth of (*hisig me-'amitat*) His existence such that the Holy One, blessed be He, was distinguished in his mind from the rest of the existent things, just as a man who has been viewed from behind (his entire body and clothing) is distinguished in one's mind from other men."[6]

Though lexically the reference to *Mishneh Torah* might work, it does not seem that Rav Kook is reacting to Moses Maimonides. It is much more likely that Rav Kook is responding to something written by Moses Mendelssohn's lifelong friend, Gotthold Ephraim Lessing. (It is accepted that Mendelssohn is the protagonist portrayed in Lessing's play *Nathan the Wise*.) In 1778, Lessing boldly asserted:

> The true value of a man is not determined by his possession, supposed or real, of Truth, but rather by his sincere exertion to get to the Truth. It is not possession of the Truth, but rather the pursuit of Truth by which he extends his powers and in which his ever-growing perfectibility is to be found. Possession makes one passive, indolent, and proud.
>
> If God were to hold all Truth concealed in his right hand, and in his left only the steady and diligent drive for Truth, albeit with the proviso that I would always and for-

ever err in the process, and offer me the choice, I would with all humility take the left hand, and say: "Father, I will take this one—the pure Truth is for You alone."[7]

To employ Lessing's imagery, it seems that Rav Kook would choose what is in the right hand of God ("Truth"), rather than what is contained in the left ("the diligent drive for Truth").

Whether Rav Kook was aware of the quote from Lessing is open to speculation. Some years ago, Eliezer Goldman published a groundbreaking article in which he investigated Rav Kook's familiarity with European philosophy.[8]

As I have written elsewhere,[9] Rav Kook was eminently familiar with the *Pantheismusstreit* (Pantheism Controversy) that broke out between Friedrich Heinrich Jacobi and Mendelssohn concerning Spinozism. What sparked the controversy was the alleged deathbed confession of Lessing, confirming his pantheistic belief. As Lessing was Mendelssohn's dearest friend, Jacobi hoped by publicizing Lessing's confession to discomfit and unseat the regnant "German Plato." Jacobi placed Mendelssohn in a bind. If Mendelssohn were to reject pantheism outright, he would thereby dishonor his departed friend's memory. If, on the other hand, he upheld Lessing's legacy, he would have to embrace Spinoza's doctrine which was widely construed as atheism. Mendelssohn tried to find a middle ground by casting Spinoza's doctrine in a different, favorable light. The grief caused Mendelssohn by Jacobi's assault on his integrity was considerable; some credit Jacobi with precipitating Mendelssohn's sudden death (at age fifty-six).

In one of Rav Kook's journals, he alluded to Moses Mendelssohn's attempt to "purify" Spinoza.[10] Did Rav Kook also look into the works of Lessing? I have no way of knowing.[11]

There is another avenue to explore in our attempt to contextualize Rav Kook's abrupt remark.

In his birthplace of Grieva, a suburb of Dvinsk, Latvia, Rav Kook was exposed at an early age to HaBaD Hasidism. His maternal grandfather, Rabbi Raphael Felman, was a Lubavitcher Hasid. (His particular allegiance was to the Rebbes of Kopyst, Rabbi Yehudah Leib Schneerson, and after his passing, his son Rabi Shelomo Zalman Schneerson, author of *Magen Avot*. These were the son and grandson of the famed *"Tsemah Tsedek,"* Rabbi Menahem Mendel Schneersohn of Lubavitch.)[12]

The *Tsemah Tsedek* recorded in his writings that his grandfather Rabbi Shneur Zalman of Liadi, the founder of the HaBaD school, could be overheard uttering these words in his meditation before commencing the morning prayer:

Ich vill zhe gor nisht.
Ich vill nit dein Gan Eden.
Ich vill nit dein Olam Habo.
Ich vill mehr nit az Dich alein.

I want nothing.
I don't want Your Garden of Eden.
I don't want Your World to Come.
I want nothing but You alone.[13]

A slightly different, lengthier version was recorded by a Hasid close to the *Tsemah Tsedek*, Rabbi Peretz Chein:

I do not want the hasagah *of the ophanim.*
I do not want the hasagah *of the seraphim.*
I do not want Your Garden of Eden.
I do not want Your World to Come.
"Who is there for me in heaven, and beside You I desire none on earth."[14]

In his *cri de coeur*, Rav Kook might have been reverberating the anguished cry of the *Alter Rebbe* ("Old Rabbi"). Just as the founder of HaBaD had no interest in the *hasagot* of the ophanim and the seraphim, so Rav Kook had no interest in the *hasagah* of truth. Like the *Alter Rebbe* who desired God alone, Rav Kook thirsted for "truth" *tout court*.

Though the word *"hasagah"* does not occur in the shorter version of Rabbi Shneur Zalman's meditation, it may be implicit in the reference to the Garden of Eden. According to the teaching of Rabbi Shneur Zalman, there is not one Garden of Eden awaiting the soul after its departure from the body, but infinitely many. And each time that the soul is about to graduate from a lower Garden (*Gan 'Eden* ha-Tahton) to a higher Garden (*Gan 'Eden ha-'Elyon*),¹⁵ it must first immerse itself in the *Nehar di-Nur*,¹⁶ the River of Fire, which results in memory loss. In order to assimilate the new *hasagot*, the new consciousness, one must first forget the old and familiar, as Rabbi Zeira who fasted one hundred fasts to forget the learning of Babylonia so that he might absorb the higher learning of *Erets Yisrael*.¹⁷ Thus, for Rabbi Shneur Zalman, the Garden of Eden is not a final destination but a station along a way with no end in sight.¹⁸

And one daresay, it was the unending process of perception upon perception, *hasagah* upon *hasagah* of truth that Rav Kook—perhaps not unlike the *Alter Rebbe*—wished to dispense with. This impassioned soul longed to bypass the process and finally, definitively arrive at—the truth.

As the *Alter Rebbe*, Rav Kook desperately desired to break the heavens wide open, to put an end once and for all to "process theology." "You alone." "The truth."

Rabbi Moshe Tsevi Neriyah, who studied under Rav Kook in his *yeshivah* in Jerusalem, recorded that during the afternoon banquet of *Simhat Torah*, a time of great exultation, Rav Kook suddenly got up from the table and began pacing the length of the hall while singing with emotion the *Alter Rebbe*'s paraphrase of the verse in Psalms 73:25:

"*Mi li va-shamayim ve-'imkha lo haftsti va-'arets.*"
Ich vill nit hoben dem Olam Hazeh,
Ich darf nit hoben dem Olam Habo,
Nor Dir alein,
*Nor Dir alein.*¹⁹

"Who is there for me in heaven, and beside You I desire none on earth."
I do not want this world,
I do not need the World to Come,
Only You,
Only You!

※

There is yet another angle to examine. Rav Kook expressed a predilection for the Talmud of *Erets Yisrael* (referred to by academicians as the "Palestinian Talmud") over the Babylonian Talmud. As he wrote to the historian Rabbi Yitzhak Isaac Halevi Rabinowitz (author of *Dorot ha-Rishonim*):

> So in *Erets Yisrael*, which is the place of prophecy, the flow of prophecy leaves a mark upon the discipline (*seder ha-limmud*), and the sense [of the text] is explained through an inner gaze and does not require such lengthy investigation....The wisdom of prophecy...was much more active in *Erets Yisrael* than in Babylonia, which is unworthy of prophecy....Now those influenced by the roots of the wisdom of prophecy—for them brevity is an advantage. The halakhic analysis and inference is accomplished by them with a wide view. For them, a subtle hint is sufficient to decide the law. This was the foundation of the discipline

(*seder ha-limmud*) of the [Talmud] *Yerushalmi*. For those fortunate to benefit from the light above, short inferences sufficed to clarify the *halakhah* (*birur ha-halakhah*). But for the Babylonians, upon whom the roots of prophecy did not exert so much influence, brevity was insufficient and there was required a lengthy discussion.[20]

The consensus among modern historians today is that the *sugyah* (Talmudic discussion) of the *Yerushalmi* is abbreviated in comparison to its Babylonian counterpart, not because of an influx of prophetic inspiration in *Erets Yisrael*, but for the more prosaic reason that the conversation in Babylonia continued for a century longer, during which time the next generations of *amoraim* had opportunity to join the discussion. In addition to that, the Babylonian Talmud underwent an editorial process by anonymous *"stammaim"* (as they are currently referred to) who provided the mortar to the bricks of the Talmud.

Yet Rav Kook persisted in his belief that the discipline of Talmudic study could yet be revolutionized in *Erets Yisrael*, "the place of prophecy." It is certainly no coincidence that in his first *yeshivah* in *Erets Yisrael* (that which existed in Jaffa when he served as rabbi there between the years 1904-1914), Rav Kook made a point of teaching Rabbi Yehudah Halevi's *Kuzari*.[21] The *Kuzari* states boldly: "Whoever prophesied did so either in the [Holy] Land, or concerning it."[22]

To the end of streamlining the process of halakhic decision-making, Rav Kook undertook the painstaking task of transcribing to the margins of the Talmud the pertinent quotes from Maimonides' code of law and Rabbi Joseph Karo's *Shulhan 'Arukh*. In his Central Universal Yeshivah in Jerusalem (today known as "Merkaz Harav"), Rav Kook rebuffed all attempts to import from Europe the type of conceptualization (*"Hasbarah"*) that was all the rage in the Lithuanian *yeshivot* of the day. (For this reason, Rav Kook was loath to endorse Rabbi Shimon Shkop's appointment as *Rosh Yeshivah*.) Instead, Rav Kook wished his students to adhere to the method of *"peshat"* (simple meaning) that was personified by the Vilna Gaon.[23] (Rav Kook himself penned a super-commentary [*Be'er Eliyahu*] to *Be'ur ha-Gra*, the Gaon's skeletal notes to *Shulhan 'Arukh, Hoshen Mishpat*.)

Today, we regard with some wonderment Rav Kook's idealization of the Talmud *Yerushalmi* over and against the *Talmud Bavli*. There is a tendency in some quarters to cut Rav Kook loose from his HaBaD roots. Scholars who are truly objective and disinterested would do well to compare Rav Kook's thoughts on the *Yerushalmi-Bavli* divide to an especially pithy passage in the writings of the *"Mitteler Rebbe"* ("Middle Rabbi"), Rabbi Dov Baer Shneuri, a master of HaBaD known for his depth.

In his work *Sha'arei 'Orah*, Rabbi Dov Baer discusses at length the protracted dialectic, the alternating stages of light and darkness, clarity and obfuscation, revelation and concealment that the sages of Babylonia would endure before they finally arrived at some halakhic conclusion. As they observed, considering their predicament: "'He sat me down in darkness.' This refers to the Talmud of Babylonia."[24] The sages of *Erets Yisrael*, on the other hand, were able to arrive at the finish line and reach halakhic decisions without the *pilpul* (dialectic). While the *Mitteler Rebbe* does not attribute this ability to the remnants or roots of prophecy as does Rav Kook, he does draw on kabbalistic tradition to account for the different disciplines of *Erets Yisrael* and Babylonia:

> This is the difference between the inhabitants of Babylonia and the inhabitants of *Erets Yisrael*: Outside the Land, the air of the nations is impure from *kelipat nogah*,[25] etc. The true light from the source of wisdom cannot come to them as it is without recourse to *pilpul*....But in *Erets Yisrael* where *kelipat nogah* does not rule in such a coarse manner (only through a thin veil, as is known), inasmuch as they are more separated from *kelipat nogah*,[26] the true light is able to be revealed in the vessels of their minds...without such lengthy *pilpul*.[27]

The *Mitteler Rebbe* describes the chiaroscuro process of the *Bavli* as one of *hasagah* mounted upon *hasagah* (or conversely as *"he'elem ahar he'elem,"* "one concealment after another"), as opposed to the *Yerushalmi*'s brilliant flash of *"emet"* (truth).

Just as Rabbi Nahman of Breslov had once told his premier disciple Rabbi Nathan of Nemirov, so Rav Kook revealed to his premier disciple Rabbi Ya'akov Moshe Harlap that they had known each other in a previous lifetime.

On another occasion Rav Kook remarked that when he and Rabbi Harlap are alone together in a room, there is only one person there, not two. Such was the intimacy and closeness of master and acolyte.

Yet at the end of the day, no two people think alike. As the Rabbis expressed it: "Just as their faces are not alike, so their opinions are not alike."[28] In stark contrast to Rav Kook's one-liner, we find in the writings of Rav Harlap this reflection:

> However, one must ponder the *hasagot* (realizations) at their foundation: Is the realization the main thing, or is seeking the realization (*bakashat ha-hasagah*) the main thing. And if one should say that seeking the realization is the main thing, one must still see if the seeking must be restricted to that which it is possible to realize, or also—and essentially—that which it is impossible to realize.[29]

Rav Harlap presents his case that what enlivens man—if you would have it, the élan vital—is not the attainment of the realization but the unceasing striving for the unattainable.[30]

As Yeshayahu Leibowitz pointed out when reading aloud from the text of Rav Harlap, the author never heard of Lessing, yet independently arrived at Lessing's conclusion.[31] These words of Rav Harlap were very dear to Leibowitz because in them he heard (or wished to hear) a resonance of his own idiosyncratic Messianic vision, one of infinite striving. In Leibowitz's reading, Messiah tarries because he must; because, by definition, his arrival must be forever delayed. In the more popular and pointed version, Leibowitz notoriously defined a false Messiah as a Messiah who comes.

When Leibowitz attempted to ascribe his controversial version of Messianism to Maimonides, he was called out by Professor Ze'ev Harvey. Harvey demonstrated that Maimonides firmly believed in "perfectibility" and in a Messiah who in fact arrives.[32]

As is well known, despite Professor Yeshayahu Leibowitz's immense respect for Rav Kook's spiritual and intellectual stature, he could never agree to his philosophy. Needless to say, Rav Kook's "thirst for truth, not the striving for truth" could never become the *"Hazon Yeshayahu,"* "the vision of Yeshayahu."[33]

---

[1] *Shemonah Kevatsim* 3:280. That particular *pensée* was first made available to the public in a collection of Rav Kook's poetry published by A.M. Habermann in *Sinai* 17 (1945). The poems were made available to Habermann by the poet's son, Rabbi Tsevi Yehudah Kook. (The ostensible dates of their composition were also provided by Rabbi Tsevi Yehudah.) In Habermann's edition, paragraphs 279 and 280 of *Shemonah Kevatsim* were conjoined (separated only by a dash) and entitled *"Merhavim, Merhavim"* ("Expanses, Expanses"), the first two words of paragraph 279.

[2] Maimonides, *MT, Hil. Yesodei ha-Torah* 1:9.

[3] Exodus 33:18.

[4] *Hil. Yesodei ha-Torah* 1:10.

[5] Exodus 33:23. Maimonides' nemesis, Rabad of Posquières, quipped: "'My face' and 'My back' is a great mystery and it is not fitting to reveal it to every man. And perhaps this author [i.e., Maimonides] did not know it." See *Hasagot ha-Rabad le-Mishneh Torah*, ed. Bezalel Naor (Jerusalem, 1985), *Hil. Yesodei ha-Torah* 1:10 (p. 15).

[6] *Hil. Yesodei ha-Torah* 1:10.

[7] *Anti-Goeze* (1778), as quoted in *God Is Not Great* (2007), by Christopher Hitchens, chap. 19.

[8] Eliezer Goldman, *"Zikato shel ha-Rav Kook la-Mahshavah ha-Eropit"* in *Yovel Orot*, ed. Binyamin Ish-Shalom and Shalom Rosenberg (Jerusalem: WZO,

1988), pp. 115-122.
9. Bezalel Naor, *The Limit of Intellectual Freedom* (Spring Valley, NY: Orot, 2011), pp. 22-23.
10. Rabbi Abraham Isaac Hakohen Kook, *Kevatsim mi-Ketav Yad Kodsho*, ed. Boaz Ofen, vol. 1 (Jerusalem, 2006), Pinkas "Rishon le-Yaffo," par. 117 (p. 146).
11. In a letter to Rabbi Ya'akov Moshe Harlap, a young Tsevi Yehudah Kook (aged nineteen) quotes a saying of Lessing. Tsevi Yehudah explains to Rabbi Harlap that Lessing (and Kant, also quoted in that letter) lived in the generation of the Vilna Gaon. The quote from Kant was heard from Tsevi Yehudah's uncle, Shaul Hanna Kook. See *Tsemah Tsevi: Iggerot Harav Tsevi Yehudah Hakohen Kook*, vol. 1 (1907-1919), ed. Landau, Neuman, and Rahmani (Jerusalem, 1991), Letter 9 (p. 25).
12. Rabbi Menahem Mendel Schneersohn of Lubavitch (1789-1866) was referred to as *"Tsemah Tsedek,"* the title of his collection of halakhic responsa.
13. Rabbi Menahem Mendel Schneersohn, *Derekh Mitsvotekha: Ta'amei ha-Mitsvot* (Poltava, 1911; photo offset Kefar Habad, 1973), Shoresh Mitsvat ha-Tefillah, chap. 40 (138a). See further ibid. Kedoshim 5562 (154a).
    Rav Kook borrowed *Derekh Mitsvotekha* (yet in manuscript) from his neighbor, Rabbi Shneur Zalman Slonim, Rabbi of the HaBaD community of Jaffa. See *Iggerot la-RAYaH* (Jerusalem, 1986), Letter 169 (p. 146): "Sometimes he borrowed from me [i.e., S.Z. Slonim] a manuscript, the *Sefer ha-Mitsvot* [Book of Commandments] by the *Tsemah Tsedek*."
14. *Ha-Mashpi'a* (biography of Rabbi Shelomo Zalman Havlin) (Jerusalem, 1982), pp. 126-127. The line of transmission went from the *Tsemah Tsedek* to Rabbi Peretz Chein to his son Rabbi David Tsevi Chein, Rabbi of Chernigov. The final line is a quote from Psalms 73:25.
15. In one recension of the *Alter Rebbe*'s meditation, he spurns the lower Garden of Eden (*Gan 'Eden ha-Tahton*) and the higher Garden of Eden (*Gan 'Eden ha-'Elyon*). See Moshe Hariton in *Heikhal ha-Besht*, no. 4, year 3 (Tishri 5766), p. 167.
16. In his vision of the "four great beasts," Daniel saw a river of fire, "*Nehar di-Nur*" (Daniel 7:10).
17. *b. Bava Metsi'a* 85a; Rabbi Shneur Zalman of Liadi, *Torah 'Or*, Yitro, s.v. *mar'eihem u-ma'aseihem*, 69c.
18. See Rabbi Shneur Zalman of Liadi, *Torah 'Or*, Mikets, 32d:

> Therefore even though in general there are but two levels, the higher Garden of Eden in [the World of] *Beri'ah* and the lower Garden of Eden in [the World of] *Yetsirah*, to be specific, there are unlimited *hasagot* (attainments)....There are innumerable *hasagot*....And each time that the soul must ascend from one Garden of Eden to another there must precede the level of *Nehar di-Nur* (the River of Fire) in order that all the previous attainments be nullified, for the previous *hasagah* is incomparable to the *hasagah* above....With each added *hasagah*, the *hasagah* below becomes inconsequential.

The *Alter Rebbe* revisits this theme several times. See Rabbi Shneur Zalman, *Torah 'Or*, Mikets, 31a-b; *Megillat Esther*, 96a; idem, *Likkutei Torah*, Beshallah, 1d; *Derushim li-Shemini 'Atseret*, 83d, 84d.

[19] Rabbi Moshe Tsevi Neriyah, *Sihot ha-RAYaH* (Tel-Aviv, 1979), p. 258. Rabbi Neriyah juxtaposed a passage in Rabbi Shneur Zalman's *Tanya*, chap. 43 (62a).

When subsequently challenged by HaBaD Hasidim who knew of no such *niggun*, Rabbi Neriyah countered that Rav Kook must have heard the tune in his youth from the Kopyster Hasidim in his hometown of Grieva. There is another possibility, namely that Rav Kook composed the melody himself, perhaps on the spur of the moment.

[20] *Iggerot ha-RAYaH*, vol. 1 (Jerusalem: Mossad Harav Kook, 1962), Letter 103 (pp. 123-124).

[21] See my edition of *Orot* (Maggid, 2015), p. 454, n. 174. See also Rabbi M.G. Barg's incomplete notes of Rav Kook's lectures on the *Book of Kuzari* delivered in Jerusalem in 1921; in *Ma'amrei ha-RAYaH*, vol. 2, ed. Rabbi Elisha Aviner (Langenauer) (Jerusalem, 1984), pp. 485-495.

[22] Judah Halevi, *Book of Kuzari*, transl. Hartwig Hirschfeld (New York: Pardes Publishing House, 1946) II, 14 (p. 78).

[23] See the response of Rabbi Ya'akov Moshe Harlap to Rabbi Hizkiyahu Yosef Mishkovksi of Krinik regarding the appointment (or dis-appointment) of Rabbi Shim'on Shkop, famous for his method of *Higayon* or Talmudic logic; in *Zeved Tov* [*Festschrift* for Rabbi Zevulun Charlop] ed. Ari S. Zahtz (New York: Yeshiva University Press, 2008), Letter 7 (p. 103). The letter is datelined "2nd Day of Rosh Hodesh Adar, 5686 [i.e., 1926], Jerusalem."

[24] Lamentations 3:6; *b. Sanhedrin* 24a. Quoted in Rabbi Dov Baer Shneuri, *Sha'arei 'Orah* (Johannisburg, n.d.; photo offset Brooklyn: Kehot, 1979), *Sha'ar ha-Hanukkah*, chaps. 54-58 (pp. 22b-24a).

[25] Literally, "shell of brightness," or "translucent shell." A Lurianic kabbalistic term for the borderline level intervening between *kedushah* (holiness) and the full-fledged *"shalosh kelipot teme'ot,"* or "three impure shells."

[26] See *Zohar* II, 140b-141a. Cf. Rabbi Abraham Azulai, *Hesed le-Avraham* (Lvov, 1863; photo offset Jerusalem, 1968), 3:9 (20a-b).

[27] *Sha'arei 'Orah*, chap. 58 (24a).

[28] *y. Berakhot* 9:1; *b. Berakhot* 58a.

[29] Rabbi Ya'akov Moshe Harlap, *Mei Marom*, vol. 1 (Commentary to Maimonides' *Shemonah Perakim*) (Jerusalem: Beit Zevul, 1982), 7:6 (p. 136).

[30] Ibid. pp. 136-139.

Cf. Rabbi Harlap's letter to a young Rabbi Yehudah Klein (who later changed his surname to "Amital"). There, the point is made that that which is incomprehensible (*bilti-mussag*) is greater than that which is comprehensible (*mussag*) and more pleasurable. The letter is datelined "6 Adar I, 5706 [i.e., 1946]." First published in *'Alon Shevut*, Year 5, no. 20 (Adar 5734), pp. 18-21, it was later included in a 64-page brochure on Rabbi Harlap issued by the Israeli Ministry of Education, edited by Rabbi Aryeh Strikovsky, no. 271 (Tishri 5767), pp. 45-46. The brochure is available online: http://meyda.education.gov.il/files/tarbut/pirsumeagaf/kitveet/271pdf.pdf?fbclid=IwAR2uIdw9XhInuL_bW8LyHDq77j9JQGkNxBgG4WorTD-jbXHulQKlgLL5l1KU

In his letter, Rabbi Harlap refers to an early work of his, *Hed ha-Hayyim ha-Yisraeliyim* (Jerusalem, 1912).

In this respect, Rav Kook and Rav Harlap would be in total agreement.

Rav Kook embraced Maimonides' "negative attributes" (*to'arei shelilah*). See *Reish Millin* (Jerusalem: Makhon RZYH Kook, 2003), Part Two (*Ha-Shorashim*), s.v. *Aleph Lamed* (p. 122):

> It is the spiritual negation, by which the logical mind negates from the highest concept (*musag*), that informs it [i.e., the mind] of its [i.e., the concept's] truth (*amitato*) and reveals its power and light.
> Negation in divine attributes is the source of truth, by which the soul stands on a basis filled with light, freedom, and eternal joy.

[31] See the video of the dialogue between Professors Yeshayahu Leibowitz and Zev (Warren) Harvey of 30/5/1993 at 28:45-32:30. Available at Youtube: https://www.youtube.com/watch?v=wkcnXAsFUgA

[32] See Warren Zev Harvey, "Leibowitz's Anti-Greek Concept of the Messiah," *Iyyun*, vol. 42 (October 1993): 517-520 (Hebrew); and the video cited in the previous note.

[33] Isaiah 1:1.

Zion and Jerusalem:
The Secular and the Sacred

Much has been written about Rav Kook's short-lived movement, *Degel Yerushalayim* (Banner of Jerusalem), which he envisioned as the complement or counterpart to the Zionist movement.[1] The bulk of the third volume and a good portion of the fourth volume of *Iggerot ha-RAYaH*, the collected letters of Rav Kook, are devoted to explicating and promoting the fledgling movement.[2] To Rav Kook's thinking, the two movements would work side by side in perfect symmetry. The secular Zionist movement founded by Herzl would address the physical building of the Land of Israel, while the movement with Rav Kook at its helm would focus on the spiritual rebirth to take place in the ancestral land.

This symmetry would be reflected in the respective names "Zion" and "Jerusalem." Zion symbolizes the political entity of statehood; Jerusalem is synonymous with the spiritual aspirations associated with the sacred place.[2*]

Historians tell us that the impetus for the movement came from none other than Nahum Sokolow, who, together with Chaim Weizmann, led the Zionist movement in London in World War One. When Rav Kook, then residing in London, pressed Sokolow to include the traditional Judaic vision in the Zionist platform, Sokolow responded in writing with the witticism, "A vessel used for the secular, may not be used for the sacred" (*"Keli she-mishtamshim bo hol, ein mishtamshim bo kodesh"*), while encouraging Rav Kook to found his own independent movement devoted solely to the sacred.[3]

What was apparent to Rav Kook's rabbinic peers was that a spiritual vacuum had been left by political Zionism. What required some explaining on Rav Kook's part was why yet another religious movement was called for. There existed already the Mizrachi (Religious Zionist) movement, founded by Rabbi Jacob Reines of Lida, and *Agudat Yisrael* (or simply the *Agudah*), founded by Jacob Rosenheim of Frankfurt. Rav Kook pointed out the shortcomings of these two movements. Mizrachi never emerged as a separate entity but always worked within the framework of Zionism, which is essentially secular in character. *Agudat Yisrael*, on the other hand, while clearly independent of and even antagonistic to Zionism, failed to make Erets Yisrael its priority.[4]

Conceptually, Rav Kook presented what appeared a coherent picture. Semantically, there was a problem with his construct, this being of a kabbalistic nature.

An acquaintance of Rav Kook from his sojourn in London during World War One, raised the following concern. According to Kabbalah, Zion represents the internal and Jerusalem the external. How, then, could Rav Kook reverse the significance of these terms, attributing the inner dimension to Jerusalem and the outer dimension to Zion?

The man who voiced this vexatious problem was Rabbi Shemariah Menashe Hakohen Adler. A native of Poland, he emigrated to Fuerth, Germany, where he engaged in commerce. At the outbreak of World War One, he arrived in London as a refugee.[5] As Rabbi Adler was an erudite Talmudist and halakhist (besides being knowledgeable in Kabbalah), he would go on to author several volumes of responsa, entitled *Mar'eh Kohen*. Unfortunately, his prodigious intellect was blighted by unattractive character traits. Shemariah Menashe Adler was known to be of a cantankerous nature. He publicly insulted Dayan Hillman,[6] and later, his successor in the London Beth Din, Dayan Abramsky.[7] Though Rabbi Shemariah Menashe Adler could be quite disdainful of celebrated rabbis, to Rav Kook's credit, it must be said that the ill-natured controversialist was quite fond of him,[8] even going so far as penning a commentary to Rav Kook's slight kabbalistic work *Reish Millin* (London, 1917). Rav Kook responded to Rabbi Adler on that occasion, complementing him on his work, while spelling out the true kabbalistic significance of the neologism *"Arieliyut"* in the introduction to the tract, *Reish Millin*, and correcting a theological error in Rabbi Adler's wording concerning the *Ein Sof*.[9]

※

Here, once again, we have Rav Kook engaging with Rabbi Adler in a kabbalistic discussion, this time concerning the terms "Zion" and "Jerusalem."[10] Although Rav Kook addresses Rabbi Adler with the customary honorifics reserved for an outstanding rabbinic scholar ("the *gaon*, sharp and encyclopedic, et cetera"), from the tone of the letter, it sounds as if Rav Kook is somewhat miffed by the challenge to his proficiency in Kabbalah: "Regarding his comment that 'Zion' is an attribute more inward than 'Jerusalem,' *this is a simple matter, and every beginner in Kabbalah knows* that 'Zion' is the attribute of *'Tsaddik Yesod 'Olam'* [i.e., *Yesod*][11] and 'Jerusalem' is [situated] in *Malkhut*...."[12] (Italics mine—BN.) In fact, the question that Rabbi Adler poses is so basic that it is only with the greatest ingenuity that Rav Kook succeeds in answering it.

What follows is nothing less than a bouleversement. Rav Kook begins by offering an instructive example:

> Just as the days of the workweek correspond to the "six edges" (*vav ketsavot*)[13] and the Sabbath is the attribute of *Malkhut* which is the last [of the ten *sefirot*], nevertheless, for this very reason, the sanctity of the Sabbath is more revealed in the world, because the height of the upper attributes [i.e., the "six edges"] does not let them reveal their sanctity in the world. Only the attribute of *Malkhut* is fitting for such, and for this reason, the sanctity of the Sabbath is so severe.

Rav Kook would have us accept that the kabbalistic scheme is actually counterintuitive. That which in the kabbalistic reckoning is "higher," manifests in our mundane world as profane (*hol*); that which is sefirotically "lower," comes across in our plane of reality as sacred (*kodesh*). Having established the topsy-turvy relation of the six days of work to the seventh day of rest, Rav Kook proceeds to elucidate the relation of Zion to Jerusalem:

> Similarly, since the attribute of "Zion" is inner, in this world it is not recognized as being sacred. Therefore, here [i.e., in this world] it is the place of the kingdom (*mamlakhah*), and not the place of the Temple (*mikdash*), as is famous to those who stand in the Holy City.[14] And certainly the innermost holiness sanctifies the earthly kingdom as well, but the attribute of "Jerusalem"—because it is external at its root, in comparison to "Zion"—manifests below [i.e., in this world] with the power of holiness, and therefore we say, "[Bring us] to Zion, Your city, and to Jerusalem, Your Holy Temple."[15]

To digest Rav Kook's reconstruction, at its root on high, the secular aspect of Erets Yisrael ("Zion") with all the trappings of statehood, is actually "higher" and more "inward." On the other hand, the sacred aspect ("Jerusalem"), that which is manifestly holy in our world, is "lower" in the sefirotic realm, and more "outward."

The implications of Rav Kook's kabbalistic analysis are bold indeed. From the view above, that which manifests in the world as secular (*hol*) is "higher" than that which is revealed on our plane as sacred (*kodesh*)![16]

The next segment in Rav Kook's epistle appears to be a *non sequitur*. Rav Kook writes:

> ... and though there is the "word of the LORD" that is prophecy,[17] from *Netsah* and *Hod*,[18] below the Written Torah, which is the attribute of *Tif'eret*,[19] nevertheless, there is also the "word of the LORD" that is the root of creation and the source of Torah from heaven (*Torah min ha-shamayim*),[20] and "By the word of the LORD the heavens (*shamayim*) were made,"[21] which includes as well the supernal heavens (*ha-shamayim ha-'elyonim*).[22] "And the matters are ancient."[23]

Rav Kook explains that the Biblical phrase, "the word of the LORD," is a homonym.[24] It can have two different meanings. On occasion it refers to the Prophets (whose status is lower than that of the Torah), but it can also refer to the primordial Word which is the root of the Creation and the source of the Torah.

Though lexically interesting, this discussion seems off-topic. Why has Rav Kook suddenly segued to defining the term "the word of the LORD"?

I would venture a guess that Rabbi Shemariah Menashe Adler challenged Rav Kook's assignation of Zion to the secular and Jerusalem to the sacred, by quoting the famous verse, "For from Zion shall go forth Torah, and the word of the LORD from Jerusalem."[25] I imagine that Rabbi Adler marshaled the verse as proof that "Zion" represents a higher spiritual level than "Jerusalem." From Zion goes out "Torah," the Written Torah (*Torah she-bi-Ketav*), whereas from Jerusalem goes out the lower level of divine inspiration, "the word of the LORD" ("*devar Hashem*"), i.e., the *Nevi'im* or Prophets.[26] Rabbi Adler might have gone so far as to translate this into kabbalistic terms: "Torah" is synonymous with *Tif'eret*; the *Nevi'im* are directly below in *Netsah* and *Hod*. Thus, Rabbi Adler found incongruous Rav Kook's equation of Zion with the material aspect of the Land, and Jerusalem with the spiritual aspect.

To counter this supposed proof, and maintain the spiritual superiority of Jerusalem over Zion, Rav Kook had to show that the "the word of the LORD" need not refer to the *Nevi'im* or Prophets, who rank below the Torah; it might as well refer to the original "word of the LORD," which registers above the Torah.

The plot thickens. In 2018, there was released *Metsi'ot Katan* (*Findings of a Minor*), one of Rav Kook's earliest works, containing his thoughts from the years 1889-1895, when he served as Rabbi of Zeimel, Lithuania.[27] There, to our surprise, Rav Kook maintains that Zion is the site of the Temple, while Jerusalem is the site of the secular court. This is borne out in the verse, "For from Zion shall go forth Torah, and the word of the LORD from Jerusalem." Writes a youthful Rav Kook:

> When Israel were in their land....there were the priests, the teachers of Torah,[28] who would judge the people based on Torah law, and the officials appointed by the government would judge the law of the land. In Zion—the place of the priests—was the seat of Torah rule, and in Jerusalem was the political rule. They too [i.e., the statesmen] would judge for the sake of heaven by stabilizing the state.[29] And when Israel were settled [in their land] and performed the will of the Omnipresent, the law of the government was also aligned with the will of the LORD,[30] though it was not exactly perfectly Torah. And so it is written, "For from Zion shall go forth Torah, and the word of the LORD from Jerusalem." So, Zion was the source of instruction that transcends human intellect, greatly surpassing it...."[31]

Rav Kook repeats his interpretation of the verse once again:

> "For from Zion shall go forth Torah, and the word of the LORD from Jerusalem." The meaning is that Zion is called the site of the Temple, as it is said in the prayer of the Temple service: "May our eyes see when You return to Zion with compassion." And in Jerusalem, the site of the secular (*hol*), there sat the Sanhedrin, for half of the Chamber of Hewn Stone (*Lishkat ha-Gazit*) was situated

ZION AND JERUSALEM

in the area of the profane, and the seating [of the Sanhedrin] was in the area of the profane.[32] And also [situated in Jerusalem were] all the kings of Israel with the power to enforce [observance of] the holy religion even by those who were disobedient.[33]

The reader will appreciate that by the time Rav Kook penned his epistle to Rabbi Shemariah Menashe Adler, he had reversed his thinking concerning the roles played by Zion and Jerusalem. In the interim, there had been born the Zionist movement, which laid claim to the secular realm, forcing Jerusalem—id est *Degel Yerushalayim*—to assume the role of the sacred. And it was necessary to explain to fellow kabbalists such as Rabbi Shemariah Menashe Adler how such a bouleversement played itself out "in all the worlds."

A few months after writing the response to Rabbi Shemariah Menashe Adler, on April 1st, 1925 (7 Nissan, 5685), Rav Kook would speak at the historic opening of Hebrew University on Mount Scopus in Jerusalem. He would conclude with the verse from the Prophets, "For from Zion shall go forth Torah, and the word of the LORD from Jerusalem."[34] Rav Kook's enemies seized the opportunity, beating his well-meant words into one more weapon in their arsenal. To invoke this prophecy in regard to the secular studies about to be taught at the University was nothing less than blasphemy! Rav Kook tried to explain that it was not in regard to the University that he waxed prophetic, rather in regard to the incipient Yeshivah with its Torah studies.[35] Indeed, an inspection of Rav Kook's letters from this period, reveals that this was the very time that he advocated for the Central Universal Yeshivah (*Ha-Yeshivah ha-'Olamit ha-Merkazit*), known today as *"Merkaz Harav."* From the time that he arrived back in the Land from his long sojourn in America, he wrote tirelessly to individuals and to the general public, begging to bring this dream to fruition.

Based on his recently released writings, we may now say that Rav Kook—unlike both the secular and religious camps—heard in the words of Isaiah's prophecy that there would issue from the Holy City—from two different locations within her, namely Zion and Jerusalem—the secular *and* the sacred, the temporal *and* the eternal.

Poignantly, the Aramaic *Targum* of Psalm 133:1 ("How good and how pleasant it is for brothers to dwell together in unity!") paraphrases: "How good and how pleasant it is for *Zion* and *Jerusalem* to dwell as two brothers yet as one!"

---

[1] See recently Rabbi Abraham Wasserman, *Koré ha-Degel* (2020).
   Incidentally, Jacob Agus entitled his biography of Rav Kook, *Banner of Jerusalem* (New York: Bloch, 1946). Later, he retitled the book, *High Priest of Rebirth* (New York: Bloch, 1972).

[2] See *Iggerot ha-RAYaH*, vol. 3 (1916-1919), ed. Rabbi Tsevi Yehudah Hakohen Kook (Jerusalem: Mossad Harav Kook, 1965); vol. 4 (1920-1925), ed. Rabbi Ya'akov Filber (Jerusalem: Makhon RZYH Kook, 1984).
   In Rabbi Tsevi Yehudah Kook's preface to the third volume, he writes that it pertains to the period of the Balfour Declaration and to the establishment of *"Degel Yerushalayim,* for the sanctification of Zionism" ("*kiddushah shel ha-*

Tsiyoniyut").

2* Rav Kook expressed this dichotomy succinctly in his address to the Agudat ha-Rabbanim in New York on 10 Iyyar, 1924, as recorded in *Ha-Tor*, year 4, no. 38, p. 12. See Yehoshua B. Be'ery, *Ohev Yisrael bi-Kedushah* (Tel-Aviv, 1989), vol. 1, p. 371; vol. 5, p. 248.

3 Nahum Sokolow's letter to Rav Kook, dated "5 Tevet, 5678" (i.e., December 20, 1917), was penned in the immediate aftermath of the Balfour Declaration of November 2, 1917. The whereabouts of the letter—once in the possession of Rav Kook's son, Rabbi Tsevi Yehudah Hakohen Kook—is today unknown. Rabbi Moshe Tsevi Neriyah excerpted the letter in his *Likkutei ha-Rayah*, vol. 1, p. 117. See further idem, *Mo'adei ha-Rayah*, pp. 396-397; *Entsiklopedia shel ha-Tziyonut ha-Datit*, p. 200. (Communication from Rabbi Zuriel Hallamish, researcher at Beit Harav, Jerusalem.)

Sokolow, who, in his youth, received the traditional Talmudic education, inverted the Talmudic saying (*b. Bava Metsi'a* 84b), "A vessel that was used for the sacred, should be used for the secular?" (*"Keli she-nishtamesh bo kodesh, yishtamesh bo hol?"*). Cf. *b. 'Avodah Zarah* 52b: "Since it was used for the sacred (*gavo'ah*) it is inappropriate to use it for the secular (*hedyot*)." However, essentially, Sokolow's statement is found in the *Tosefta, Megillah*, chap. 3 (Zuckermandel ed., p. 224); and *Menahot*, end chap. 9 (Zuckermandel ed., p. 526), though the wording differs: "Vessels that were made originally for the secular (*hedyot*), we may not make them for the sacred (*gavo'ah*)." The *Tosefta* is quoted verbatim in Maimonides, *MT, Hil. Beit ha-Behirah* 1:20.

4 *Iggerot ha-RAYaH*, vol. 4, Letter 1000 (p. 32). The letter, datelined "25 Kislev, 5680 [i.e., 1920]," is addressed to Rabbi Mendel Yitzhak Behrman and the members of *Degel Yerushalayim* in Manchester, England.

5 See the introduction to Rabbi Shemariah Menashe Hakohen Adler, *Mar'eh Kohen, Mahadura Telita'ah*, vol. 1 (Piotrków, 1931), 3b.

6 Rabbi Shemariah Menashe Adler unsuccessfully attempted to convince Rabbi Joseph Hayyim Sonnenfeld of Jerusalem that Dayan Shmuel Yitzhak Hillman should be disqualified as *Av Beit Din* based on the ignorance displayed in his Talmudic commentary *'Or ha-Yashar*! See *Mar'eh Kohen, Mahadura Telita'ah*, vol. 2 (Warsaw, 1933), nos. 130-131.

For a discussion of Rabbi Sonnenfeld's diplomacy in general, and vis-à-vis Rabbi Adler in particular, see Eitam Henkin's study of Rabbi Joseph Shapotshnick, *"Ki hekhin beit haroshet lehatir 'agunot," Asif* 2 (2015), pp. 379-382.

Rabbi Adler feigned surprise when Rabbi Dr. Isaac Halevi Herzog of Dublin, Dayan Hillman's son-in-law, returned the book (*Mar'eh Kohen, Mahadura Telita'ah*) to its sender! See Rabbi Shemariah Menashe Hakohen Adler, *'Emek ha-Bakha* (Keidan, 1935), 10:1 (p. 138). *'Emek ha-Bakha* is an attempt to prohibit the recent Soncino translation of the Talmud to English under the editorship of Rabbi Isidore (Yehezkel) Epstein of Jews' College. In lieu of a *haskamah* (approbation), Adler prefaced his work with a letter from the famed Rogatchover Gaon, Rabbi Joseph Rosen of Dvinsk, forbidding teaching Talmud to non-Jews. The letter is reprinted in *She'elot u-Teshuvot Tsafnat Pa'ne'ah ha-Hadashot*, vol. 2 (Modi'in 'Ilit, 5772/2012), nos. 109-110 (pp. 304-313). Unfortunately, both the Rogatchover and the editor of the new edition of his collected responsa accepted at face value Rabbi Adler's libelous accusation that the Soncino translation of the Talmud was directed primarily at non-Jews; see ibid., the bold print in note 48 on page 313.

Adler's work, *Maror de-Rabbanan* (*Bitter Herb of the Rabbis*), appended to *Mar'eh Kohen Tinyana* (London, 1928), is a diatribe against the Chief Rabbi and the London Beth Din.

[7] For starters, in the introduction to *Mar'eh Kohen, Mahadura Hamisha'ah* (London, 1945), p. 20, the author trashes Dayyan Abramsky's work on the *Tosefta, Hazon Yehezkel*. (See earlier, *'Emek ha-Bakha*, 10:12 [p. 158], where Adler is just "warming up" for the full-blown attack on *Hazon Yehezkel*.) In a later volume of *Mar'eh Kohen*, concerning the *Herem de-Rabbeinu Gershom* (London, 1953), the author once again spews venom on Rabbi Abramsky, who by that time no longer resided in England but in Erets Yisrael, and may merely have acted in a consultant capacity on a visit to London. In the introduction to that volume (p. 3), Rabbi Adler records a dream in which the *Sefat Emet* appeared to him. (Prof. Marc B. Shapiro informs me that Rabbi Adler was a *hasid* of the Gur dynasty.) The volume deals with the problem of men whose wives disappeared in the Holocaust. Rabbi Adler, based on a responsum of the *Hiddushei ha-RIM* (founder of the Gur Hasidic dynasty) to Rabbi Hayyim Halberstam of Sanz (author of the responsa *Divrei Hayyim*), required a *heter me'ah rabbanim* (permission of one hundred rabbis) to allow the husbands to remarry. He accused Dayan Abramsky of obviating the requirement.

[8] In letters to Rav Kook published in the first volume of *Mar'eh Kohen* (London, 1919), nos. 30, 32 (pp. 91, 96), Rabbi Adler addresses him as *"Ha-Rav ha-Ga'on ha-Tsaddik."* So too in the header to Rav Kook's approbation in *Zikhron Elhanan* (London, 1920), and ibid. pp. 5-6.

However, after Rav Kook's refusal to get involved in Rabbi Adler's campaign to unseat Dayan Hillman, one senses deep disappointment on the part of Rabbi Adler, if not outright bitterness. (Rav Kook's title, *"Tsaddik,"* conveniently disappears.) Rabbi Adler had hoped that in 1924, when Rav Kook stopped off in London on his way back from America, he would adjudicate the matter, but that did not happen. Rabbi Adler quotes Rav Kook as having told him in Yiddish on that occasion: *"Ikh kon mikh nisht shtellen mit dem Beis Din de-London veil Ikh broikh fun zei shtitze in fershidene inyonim."* ("I cannot get involved with the London Beth Din as I need from them support in various matters.") Rabbi Adler reminds Rav Kook of his past kindnesses, how during World War One, he had once hosted the Rav and Rebbetsin in his home in Oxford, at which time he served them personally. He also brought up the fact that it was he who publicly defended Rav Kook and the other rabbis in the press when the madman Joseph Shapotshnick defamed them. See *Mar'eh Kohen, Mahadura Telita'ah*, vol. 2 (Warsaw, 1933), nos. 132-133:1, 4 (f.231, 232d). The exchange of letters between Rabbis Kook and Adler took place at the end of 1928. For Rav Kook's experience with Shapotshnick, see Henkin, op. cit.

[9] See *Iggerot ha-RAYaH*, vol. 3, Letter 896 (pp. 207-208); *Haskamot ha-RAYaH* (1897-1928), ed. Rabbis Ari Yitzhak Shvat, Zuriel Hallamish, and Yohanan Fried (Jerusalem: Beit Harav, 2017), no. 81 (pp. 174-176). See further Bezalel Naor, "Reish Millin—Mekorot ve-He'arot," *Sinai* 97 (Nissan-Ellul 5745/1985), pp. 69-76; also issued as *Zikhron RAYaH* (Memorial Volume on Rav Kook's Fiftieth *Yahrzeit*), ed. Yitzhak Rafael (Jerusalem: Mossad Harav Kook, 1986).

Rav Kook's letter to Rabbi Adler is datelined *"Erev Rosh Hodesh Mena-*

hem-Av, 5678 [i.e., 1918], Harrogate." During the summer months, Rav Kook, suffering from poor health, would rest in the famed spa town.

Years later, Rabbi Adler later confronted Rav Kook with the fact that Rav Kook had once written to him in a letter that his work *Reish Millin* came about in a revelatory manner (*"be-derekh hofa'ah ve-hitnotsetsut"*). See *Mar'eh Kohen, Mahadura Telita'ah*, vol. 2 (Warsaw, 1933), no. 133:1 (231c).

Rabbi Tsevi Yehudah Kook told the present writer (BN) that his father had received a *"tsav"* ("command") from above to write *Reish Millin* and also the more prosaic work, *Halakhah Berurah*.

Rabbi Adler's commentary to *Reish Millin* ran to some three hundred pages. Sometime after 1925, he offered it to Rabbi Yitshak Arieli of Jerusalem for publication. When Rabbi Arieli consulted with Rav Kook, his response was: "It is a commentary based on the kabbalistic side but does not touch on the philosophical side." See *'Eynei Yitzhak* (biography of Rabbi Yitzhak Arieli), ed. Aharon Ilan (Jerusalem, 2018), p. 177.

Despite that supposed disparagement, evidently the Rav's son, Rabbi Tsevi Yehudah Kook, thought highly enough of the commentary that on the 6th of Tishri, 5696 [i.e., 1935], barely a month after his father's passing (on the 3rd of Ellul), he reached out in writing to Rabbi Adler, requesting a copy of the commentary in its entirety, with an eye to its publication. See the introduction to the recently issued *Iggerot ha-RAYaH*, vol. 5 (1922), ed. Ze'ev Neuman (Jerusalem: Makhon RZYH Kook, 2019), pp. 10-11. See also *Iggerot ha-RAYaH*, vol. 3, Letter 874 (p. 162).

In *Iggerot ha-RAYaH*, vol. 3, Letter 916 (p. 228) consists of a *haskamah* (approbation) to an unnamed work by Rabbi Adler, datelined "London, 1st day of *Rosh Hodesh* Marheshvan, 5679" [1918]. Rav Kook's *haskamah* was published in Rabbi Adler's *Kuntres Zikhron Elhanan* (London, 5680). (However, the colophon of the book reads: Marheshvan, 5681 [i.e., 1920].) Zikhron Elhanan consists of notes to *Shulhan 'Arukh, Even ha-Ezer*, composed during the rabbi's three-week incarceration. The *haskamah* has been reprinted in *Haskamot ha-RAYaH* (1897-1928), no. 82 (p. 177) under the header, *"Peirush 'al Sefer Reish Millin"* (Commentary to *Reish Millin*). Actually, according to Rabbi Adler, Rav Kook's *haskamah* was an endorsement of his work, *Keter Torah*, on the *Otiyot de-Rabbi Akiva* (*Zikhron Elhanan*, p. 6). (Parenthetically, in the version printed in *Zikhron Elhanan*, the words *"bi-netivot lo yad'u,"* missing from the verse in Isaiah 42:16, have been supplied.)

Later, on the 18th of Tevet, 5681 [i.e., December 29, 1920], at the height of the controversy surrounding Rav Kook's seminal work, *Orot*, Rav Kook penned an additional *haskamah*, published in Rabbi Adler's sequel volume of *Mar'eh Kohen* (London, 1928). See *Haskamot ha-RAYaH* (1897-1928), no. 95 (p. 198).

Several years ago, I asked the renowned bibliophile Abraham Halevi Schischa of London if he knew what became of Rabbi Menashe Adler's manuscript of the commentary to *Reish Millin*. Sometime later, Schischa reported back to me that by sheer serendipity he "bumped into" a descendant of Rabbi Adler who said that the rabbi's sons did not care much for their father and after his passing, destroyed his manuscripts!

Recently, I published on the Orot website a facsimile of a letter from Rav Kook to Rabbi Yehudah Newman. Datelined "London, 21 Tevet, 5679" [i.e.,

December 24, 1918], the letter mentions *en passant* a Talmudic interpretation of Rav Kook's friend, R[abbi] S[hemariah] M[enashe]. The postscript contains a reference to *"histadruteinu ha-kedoshah"* ("our holy organization"), clearly *Histadrut Yerushalayim*, or the Jerusalem Organization, as it was known. See http://orot.com/newly-acquired-manuscript-rav-kook/

[10] *Iggerot ha-RAYaH*, vol. 4, ed. Rabbi Ya'akov Filber (Jerusalem: Makhon RZYH Kook, 1984), Letter 1277 (p. 217). The letter is datelined "23 Tevet, [568]5" (i.e., January 19, 1925). Rav Kook mentions that he has not yet had time to rest up from his journey. Evidently, the reference is to Rav Kook's fundraising mission to America, where he spent the better part of the year 1924. See Rabbi Joshua Hoffman, "Rav Kook's Mission to America," *Orot: A Multidisciplinary Journal of Judaism*, vol. 1 (5751/1991), pp. 78-99. On the way back from America to Erets Yisrael, the indefatigable Rav Kook stopped over in London (where he made an appeal for his colleague Rabbi Nahman Shlomo Greenspan's Yeshivah 'Ets Hayyim) and Paris (where he persuaded Baron Edmond de Rothschild to halt desecration of the Sabbath on the newly installed train from Ras al-'Ayn to Petah Tikvah). See *Iggerot ha-Rayah*, vol. 4, Letter 1268 (pp. 211-212) and Letter 1266 (pp. 210-211).

[11] See Rabbi Meir Poppers, *Me'orei 'Or*, *Tsade*-15, s.v. *"Zion,"* that Zion has the numerical value of "Yosef." Joseph is identified with the *sefirah* of Yesod.

[12] See Rabbi Joseph Gikatilla, *Sha'arei Orah*, ed. Joseph Ben-Shlomo (Jerusalem: Bialik Institute, 1970), vol. 1, *Sha'ar Hamishi* (p. 205), note 53; idem, *Gates of Light*, transl. Avi Weinstein (San Francisco, CA: HarperCollins, 1994), Fifth Gate, p. 176 (regarding Psalm 135:21); *Zohar* III, 31a; 171a; 296 (*Idra Zuta*); Rabbi Moses Cordovero, *Pardes Rimonim*, Gate 23 (*Sha'ar 'Erkei ha-Kinuyim*), s.v. *Yerushalayim* and s.v. *Zion*; Rabbi Hayyim Vital, *'Ets Hayyim*, Gate 35 (*Sha'ar ha-Yare'ah*), chap. 3; Gate 34 (*Sha'ar Tikkun ha-Nukva*), chap. 2, *kelal* 18; idem, *Peri 'Ets Hayyim*, *Sha'ar ha-Lulav*, chap. 4; Rabbi Elijah Gaon of Vilna, *Likkutei ha-GRA 'al Seder Alpha Beta*, ed. Rabbi Nehemiah Feffer (New York, NY: Makhon HaGRA, 1999), *Tsade*-2, s.v. *Tsiyon vi-Yerushalayim*; Rabbi Menahem Mendel Schneerson ("*Tsemah Tsedek*"), *Reshimot 'al Shir ha-Shirim, Rut, Kohelet* (Brooklyn, NY; Kehot, 1960), *"Tse'enah u-Re'enah"* I (p. 79); Rabbi Levi Isaac Schneerson, *Likkutei Levi Yitzhak: Iggerot Kodesh* (Brooklyn: Kehot, 2004), Letter datelined "Dnepropetróvsk, 9 Kislev, 5695 [i.e., 1934]," pp. 340-341.

[13] The six *sefirot* of *Hesed, Gevurah, Tif'eret, Netsah, Hod* and *Yesod* are referred to as the "six edges (or extremities)" (of a cube). The term is taken from *Sefer Yetsirah* 1:13.

[14] Zion was associated with the City of David and the ancient seat of government, as opposed to the Temple Mount, which was the place of worship. See 1 Kings 8:1, and *Seder 'Olam Rabbah*, ed. Moshe Ya'ir Weinstock (B'nei Berak, 1990), chap. 14, in commentary "*Seder Zemanim,*" pp. 230-231. (According to the very latest archeological findings, during the reign of King Hezekiah—who was a contemporary of the Prophet Isaiah—the administrative headquarters were outside of the City of David.)

However, see below the quotations from the earlier work, *Mets'iot Katan*, where Rav Kook wrote the exact opposite, that Zion is the site of the Temple and Jerusalem the site of the secular government.

[15] *Mussaf* (Additional Prayer) for festivals.

[16] In broad terms, one might say that this kind of inversion, whereby the "root" of the secular is higher than the "root" of the sacred, is reminiscent of HaBaD Hasidic teaching.

See, for example, Rabbi Shneur Zalman, *Tanya*, Part Four [*Iggeret ha-Kodesh*], chap. 20, where the root of the *mitsvot*, or commandments, is higher than the root of the Torah. In that regard, the *Tanya* employs the image of "a seal in reverse" (*hotam ha-mit-hapekh*), and quotes from *Sefer Yetsirah* (1:7): "Their beginning is embedded in their end."

An expression that has gained great currency is: "The root of the vessels is higher than the root of the lights." See Rabbi Aaron Halevi Hurwitz of Staroshelye, *Sha'arei ha-Yihud ve-ha-Emunah* (Shklov, 1820), Fourth Gate (*Sha'ar Orot ve-Kelim*), chap. 14 (15b); and chap. 29 (where it is explained that the root of the vessels is from the *"reshimu"* and the root of the lights is from the *"kav"*). In the latter regard, see also Rabbi Shneur Zalman of Liadi, *Likkutei Torah*, *Hosafot* (Addenda) to the Book of Leviticus, s.v. *Lehavin mah she-katuv be-'Otserot Hayyim*, 54a; Rabbi Menahem Mendel Schneersohn of Lubavitch ("*Tsemah Tsedek*"), *'Or ha-Torah*, *Tetse*, vol. 2, *Derush Kan Tsipor* (pp. 924-925) (transcribed in M.M. Laufer, *Ha-Melekh bi-Mesibo*, vol. 2, pp. 284-285); and Rabbi Isaac Dov Baer Schneerson of Liadi, *Siddur MaHaRID* (Berdichev, 1913; facsimile edition Kefar Habad, 1991), Part 2, *Mussaf le-Shabbat*, 69b, s.v. *u-be-Siddur ha-ARI z"l*.

In his famous essay, "The Souls of the World of Chaos," reprinted in the 1950 edition of *Orot*, Rav Kook writes: "The souls of Chaos (*neshamot de-Tohu*) are higher than the souls of Establishment (*neshamot de-Tikkun*)" (*Orot*, "*Zer'onim*," chap. 3 [p. 122]). In an endnote (on the final page of the volume, p. 192), the editor, Rabbi Tsevi Yehudah Kook, sourced this statement in RSZ, *Torat Hayyim*, *Vayyishlah*. *Torat Hayyim*, misattributed to Rabbi Shneur Zalman, is actually by his son, Rabbi Dov Baer, known in Lubavitch circles as the *"Mitteler Rebbe,"* or "Middle Rabbi." In that work of HaBaD Hasidism, we learn that the soul of Esau (*Tohu*) is higher than that of Jacob (*Tikkun*).

And see below, note 22, the inversion of the Written Torah and the Oral Torah.

Yet, to the best of my knowledge, the application to the particular realms of *kodesh* versus *hol*, is without precedent in the annals of Kabbalah and is uniquely Kookian. One might say that it is the response of a Kabbalist to the secular age in general, and specifically to the phenomenon of secular Zionism.

For the influence of HaBaD Hasidism upon the development of Rav Kook's thought, see my essay, "The Curtains of the Tabernacle: R. Shelomo Zalman of Kopyst," in *Orot: A Multidisciplinary Journal of Judaism*, vol. 1 (1991), pp. 33-41.

[17] See e.g. 1Samuel 3:1. Also, b. *Shabbat* 138b.

[18] According to Kabbalah, the source of the Prophets' inspiration is from the *sefirot* of *Netsah* and *Hod*. See Rabbi Joseph Gikatilla, *Sha'arei Orah*, Gates 3-4 (Ben-Shlomo ed., vol. 1, p. 158; Weinstein ed., p. 130); *Tikkunei Zohar* with commentary of Vilna Gaon (Vilna, 1867), Introduction, 13a, and *Tikkunim mi-Zohar Hadash*, 46b; Rabbi Moses Cordovero, *Pardes Rimonim* 6:6, 13:6, and 23:14 (s.v. *nevi'ei ha-emet*).

[19] See Rabbi Joseph Gikatilla, *Sha'arei Orah*, Fifth Gate (Ben-Shlomo ed., vol.

1, p. 248; Weinstein ed., p. 220).

Cf. Rav Kook's commentary to *The Legends of Rabbah bar Bar Hannah*, ed. Bezalel Naor (Monsey, NY: Orot/Kodesh, 2019), English, p. 91; Hebrew, p. 20.

One should add that halakhically, as well, the status of the Prophets (*Nevi'im*) is below that of Torah. For this reason, one must not place the Prophets on top of the Torah. See *t. Megillah* 4:20 (Zuckermandel ed., p. 227); *y. Megillah* 3:1; *b. Megillah* 27a; Maimonides, MT, *Hil. Sefer Torah* 10:5.

[20] *m. Sanhedrin* 10:1. See Rabbi Abraham Isaac Hakohen Kook, *Shemonah Kevatsim* 1:633.

In the present context, *"Torah min ha-shamayim"* means that the Written Torah emanates from the *sefirah* of *Tif'eret*, which is symbolized by *"shamayim,"* or heaven.

[21] Psalms 33:6. See Introduction to *Zohar* I, 5a.

[22] In the kabbalistic lexicon, the heavens (*shamayim*) are synonymous with the *sefirah* of *Tif'eret*, which, as Rav Kook explained earlier, is where the Written Torah (*Torah she-bi-ketav*) is situated. On the other hand, earth (*erets*) is synonymous with the *sefirah* of *Malkhut*, the location of the Oral Torah (*Torah she-be-'al-Peh*).

Rabbi Joseph Ibn Waqar quotes Rabbi Azriel of Gerona that in the verse in 1 Chronicles 29:11, *"shamayim"* signifies *Tif'eret* and *"arets"* signifies *Malkhut*. (This verse is basic to Kabbalah, as it provides the names of five *sefirot*: *Gedulah* [i.e., *Hesed*], *Gevurah*, *Tif'eret*, *Netsah*, *Hod*.) See Rabbi Joseph B. Abraham Ibn Waqar, *Shorashei ha-Kabbalah* (*Principles of the Qabbalah*), ed. Paul B. Fenton (Los Angeles: Cherub Press, 2004), p. 152, s.v. *limmudei Hashem*. Cf. *Zohar* I, 31; II, 116a.

It is explained that the Hebrew word *"shamayim"* is a combination of *esh* (fire) and *mayim* (water). See *b. Hagigah* 12a; *Genesis Rabbah* 4:7; Rashi, Genesis 1:1, 8. Since water is the symbol of *Hesed* and fire is the symbol of *Gevurah*, their synthesis, *shamayim*, symbolizes the synthesis of those two attributes: *Tif'eret*. See Rabbi Joseph Gikatilla, *Sha'arei Orah*, Gates 3-4 (Ben-Shlomo ed., p. 156; Weinstein ed., p. 127).

In *Shemonah Kevatsim* 1:98, Rav Kook writes: "The Written Torah is the attribute of 'Heaven' (*'shamayim'*)." The kabbalistic association of the Written Torah with Heaven (*"Tif'eret"*) and the Oral Torah with Earth, is borne out in the first chapter of *Orot ha-Torah* ("The Written Torah and the Oral Torah"), culled by the editor, Rabbi Tsevi Yehudah Hakohen Kook, from various passages in *Shemonah Kevatsim*.

The first paragraph in the chapter was taken from *Shemonah Kevatsim* 2:56, 57. By the way, in the very first line of *Orot ha-Torah*, the word *"ha-tsinor"* ("the pipeline") now reads *"ha-tsiyyur"* ("the conception"). This alteration was unnoticed by the editor of *Shemonah Kevatsim* in the *"He'arot Nusah"* or *variae lectiones* at the end of the volume.

The second paragraph in the chapter (taken from *Shemonah Kevatsim* 2:223) makes the point that the root of the Oral Law is higher than the root of the Written Law (yet another example of the topsy-turvy in Rav Kook's Kabbalah). In this connection, Rav Kook quotes the saying of the *Talmud Yerushalmi* (*Berakhot* 1:4; *Sanhedrin* 11:4; *'Avodah Zarah* 2:7): "The words of the scribes are more beloved than the words of the Torah." This *pensée* may have been inspired by a teaching of the *"Alter Rebbe,"* Rabbi Shneur Zaman of Liadi, founder of HaBaD Hasidism. See Rabbi Shneur Zalman, *Likkutei Torah, Shir ha-Shirim,* s.v. *Shehorah Ani ve-Navah* II, par. 3 (7a). Rav Kook once remarked to Rabbi Shim'on Glitzenstein—the HaBaD Hasid who served as his secretary during the years in London—regarding this particular *ma'amar* in *Likkutei Torah*: *"Do iz ofener ru'ah ha-kodesh."* (Yiddish, "Here is open divine inspiration.") Quoted in Rabbi Moshe Tsevi Neriyah, *Sihot ha-RAYaH* (Tel-Aviv, 1979), p. 256. According to Rabbi Glitzenstein's description, Rav Kook was so enraptured by the Hasidic discourse that he was pacing the length of his study in an emotional state!

In this paragraph, as well, the variants have gone unnoticed by the editor of *Shemonah Kevatsim*. *"Mats'ah et darkah"* ("she found her way") has become *"mats'ah et birkatah"* ("she found her blessing"); *"segulah 'ofit"* ("characteristic treasure") is rendered *"segulah Elohit"* ("Godly treasure").

23 1 Chronicles 4:22. This is an expression for the arcane.

24 See *b. Shabbat* 138b, where three different interpretations of *"devar Hashem"* ("the word of the LORD") are given.

25 Isaiah 2:3; Micah 4:2; *y. Nedarim* 6:8; *b. Berakhot* 63b.

26 Cf. Malbim's interpretation of the verse in Isaiah 2:3, whereby "Torah" refers to the judgment of the Sanhedrin in the Chamber of Hewn Stone (*Lishkat ha-Gazit*), as opposed to the "word of the LORD," which refers to the inspiration of the prophets, who did not sit in the Chamber of Hewn Stone, but circulated throughout the entire city of Jerusalem.

27 Rabbi Abraham Isaac Hakohen Kook, *Metsi'ot Katan*, ed. Harel Cohen (Israel: Maggid, 2018).

As Rav Kook was born in 1865, he was between the ages of 24 and 30 when he penned *Metsi'ot Katan*.

28 Hebrew, *tofesei ha-Torah*. See Jeremiah 2:8.

29 See Rabbeinu Nissim Gerondi, *Derashot ha-RaN*, ed. Leon A. Feldman (Jerusalem: Shalem, 1973), *derush* 11 (189ff.). According to Rabbeinu Nissim, the Torah provided for two parallel systems of jurisprudence: strict Torah law (*mishpat ha-Torah*) and the law of the monarchy or state (*mishpat ha-melukhah*).

Earlier, Rabbi David Kimhi envisioned the covalent institutions of King Messiah, the temporal authority, and the Aaronide High Priest, who would provide instruction in Torah law. See the commentary of RaDaK to Psalm 133. In this scheme, "Zion" is the seat of the monarchy.

30 Rav Kook understands the "word of the LORD" to refer in this context to the judgment rendered not strictly according to Torah law but nonetheless aligned to the will of the LORD.

31 *Metsi'ot Katan*, par. 99 (pp. 167-168). Rabbeinu Nissim made the point that the laws of the Torah transcend logic; see *Derashot ha-RaN*, loc. cit. (pp. 190-191).

32 *m. Middot* 5:4; *b. Yoma* 25a; *Sanhedrin* 88b. Rav Kook's scheme diverges from that of Rabbeinu Nissim (p. 191), who understood that the Sanhedrin sat in the Chamber of Hewn Stone in order to be in the place of divine inspiration (as opposed to the kings who sat in judgment at a far remove from the Temple Mount).

33 *Metsi'ot Katan*, par. 155 (pp. 249-250). See *Derashot ha-RaN*, cited in the

previous note.

[34] See *Ma'amrei ha-RAYaH*, vol. 2, ed. Elisha Aviner (Langenauer) (Jerusalem, 1984), pp. 306-308; English translation in *When God Becomes History: Historical Essays of Rabbi Abraham Isaac Hakohen Kook*, ed. Bezalel Naor (New York, NY: Kodesh Press, 2016), pp. 141-145.

[35] Ibid. pp. 147, 150.

In 1924, Rav Kook issued a 12-page prospectus, *Ha-Yeshivah ha-Merkazit ha-'Olamit bi-Yerushalayim*. Evidently, the booklet was issued simultaneously in New York and Jerusalem (at the press of Y.A. Weiss). The final line of the brochure is the verse, "For from Zion shall go forth Torah, and the word of the LORD from Jerusalem." See *Ma'amrei ha-RAYaH*, vol. 1 (Jerusalem, 1980), pp. 62-65. In the Jerusalem edition, the verse also appears alone as the motto on page (2).

Rav Kook's Shattered Vessels and Their Repair

Undoubtedly, Rav Kook's most important discussion of the *Zohar*'s Myth of the Primordial Kings (*Sod Malkin Kadma'in*), is the passage in *Shemonah Kevatsim* (1:164). In *Orot ha-Kodesh*, it was aptly titled, *"Shevirat ha-Kelim ve-Tikkunam"* ("The Shattering of the Vessels and Their Repair") by the editor, Rav Kook's disciple, Rabbi David Cohen, "the Nazirite."[1]

Recognizing the significance of this passage, the great researcher of Kabbalah, Yosef Avivi, devoted an entire chapter of his work, *Kabbalat ha-RAYaH*, to parsing it.[2] Avivi retitled the *pensée*, *"Kilkul ve-Tikkun,"* or "Corruption and Correction."[3] He then divided the material in two thematically, subtitling the first half, *"Mishtabrim ha-Kelim, Metim ha-Melakhim"* ("The Vessels Shatter, the Kings Die"), and the second half, *"Hesed 'Olamim ve-'Or Hadash"* ("Eternal Love and a New Light"). I have followed suit and divided the piece in two. The first half is Rav Kook's narrative of the shattering of the vessels; the second half is the story of their repair.

The account of the Kings of Edom occurs at the end of *Vayyishlah* (Genesis 36:31-39): "And these are the kings who reigned in the land of Edom before any king reigned over the Children of Israel...." There follow seven kings who reign and die (*"Vayyimlokh ... vayyamat"*), until finally, we come to the eighth king, Hadar, who reigns and does not die. This signifies that his reign is permanent. The previous seven kings, whose reign is fleeting and unstable, symbolize the previous world order which came crashing down, the '*Olam ha-Tohu*, the World of Chaos. Hadar will come to signify the new world order, noted for its stability and integrity, '*Olam ha-Tikkun*, the World of Establishment. The portion of the *Zohar* which treats this myth is called the *Idra*.[4] This is what we would call a creation myth. Roughly, it runs along the lines of the Midrash that God was "building worlds and destroying them."[5]

For Rav Kook, the mystery of the Death of the Kings is a trope for the death of the gods. As Rav Kook writes: "The vessels shatter, the kings die, the gods die...." (*"Mishtabrim ha-kelim, metim ha-melakhim, metim ha-elim...."*)

What does Rav Kook mean by the death of the gods? Is it merely that the names that mortals have assigned to the deity no longer serve their purpose, no longer signify what they were once intended to? The mystic loses patience with these signifiers that have worn thin. None of the names can satisfy the seeker's relentless quest for that which is ultimately beyond names. Thus, we have a breakdown of language.[6]

Or is it something deeper, something much more profound than the letters coming apart? Not only the various names of God come undone, but the gods themselves are dead to us. And here, various possibilities open up.

Is Rav Kook saying that the Kings of Edom were thought to be divine? Rav Kook may have had a historiosophical sense that the age of the gods had passed. Was Rav Kook familiar with the philosophy of history espoused in Vico's *Scienza Nuova* (1725)? Rav Kook's disciple, Rabbi David Cohen ("the Nazirite") speculated that Rabbi Moshe Hayyim Luzzatto had imbibed some of the theory of his countryman, Giambattista Vico (1668-1744).[7]

Or, might Rav Kook—like the modern Hebrew writers with whom he contended (Berdichevsky, Brenner, Tchernichovsky, even Zeitlin)—have been feeling the sting of Nietzsche's "death of God." Is *"metim ha-elim"* Rav Kook's Hebrew rendition of Zarathustra's barbed statement, *"Gott is tot"* ("God is dead")?[8]

In Rav Kook's writings (that have surfaced to date), there is but a single mention of Nietzsche's name. Juxtaposing Nietzsche to Shabbetai Tsevi, Rav Kook states the obvious, that "Nietzsche took leave of his senses."[9] However, in an all-important essay entitled, *"Yissurim Memarkim"* ("Purifying Tribulations"),[10] Rav Kook maintains that the modern phenomenon of atheism is a necessary stage in the spiritual evolution of mankind, whereby all the dross (Rav Kook employs the kabbalistic image of the *"kelipah,"* or outer shell) that has managed to creep into the conception of the *Ein Sof*, the Infinite, is purged. Playing on the Hebrew word for atheism, *"kefirah,"* and the word for frost, *"kefor,"* Rav Kook waxes poetic:

One who recognizes the inside of *kefirah*, sucks its honey, and returns it to the root of its holiness; and beholds the majesty of "the terrible ice" ("*ha-kerah ha-nora*")[11]—"the frost of heaven" (*kefor shamayim*).[12]

In his poetic rendition of the Myth of the Primordial Kings, Rav Kook has given us to understand that the movement from *Tohu* to *Tikkun* is not linear but cyclical.[13] Time and time again the vessels (the divine names) are shattered, emptied of meaning, only to be repaired and reconstructed once again, which is to say, invested with new significance and infused with new divine soul. As Rav Kook expressed it, "as [man's] soul lifts higher and higher" ("*be-hinasé nishmato le-ma'alah le-ma'alah*").

⁂

Though one cannot be certain, there appears to be Kantian influence in this musing of Rav Kook. We are struck by his ardent desire to break free of the phenomenon ("the light of God through the world, through existence, that penetrates into the eyes") and somehow latch on to the noumenon, the *Ding an sich* ("*emet she-hu le-'atsmo*," or "truth in itself").[14]

In Lurianic Kabbalah, the *shevirah*, or shattering, occurred in the light of the eyes of *Adam Kadmon*.[15] For Rav Kook, the eyes are a symbol of the phenomena (as opposed to the noumena). For Rav Kook's disciple, "the Nazirite," the eye symbolizes Western thinking, which is visual, as opposed to the ear, which symbolizes

Hebrew prophetic acoustic logic (*ha-higayon ha-'Ivri ha-shim'i ha-nevu'i*).[16]

Before we embark on a study of this seminal *pensée*, I must state at the onset that I differ with Avivi in terms of general orientation. Where Avivi situates Rav Kook's script solidly within the tradition of Lurianic Kabbalah, I understand Rav Kook's *Sitz im Leben* to be much more eclectic than that of the "lion whelps" (*gurei ha-ARI*). While Rabbi Isaac Luria certainly provided the template, in the relatively free atmosphere created by Rav Kook's creative writing (which forever oscillates between the wavelengths of poetry and prose) there is room aplenty for improvisation and variations on the theme. To state it differently, though Lurianic Kabbalah is the mainstream which comes gushing through the sluice of Rav Kook's mystical experience, that stream is fed by many unnamed tributaries yet identifiable by telltale signs. A suggestive phrase, sometimes a single word, is sufficient to uncover a hidden sphere of influence. Rav Kook read widely and many souls are nested within this *neshamah kolelet*: Rabbi Moses Cordovero, Rabbi Isaac Luria, Abraham Herrera, the Vilna Gaon and his disciples, the Ba'al Shem Tov and his disciples. All these distinguished visitors to the Kook residence left their calling cards.[17]

I should like to discuss two important points left unaddressed by Avivi.

In the first half, from the stress that Rav Kook places upon the words *"mit-hader, mehader,"* it is apparent that he alludes to the eighth king of Edom, Hadar. But then, the very next sentence, *"Molekh ve-met"* ("Reigns and dies") is mystifying, for in Genesis 36:39, the eighth and last king of Edom, Hadar, does not die. This is crucial to the symbolism of the *Idra*.[18]

For lack of a better solution, I suggest that Rav Kook alludes to a profound teaching of his mentor in Kabbalah, Rabbi Shelomo Eliashov. Rabbi Eliashov (author of the series, *Leshem Shevo ve-Ahlamah*) lavished much attention on the discrepancies between the accounts in Genesis 36:31-39 and 1 Chronicles 1:43-51, chief of which may be the fact that in Chronicles, Hadad (not Hadar) dies.[19]

In the second half, Rav Kook writes the phrase *"hesed 'olamim."* Obviously, Avivi understood what a crucial part it plays, for he incorporated it in his subtitle. Yet he chalked it up to a *"kinnui mehuddash,"* or neologism, of Rav Kook.[20] In fact, in the text of the *Idra* (*Zohar* III, 142a), *"hesed"* (albeit *"hesed 'ila'ah,"* not *"hesed 'olamim"*) is of paramount importance in effecting *Tikkun*. Elsewhere, Avivi has discussed the significance of *hesed 'ila'ah* in this context.[21]

This *pensée*, fraught with kabbalistic symbolism and terminology, was included in A.M Habermann's collection of Rav Kook's poetry that appeared in the journal *Sinai*.[22] The poems (and their supposed dates of composition) were transmitted to Habermann by the Rav's son, Rabbi Tsevi Yehudah Kook. Our poem was dated "5672?" (i.e., "1912?").

Subsequently, Habermann's collection comprised the section of *Poems* in Ben Zion Bokser's anthology, *Abraham Isaac Kook*.[23] The translation which follows is my own. In a couple of instances, I noted Bokser's translation of a twist of language where I found it apposite.

BN

Text

I am full of love for God. I know that what I seek, what I love, is not called by any name. That which is more than all, more than the good, more than the essence, more than existence. And I love. And I say, I love God.

The light of *Ein Sof*[24] resides in the expression of the name, in the expression of "God," and in all the names and epithets that the heart of man conceives and utters, as his soul lifts higher and higher.

I cannot satisfy my soul with that love that comes from the knots of logic,[25] from searching the light of God through the world, through existence, that penetrates into the eyes.[26]

There are born in our souls, godly lights, many gods (*elohim rabbim*) in the vision of our spirit; one true God, "and before one"[27] in the depth of its truth.[28] God is revealed, controls us, conquers all our spirit, the spirit of all being. Wherever there is an idea, a feeling, a thought, a will; wherever there is exalted spiritual life—there a godly light reigns (*molekh*), rules (*moshel*),[29] conquers, sparkles, is beautiful (*mit-hader*), beautifies (*mehader*)[30] and glorifies,[31] enlivens, uplifts—all through the clarity of the light of existence. [The godly light] reigns and dies. The kingdom is limited, as long as it comes from the midst of the world, from the midst of existence.

Sometimes the light is overpowering. The will desires a light that is more refined, more inward, more truth in itself (*emet she-hu le-'atsmo*),³² more mightful in the content of its inwardness. The light appears upon the vessel, the thought (*ha-mahshavah*)³³ upon existence—the situation cannot endure, the content does not fit. The vessels shatter, the kings die, the gods die. Their soul departs, taking flight to the heavens.³⁴ The bodies descend to the World of Separation (*'Alma de-Piruda*).³⁵ Existence stands naked, lonely, torn, scattered.

※

In [existence's] interior, there is hidden an eternal desire for a supernal light. In the broken vessels, an eternal love (*hesed 'olamim*) has deposited its light, its sparks. In every movement, in every life form, in every "is" (*yesh*), there is a spark, a spark of a spark (*nitsots shel nitsots*), finer than fine.

The inner light, the supernal light of God, builds and founds (*meyased*),³⁶ gathers in the dispersed, repairs worlds without end, arranges and pieces together. There is revealed an eternal kingdom (*malkhut*),³⁷ from the light of *Ein Sof* that is in the inwardness of the soul, from God to the world.³⁸ A new light is born,³⁹ the light of the splendor of the beauty (*hadar*)⁴⁰ of the Face of God (*p'nei El*).⁴¹

---

[1] See *Orot ha-Kodesh*, vol. 4, ed. Rabbis David Cohen and Yohanan Fried (Jerusalem: Mossad Harav Kook, 1990), pp. 400-401, "*Shevirat ha-Kelim ve-Tikkunam.*"

   Those exact words occur in the classic, *KaLaH Pithei Hokhmah* (attributed to Rabbi Moshe Hayyim Luzzatto), *petah* 37.

[2] See Yosef Avivi, *The Kabbalah of Rabbi A. I. Kook* (Hebrew) (Jerusalem: Yad

Ben-Zvi, 2018), vol. 3, chap. 39 (pp. 851-870).
3 This too is in conformity to *petah* 37 of the *KaLaH*. (See above note 1.)
4 The Greater *Idra*, or *Idra Rabbah*, is printed in *Naso*; the Lesser *Idra* or *Idra Zuta* is printed in *Ha'azinu*.
  One notes with interest that Maimonides (*Guide* III, 50) considered the account of "the kings who reigned in the land of Edom" (Genesis 36:31) as belonging to the "mysteries of the Torah" *("sitrei Torah")* (Pines translation, p. 613). However, as is evident, Maimonides' understanding of this mystery is totally different from that of the *Zohar*.
5 *Genesis Rabbah* 3:7.
6 Of late, there is much speculation in literary circles that the Lurianic myth of the shattering of the vessels may have influenced the thinking of the celebrated critic Walter Benjamin (who would have been introduced to the imagery by his friend Gershom Scholem). The passage in question reads (in the translation of Harry Zohn):

> Fragments of a vessel that are to be glued together must match one another in the smallest details, although they need not be like one another. In the same way a translation, instead of imitating the sense of the original, must lovingly and in detail incorporate the original's way of meaning, thus making both the original and the translation recognizable as fragments of a greater language, just as fragments are part of a vessel.
> (Walter Benjamin, "The Task of the Translator," in *Walter Benjamin: Selected Writings*, vol. 1 [1913-1926], ed. Marcus Bullock and Michael W. Jennings [Cambridge, Mass.: Harvard University Press, 1996], p. 260)

  See further Naomi Seidman, *Faithful Renderings: Jewish-Christian Difference and the Politics of Translation* (Chicago: University of Chicago Press, 2006), pp. 187-198.
7 See Rabbi David Cohen, *Kol ha-Nevu'ah* (Jerusalem: Mossad Harav Kook, 1979), p. 307, n. 452. (For some reason, the names of both Leibniz and Vico have been elided in that footnote.)
8 Friedrich Nietzsche, *Also Sprach Zarathustra (Thus Spoke Zarathustra)*, in *Nietzsche*, ed. Walter Kaufmann (New York, 1968), II, p. 202; IV, pp. 373, 375, 398, 399. See Bezalel Naor, "Rav Kook and Emmanuel Levinas on the 'Non-Existence' of God," in idem, *From a Kabbalist's Diary* (Spring Valley, NY: Orot, 2005), pp. 75-90.
9 Rabbi Abraham Isaac Hakohen Kook, *Kevatsim mi-Ketav Yad Kodsho*, vol. 1, ed. Boaz Ofen (Jerusalem, 5766/2006), *Pinkas "Aharon be-Boisk,"* par. 40 (p. 56).
  Rabbi Tsevi Yehudah Hakohen Kook, on the other hand, mentioned Nietzsche by name on several occasions. See *Tsemah Tsevi* (Jerusalem, 1991), Letter 71 (p. 181); quoted in my introduction to *Orot* (Maggid, 2015), in the section entitled, "The Man Who Wore *Tefillin* All Day—And Nietzsche?" See ibid., pp. 63-64 and p. 450, n. 128.
  Recently, there came to my attention that a line in a letter of Rabbi Tsevi Yehudah was censored. See *Tsemah Tsevi*, Letter 41 (p. 109). The letter, addressed to his father, Rav Kook (then in London), was written from Basel,

Switzerland in 1916. In the crucial passage, Rabbi Tsevi Yehudah quotes Rabbi Nahman of Breslov's famous statement regarding Erets Yisrael: *"Ich mein takeh dos Erets Yisroel mit die shtieber, mit die heizer."* ("I mean this Land of Israel with these homes, with these houses.") The omitted sentence reads: "In this respect, one may find basis for the comparison of [Rabbi Nahman] with Nietzsche, that was expressed in the new literature." See the facsimile on page 98 of Moshe Nahmani's *Shnei ha-Me'orot* (2019).

Probably, by "the new literature," Rabbi Tsevi Yehudah intended the writings of Hillel Zeitlin, who was wont to juxtapose Rabbi Nahman and Nietzsche. (Rabbi Tsevi Yehudah was very fond of Hillel Zeitlin, as was conveyed to this writer [BN] in oral conversation. See Rabbi Tsevi Yehudah's eulogy of Zeitlin, *"Zekher le-Mikdash ke-Hillel,"* which touches on Zeitlin's faithful presentation of Rabbi Nahman of Breslov. *"Zekher le-Mikdash ke-Hillel"* was reprinted in the collection of Rabbi Tsevi Yehudah's essays, *Li-Netivot Yisrael*, vol. 2 [Jerusalem, 1979], pp. 24-27.) Zeitlin saw similarities between Nietzsche's *Ubermensch* and Rabbi Nahman's *"Tsaddik,"* inasmuch as both enjoy a freedom denied lesser men. See Jonatan Meir's annotated edition of Zeitlin's 1910 essay, *"Rabbi Nahman mi-Breslov: Hayyav ve-Torato,"* chap. 16, p. 59, n. 117. In *Rabbi Nahman of Bratslav: World Weariness and Longing for the Messiah: Two Essays by Hillel Zeitlin*, Introduction and Critical Notes by Jonatan Meir (Hebrew) (Jerusalem, 2006). Meir noted that Aaron Zeitlin deleted the term *"adam ha-'elyon"* when he reissued his father's essay, because of its Nietzschean association.

[10] The essay was included in the collection *"Zer'onim,"* which first appeared in the literary journal *Ha-Tarbut ha-Yisraelit* in 1913. Subsequently, the chapters of *"Zer'onim"* were included in the 1950 edition of *Orot*. One may now consult the original texts that comprised *"Yissurim Memarkim"* in *Shemonah Kevatsim (Eight Journals)*.

Ben Zion Bokser translated the title of the essay as "The Pangs of Cleansing." See Bokser, *Abraham Isaac Kook* (Mahwah, NJ: Paulist Press, 1978), pp. 261-269.

[11] Ezekiel 1:22.

[12] Job 38:29.

Rabbi Abraham Isaac Hakohen Kook, *Orot* (Jerusalem: Mossad Harav Kook, 1963), p. 127; *Shemonah Kevatsim* 1:179.

This is comparable to Rabbi Nahman of Breslov's interpretation of Numbers 23:21, as transmitted by his disciple Rabbi Nathan Sternhartz:

> "and the shouting for the King is in him" *("u-teru'at melekh bo")*— *Teru'ah* is an expression of breaking, as it says, *"tero'em be-shevet barzel"* ("You shall break them with a rod of iron") (Psalms 2:9). This is to say that when we break *kefirot* (denials), then the King is in it. In other words, we discover the King, blessed be He, even within the denials themselves, for even in the denials themselves is garbed His vitality, blessed be He.
>
> (*Sihot ha-RaN*, par. 102)

Rav Kook gratefully acknowledged receipt of the work *Sihot ha-Ran* (from his son Tsevi Yehudah), which he read. See Moshe Nahmani, *Shnei ha-Me'orot* (2019), pp. 93-94. On page 25, Nahmani wrote that the letter of acknowledgment was written in 1906 (when Tsevi Yehudah was fifteen).

[13] One might glean this sense from reading Rabbi Yitzhak Eizik Haver's *Pithei She'arim*, Part One, *Netiv 'Olam ha-Tikkun*, chap. 5 (66a): "Close to the end of the sixth millennium, evil will grow very strong... and then there will reincarnate sparks of the *'Olam ha-Tohu*, the brazen-faced of the generation who are from the side of the Mixed Multitude *('Erev Rav)*; and heresy and informing will wax; and 'impudence *(hutspah)* will increase' [*m. Sotah* 9:15]." This reference was provided in the notes to Rav Kook's essay, "*Neshamot shel 'Olam ha-Tohu*" ("Souls of the World of Chaos"); see *Orot* (Jerusalem: Mossad Harav Kook, 1963), p. 181.

[14] Rav Kook discusses the Kantian revolution in philosophy in a letter to Samuel Alexandrov of Bobruisk, published in *Iggerot ha-RAYaH*, vol. 1 (Jerusalem: Mossad Harav Kook, 1962), Letter 44 (pp. 47-48); available in the English translation of Tzvi Feldman, *Rav A.Y. Kook: Selected Letters* (Ma'aleh Adumim, 1986), p. 92.

[15] Rabbi Hayyim Vital, *'Ets Hayyim* 8:1.

[16] See Rabbi David Cohen, *Kol ha-Nevu'ah*, pp. 225-226 ("*Shevirat ha-Kelim ve-Tikkunam*").

Cf. Rabbi Tsevi Elimelech of Dynów, *Igra de-Pirka*, chap. 297 (who equates "seeing" with *hakirah* or philosophical investigation, as opposed to simple faith, symbolized by "hearing"); quoted in Rabbi David Yitzhak Eizik Rabinowitz of Skolya-Vienna-Brooklyn, *Mekor ha-Berakhah* (Brooklyn, 1967), Introduction, 4a, and *Hashmatah* from Introduction, 11a.

[17] Rav Kook's eclectic approach was attested to by the Lithuanian kabbalist Rabbi Shelomo Eliashov, author of *Leshem Shevo ve-Ahlamah*:

> Once in conversation, the name of Rav Kook came up. Rabbi Shelomo [Eliashov] said to me: "Just as there are different lines *(shitot)* in Halakhah, so there are lines in Kabbalah, as well. RABaD [of *Posquières*] has a specific way and so does Nahmanides. The line of Rabbi Isaac Luria is different from that of Rabbi Moses Cordovero. And so throughout the generations: Rabbi Menahem Azariah of Fano, Rabbi Moshe Hayyim Luzzatto, the Vilna Gaon. However, Rav Kook encompassed and knew all the lines together, and in regard to him, one can say: 'No mystery escapes him.'"
>
> (Rabbi Aryeh Levine, quoted in Rabbi Moshe Tsevi Neriyah, *Sihot ha-RAYaH* [Tel-Aviv, 1979], p. 164)

The Jerusalemite saint ("*Tsaddik Yerushalmi*") Rabbi Aryeh Levine was very close to Rabbi Shelomo Eliashov. Eventually, Rabbi Levine's daughter was wed to Rabbi Eliashov's grandson, Rabbi Yosef Shalom Elyashiv. (Rav Kook was the *shadkhan*, or matchmaker, and *mesader kiddushin*, which is to say that he officiated at their wedding ceremony.)

[18] See *Idra Rabba* in *Zohar* III, 142a, and *Idra Zuta* in *Zohar* III, 292a.

[19] See Rabbi Shelomo Eliashov, *Sefer ha-De'ah* [=*Hu Derushei 'Olam ha-Tohu*] (Piotrków, 1912), Part 1, *ma'amar kelali*, par. 1 (1a); and Part 2, *derush* 1, 2:3-3:4 (4a-5b). See also Rabbi Reuven Margaliyot, *Nitsutsei Zohar* to *Zohar* III, 142a (*Idra Rabba*), note 6; Rabbi Menahem Menkhin Heilprin, *Hagahot u-Be'urim* to Rabbi Hayyim Vital, *'Ets Hayyim* (Warsaw, 1891), 10:3 (*Mahadura Tinyana*), note 9; and the ingenious solution of Malbim, 1 Chronicles

1:43. And see Rabbi Gedaliah Levi, *"Kibbuts Derushei ha-Melakhim de-Mitu,"* in Rabbi Jacob Tsemah, *Kol be-Ramah,* ed. Eliyahu Attiah (Jerusalem: Makhon B'nei Yissachar, 2001), p. 232ff.

[20] *The Kabbalah of Rabbi A. I. Kook,* p. 864.

[21] See Yosef Avivi, *Kabbalat ha-GRA* (Jerusalem, 1993), p. 85.

The Vilna Gaon juxtaposes the Idra's *"hesed 'ila'ah"* to the verse in Psalms 89:3: *"'Olam hesed yibaneh."* See *Sifra di-Tseni'uta* with *Be'ur ha-GRA,* ed. Samuel Luria (Vilna, 1882), chap. 1 (4a-b). Rav Kook's neologism, *"hesed 'olamim,"* is referential to the verse in Psalms.

[22] A.M. Habermann, *"Shirat Harav," Sinai,* 17 (5705/1945).

[23] See Abraham Isaac Kook, ed. B.Z. Bokser (Mahwah, NJ: Paulist Press, 1978), pp. 367-386. Our poem appears there on pages 373-374.

[24] Literally, "Without End," "Infinite." The kabbalistic term for the deity.

[25] Hebrew, *"kishrei ha-higayon."* Ben Zion Bokser translated loosely, "the web of logic."

There is the remote possibility that this phrase is an echo of the *Zohar*'s play on the verse in Song of Songs 7:6: *"melekh assur ba-rehatim"* ("the King is bound by the tresses")—*"bi-rehitei moha"* ("by the channels of the mind"). The *Zohar* (and later *Tikkunei Zohar*) refer to the phylacteries (*tefillin*) by which God is, as it were, bound. (The allusion is to the channels [*rehatim*], or troughs of water, of Jacob in Genesis 30:38.) Cf. *Leviticus Rabbah* 31:4 and *Song of Songs Rabbah* to Song 7:6 (*"rehitin shel Ya'akov Avinu"*).

See *Hakdamat Sefer ha-Zohar, Zohar* I, 14a (*"kashir 'ihu ve-'ahid be-'inun batei"*); *Zohar* III, 136a (*Idra Rabba*); 269b; 293a-b (*Idra Zuta*); *Tikkunim* appended to *Tikkunei Zohar 'im Be'ur ha-GRA* (Vilna, 1867), *tikkuna shetita'ah* (169a); Rabbi Shneur Zalman of Liadi, *Tanya, Iggeret ha-Teshuvah,* chap. 7 (96b).

Remarkably, this image of God bound by phylacteries was appropriated by the Hebrew poet Shaul Tchernichovsky in his poem "Before the Statue of Apollo" (1899). Tchernichovsky bemoans the fact that "the people has grown old—its God grown old with it." He calls for the "light of *Yah* and life" (*"'or-Yah ve-hayyim"*). The last two lines deliver the punch. Tchernichovsky longs for

> God, God of the conquerors of Canaan by storm—
> And they bound Him in straps of phylacteries
> (*va-ya'asruhu bi-retsu'ot shel tefillin*).

Written at the *fin siècle* back in Odessa (and Heidelberg), this sentiment (shall we call it Nietzschean?) would resonate in secular circles for generations to come. Eventually, there arose in Israel a movement known as "Canaanites" (*"Kena'anim"*). Like the poet Tchernichovsky, these "neo-Canaanites" sought to return to a pre-Israelite rootedness in the land and nature. Their neo-pagan deity would be freed of the fetters of Judaic religion (symbolized by the "straps of *tefillin*").

It is more than likely that Rav Kook's famous poem *"Lahashei Havayah"* ("Whispers of Existence"), first published in the journal *"Ha-Tarbut ha-Yisra-elit"* in 1913, was in some sense a direct response to Tchernichovsky's poem. Rav Kook too hears the call of life (*"hayyim"*) emitting from the Land, but the Land issues a stern warning against those who come to her with impure intentions. She spurns suitors who are aroused by her beauty to paganism ("a for-

eign fire, *"esh zarah"*): "Get away from me! Get! To you I am forbidden." She accepts only that suitor who is filled with the light of holiness; in his ear she will whisper her secret, the mysteries of existence: "My chosen, to you I am permitted." See Avi Batt, *"Lahashei ha-Havayah,"* available at:
https://bmj.org.il/wp-content/uploads/2019/12/2.51.BAT_.pdf

It is told that Rav Kook's son, Rabbi Tsevi Yehudah Kook once encountered Shaul Tchernichovsky aboard a ship voyaging from Europe to Erets Yisrael. Tchernichovsky attempted to engage Rabbi Tsevi Yehudah in conversation. Tchernichovsky pressed, saying, "Doesn't your father attempt to bridge the gap between *kodesh* and *hol*, between the sacred and the secular?" Young Rabbi Kook shot back: "Yes, indeed, but not the gap between *kodesh* and *tum'ah*, between the sacred and the impure!"

26 According to Lurianic Kabbalah, the *shevirah* (shattering) occurred in the light of the eyes of *Adam Kadmon*. See *'Ets Hayyim* 8:1; Rabbi David Cohen, *Kol ha-Nevu'ah*, pp. 225-226.

27 Hebrew, *"ve-lifnei ehad."* A quote from *Sefer Yetsirah* 1:2: "And before one (*ve-lifnei ehad*), what do you count?"

28 In Lurianic Kabbalah, the shattering of the vessels produces a diffuse state of *"reshut ha-rabbim"* (the public domain); after the *Tikkun*, this is transformed into a *"reshut ha-yahid"* (private domain; literally "domain of the one"). See Rabbi Yitzhak Eizik Haver, *Pithei She'arim*, Part One (Warsaw, 1888; photo offset Tel-Aviv, 1964), *Netiv Shevirat ha-Kelim*, chap. 13 (54a); Avivi, p. 855. Further in *Netiv Shevirat ha-Kelim*, chap. 15 (56a), the author returns to the theme of the *reshut ha-rabbim*, juxtaposing it to the saying of the Rabbis (*Hullin* 60b) "that they desired many gods" (*"she-'ivvu le-'elohot harbeh"*).

29 The Vilna Gaon differentiated between the Hebrew synonyms *melekh* and *moshel*, as follows. *Melekh* is one who rules with the consent of the people; *moshel* is one who rules by force, against the will of the people. See *Be'ur ha-Gra* to *Sefer Mishlei*, edited by his disciple Rabbi Menahem Mendel of Shklov, Proverbs 27:27. See too the commentary of the Gaon's son, Rabbi Abraham, to Psalms 89:10, 95:1; in *Sefer Tehillim 'im peirush...Be'er Avraham*, ed. Samuel Luria (Warsaw, 1887), 81b, 86.

The Gaon was preceded in this differentiation by Rabbi Abraham Ibn Ezra to Genesis 37:8 (also quoted and rejected by Nahmanides ad loc.). See also Rabbi Isaac Dov Baer Schneerson of Liadi, *Siddur 'im Peirush MaHaRID* (Berdichev, 1913; photo offset Kefar Habad, 1991), vol. 2, *Sha'ar ha-Hanukkah*, s.v. *Ha-Malokh timlokh 'aleinu*, 178a.

It is possible that Rav Kook was influenced by Maimonides' reading of the Kings of Edom, whereby they were, in fact, foreign tyrants who imposed their rule upon the nation of Edom. See *Guide of the Perplexed* III, 50 (Pines translation, p. 615).

30 *Mit-hader* and *mehader* both conjure up the eighth king of Edom, Hadar (Genesis 36:39).

Rabbi Tsevi Elimelekh Spira of Dynów explained the term *"mehadrin"* in regard to the kindling of the Hanukkah lights (*b. Shabbat* 21b) as an allusion to Hadar, the eighth of the primordial Kings, who represents *Tikkun* and the ascent of the sparks from the shattering. See *B'nei Yissachar, Ma'amrei Hodshei Kislev-Tevet*, *ma'amar* 3, par. 27. So too Rabbi Shelomo Hakohen of Radomsk, *Tif'eret Shelomo 'al Mo'adim* (Jerusalem, 1992), *Le-Zot Hanukkah*, s.v. *Zot hanukkat ha-mizbe'ah*, 165b; Rabbi Yitzhak Dov Baer Schneerson of Liadi, *Siddur 'im Peirush MaHaRID*, vol. 2, *Sha'ar ha-Hanukkah*, s.v. *Ha-Mehadrin*, 177b; Rabbi Shemariah Noah Schneerson of Bobruisk, *Shemen la-Ma'or* (Kefar Habad, 1964), *Hanukkah*, 58a.

[31] Elsewhere, Rav Kook expressed his glowing admiration for the Spanish work of Abraham Herrera, *Puerta del Cielo*, known to Rav Kook in Rabbi Isaac Aboab da Fonseca's Hebrew translation as *Sha'ar ha-Shamayim*. See *Pinkesei ha-RAYaH*, vol. 4, ed. Z.M. Levin and B.Z. Kahana-Shapira (Jerusalem, 5777/2017), *Pinkas ha-Dapim* 1:34 (pp. 88-92). My English translation of that piece appears in the present collection of essays under the title, "The Hasidism of Rav Kook."

In *Iggerot ha-RAYaH*, vol. 2 (Jerusalem: Mossad Harav Kook, 1961), Letter 447 (p. 91), Rav Kook includes Herrera's *Sha'ar ha-Shamayim* in a roster of kabbalistic works that speak of Erets Yisrael and the redemption. The footnote refers the reader to *Sha'ar ha-Shamayim* 6:9.

In *Iggerot ha-RAYaH*, vol. 3 (Jerusalem: Mossad Harav Kook, 1965), Letter 896 (p. 208), Rav Kook quotes a teaching from Herrera's other work, *Beit Elohim*, in order to drive home a point to Rabbi Shemariah Menashe Hakohen Adler. The subject is the utter indescribability of *Ein Sof*. (See *Beit Elohim* [Jerusalem, 2007], gate 1, chap. 3 [p. 6].)

Totally unrelated to King Hadar, Herrera characterized the *sefirot* as *hadar* in the sense of beauty. As explained by Yosha, Herrera was influenced in this regard by Marsilio Ficino's commentary on Plato's *Symposium*. See *Sha'ar ha-Shamayim* (Jerusalem, 2006), *ma'amar* 7, chap. 6 (pp. 163-165); Nissim Yosha, *Myth and Metaphor: Abraham Cohen Herrera's Philosophic Interpretation of Lurianic Kabbalah* (Hebrew) (Jerusalem: Magnes Press, 1994), pp. 256-257.

[32] Bokser translated, "the truth as it is in itself." Rav Kook's usage of the term is reminiscent of Kant's *Ding an sich*.

On the other hand, the thought occurs to this writer that the phrase *"emet she-hu le'atsmo"* may betray Breslov influence. During the years in Jaffa, Rav Kook took a keen interest in Breslov Hasidism. In Rabbi Nahman of Breslov's *Likkutei MOHaRaN* I, 9 (*"Tehomot yekhasyumu"*) we read:

> Know, that all is according to the greatness of the truth, for the main light is the Holy One, blessed be He, and the Holy One, blessed be he, is the essence of truth (*'etsem ha-emet*), and the main longing of God is only for truth.

The term *"'etsem ha-emet"* echoes in the disciple, Rabbi Nathan's *Likkutei Tefillot* (chap. 9). (Regarding *Likkutei Tefillot*, see the Letters of Rabbi Tsevi Yehudah Hakohen Kook, *Tsemah Tsevi* [Jerusalem, 1991], p. 26.) The themes in this Torah recur in *Likkutei MOHaRaN* I, 112 (*"Tsohar ta'aseh la-teivah"*). There we find the term *"emet ha-amiti"* ("the true truth"). There too, Rabbi Nahman issues the bold challenge: "One should pray all one's days that one merit once in one's lifetime to speak one word of truth before the LORD!"

In Rabbi Nathan's *Likkutei Halakhot, Hil. Hanukkah, halakhah* 6 (which parallels *Likkutei MOHaRaN* I,9), the thought is given this expression: "And truth is the light of the LORD Himself" (*"Ve-Emet hu 'or Hashem, yitbarakah, be-'atsmo"*) (par.1). Finally, the ascending number of Hanukkah candles is interpreted symbolically: "Every day the light increases, for every day the truth illuminates more" (par. 9).

[33] Rav Kook may be referencing the Cordoveran interpretation of the *Idra*. As opposed to Rabbi Isaac Luria's Kabbalah which tends to the mythic, his predecessor, Rabbi Moses Cordovero, developed an intellectual approach to Kabbalah. Specifically, the death of the primordial kings is viewed as a description of the intradivine intellectual process, whereby a thought was aborted. As Rabbi Moses Cordovero points out: "Do not say that they died, rather they were suppressed" (Aramaic, "*its-tan'u*," literally, "hidden away"). Furthermore, Cordovero understands *"melakhim"* in this context as *"'etsot,"* advice or counsel, as in the Aramaic verse in Daniel 4:24: *"milki yishpar 'alakh."* These divine thoughts (Cordovero coins the term, *"kohot mahshaviyot,"* "thought potentialities") are fleeting, as they are subject to revision. See Rabbi Moses Cordovero, *Elimah* (Lvov, 1881), 4:1:20 (109b-d). Cf. idem, *Shi'ur Komah* (Warsaw, 1883), s.v. *boneh 'olamot u-maharivan* (65c-66a). Earlier, in his magnum opus, *Pardes Rimonim*, Cordovero translates the Aramaic *its-tan'u* into Hebrew, *ne'elmu*; see *Pardes Rimonim* (Munkatch, 1906?; photo offset Jerusalem, 1962), 5:4 (25d).

Rav Kook, as his mentor in Kabbalah, Rabbi Shelomo Eliashov (author of *Leshem Shevo ve-Ahlamah*) made ample use of Cordoveran Kabbalah, as well as Lurianic Kabbalah (as opposed to those kabbalists who held that the latter had obsoleted the former). See Bezalel Naor, *Kana'uteh de-Pinhas* (Spring Valley, NY: Orot, 2013), pp. 25, 106-107.

(An aside: one speculates that the Cordoveran term *"kohot mahshaviyot"* and the like later influenced the development of Nathan of Gaza's theology of *'or she-yesh bo mahshavah* versus *'or she-'ein bo mahshavah*.)

[34] Cf. the Vilna Gaon's Hebrew description of the death of the kings: "...Their soul returned above to their place (*ve-nishmatam hazrah lema'alah bi-mekomam*), and their vessels below, which is the mystery of 'death'" (*Sifra di-Tseni'uta* with *Be'ur ha-GRA*, ed. Samuel Luria [Vilna, 1882], chap. 1 [11a]). See also Rabbi Yitzhak Eizik Haver, op. cit., *Netiv Shevirat ha-Kelim*, chap. 29 (62b).

[35] A kabbalistic term.

[36] An allusion to the *sefirah* of *Yesod*. In the Vilna Gaon's commentary to *Sifra di-Tseni'uta*, Hadar is equated with *'Ateret ha-Yesod*. See *Sifra di-Tseni'uta* with *Be'ur ha-GRA*, chap. 1 (10a).

[37] An allusion to the *sefirah* of *Malkhut*. In *Idra Zuta* (printed in *Zohar* III, 292a), Hadar is equated with *"peri 'ets hadar."* In the *Zohar*, *"peri 'ets hadar"* (Leviticus 23:40), identified by the Sages as the *etrog*, or citron, symbolizes *Malkhut*. For the Vilna Gaon's understanding of this passage in the *Idra*, see the note above. (The Gaon differentiates between the *Malkhut di-Ze'ir Anpin* and *Malkhut de-'Eser Sefirot*, which is to say that Hadar is the *Malkhut* of *Ze'ir Anpin* [i.e., *'Ateret ha-Yesod*], but not the *Malkhut* of the Ten *Sefirot*.)

In the Gaon's understanding, there is no *Malkhut* per se in the World of *Tohu*. The revelation of *Malkhut* (*gillui Malkhut*) is the new dimension of the World of *Tikkun*. For the symbolism of this statement, see Rabbi Yitzhak Eizik Haver, *Pithei She'arim*, *Netiv Shevirat ha-Kelim*, chap. 18 (58a).

[38] A letter written by Tsevi Yehudah Kook (aged nineteen) to Rabbi Ya'akov Moshe Harlap, might shed some light on the direction his father Rav Kook is taking in our *pensée*:

In regard to what I wrote about the concept of good and the concept of love from the perspective of the height of universality (*kelaliyut*), it seems to me that this is the true intention of the saying of the Sages, of blessed memory: "Great is the power of the prophets, that they compare the form to its Creator." (But I still do not know whether this fits properly the context of the words, for I have forgotten their location.)

In the eyes of many, these words are inscrutable. What is the comparison of the form to the Creator? On the contrary, the prophets compare the Creator to the form, not the opposite. Also, the "greatness" is not so understandable.

But in truth, this is the main greatness of prophets, that they do not scholastically infer from the creation to the Creator—which is merely the way of human investigation—rather, since their soul ascends to the heights of the heavens of the LORD, from the higher awareness of the might of the LORD; [from] the awareness of the universality (*kelaliyut*) of existence and the love; in short, from their proximity to the LORD, to the Creator, from this, precisely from this, they are able to understand and recognize, to view and know the form, the creation....

Precisely from their ascent to the "higher worlds" and from their recognition and love of the Creator, the source of the form, they come to love and recognize the form. This is above the aspect of "From my flesh, I shall see God" [Job 19:26]. The opposite: From the vision of God, I shall know my flesh. Only from recognition and love of the divinity, the universality (*kelaliyut*) and the eternal, will the individual, finite existents come to [the prophets'] awareness and love.... Without the light of God that appears within its midst, life remain a riddle without solution, something lacking all attraction.

So, once again: They compare the form to the Creator; the creation corresponds for them to the system of God, the Creator; the specifics correspond for them to the generalities; "Jerusalem below" corresponds to "Jerusalem above" [*b. Ta'anit* 5a]....—This is the special value of the prophets; this is their great power.

(Rabbi Tsevi Yehudah Hakohen Kook, *Tsemah Tsevi* [Jerusalem, 1991], Letter 9 [datelined "Jaffa, 16 Av 5670," i.e., 1910], pp. 24-25)

Like his father, Rabbi Tsevi Yehudah believed that rather than proceeding from the world to God ("from searching the light of God through the world, through existence, that penetrates into the eyes"), as do the philosophers, those truly close to God (i.e., the prophets) are able to proceed "from God to the world."

The Midrash quoted by young Tsevi Yehudah ("Great is the power of the prophets, that they compare the form to its Creator") is from *Genesis Rabbah* 27:1. For a recent discussion of the import of the Midrash attributed to Rabbi Yudan, see Yair Lorberbaum, "Anthropomorphisms in Early Rabbinic Literature: Maimonides and Modern Scholarship," in *Traditions of Maimonideanism*, ed. Carlos Fraenkel (Leiden: Brill, 2009), pp. 334-340.

[39] The new light is the new name MaH (*millui de-Alphin*); see *'Ets Hayyim* 10:2 (*Mahadura Tinyana*); Avivi, p. 869.

⁴⁰ An allusion to Hadar, the eighth king of Edom (Genesis 36:39), who, in the kabbalistic interpretation of the *Idra*, represents *Tikkun* (Repair).

⁴¹ Cf. Genesis 32:31: "And Jacob called the name of the place *Peniel*, 'for I have seen God face to face, and my life was preserved.'"

Rabbi Yitzhak Eizik Haver discusses the light of Peniel, based on the teachings of the Gaon (in his commentary to the *Heikhalot* in *Zohar, Pekudei*). *'Or Peniel* has the numerical value of *malbush* and of *hashmal* (378). See *Pithei She'arim, Netiv Shevirat ha-Kelim*, chap. 16 (f.56); Elijah Gaon of Vilna, *Yahel 'Or*, ed. Naphtali Herz Halevi of Bialystok (Vilna, 1882), *Be'ur ha-Heikhalot, Heikhal* 2 (*Zohar* II, 247a), s.v. *hakha kaymin kol inun levushin*: "*Hashmal, Orpeniel*, and *malbush* all have one [numerical] amount" (bottom 20a). And See Rabbi Reuven Margaliyot, *Mal'akhei 'Elyon* (Jerusalem: Mossad Harav Kook, 1988), s.v. *Orpeniel*, pp. 10-11.

VIII

RAV KOOK: HISTORICAL STUDIES

The Mysterious "Meir": Rav Kook's Missing Student[1]

Recent years have seen a breakthrough regarding the elusive identity of "Monsieur Chouchani," the mysterious vagabond who, in the capacity of mentor, exerted such an incredibly profound effect upon the Nobel-laureate novelist Elie Wiesel as well as the philosopher Emmanuel Levinas in the postwar, post-Holocaust years in France. I am referring to the identification of Chouchani as none other than Hillel Pearlman, an early student of Rav Kook in his short-lived Jaffa *Yeshivah*.[2]

Pivotal to the identification (which we shall not enter into here) is a letter that Rav Kook penned from exile in St. Gallen, Switzerland, to two students of the *Yeshivah*. We offer the letter in our English translation:

> With the help of God
> 6 Tishri 5676 [i.e., 1915]
> A good conclusion[3] to my beloved soul-friends, each man according to his blessing,[4] the dear "groom," the Rabbi, sharp and encyclopedic, crowned with rare qualities and character traits, our teacher, Rabbi **Hillel**, may his light shine; and the dear "groom," exceptional in Torah and awe of heaven, modest and crowned with rare character traits, Mr. **Meir**, may his light shine.

Peace! Peace! Blessing with abundant love.

My dear friends, for too, too long I delayed the response to your dear letter. In your goodness you will give me the benefit of the doubt. Only as a result of the preoccupation brought on by the pain of exile and the heart's longing produced by the general situation (God have mercy), were things put off.

Many thanks to you, our dear Mr. **Meir**, for your detailed letter, whereby you deigned in your goodness to write to us in detail the state of our family members in the Holy Land, especially the state of the girls, may they live.[5] May the LORD repay your kindness and gladden your soul with every manner of happiness and success, and may we together rejoice in the joy of the Land of Delight upon the holy soil, when the LORD will grant salvation to His world, His land and His inheritance, speedily, speedily, soon.

And you, my beloved Mr. **Hillel**, all power to you for your dear words, upright words, pronounced with proper feeling and the longing of a pure heart. We are standing opposite a great and powerful vision previously unknown in human history. There is no doubt that changes of great value are hidden in the depths of this world vision. There is also no doubt that the hand of Israel through the spirit, the voice of Jacob,[6] must be revealed here. Far be it from us to treat as false all the deeds and events, the longing for general life, that we experienced the past years. As much as they are mixed with impurities; as much as they failed to assume their proper form, their living description, their true life—we see in them in the final analysis, correspondence to the holy vision, unmistakable signs that things are happening according to a higher plan. The hand of the LORD holds them, to pave a way for His people, weary from its multitudinous troubles, and also for His world, crouching under the weight of confused life.

It is certainly difficulty at this time to trace which is the way of the process, but in this respect we may be certain: The terrible wandering of such great and essential portions of our nation residing in Eastern Europe, where the spiritual life of Israel is concentrated, and the necessity of rebuilding physically and spiritually new communities, educational institutions and Torah academies—will bring numerous new results, certainly for good. From those new winds that have been blowing in our world for the past half-century and more, something is to be derived, if we can purify them, erecting them upon foundations of purity and holiness. The opinions and longing for spiritual and physical building of Israel; the mighty desire of building the Land and the Nation, despite external and internal obstacles; the visions tucked away in the hearts of numerous thinkers to uplift the horn of Israel and its spirit, to bind together the strength of life with the sanctity of the soul, the talent of understanding with the depth of faith, immediate implementation with longing for salvation—all these are things that will bear fruit, and the Master of Wars, blessed be He, will grow from all of them His salvation.[7]

One thing we know for certain, that we are invited to great projects: philosophic projects; literary and publicistic projects; practical and social projects; projects at the interior of eternal life and projects of temporal and secular life; projects that remain within the border of Israel; and projects that overflow and touch the streams of life of the world at large and their many relations with the world of Israel, which was, is, and will be a blessing to all the families of earth,[8] as the word of the LORD to our ancestor [Abraham] in antiquity.

My beloved, I request that you write to us whatever is [happening] to you, your situation in detail, whether in spiritual or material matters; whatever you imagine might interest us, whether of private or public affairs. For all I will be exceedingly grateful to you, with God's help.

I am your fast friend, looking for your happiness and success, and your return together with all our scattered people to the holy soil in happiness and success. May the LORD bless you with all good and extend to you peace and blessing and a good conclusion, as is your wish and the wish of one who seeks your peace and good all the days, longing for the salvation of the LORD,

                Abraham Isaac Ha[Kohen] K[ook][9]

In order to understand the contents of the letter, the better to grasp the identities of its two recipients, we must first acquaint ourselves with the circumstances in which it was written.

For one decade, from 1904 to 1914, Abraham Isaac Hakohen Kook served as Rabbi of the port city of Jaffa (precursor to Tel-Aviv). During those years in Jaffa he taught a select group of students in a *yeshivah* of his own making. (This *yeshivah* is not to be confused with the famous Yeshivah Merkaz Harav founded by Rav Kook in Jerusalem in the early 1920s.) In summer of 1914, Rav Kook set sail for Europe to attend the *Knessiyah Gedolah* or World Congress of the recently organized Agudath Israel movement. Due to the outbreak of World War One (on Tish'ah be-Av of that year), the conference was cancelled. Unable to return to Jaffa, Rav Kook remained stranded in Europe for the duration of the War, first in St. Gallen, Switzerland, where his needs were provided for by a sympathetic Mr. Abraham Kimhi, and later in London, where Rav Kook served as Rabbi of the Mahzikei Hadat synagogue in London's East End.[10]

Much concerning the Jaffa *yeshivah* remains shrouded in mystery. No archive remains of this short-lived institution.[11] Thus we are pretty much left in the dark as to the curriculum,[12] enrollment, and even location. Fortunately, significant headway has been made in this direction in the recent article by Moshe Nahmani of the Yeshivat Hesder of Ramat Gan, *"She'areha Ne'ulim—Yeshivat Harav Kuk be-Yaffo"* ("Closed Gates—The *Yeshivah* of Rabbi Kook in Jaffa").[13] Through painstaking research, the author was able to put together a list of students. Researchers had no difficulty identifying the "Hillel" of the letter as Hillel Pearlman. It was merely a case of "connecting the dots."[14] But Nahmani was baffled by the "Meir" who is one of two co-addressees in our letter.[15]

I believe that I have solved the mystery of the missing Meir. In 1977, I was a visitor to the home of Rabbi Mayer Goldberg of Oakland, California. Rabbi Goldberg was a successful businessman (at that time in real estate) and a Jewish philanthropist, especially supportive of *yeshivot* or rabbinical academies. Rabbi Goldberg revealed to me that he had studied under Rav Kook in Jaffa.[16] He then went on to share with me a teaching of Rav Kook that I have since repeated on many an occasion. He said that before being exposed to Rav Kook's teaching, the term *"yir'at shamayim"* ("fear of heaven") had only a restrictive, narrowing connotation. Rav Kook explained the term in a totally different light. By the term *"yir'at shamayim,"* Rav Kook conveyed to his young listeners the vastness, the enormity, the infinitude of the universe.

Reading Moshe Nahmani's article concerning Rav Kook's *yeshivah* in Jaffa, and his bafflement as to the full identity of the student named simply "Meir," I recalled my meeting with Rabbi Mayer Goldberg. I resolved that during my forthcoming visit to the East Bay area (as it has come to be known) I would meet with the late Rabbi's children to learn from them more details of their father's involvement with Rav Kook. What emerged from our discussion (conducted on February 14, 2013) is the following reconstruction of events.

Missing Student

Mayer Vevrick was born circa 1890 "near Kiev."[17] At some time before World War One, Mayer boarded a ship from Odessa to Jaffa. In the words of his daughter Rachel Landes:

> Once he arrived in Jaffa, he sought out the yeshiva of Rabbi Kook. Rabbi Avraham Kook was a world renowned scholar and it was there my father headed to study further. He became a "hasid," a follower of the Rabbi, and thoroughly enjoyed his studies there. He lived in Rabbi Kook's home.[18] He studied Talmud...with Rashi and the commentaries, for many hours a day with the other young men. These were the happiest days of his life, with uninterrupted Torah study, and the joy of learning with Rabbi Kook. Mayer adopted [Rabbi] Kook's philosophy and was guided by it for the rest of his life.[19]

In World War One, Mayer left Jaffa for Egypt. There he was held by the British in an internment camp. Eventually, with some ingenuity, he was able to book passage on a boat to the United States.[20] Initially he resided on the East Coast. In Boston, he received a *ketav semikhah* (writ of ordination) from Rabbi Joseph M. Jacobson. The *semikhah* was written by Rabbi Jacobson on the spot in recognition of Mayer's knowledge of Torah.[21] Later, Rabbi Mayer relocated to the West Coast, first to Washington State and finally to California.[22]

What becomes apparent from the letter of Rav Kook is that "Meir" remained in Jaffa after Rav Kook's departure for Europe (followed almost immediately by the outbreak of World War One), and thus was in a position to give the Rav an update on the welfare of his daughters left behind in Jaffa. What also becomes apparent is that in the fall of 1915, "Meir" and his companion Hillel were no longer in the Land of Israel but somewhere else, for in his concluding remarks Rav Kook expresses the wish that they return to the Holy Land. This is consistent with Rabbi Goldberg's biography, whereby he (along with countless other Jews of Erets Israel) was forced to flee the Holy Land at that time.[23] This also coincides with the reconstructed biography of Hillel (Pearlman). Both students of Rav Kook, Hillel (Pearlman) and Meir (Goldberg) ended up in the United States in World War One. Whereas we are being told that Hillel (Pearlman) later left the United States for Europe and North Africa, reinventing himself as the mysterious "Monsieur Chouchani," Mayer Goldberg remained in the United States.

Rabbi Mayer Goldberg passed away on September 25, 1992, a centenarian.[24] Shortly before his passing, Rabbi Goldberg had published in Jerusalem a collection of kabbalistic insights (culled from his marginalia in the books of his library), entitled *Margaliyot shel Torah (Pearls of Torah)*. Much of the material in the book is attributed to the kabbalistic work *Yalkut Re'uveni*.[25] My attention was riveted to an unattributed piece, which would appear to originate with Rabbi Mayer Goldberg himself:

In Exodus 2:12 we read that Moses slew the Egyptian (who was beating a Hebrew) and buried him in the sand. The Hebrew words are: *"Vayyakh et ha-mitsri vayyitmenehu ba-hol."*

Rabbi Goldberg observes that the word *"ha-mitsri"* ("the Egyptian") has the same numerical value (*gematria*) as the word *"Moshe"* ("Moses"): 345. In other words, Moses slew himself! The Rabbi then goes on to explain that what is truly conveyed by the verse, is that Moses slew the opinions of Egypt. Moses, growing up in the house of Pharaoh, had imbibed secular knowledge stripped of Godliness. So in other words, on a deeper level, what Moses was actually slaying was himself, or a part of himself that was thoroughly Egyptian in outlook. He then buried that secular learning devoid of Godliness "in the sand." Here the Rabbi plays on the word *"hol,"* which may have another meaning besides "sand": the secular. This is to say, Moses buried that tainted learning in the secular realm.[26]

---

[1] The writer wishes to express his gratitude to Eve Gordon-Ramek and Robert H. Warwick, children of the late Rabbi Mayer Goldberg, for their invaluable contribution to the preparation of this article.

[2] Prof. Shalom Rosenberg, Professor of Jewish Philosophy at Hebrew University in Jerusalem, who was present at the time of Chouchani's death in Uruguay, was so convinced of the identification that he named his son "Hillel" after his revered master. See Moshe Nahmani, *"Mi Kan Hillel,"* Mussaf Shabbat, Makor Rishon, 3 Ellul, 5771 [2.9.2011]; Yair Sheleg, "Goodbye, Mr. Chouchani," *Haaretz*, Sept. 26, 2003; Solomon Malka, *Monsieur Chouchani: L'énigme d'un maitre du XXème siècle* (Paris, 1994). Recently, a website has been devoted exclusively to Chouchani. At www.chouchani.com we are told that Michael Grynszpan is in the process of producing a documentary film on the life of M. Chouchani.

I have two anecdotes to contribute to the growing literature on Chouchani, the first heard from Prof. Andre Neher (1914-1988), the second from Rabbi Uziel Milevsky (former Chief Rabbi of Mexico).

• My dear friend André (Asher Dov) Neher, z"l, had been a distinguished professor of Jewish studies at the University of Strasburg. I knew him in his last years after his retirement to Jerusalem. Neher told me that in his youth, his father had hired Chouchani to teach him Talmud. At their initial meeting it was decided that they would study Tractate *Beitsah*. Chouchani said to the young Neher: "In the next hour I can either teach you the first folio of the Tractate, or sum up for you the entire Tractate!"

• Similarly, in the final phase of Chouchani's career (in Montevideo, Uruguay), Rabbi Aaron Milevsky (1904-1986), Chief Rabbi of Uruguay, hired Chouchani to tutor his young son Uzi in Talmud. Chouchani rewarded Uzi's diligence by allowing him to quiz him on any entry in the dictionary. Uzi asked Chouchani for the Latin name of some obscure butterfly, which Chouchani was able to supply without hesitation! (Heard from Rabbi Nachum Lansky of Baltimore, shelit"a, quoting Rabbi Uziel Milevsky, z"l.)

At the onset of this article I wish to clarify one point. Should the identification of Hillel Pearlman with "Monsieur Chouchani" one day prove incorrect, that would in no way affect the positive identification of Rav Kook's addressee "Meir" as Rabbi Mayer Goldberg of Oakland, California. The identification of the mysterious "Meir" as Rabbi Meir Goldberg is in no way contingent upon the identification of Hillel Pearlman as "Chouchani," but rather stands on its own merits.

[3] Traditional blessing for the New Year uttered between Rosh Hashanah and Yom Kippur.

[4] Cf. Genesis 49:28.

[5] While Rav Kook and his Rebbetzin (as well as their only son Tsevi Yehudah) were together in Europe, their daughters were left behind in Jaffa, and Rav Kook was most anxious as to their welfare. The family would not be reunited until after World War One, when Rav Kook returned from European exile to the Holy Land.

[6] Genesis 27:22.

[7] Allusion to the conclusion of the *Yotser* prayer recited in the morning service: "ba'al milhamot, zore'a tsedakot, matsmi'ah yeshu'ot" ("Master of wars, planter of righteousness, grower of salvations"). A year into World War One, Rav Kook already envisioned that the outcome of the War would be a shifting of the center of Jewish life from Eastern Europe elsewhere, as well as the further advancement of the building of the Holy Land.

[8] Genesis 12:3.

[9] *Iggerot ha-RAYaH*, vol. 3 (Jerusalem: Mossad Harav Kook, 1965), Letter 740 (pp. 2-3).

[10] Mr. Jacob Rosenheim, organizer of the *Knessiyah Gedolah*, subsequently penned a letter of apology to Rav Kook, for by extending the invitation to him to attend the conference, Rosenheim had indirectly brought about Rav Kook's misfortune.

[11] Moshe Nahmani posits that it existed for 6-7 years from 1909/10-1915.

[12] We do know that one subject on the curriculum, namely *Kuzari* by Rabbi Judah Halevi, aroused the ire of the Jerusalem zealot Rabbi Yeshayah Orenstein. See my edition of *Orot* (Maggid, 2015), p. 454, n. 174.

[13] Available on the website www.shoresh.org.il, dated 4/17/2012 or 25 Nissan, 5772.

According to Moshe Nahmani, the true reason that so little is known of this earlier *yeshivah* of Rav Kook is that Rav Kook himself suppressed publicity concerning its inner life, for fear that should word of the curriculum leak out, the *yeshivah* would come under attack from the ever vigilant rabbis of Jerusalem. (In fact, Rav Kook's teaching of *Kuzari* to the students was sharply criticized by the zealous Rabbi Yeshayah Orenstein of Jerusalem.) Nahmani believes that Rav Kook was dispensing the arcane wisdom of Kabbalah to the students—sufficient grounds for keeping publicity away from the *yeshivah*. (But the Kabbalah may not have been the standard Kabbalah as taught in Jerusalem. We know that one of the instructors in the *yeshivah* was Shem Tov Geffen [1856-1927], an autodidactic genius who fused the study of Kabbalah together with mathematics and physics.) Of course, this is mere speculation on Nahmani's part. What is factual, is that Rav Kook taught in Jaffa the *Kuzari* of Rabbi Judah Halevi and Maimonides' *Eight Chapters* (Maimonides' introduction to his commentary to Tractate *Avot* or Ethics of the Fathers)—which in themselves represented a departure from the standard curriculum of the contemporary *yeshivot*.

In a letter to Shem Tov Geffen, then fundraising for the Jaffa *yeshivah* in Russia, Rav Kook reported that he had added to the curriculum lectures in *Kuzari* three times a week. Rav Kook refers to this study as "the beloved and fundamental subject of the inner wisdom of our holy religion." See *Iggerot ha-RAYaH*, vol. 2, ed. RZYH Kook (Jerusalem: Mossad Harav Kook, 1961), Letter 339 (p. 4). The letter is datelined "Jaffa, 22 Marheshvan 5671 [i.e., 1910]." The letter was reprinted in Yedidyah Wengrover, *R' Shem Tov Geffen* (Metula: Nezer David, 2017), Letter 29 (p. 137). And see ibid. Letter 25 (p. 131, n. 436). More than two years later (in 1913), the *shi'urim* in *Kuzari* a few times a week, were still going on. Rav Kook explained to his brother (Rabbi Dov Kook?) that he used the book as a springboard for discussion of *"hilkhot de'ot,"* or theological issues. See *Iggerot ha-RAYaH*, vol. 2, Letter 501 (p. 139).

14 In one day, 26 Iyyar, 5675, Rav Kook sent two letters from St. Gallen to America (*Iggerot ha-RAYaH*, vol. 2 [Jerusalem: Mossad Harav Kook, 1961], Letters 733-734 [pp. 329-330]). The first letter is addressed to Rabbi Meir Berlin asking that he lend assistance to Rav Kook's student, newly arrived immigrant Hillel Pearlman. The second letter is addressed to Hillel Pearlman himself, expressing pain that he too was exiled from the Holy Land, and offering encouragement, as well as the practical suggestion that he establish contact with Rabbi Meir Berlin, and with Rav Kook's staunch friend Dr. Moshe Seidel, who might be in a position to help. In a postscript, Rav Kook, noting that Hillel Pearlman had spent some time in the house after Rav Kook's own absence, asks for details concerning the welfare of the two Kook daughters left behind in Jaffa, Batyah Miriam and Esther Yael. Logic dictates that our Hillel is Hillel Pearlman of the earlier letters. What eventually became of Hillel Pearlman and whether he in fact "morphed" into "Monsieur Chouchani" remains something of a mystery. See Moshe Nahmani, *"Mi Kan Hillel?"*

15 *"She'areha Ne'ulim—Yeshivat Harav Kuk be-Yaffo,"* Part II, note 51. So too in Nahmani's earlier article *"Mi Kan Hillel?"*

16 Meir Goldberg told this writer (BN) that before arriving in Jaffa from his native Russia, he had studied under the *"Gadol* of Minsk." (That would have been Rabbi Eliezer Rabinowitz [1859-1924], who inherited the rabbinate of his deceased father-in-law, Rabbi Yeruham Yehudah Leib Perlman [1835-1896]. Both men were referred to by the sobriquet *"Ha-Gadol Mi-Minsk."*)

According to the memoir of Rabbi Goldberg's daughter, Rachel Landes, "My Father, Mayer Goldberg" (October 15, 2009), her father grew up in Krementchug, Ukraine. She also writes that at one point in his career, her father studied in a *yeshivah gedolah* under Rabbi Zimmerman. Though Landes does not specify that the *yeshivah* was located in Krementchug (to the contrary she writes that the *yeshivah* was in Kiev), one ventures a guess that this *yeshivah* of Rabbi Zimmerman was actually that of Rabbi Abraham Isaac Halevi Zimmerman, Rabbi of Krementchug.

Rabbi Abraham Isaac Halevi Zimmerman of Krementchug was the paternal grandfather of Rabbi Dr. Aharon Chaim Halevi Zimmerman (1915-1995), *Rosh Yeshivah* of Beit ha-Midrash le-Torah (Hebrew Theological College) in Skokie, Illinois. (Rabbi Dr. Zimmerman's father, Rabbi Ya'akov Moshe Halevi Zimmerman was the son of Rabbi Abraham Isaac Halevi Zimmerman of Krementchug.) Rabbi Chaim Zimmerman published a collection of his grandfather's novellae on Maimonides' *Mishneh Torah*, two volumes of *Hiddushei ha-RAYaH* (Jerusalem, 1988).

(According to Rabbi Chaim Zimmerman, a young Menahem Mendel Schneerson, the son of the Rabbi of Yekaterinoslav [later Dnepropetrovsk], who would one day become the Lubavitcher Rebbe, briefly visited the *yeshivah* of Rabbi Zimmerman in Krementchug, though he was never officially enrolled there. I have been unable to corroborate this story from other sources.)

Rabbi Abraham Isaac Halevi Zimmerman of Krementchug was the father-in-law of Rabbi Baruch Baer Leibowitz (*talmid muvhak*, or premier disciple, of Rabbi Hayyim Halevi Soloveitchik, known as "Rabbi Hayyim of Brisk"). Rabbi Baruch Baer Leibowitz served as *Rosh Yeshivah* of Knesset Beit Yitzhak, originally located in Slabodka, a suburb of Kovno, Lithuania, and between the two World Wars in Kamenets. During World War One, Knesset Beit Yitzhak was located in Krementchug, where the Rosh Yeshivah, Rabbi Baruch Baer Leibowitz, acted also as Rabbi of the community. See Shulamit Ezrahi's biography of her father, Rabbi Meir Hadash, *Ha-Mashgi'ah Rabbi Meir* (Jerusalem: Feldheim, 2001), p. 93.

[17] According to Rachel Landes' memoir, her father was born in Krementchug. In his Application for a Certificate of Arrival and Preliminary Form for Petition for Naturalization (1940), Mayer writes that he was born in "[illegible] near Kiev." Mayer adopted the surname "Goldberg" in the United States.

[18] The fact that Meir (or Mayer) resided in the Kook home would explain how he was able to supply Rav Kook with information concerning the Rav's daughters. Nahmani noted that Rav Kook had earlier asked Hillel Perlman for details concerning the girls, the assumption being that Hillel Perlman had resided in the Rav's home (though that is not explicitly stated in Rav Kook's letter to Hillel Pearlman). See Moshe Nahmani, *"Mi Kan Hillel?"*

[19] Rachel Landes, "My Father, Mayer Goldberg" (2009), p. 2.

[20] According to Mayer Warwick Goldberg's Application for a Certificate of Arrival and Preliminary Form for Petition for Naturalization (1940), he booked passage on a Greek steamship from Alexandria, Egypt to New York under the assumed name "Othniel Kaplan" in spring of 1915 or 1916. Writing twenty-five years after the fact, Mayer could no longer recall the precise date, whether the arrival in New York had taken place in spring of 1915 or spring of 1916. We are now in a position to aid his memory. We know from Rav Kook's letters to Rabbi Meir Berlin and to Hillel Pearlman, both datelined "St. Gallen, 26 Iyyar 5675," that as of spring 1915, Hillel Perlman was in America.

In order for Rav Kook's letter of 6 Tishri, 5676, to be addressed jointly to Hillel and Meir, Meir too would have had to reside in America by fall of 1915. That could only be so if Meir (or Mayer) arrived in New York in spring of 1915—not 1916!

[21] The fact that Rav Kook does not address Meir by the title "Harav" in the salutation (as he does Hillel) indicates that Meir was not yet an ordained rabbi in the fall of 1915.

[22] According to information supplied in his 1940 Application for Naturalization, Mayer resided in New York City and Brooklyn from 1916 to 1917; in New Haven and Colchester, Connecticut from 1917 to 1919; in Seattle and Tacoma, Washington from 1919 to 1922; in San Francisco from 1922 to 1930; and in Oakland from 1930 to 1940.

[23] To quote from Rachel Landes' memoir (p. 2): "...World War I broke out. The Turks, who were in control of Palestine, sided with Germany, and Russia was on the side of the Allies. My father, being from Russia, found himself classified as an enemy alien. The Turks began to round up all foreign nationals. It became clear that my father could not stay there."

[24] At the 24th Annual Banquet of the Hebrew Academy of San Francisco, held on Sunday, December 6, 1992, a moving tribute was paid to the recently departed Rabbi Mayer Goldberg.

[25] *Yalkut Re'uveni* (Wilmersdorf, 1681), by Reuben Hoshke HaKohen (Sofer) of Prague (died 1673), is a kabbalistic collection on the Pentateuch.

[26] Rabbi Mayer Goldberg, *Margaliyot shel Torah* (Jerusalem, 5750), p. 112. The Hebrew original reads:

וי"ך – כמנין ל"ו כריתות [משנה, כריתות א, א], משה כרת את המצרי, כרת את החיצונים, וטמינם בחולין. המצרי שהרג משה – הדעות של מצרים שמשה למד, חיצוניות בלי אלוהות – הרג וטמן בחולין, כי מש"ה בגימטריא המצר"י".

When Rav Kook Was the Zealot *(Kannai)* and His Opponent the Advocate *(Melits Yosher)*[1]

In 1891, there appeared in Warsaw an anonymous work[2] entitled *Hevesh Pe'er*,[3] whose sole objective was to clarify for the masses the proper place on the head to don the *tefillah shel rosh* or head-phylactery. According to *halakhah*, the *tefillah* must be placed no lower than the hairline and no higher than the soft spot on a baby's head (i.e., the anterior fontanelle).[4] In ancient times, there were sectarian Jews who deliberately placed the *tefillah* on the forehead, as attested to by the *Mishnah*: "If one placed it [i.e., the *tefillah*] on his forehead, or on his hand, this is the way of sectarianism *(minut)*."[5] These Jews interpreted literally the verse, "You shall bind them for a sign upon your hand, and they shall be for frontlets between your eyes."[6] Adherents to Rabbinic Judaism are punctilious about placing the hand-phylactery on the biceps of the forearm opposite the heart,[7] and the head-phylactery above the hairline. East European Jews who placed their phylacteries on the forehead did so not out of conviction, as the Sadducees of old, but out of sheer ignorance of the law. The slim book (all of 24 leaves or 48 pages) was thus an elaborate educational vehicle to educate the masses how to properly observe the law.[8]

According to the approbation to *Hevesh Pe'er* by Rabbi Elijah David Rabinowitz-Te'omim (ADeReT) of Ponevezh, the book was published [but not authored] by his former son-in-law (presently his brother's son-in-law), Rabbi Abraham Isaac Hakohen Kook of Zeimel.[9]

Wares in hand, the young rabbi of Zeimel (aged twenty-six) assumed the role of an itinerant bookseller, travelling from town to town in Lithuania. Wherever he went, he preached concerning the importance of fulfilling the commandment of *tefillin*. Historically, there was precedent for a rabbi promoting that specific *mitsvah*. In the thirteenth century, Rabbi Moses of Coucy (author of *Sefer Mitsvot Gadol* or *SeMaG*), circulating in the communities of France and Spain, was able to turn the tide and convince Jews, hitherto lax in their observance of the commandment, to don *tefillin*.[10] As for an author posing as an itinerant bookseller, Rav Kook's older contemporary, Rabbi Israel Meir Kagan of Radin, had done exactly that, thus earning himself the sobriquet *Hafets Hayyim*, after the book by that name that he peddled. (*Hafets Hayyim* tackles the problem, halakhic and otherwise, of malicious gossip.)

It is recorded that Rav Kook's sermons had such a positive influence upon his audience that the Rebbe of Slonim, Rabbi Shmuel Weinberg, offered to support him if he would devote himself full-time to acting as a *maggid* or peripatetic preacher.[11]

One would never have imagined that this halakhic work would meet with any rabbinic opposition.[12] The point it makes that wearing the head-phylactery below the hairline on the forehead invalidates the performance of the commandment, seems rather clear-cut in the sources. (In fact, but a few years earlier, in 1884, Rabbi Israel Meir Kagan in his work *Mishnah Berurah* had advised wearing the phylactery higher on the head, at a remove from the hairline, just to be on the safe side.)[13]

However, five years later, Rabbi Ze'ev Wolf Turbowitz of Kraz (Lithuanian, Kražiai; Yiddish, Krozh)[14] devoted the very first of his collected responsa, *Tif'eret Ziv*, to pummeling the anonymous work *Hevesh Pe'er*.[15] Rabbi Turbowitz prefaces his remarks by saying: "The intention of this author [i.e., the author of *Hevesh Pe'er*] is for [the sake of] Heaven, but nonetheless he has spoken shabbily of the people of the LORD. May the LORD forgive him. For Israel, 'if not prophets, are the children of prophets.'"[16] Rabbi Turbowitz goes on to argue that the commandment is invalidated only if the majority of the phylactery is placed below the hairline. If, on the other hand, the majority is situated above the hairline and only a minority below, then the halakhic principle of *"rubbo ke-khullo"* ("the majority as the whole") applies, and the commandment is fulfilled.[17] One of the rabbi's supposed proofs is the ruling of the *Turei Zahav* that one must recite the blessing once again only in a case where the entire phylactery or the majority thereof has slipped down, but if only a minority of the phylactery has been displaced, with the majority still within the prescribed area, one does not recite another blessing upon readjusting the phylactery.[18]

Rav Kook (now outed as the author of *Hevesh Pe'er*) responded to the onslaught of *Tif'eret Ziv*. His lengthy rejoinder, entitled *"Kelil Tif'eret,"* appeared in the periodical *Torah mi-Zion* (Jerusalem, 1900).

In *"Kelil Tif'eret,"* Rav Kook makes a strong case that the principle of *rubbo ke-khullo* cannot justify a minority of the head-phylactery descending below the hairline onto the forehead. *Rubbo ke-khullo* has no bearing on *shi'urim* or measurements. In support of his position, Rav Kook quotes two sources: Rabbi B.H. Auerbach's *Nahal Eshkol*,[19] and the recent responsa of Rabbi Eliezer Don-Yahya of Lutzin, *Even Shetiyah*.[20] (Rav Kook seems to have overlooked the earlier authority Rabbi Moses Schreiber, who writes explicitly: "We do not say in regard to *shi'urim* [the principle of] '*rubo ke-khullo.*'")[21]

Rav Kook dismantles Rabbi Turbowitz's supposed proof from the fact that another blessing is unwarranted as long as the majority of the phylactery is still in its proper place. Rav Kook reasons that we must distinguish between the essential commandment ("*'etsem ha-mitsvah*") and the action of the commandment ("*ma'aseh ha-mitsvah*"). The fact that one does not recite an additional blessing does not necessarily mean that the commandment ("*'etsem ha-mitsvah*") is still being fulfilled. What it does imply, is that the action of the commandment ("*ma'aseh ha-mitsvah*") is ongoing. The blessing addresses renewed action ("*ma'aseh ha-mitsvah*"). In a case where only a minority of the phylactery has been displaced, the action required to readjust it does not warrant a blessing. "And the *Turei Zahav*[22] holds that since in the entire Torah, '*rubbo ke-khullo,*'[23] once most of the action has been nullified, the action as a whole is nullified, but if most of the action remains, even though the commandment has been nullified, still the action exists..."[24]

As is typical for Rav Kook, he signs himself, "Abraham Isaac Hakohen Kook, servant to the servants of the LORD...Bausk."[25]

Evidently, Rabbi Turbowitz was not one to take something lying down. He came back at Rav Kook with a stinging reply, integrated into *Ziv Mishneh*, his commentary to Maimonides' *Mishneh Torah*.[26] There, in *Hilkhot Tefillin* (4:1), he maintains that since "*rubbo ke-khullo* is a universal principle in the entire Torah,"[27] this applies to *tefillin* as well. He reiterates once more his proof from the *Turei Zahav*, who ruled that the blessing is recited once again only in a scenario where the *tefillin* are totally displaced. He mentions the opinion of "one wise man" ("*hakham ehad*") who wrote that even the slightest deviation disqualifies the *mitsvah*, and disagrees. According to Rabbi Turbowitz, *lekhathillah* (*ab initio*), the entire phylactery should be above the hairline with none of it extending down to the forehead, but *be-di-'avad* (*ex post facto*), if a minority of the phylactery is below the hairline, one has nonetheless fulfilled the commandment. And therefore, the anonymous sage was wrong to criticize the masses, who are remiss in this respect, and their spiritual leaders, who look the other way and do not protest. "He spoke shabbily of the people of the LORD and will in the future be called to judgment!" After summing up rather concisely the position he took earlier in *Tif'eret Ziv*, Rabbi Turbowitz now lambastes Rav Kook for what he wrote in *Torah mi-Zion* (Jerusalem, 1900), no. 4, chap. 4, accusing Rav Kook of deliberately misquoting him.

In 1925, two disciples of Rav Kook, Rabbi Yitzhak Arieli[28] and Rabbi Uri Segal Hamburger,[29] reissued *Hevesh Pe'er* in Jerusalem with Rav Kook's permission.[30] Appended to the work was Rav Kook's rebuttal *"Kelil Tif'eret."* (In addition, this edition was graced by the comments of Rav Kook's deceased father-in-law, ADeReT, and of Rav Kook's admirers in Jerusalem: Rabbis Tsevi Pesah Frank, Ya'akov Moshe Harlap, and Yehiel Mikhel Tukachinsky. Finally, there are the substantial "Comments upon Comments" ["He'arot le-He'arot"] of the editor, Rabbi Yitzhak Arieli.)[31]

In 1939, Rabbi Yosef Avigdor Kesler of Rockaway (Arverne to be precise)[32] published a second collection of his deceased father-in-law, Rabbi Ze'ev Turbowitz's numerous responsa. Whereas the first collection of *Tif'eret Ziv* covered only *Orah Hayyim*, this collection covered all four sections of *Shulhan 'Arukh*.[33] In addition, it contained a supplement (*Kuntres Aharon*) entitled *"Mele'im Ziv."* In the supplement, Rabbi Kesler published a letter from ADeReT to Rabbi Turbowitz that turned up in the latter's papers.

ADeReT's letter is datelined "Monday, *Vayyetse*, 5657 [i.e., 1896]." In the letter, ADeReT gratefully acknowledges receipt of the recently published book *Tif'eret Ziv*. Regretting that he is unable to send monetary payment for the book because he is presently inundated with works of various authors, ADeReT nonetheless wishes to at least offer some comment on the contents of the book.[34]

Referring to the very first responsum in *Tif'eret Ziv*, ADeReT rejoices that Rabbi Turbowitz sought to advocate on behalf of the Jewish People regarding the commandment of *tefillin*. He is especially overjoyed that Rabbi Turbowitz was not cowed, but dared to differ. ADeReT holds up as role models Rabbi Zerahyah Halevi (*Ba'al ha-Ma'or*) who critiqued Rabbi Isaac Alfasi (RIF), only to be attacked himself by RABaD of *Posquières*; RABaD of *Posquières* who critiqued Maimonides; et al. Since this is the "way of Torah" (*darkah shel Torah*), why should he harbor any resentment toward Rabbi Turbowitz for disagreeing with him?[35] (ADeReT, though not the author of *Hevesh Pe'er*, had wholeheartedly endorsed and sponsored its publication.)

The sterling character of ADeReT is best summed up in the following lines:

> God forbid, I am not deluded to think that truth resides with me. I wholeheartedly acknowledge the truth. I have not a thousandth part of resentment towards one who differs with me. And the opposite, I love him with all my soul when he points out to me the truth.[36]

Since Rabbi Turbowitz acted as a true *talmid hakham* (Torah scholar) who uninhibitedly speaks truth, ADeReT wonders why he failed to mention the name of the work he critiqued, *Hevesh Pe'er*. This would have provoked neither the author nor ADeReT.[37]

In this vein of truth-seeking, ADeReT proceeds to explain why the argument presented in *Tif'eret Ziv* failed to dissuade him from the position adopted both by him and by the author of *Hevesh Pe'er*. Since the *shi'ur* or measurement of the area on the head where the phylactery is to be placed is *Halakhah le-Moshe mi-Sinai* (a law to Moses from Sinai), the principle of *"rubbo ke-khullo"* is of no consequence in this regard.[38]

Realizing the historic importance of the contents of the letter, Rabbi Kesler provided a photograph of the crucial passage in the letter, which reads as follows:

> About two years ago, the thought occurred to me to reprint the booklet *Hevesh Pe'er*. I wrote to its author, my son-in-law, my soul-friend (today the Rabbi of Bausk, may he live) and asked him if he has anything new to add to it. He wrote me an article, brief in quantity but great in quality, that it is possible to say *"rubbo ke-khullo."* In the summer of 5655 [i.e., 1895] when I was in Warsaw, I already spoke with a printer and also notified the [government] censor, and I was thinking to print. But after this, I reversed myself, and the two of us [i.e., ADeReT and Rav Kook] agreed that it is not worthwhile to print leniencies (*kulot*).[39]

ADeReT explains that if we show any leniency, it will prove a slippery slope. He reveals to Rabbi Turbowitz his unusual experience with Hasidim in particular: "From this, there came about in places where the Hasidim reside [the custom] to wear large *tefillin*.[40] Not one in a thousand bears most of the *tefillah* within the hairline. In most cases, but a small fraction (*mi'uta de-mi'uta*) [is within the hairline]. I have seen with my own eyes the entirety upon the forehead. They laughed at my rebuke, saying: 'Thus is the *mitsvah*.' 'So we saw our fathers doing.'"[41]

The letter concludes with this salutation:

His friend who is honored by his love, appreciates his genius and his Torah, and blesses him with all good,

Elijah David Rabinowitz Te'omim

...Mir[42]

---

[1] These are the exact words of Rabbi Joseph Avigdor Kesler in the introduction to his father-in-law Rabbi Ze'ev Wolf Turbowitz's work of responsa, *Tif'eret Ziv* (Brooklyn: Moinester Publishing Company, 1939), p. 7, par. 5.

By the time of his passing in 1935, Rav Kook would be immortalized as a twentieth-century Rabbi Levi Isaac of Berdichev, the great advocate of the Jewish People, forever defending their practices in the heavenly tribunal. Today, Rav Kook is famous for his leniency concerning the *Shemittah* or Sabbatical year, the *heter mekhirah*, which allows sale of the land to a non-Jew for the duration, whereby agricultural work, or at least some forms thereof, may take place. The model for this contract is the prevalent *mekhirat hamets* or sale of leaven to a non-Jew before Passover, so that it need not be removed from the home of the Jew.

However, in general, if one studies the *teshuvot* (responsa) of Rav Kook, he does not come across as extraordinarily lenient in his *pesakim* or halakhic decisions. *Par contre*, someone whose work is chock-full of startling leniencies is Rabbi Aryeh Tsevi Frumer of Kozhiglov, *Hashem yikom damo* (1884-1943), *Rosh Yeshivah* of Yeshivat Hakhmei Lublin and a disciple of Rabbi Abraham Bornstein (the author of responsa *Avnei Nezer*). Rabbi Fromer designed his work of responsa, *Erets Tsevi* (Lublin, 1938), to be *melammed zekhut*, to find some halakhic justification (however farfetched) for certain otherwise anomalous practices within the Jewish community. This is apparent from the very first responsum, where the author attempts to justify the prevalent practice of wearing a *tallit katan* that fails to meet the prescribed *shi'ur* or measurement.

[2] The title page credits as author: "KDY (*Kohen Da'ato Yafah*)." The expression "*kohen she-da'ato yafah*" comes out of the *Mishnah*, *'Avodah Zarah* 2:5. Thus, the title alludes to the author being a *kohen* or member of the priestly caste.

The thought occurs to this writer (BN) that *"Yafah"* might be an allusion to Rav Kook's descent from Rabbi Mordechai Yaffe (author of the *Levush[im]*). Rav Kook was immensely proud of his pedigree which reached back to the *Levush*. The pedigree to the *Levush* was something that Rav Kook had in common with his father-in-law ADeReT (who was the *éminence grise* of the publication). See Rabbi Moshe Tsevi Neriyah, *Sihot ha-RAYaH* (Tel-Aviv, 1979), note on p. 134; and idem, *Tal ha-RAYaH* (Tel-Aviv, 1993), p. 75.

In the letter written by Rav Kook's paternal great-uncle, Rabbi Mordechai Gimpel Yaffe of Rozhinoy, to the Trisker Maggid, Rabbi Abraham Twersky, Rabbi Yaffe mentions their remote common ancestor, the *Levush*. See *The Legends of Rabbah bar Bar Hannah with Commentary of Rabbi Abraham Isaac*

Kook, ed. Bezalel Naor (Orot/Kodesh, 2019), pp. 202-203.

³ The title is taken from the verse in Ezekiel 24:17: *"Pe'erkha havosh 'alekha"* ("Bind your head-tire upon you"). The Rabbis interpreted the head-tire as a reference to the head-*tefillah*; see *b. Mo'ed Katan* 15a.

⁴ *y. 'Eruvin* 10:1; *b. Menahot* 37a; Maimonides, *MT, Hil. Tefillin* 4:1; Rabbi Joseph Karo, *Shulhan 'Arukh, Orah Hayyim* 27:9.

⁵ *m. Megillah* 4:8.

⁶ Deuteronomy 6:8.

⁷ *Shulhan 'Arukh, Orah Hayyim* 27:1.

⁸ In *Hevesh Pe'er*, chap. 2, the author points out that there already appeared in print a small booklet with diagrams, *"Tikkun 'Olam 'im tsiyurim,"* but writes that the error persists depite that.

⁹ Rav Kook's first wife, Alta Batsheva, daughter of ADeReT, died at a young age, leaving him to raise their infant daughter, Freida Hannah. ADeReT suggested to Rav Kook that he marry Reiza Rivkah, ADeReT's niece, daughter of his deceased twin brother, Tsevi Yehudah, Rabbi of Ragola. ADeReT had raised Reiza Rivkah in his home after her father's death.

¹⁰ Rabbi Jacob of Coucy, *Sefer Mitsvot Gadol*, positive commandment 3; *Hevesh Pe'er*, chap. 2. At the end of positive commandment 3, Rabbi Jacob gives the exact year of his campaign in Spain: 4996 *anno mundi* or 1236 C.E.

Urbach writes that this role of the itinerant preacher, or *darshan*, is without precedent among the French Tosafists. He conjectures that in this respect, Rabbi Moses of Coucy came under the influence of *Hasidei Ashkenaz*. See E.E. Urbach, *Ba'alei ha-Tosafot* (Jerusalem: Bialik Institute, 1995), pp. 466-470. Concerning specifically French Jewry's laxity when it came to observing the commandment of *tefillin*, see ibid. p. 469, n. 13 (citing *Tosafot, Shabbat* 49a, s.v. *ke-Elisha Ba'al Kenafayim*, and *Rosh Hashanah* 17a, s.v. *karkafta de-lo manah tefillin*). The *SeMaG* refutes Rabbenu Tam's understanding of *"karkafta de-lo manah tefillin."*

¹¹ Rabbi Ya'akov Moshe Harlap, quoted in Rabbi Moshe Tsevi Neriyah, *Sihot ha-RAYaH* (Tel-Aviv, 1979), p. 191, and idem, *Tal ha-RAYaH* (Tel-Aviv, 1993), p. 116. According to Rabbi Harlap, the Slonimer Rebbe reached out to ADeReT, hoping that he could prevail upon his former son-in-law (and present nephew by marriage) to accept this magnanimous offer.

¹² Rav Kook's erstwhile mentor in the Volozhin Yeshivah, Rabbi Naphtali Tsevi Yehudah Berlin (NeTsIV), was so enamored of *Hevesh Pe'er* that he kept it in his *tallit* bag. See the Introduction of Rabbis Yitzhak Arieli and Uri Segal Hamburger to the Jerusalem 1925 edition of *Hevesh Pe'er*, p. 2.

¹³ See Rabbi Israel Meir Kagan, *Mishnah Berurah* (Warsaw, 1884) to OH 27:9. In the *Be'ur Halakhah*, Rabbi Kagan sought support for this prescription in the manuscript glosses of "the Gaon Rabbi El'azar Harlap" to *Ma'aseh Rav* (a collection of the practices of the Vilna Gaon). If I am not mistaken, these notes would have been penned by the Gaon (and *Mekubbal*) Rabbi Ephraim Eliezer Tsevi Harlap of Mezritch.

¹⁴ Rabbi Ze'ev Wolf Turbowitz was born *Rosh Hodesh Iyar*, 1840 in Baboina near Kletsk and was known in his youth as the *"'Illui* of Baboina." His first wife was from Izilian. After his marriage, he devoted himself exclusively to study of Torah, whereby he was then known as the *"Porush* of Izilian." At a tender age he began to study Kabbalah. (Among his writings was found a work on

Zohar.) In 1863, he was appointed as a *rosh metivta* in Minsk. In 1866, he received his first rabbinical position in Swislowitz. In 1875, he assumed the rabbinate of Kletsk. Afterward, he served a stint in Wolpa. And finally in 1889, he was elected rabbi of Kraz, where he served until his death on the 14th of Kislev, 5682 [i.e., 1921]. These biographical details were gleaned from his son-in-law Rabbi Yosef Kesler's introduction to the Brooklyn 1939 edition of *Tif'eret Ziv*, p. 4.

Rabbi Eitam Henkin, *Hashem yikom damo*, wrote of the interface between Rabbi Turbowitz and Rabbi Eliyahu Goldberg, mentor of Rabbi Yehiel Mikhel Epstein (author of *'Arukh ha-Shulhan*). Besides corresponding with Rabbi Goldberg in halakhic matters, Rabbi Turbowitz delivered a moving *hesped* (eulogy) for Rabbi Goldberg in 1875 in the town of Kletsk, Rabbi Goldberg's birthplace. See Rabbi Eitam Henkin, *Ta'arokh Lefanai Shulhan* (Israel: Maggid, 2018), pp. 359-360, 363.

[15] See Rabbi Ze'ev Wolf Turbowitz, *Tif'eret Ziv* (Warsaw, 1896), no. 1. Ziv is an acronym for *Ze'ev Yekhuneh Volf*.

The responsum is datelined "Wednesday, 16 Tammuz, 5651 [1891]," which means that it was penned the same year that *Hevesh Pe'er* was published. Rabbi Turbowitz does not mention the book by name, referring to it as "a new book that has appeared" (*"sefer ehad hadash she-yatsa la-'or"*).

By the same token, in responsum 12 of *Tif'eret Ziv*, where Rabbi Turbowitz engages with another early work of Rav Kook (in fact, his first), *'Ittur Soferim*, he refers to that work obliquely as *"sefer ehad katan"* ("a small book"). Rabbi Abraham Joshua of Pokroi had raised the question whether one who becomes *bar mitsvah* at night must recite once again the blessing for studying Torah (*birkat ha-Torah*), though he already recited it that morning. The editor, Rav Kook, devoted a few pages to resolving this problem. See *'Ittur Soferim*, Part Two (Vilna, 1888), 9a-10b. Rabbi Turbowitz made short shrift of the question. At the same time, he tackled the Vilna *dayan*, Rabbi Shelomo Hakohen, who had also raised the question in his work, *Binyan Shelomo*. In the Brooklyn 1939 edition of *Tif'eret Ziv*, the first two responsa are to Rabbi Shelomo Hakohen, who had defended his position to Rabbi Turbowitz.

According to Rabbi Turbowitz's son-in-law, Rabbi Yosef Avigdor Kesler, the famous "*Gadol* of Minsk" (i.e., Rabbi Yeruham Yehudah Perlman) read Rabbi Turbowitz's responsum concerning the placement of the head-phylactery before it went to print and approved its contents. See the supplement to the Brooklyn 1939 edition of *Tif'eret Ziv*, *Kuntres Aharon*, *"Mele'im Ziv,"* 2d-3a, footnote.

[16] *Tif'eret Ziv*, 6a. The quote is from *b. Pesahim* 66b: "Leave Israel alone! If they are not prophets, they are the children of prophets." Rabbi Turbowitz's remark is quoted in Yehudah Mirsky, *Rav Kook: Mystic in a Time of Revolution* (New Haven: Yale University Press, 2014), p. 23.

[17] *Tif'eret Ziv* 1:3 (6c).

[18] *Tif'eret Ziv* 1:16-21 (8c-9b). See Rabbi David Halevi (*TaZ*), *Magen David* to OH 8:15; cited in *Mishnah Berurah* to OH 25:12.

[19] Rabbi B.H. Auerbach, *Sefer ha-Eshkol* with commentary *Nahal Eshkol*, Part Two (Halberstadt, 1868), *Hil. Tefillin*, pp. 92-94.

[20] Rabbi Eliezer Don-Yahya, *Even Shetiyah* (Vilna, 1893), nos. 12-13.

As a teenager, Rav Kook came under the influence of Rabbi Eliezer Don-Yahya (1838-1926) in Lutzin (Latvian, Ludza). See Rabbi Moshe Tsevi Neriyah, *Sihot ha-RAYaH* (Tel-Aviv, 1979), pp. 58-65; idem, *Tal ha-RAYaH* (Tel-Aviv, 1993), pp. 20-21; idem, *Bi-Sdeh ha-RAYaH* (Tel-Aviv, 1991), pp. 526-528, 537-540; and *Haskamot ha-RAYaH*, ed. Y.M. Yismah and B.Z. Kahane (Jerusalem, 1988), nos. 79, 94 (pp. 97, 112). In *"Kelil Tif'eret,"* Rav Kook refers to Rabbi Eliezer Don-Yahya as "my friend" (*"yedidi"*). This is explained by the fact that the Rabbi of Lutzin related to the young men who studied there not as an authority figure but "as an older brother." So wrote his son Rabbi Benzion Don-Yahya; see *Sihot ha-RAYaH*, pp. 62-63.

This writer (BN) had the privilege of enjoying the friendship of Rabbi Eliezer Don-Yahya's grandson, Shabtai Don-Yahya, a disciple of Rav Kook in Merkaz Harav. As editor of *Ha-Tzofeh*, he would sign his articles with the *nom de plume*, "Shin Daniel." (The Hebrew surname "Daniel" was bestowed upon him by Rabbi David Cohen, the "Nazirite.")

For other members of this distinguished rabbinical family, see below, "The Religious-Zionist Manifesto of Rabbi Yehudah Leib Don Yahya."

[21] *She'elot u-Teshuvot HaTaM Sofer, Orah Hayyim*, no. 140. See also the discussion of *"Rubo ke-khullo"* by Rabbi Hayyim Soloveitchik (and the proof brought by Rabbi Zelig Reuven Bengis), in *Hiddushei ha-GRaH he-Hadash*, vol. 3 (stencil, Jerusalem, 1967), p. 90.

[22] See above note 18.

[23] It may strike the reader as ironic that Rav Kook introduced at this point in the discussion the concept of *rubbo ke-khullo* when he had earlier rejected its application. But from Rav Kook's standpoint (and that of his father-in-law ADeReT, see below note 38), that principle simply could not be applied to the *area* of the phylactery with its precise dimensions. "*Shi'urim halakhah le-Moshe mi-Sinai*," "Measurements are a law to Moses from Sinai" (*y. Pe'ah* 1:1, *Hagigah* 1:2; *b. 'Eruvin* 4a, *Yoma* 80a, *Sukkah* 5b).

[24] Rabbi Abraham Isaac Hakohen Kook, *"Kelil Tif'eret"* in *Hevesh Pe'er*, ed. Rabbis Yitzhak Arieli and Uri Segal Hamburger (Jerusalem: Mossad Harav Kook, 1985), p. 46. Of course, the element of *hesah ha-da'at*, i.e., whether one has "removed one's awareness," plays a crucial part in determining whether one must recite the blessing on the *tefillin* once again. See ibid.

Rav Kook's *hilluk* (differentiation) between *"'etsem ha-mitsvah"* and *"ma'aseh ha-mitsvah"* (especially the terminology) is somewhat remarkable, issuing as it did from the pen of Rav Kook, who studiously avoided the school of *Hasbarah* with its abstract constructs and neologisms, then in vogue in the Lithuanian *yeshivah* world. The most famous proponent of *Hasbarah* was Rabbi Hayyim Soloveitchik (who would one day inherit his father Rabbi Yosef Dov Soloveitchik's rabbinate in Brisk, whereupon he would be known as "Reb Hayyim Brisker"). The latter's methodology of Talmudic analysis came to be known as the *"Brisker derekh [ha-limud],"* "the Brisker way [of learning]."

Rav Kook's biographers have duly noted that his first mentor back in Dvinsk (since Rav Kook's *bar mitsvah*), Rabbi Reuven Ha-Levi Levin (known as "Reb Ruvaleh Denaburger") had, so to speak, "immunized" Rav Kook against the trend of *"sevarot"* or newfangled "concepts." Rabbi Reuven Levin was highly suspicious of *sevarot* that had not been enunciated already by the *rishonim*, the medieval authorities. (See Rabbi Kesler's introduction to *Tif'eret*

Ziv, Brooklyn 1939, p. 8, par. 9, quoting Rabbi Reuven Levin, and ibid. sec. *Hoshen Mishpat*, responsum 46:6 [116c]: "It is not my way to say *sevarot* of my own cognizance.")

And thus, when later Avraham Yitzhak Kook arrived at Volozhin, "the mother of *yeshivot*," he gravitated to the elder *Rosh Yeshivah*, Rabbi Naphtali Tsevi Yehudah Berlin (NeTsIV), known as a *pashtan*, a champion of the simple understanding of the text, rather than to his grandson-in-law, Rabbi Hayyim Soloveitchik, who was surrounded by budding scholars attracted to the exciting new method of Talmudic analysis that he was developing.

Although Rav Kook was never so outspoken as Rabbi Ya'akov David Wilovsky (or "Reb Yankel Dovid Slutsker"), known by the acronym RIDBaZ, who satirized the new method as "chemistry," Rav Kook was clearly on the other side of the great divide between Lithuanian Talmudists. This aversion of Rav Kook to the method of *"hasbarah"* was given eloquent testimony in recently unearthed correspondence concerning the unsuccessful attempt of Rabbi Shim'on Shkop (a *rosh yeshivah* in Telz and later head of his own *yeshivah* in Grodno) to be accepted as *Rosh Yeshivah* of Merkaz Harav in Jerusalem. Speaking in Rav Kook's name, his devoted disciple Rabbi Ya'akov Moshe Harlap conveyed to Rabbi Hizkiyahu Yosef Mishkovski of Krinik (who had interceded on Rabbi Shim'on Shkop's behalf) the following laconic response:

> Regarding the proposal concerning the Gaon Rabbi Shim'on Shkop, may he live, to accept him as *Rosh Yeshivah* of Merkaz Harav, there is certainly nothing to discuss, for since the founding of the *Yeshivah*, this position is reserved for *Maran* [our master, i.e., Rav Kook], may he live, who plans to fill it himself. For *Maran*, may he live, wishes—and this is a strong desire—that the main method of learning of the *Yeshivah* be according to the order and method of the GRA [i.e., the Gaon Rabbi Elijah of Vilna], of blessed memory. Though he [i.e., Rav Kook] knows and feels also the great necessity of developing the methods of *"hasbarot"* (conceptualizations) and *"havanot hegyoniyot"* (logical understandings), he wants the main spirit of the *Yeshivah* to be based on his method, etc. Today I showed *Maran*, may he live, his honor's letter, and what I wrote here is his response.

Rabbi Harlap's letter is datelined "Monday, 2nd day of *Rosh Hodesh Adar*, 5686 [i.e., 1926], Jerusalem." It was published in a *Festschrift* for his grandson, Rabbi Zevulun Charlop, *Zeved Tov*, ed. Ari S. Zahtz (New York: Yeshiva University Press, 2008), p. 103.

Inter alia, "Z. Wein" mentioned in the letter from Rabbi Shkop to Rabbi Tobolsky, expressing Rabbi Shkop's desire to settle in the Holy Land (ibid. p. 101), is none other than [Rabbi] Ze'ev Wein, *a"h*, father of Rabbi Berel Wein, *shelit"a*. Rabbi Ze'ev Wein (1906-2004), a disciple of Rabbi Shkop, went on to study in Rav Kook's Merkaz Harav in Jerusalem. He served for many years as a distinguished rabbi in Chicago.

Rabbi Shim'on Shkop was famous for his method of *"higayon"* (logic), displayed in his magnum opus, *Sha'arei Yosher*. (Rabbi Hershel Shachter, *shelit"a*, revealed to this writer [BN] that his father-in-law, Rabbi Yeshayah Shapiro, a *rosh yeshivah* at Torah Vodaath in Brooklyn, was instrumental in writing that work.)

This is not the place to discuss in any depth the differences between

Rabbi Shim'on Shkop's method and that of Rabbi Hayyim Brisker and his heirs. Two anecdotes should suffice. The Briskers quipped that Rabbi Shim'on "had looked at the world and created the Torah" ("*Istakel be-'alma u-vara 'oraita*"), a reversal of the *Zohar*'s adage, "[God] looked at the Torah and created the world" ("*istakel be-'oraita u-vara 'alma*"). On one occasion, Rabbi Yitzhak Ze'ev Soloveitchik ("Reb Velvel," known as the "Brisker Rov," for he inherited from his father Rabbi Hayyim the rabbinate of Brisk) met Rabbi Shim'on Shkop and told him: "I removed from your student Rabbi Leib Malin the last sinew (*gid*) left from your teaching." (The imagery is that of de-veining or *nikkur*. Reb Velvel probably used the Yiddish verb, "*treiberen.*") Both anecdotes were heard from Rabbi Shelomo Fisher, *shelit"a*, of Jerusalem.

25 In 1895, Rav Kook left the town of Zeimel for the large city of Bausk, Latvia.

26 Rabbi Ze'ev Wolf Turbowitz, *Ziv Mishneh* (Warsaw, 1904). The author has the rather unique distinction of viewing Maimonides as a kabbalist and finding kabalistic "sources" for his rulings. (Similarly, the introduction to the Warsaw 1896 edition of *Tif'eret Ziv* demonstrates the author's proficiency in Lurianic kabbalah.) Though not unique in this respect, Rabbi Turbowitz is perhaps the most outspoken proponent of this peculiar methodology of studying Maimonides' *Mishneh Torah*. Another Maimonidean commentator who occasionally resorts to this method of sourcing is Rabbi Joseph Rosen (the Rogatchover Gaon). See his *Tsaphnat Pa'ne'ah*, Hil. 'Avodah Zarah 12:6. Nowadays, Rabbi Hayyim Kanievsky's *Kiryat Melekh*, a work that provides sources for *Mishneh Torah*, is replete with references to *Zohar*.

27 b. *Horayot* 3b; and Rashi, *Zevahim* 26a, s.v. *hikhnis rosho ve-rubbo*. Both are referenced by Rabbi Turbowitz.

28 Rabbi Yitzhak Arieli was one of the founders of Yeshivat Merkaz Harav and acted in the official capacity of *"Mashgiah"* of the *Yeshivah*. He is most famous for his work on the Talmud, *'Eynayim le-Mishpat*. Recently, Aharon Ilan, a great-grandson of Rabbi Yitzhak Arieli, brought out his biography, *'Eynei Yitzhak* (Jerusalem, 2018).

29 Rabbi Uri Segal Hamburger was a descendant of Rabbi Moshe Yehudah Segal Hamburger of Novemeste (a disciple of the *HaTaM Sofer*) who came to *Erets Yisrael* in 1857. Rabbi Uri Segal Hamburger resided in the Old City of Jerusalem until its conquest by the Jordanians in 1948. He penned a memoir of that tragic event, *"Be-Tseiti mi-Yerushalayim."* One may find a short biography and a photograph of Rabbi Hamburger in *'Eynei Yitzhak*, pp. 136-137.

30 Rav Kook's biographer and disciple, Rabbi Moshe Tsevi Neriyah, records that Rav Kook wrote in his *haskamah* (letter of approbation) to the publishers the following disclaimer: "In our holy land, which thank God, is full of Torah and fear of heaven, the admonition (*azharah*) is not so necessary. Nevertheless, I have not prevented re-issuing the book, for the benefit of our brothers in the Diaspora, in areas where the matter is yet in need of correction" (*Sihot ha-RAYaH* [Tel-Aviv, 1979], pp. 189-190). This disclaimer does not appear in the printed version of the *haskamah*. Where did Rabbi Neriyah obtain it? The mystery was cleared up in the new edition of *Sihot ha-RAYaH* (2015) published after Rabbi Neriyah's passing. Rabbi Arieli's son, Prof. Nahum Arieli, wrote to Rabbi Neriyah that he has in his possession much material that went into the making of the Jerusalem edition of *Hevesh Pe'er* edited by his father, including a *"petek"* (note) with those exact words. Rabbi Neriyah's daughter,

Tsilah Bar-Eli, granted Aharon Ilan permission to include a facsimile of Nahum Arieli's letter to her father (on stationery of Bar-Ilan University) in the biography of Rabbi Arieli, *'Eynei Yitzhak*, p. 139.

[31] Rabbi Arieli's promised *"Kuntres Aharon"* was never published. Remnants of the manuscript are in the possession of his heirs. Rabbi Neriyah speculated that financial considerations prevented its publication in *Hevesh Pe'er*. See *'Eynei Yitzhak*, p. 138, n. 102.

[32] On the inside of the book, Rabbi J. Kesler's address is given as: "146 Beach 74th Street, A[r]verne, Long Island."

[33] It is important to note that the two collections do not overlap. The responsa on *Orah Hayyim* that appeared in the Warsaw 1896 edition of *Tif'eret Ziv*, were not included in the Brooklyn 1939 edition. In their stead, appear more recent responsa on *Orah Hayyim*. In terms of sheer quantity, the second collection by far outstrips the first. The first Warsaw edition has 122 pages; the second Brooklyn edition, 488 pages.

[34] *"Mele'im Ziv,"* 2a-b.

[35] *"Mele'im Ziv,"* 2b-2c.

[36] *"Mele'im Ziv,"* 2d.

[37] *"Mele'im Ziv,"* 3a.

[38] *"Mele'im Ziv,"* 3a-b.

[39] The facsimile occurs in Rabbi Kesler's introduction to the book on p. 7. It is transcribed in *"Mele'im Ziv,"* 3b.

If not for the evidence of the facsimile, it would indeed be difficult to accept that Rav Kook once entertained even the remote possibility of invoking the principle of *rubbo ke-khullo* in this regard.

[40] To this day, Lubavitcher Hasidim wear very large *tefillin*.

[41] *"Mele'im Ziv,"* 3b-c.

[42] *"Mele'im Ziv,"* 3d.

In 1893, ADeReT left the community of Ponevezh to assume the rabbinate of Mir.

IX

MESSIAH

THE TWO FACES OF MESSIANISM[1]

In Messiah Son of Joseph is revealed the characteristic of Israel's nationalism per se. However, the ultimate goal is not the isolation of nationalism, but the longing to unite all the inhabitants of the world into a single family, that all may call upon the name of the LORD. And despite the fact that this too requires a special center, nonetheless the intention is not the center, but its effect upon the great collective. Now when the world must transition from the concept of nationalism to universalism, there must be a sort of destruction of the things that were rooted in narrow nationalism, which carries with it the drawbacks of excessive self-love. Therefore in the future, Messiah Son of Joseph will be killed, and a true and enduring kingdom will be [that of] Messiah Son of David.

(Rabbi Abraham Isaac Hakohen Kook)[2]

In this brief pensée, our great teacher Rav Kook (1865-1935) has provided the key to at once penetrate the arcane mysteries of the Rabbinic tradition (with its oblique references to two Messiahs, "Messiah Son of Joseph" and "Messiah Son of David") and unlock the secrets of the human heart. Every individual human and every nation on this planet of ours must somehow come to terms with the sometimes seemingly insurmountable conflict between the ideals of nationalism and universalism, peoplehood and humanity. We are at once citizens of our respective nations and of Planet Earth. The conflict is not a particularly Jewish one; it affects everyone on the globe. (Although historically, the conflict may have been intensified in the nation of Israel—even before the advent of Zionism.)

By decoding "Messiah Son of Joseph" as nationalism (though unstated, the reference is likely to Jewish nationalism or even Zionism) and "Messiah Son of David" as universalism, Rav Kook envisioned a humanity transitioning from a tribal or ethnocentric consciousness to a global or planetary consciousness. The present writer on the other hand, is disinclined to view mankind's historical process as a unilateral progression from the confines of nationalism to the expanses of universalism, and proposes an alternate model, whereby there is at work here a dialectic between the two poles of nation and planet.

The genesis of our essay is itself instructive in this regard. It came as a reverie to a young man traipsing about Switzerland, *en route* from West to East; from Berkeley, California, to Jerusalem, Israel. The geography is pregnant with symbolism. In Berkeley, the writer was exposed to a broad, global perspective. Yet he was travelling to Jerusalem to seek out a teacher of the Kabbalah, an esoteric discipline restricted to Jews, and then to only the most pious among them. The thought uppermost in the seeker's mind was: Would it be possible to find a teacher who could show the way to integrate the most expansive spiritual realizations with the treasures of the ancient tradition?

On his second day in Jerusalem, the writer (then in his early twenties) found himself sitting face to face with an octogenarian rabbi by the name of Tsevi Yehudah Hakohen Kook (1891-1982), only son of the famed Chief Rabbi. Thinking to impress the elderly gentleman with a good opening line, the writer blurted out: "How much *Ahavat Yisrael* (love of the Jewish People) your father had!"

Rabbi Tsevi Yehudah's response was a spontaneous outburst of hearty laughter. When he regained his composure, the ancient sage revealed what in that statement precipitated the sudden mirth:

"Ahavat Yisrael? Love of Israel? My father loved the entire world!"[3]

Rabbi Tsevi Yehudah then proceeded to retrace the great chain of being. *"Afilu tsome'ah!"* ("Even the vegetable kingdom!")

And then reaching down to rap on the stone floor for emphasis, he added, *"Afilu domem!"* ("Even the mineral kingdom!")

In the writings of Rav Kook, the present essayist, as many other seekers (Jews and non-Jews), discovers a master, who, torn as his soul may be (by his own admission),[4] brings to the esoteric discipline of Kabbalah the clever wisdom of the adult and the simple faith of the child, and attempts to synchronize the "little picture" with the "big picture," as he zooms in and out of a Cosmos[5] longing to be redeemed from Chaos; all the while envisioning a World of *Tikkun* bringing integration (*hitkalelut*) to a World of *Tohu* inhabited by primordial kings and self-mythologizing gods.[6]

Finally, a word about the style. The author traces the ongoing oscillation of Judaism between the tribal and the universal, utilizing raw materials of Bible, Midrash, Talmud, medieval philosophy, Kabbalah and Hasidism. The essay is written in a lyrical style not readily comprehensible to those seeking political analysis. In this respect, the author's role model was Rabbi Abraham Isaac Hakohen Kook.

MESSIAH

GENEALOGY

PARTICULARISM	UNIVERSALISM
RACHEL	LEAH
JOSEPH (AND BENJAMIN)	JUDAH
SAUL	DAVID
JEROBOAM	SOLOMON
MESSIAH SON OF JOSEPH	MESSIAH SON OF DAVID

MESSIAH SON OF JOSEPH
AND MESSIAH SON OF DAVID

The history of the human race may be compared to a giant field through which the mighty winds of unification and atomization blow back and forth. Nations come together, confederate, aspire to commonality and cooperation, and once again there is raised the demand of nationalism or tribalism, and the member nations return "each man to his camp and to his flag."[7] So it has been throughout time. These two opposite *Zeitgeisten* are forever circulating in the unconscious and sometimes conscious thinking of those who shape the dominant ideas of any given historical period.

Messiah Son of Joseph is the atomizer, the separatist; Messiah Son of David is the unifier. Messiah Son of Joseph carries within his head a vision drawn along coordinates of national boundaries and bloodlines; Messiah Son of David envisions a reality that is supra-nationalist and planetary.

In the Book of Genesis we learn that Joseph, Viceroy of Egypt, would divine events by gazing into his goblet.[8] The Hebrew word for goblet is *gavi'a* (גביע). Broken down into its component letters, *gimmel, bet-yod, 'ayin* (ג-ב-י-ע), the word signifies the three patriarchs, twelve tribes and seventy souls that culminated in the formation of the Israelite nation.[9] This is what we might expect of the clairvoyance of Joseph (prototype of Messiah Son of Joseph). Within the statecraft of Joseph runs the desire to preserve national identities and narratives.

Joseph views a national entity (in this case, his own people of Israel) through the lens of biology. Israel descends from three patriarchs (Abraham, Isaac and Jacob), develops into twelve tribes (Reuben, Simeon, Levi, Judah, etc.), and at a later, critical stage of its evolution (the descent into Egypt), evolves into "seventy souls."[10] It is not mere happenstance that Joseph seats Egyptians and Hebrews separately at his dinner table,[11] or that later, he arranges that his brethren come to reside in the separate province of Goshen, apart from mainstream Egyptian life.[12] Joseph was identified as a "Hebrew man."[13] According to the Midrash, it was in this merit that Joseph was later buried in the Land of the Hebrews. (On the other hand, Moses who was identified as an "Egyptian man,"[14] did not merit interment in the land. As the Midrash expressed it so succinctly, "He who admitted to his land, was buried in his land; he who did not admit to his land, was not buried in his land."[15] But we are getting ahead of ourselves.)

Vastly different is the statecraft of David and his successor Solomon. Joseph *speaks* seventy languages; Solomon *marries* seventy languages. David, but even more so Solomon, are thinking in terms of global expansion, but ultimately—world union.

The comprehensive vision of unity has traditionally been the domain of the individual, of the gifted few. The atomistic, divided view of reality on the other hand, seems to fall quite naturally into the public domain. David's expansionist worldview prompts him to conquer Syria. The *Sifré* (a third-century halakhic commentary to the Book of Deuteronomy) censures David's conquest: "You did not lay claim to the immediate vicinity of your palace [in Jerusalem], yet you go and conquer Aram-Naharayim and Aram-Tsobah?"[16] The contentious conquest of Syria, a relic of Davidic ambition, would forever be subjected in the annals of the Talmud to the dubious distinction of a *"kibbush yahid,"* "a one-man conquest," unsanctioned by proper parliamentary procedure.[17] The collective Jewish People had its eyes trained on Jerusalem; it was that rare individual David (forerunner of Messiah Son of David) whose vision expanded to enfold an entire world. The "one-man conquest" forever remains a mystery.[18]

"HEAR O ISRAEL, THE LORD OUR GOD, THE LORD IS ONE" (DEUTERONOMY 6:4)

The most basic utterance of Jewish faith, the *Shema'*, the first thing that we are taught as children, and the last thing that we recite before dying, reads: "Hear O Israel, the LORD our God, the Lord is one." As a declaration of divine unity, the sentence is strangely disjointed. Rashi, a native of medieval Troyes (France), most beloved of Bible commentators, attempted to smooth over the disruption in thought: "The LORD Who is today our God [i.e., the God of Israel], will one day be one LORD over all the nations."

"The LORD our God" is the call of Messiah Son of Joseph. "The LORD is one" is the call of Messiah Son of David.

If we should be even more exacting, the word "one" itself is given to two opposite interpretations: "One," in the sense of uniqueness, to the exclusion of all others; as opposed to "one" in the sense of unity, comprehending and including all.[19]

From an historic perspective, the Messianisms of Joseph and David interact and reciprocate, and the relations between them as well as their concatenations tend to be extremely complex. Nonetheless, we shall attempt to point out a few directions that these interactions have taken over the centuries.

"MOSES TOOK THE BONES OF JOSEPH WITH HIM" (EXODUS 13:19)

If ever there was a man deserving of the title "cosmic visionary," it was Moses. Could it be otherwise? Is it conceivable that the prophet unequalled in having spoken to the LORD "face to face," was not privy to some sense of the eternal destiny of the globe? The God of Moses, *Ehyeh asher Ehyeh* ("I am that I am," or "I shall be that I shall be," as it is variously translated into English) is not a local, regional deity, but the LORD of Necessary Existence (as Maimonides explained so well),[20] an existence at once simple and abstract. And yet, paradox of paradoxes, this prophet of cosmic proportions, a "Davidic" Messiah if ever there was one, is sent to perform a mission purely "Josephic" in character, namely that of national liberation. He is dispatched to Egypt to take the oppressed Hebrew nation out of the House of Bondage. "Moses took the bones of Joseph with him." In Hebrew, the word for "bones," "*atsmot*," slightly re-vocalized becomes "*atsmut*" or "essence." Moses took the essence of Joseph with him. "There was in Jeshurun a king. When the heads of the people assembled. The tribes of Israel together."[21] According to some commentators, the "King" of Jeshurun refers to Moses.[22] Moses acted in the capacity of a monarch over Israel.[23]

But at the end of Moses' career, there is revealed retroactively who Moses truly is. Moses is relieved of his duties as national liberator. The actual entry into the Promised Land will not be accomplished by Moses. Rather, the national deliverance is entrusted to Moses' successor Joshua, appropriately enough an Ephraimite, descended from Joseph. It is Joshua, not Moses, who will complete the mission, the *"mitsvah,"* of depositing the bones of Joseph in their final resting place in Shechem.

Rather than meriting burial in Israel, Moses' mysterious crypt is situated rather nebulously "opposite Beit Pe'or,"[24] a site tied to the idolatrous cult of Pe'or. At day's end, we find Moses working to uplift cosmic sparks dispersed in the depths of depravity, rather than being entombed in sacred soil.

One may almost palpably feel Moses' final frustration, his anxiety, his discomfiture. More than most of us, he is torn between the godly and the all too human. *"'The man of God.'* Said Rabbi Abin: From the waist down, man; from the waist up, God."[25] The prophet who looks through a "clear speculum,"[26] is godly; the national liberator, is human. Moses must descend from the Mountain of God illuminated in eternal light, to the camp of the Hebrews, in order to set in motion events that will birth a nation of Israel. However, as the curtain closes on his career, Moses is informed from on high that he will not be granted the privilege of completing this national mission; he will not enter into the land. A prophet of Moses' caliber must be ready to abandon his "humanity" and revert back to his "divinity," expressed symbolically in death by the kiss of God[27]—in the very middle of the act.[28]

MESSIAH SON OF JOSEPH IS KILLED

Throughout its history, the Jewish People is forced to battle enemies. Joshua battles Amalek; Saul, Agag and his people; Mordechai and Esther, Haman; and at the End of Days, Messiah Son of Joseph contends with Armilus the Wicked.[29] (Some say that Armilus is a thinly veiled reference to Romulus, the legendary founder of Rome.)[30] "The House of Jacob shall be a fire, and the House of Joseph a flame; and the House of Esau straw; and they shall burn them and consume them."[31]

It is the job of Josephic Messianism to protect the Israelite character from inimical forces and currents. This mission is entrusted to the Children of Rachel.[32] In Kabbalah, Rachel symbolizes "the Revealed World" (*'Alma de-Itgalya*)—the world of division and differentiation—and the *sefirah* (attribute) of *Malkhut* (Kingship). At the opposite pole, Messiah Son of David descends from Rachel's sister Leah, who, in turn, symbolizes "the Hidden World" (*'Alma de-Itkasya*), a world of unity associated with the *sefirah* (attribute) of *Binah* (Understanding).

Before the arrival of Messiah Son of David, there precedes him Messiah Son of Joseph, which is to say in so many words, before there will commence in earnest a cosmic unification, there will precede an arousal of particularist nationalism. The Talmud describes the death of Messiah Son of Joseph.[33] Yet the greatest kabbalist of all time, Rabbi Isaac Luria, prescribed a prayer (to be recited during the silent devotion, the *Shemoneh 'Esreh* or *'Amidah*) asking that Messiah Son of Joseph be spared death on the battlefield at the hand of Armilus the Wicked.[34] As Maimonides judiciously wrote concerning the Days of Messiah, ours is not to know "the order of these events, nor their specifics,"[35] but this much we do know. The discussion in the Talmud and in the Lurianic writings revolves around this question: What will be the nature of the transition from the particularist to the universalist; from the nationalist to the global? Must the epoch of Messiah Son of Joseph die a violent death in order to pave the way for the epoch of Messiah Son of David? Or is it possible (as was the fervent prayer of Rabbi Isaac Luria) that there might develop a peaceful coexistence of Joseph and Judah, Saul (the Benjaminite, descendant of Rachel) and David (the Judahite, descendant of Leah); that in the imagery of the Talmud, there might result a seamless, uninterrupted transition from "redemption" to "prayer" (*semikhat ge'ulah li-tefillah*)?[36] To put it into our contemporary jargon, must there be violent revolution, or can the "birth pangs of Messiah" take the form of peaceful evolution?

JUDAH AND JOSEPH

> Judah approached him [Joseph] and said, "Please, my master (*bi adoni*)." (Genesis 44:18)
>
> (Or translated differently, "Mine the mastery [*bi adoni*]!")

Two Faces of Messianism

What is the nature of the struggle, the conflict that erupted between Judah and Joseph? Joseph is an acculturated Hebrew who works for the cause of the nationalist dream; Judah conversely is a *"heimishe Yid"* (Yiddish, a homey Jew), whose progeny will take up global concerns. The hermeneutic method of Joseph is from the universal to the particular; the method of Judah, from the particular to the universal. The line of Judah is a series of endogamous, even incestuous relations: Lot and his daughters, Judah and his daughter-in-law Tamar. It would be hard to find a more inbred family. Yet, from these unions emerges King David, who aspires to redeem the world at large in all its breadth and externality. The turning point from endogamy to exogamy was the intermarriage of Boaz and Ruth the Moabitess. (Rabbinic tradition made Ruth's adventure the very paradigm of halakhic conversion to Judaism.)[37] In Kabbalah, their union bespeaks the marrying of "redemption" (Boaz the Redeemer) to "prayer" (Ruth, grandmother of David, "who satiated [*rivah*] the Holy One, blessed be He, with songs and praises").[38] Boaz represents ancestral land claims, while Ruth, a landless alien, symbolizes the universal.

The tribes of Judah and Joseph would evolve into two kingdoms: the Kingdom of Joseph (consisting of ten tribes) in the North and the Kingdom of Judah (consisting of two tribes, Judah and Benjamin) in the South. Which of the two kingdoms was more universalist in scope; which more particularist or nationalist? Reading the Bible, it becomes apparent that the Northern Kingdom was more prone to adopting surrounding idolatries. Yet this steady seduction to the worship of Baʻal and Asherah does not seem to have bestowed a more cosmopolitan outlook. The Kingdom of Judah on the other hand, centered on Solomon's Temple in Jerusalem, might actually have been less parochial in outlook.

Take the Tree of Joseph and the Tree of Judah, and they shall be as one in your hand.[39]

MORDECHAI: A BENJAMINITE JUDEAN

Before we analyze his personality, we must develop somewhat the historical and political backdrop from which Mordechai emerges.

The Scroll of Esther is dominated by King Ahashverosh. This near-mythic king heads a list of several "cosmocrats" (to employ the Greek loanword *"kosmokrator"* imported by the Rabbis of the Midrash).[40] The "dark side" of cosmocracy usually spells trouble for the Jews. What about the "bright side" of this phenomenon? How does Judaism fare under a "benevolent despot" such as Alexander the Great, or Napoleon, for that matter?

To this day, devout Jewish men bear the name "Alexander" (bestowed upon them at the time of their circumcision). That itself is indication of a fondness for this historic figure. The Talmud tells a charming tale of an encounter in Erets Israel between Alexander the Macedonian and the leader of the Jews, the High Priest Simeon the Just. Alexander was astonished to behold the visage of the saintly man. It was that very face that would appear to Alexander in dream on the eve of a major victory. Thus positively predisposed,

Alexander granted Simeon his request that the Temple in Jerusalem be spared destruction.[41]

Moving on to Napoleon and the Jews, there are many different versions of this complex relationship. Tomes have been written concerning this intriguing chapter in history. Was Napoleon bent on the extirpation of Judaism and the forceful absorption of the Jews into European civilization? Was he sympathetic to the Jews' return to their land?

As romantically told by Martin Buber in the historic novel *For the Sake of Heaven* (entitled in Hebrew, *Gog u-Magog*), the great Hasidic masters of Russia and Poland were divided in their opinions of Bonaparte. While some Rebbes viewed him as a gentile Messiah, a modern-day Cyrus,[42] others looked upon him as Satan incarnate. Rabbi Shneur Zalman of Liadi was shown on the first day of Rosh Hashanah (before *Mussaf*) that Napoleon's victory would bring economic prosperity to the Jews while spelling spiritual destruction. Contrariwise, Tsar Alexander's victory would bring economic ruin to the Jews, yet their faith would survive intact. Rabbi Shneur Zalman opted for the latter and was forced to flee to the interior of Russia, always one step ahead of the *Grande Armée*. Finally, the Old Rabbi succumbed in the remote village of Piena.[43]

The Messiah and the cosmocrat share much in common. How did Alexander and Napoleon hope to juggle the opposed currents of union and diversity, empire and nationalism? In the Scroll of Esther, Ahashverosh, "who rules from India to Ethiopia over a hundred and twenty-seven states,"[44] encourages each man to "speak the language of his people."[45] If language is an indication, then Alexander and Napoleon lie at the opposite end of the spectrum from the Persian emperor Ahashverosh, the one imposing Hellenization, the other Gallicization upon the subjects of their respective realms. Assimilation to the dominant culture was the price of admission to these latter two cosmocracies. Napoleon's bold new synthesis, while tearing down the walls of the ghetto, sought to homogenize ethnic Jews into Frenchmen of the Mosaic faith.

Back to Mordechai. When confronted with the dark side of the Persian Empire, with "Haman," Mordechai functions as a Josephic Messiah (though technically not descended from Joseph, but from Benjamin, Rachel's younger son),[45*] throwing all the forces at his disposal—both physical and spiritual—into the fray against Haman the Agagite. As for the bright side of the Empire, Mordechai, as Joseph before him, serves as viceroy to the King. According to rabbinic tradition, Mordechai of the *Megillah* is one and the same as Mordechai Bilshan (Mordechai the Linguist) of Ezra 2:2 and Nehemiah 7:7, whereby it was deduced that he was a gifted linguist.[46]

Mordechai is in the final analysis a hybrid: a Benjaminite Judean. As a Benjaminite, he falls into the tradition of Messiah Son of Joseph; as *"Mordechai ha-Yehudi"* ("Mordechai the Judean") he longs for a world of unity. Drawing on the interchangeability of the letters *hé* and *ḥet*, the Midrash is able to interpret *Yehudi* (יהודי), or Judean, as *Yiḥudi* (יחודי), or Unifier.[47]

"THE SCEPTER SHALL NOT DEPART FROM JUDAH, NOR THE RULER'S STAFF FROM BETWEEN HIS FEET, UNTIL SHILOH COMES" (GENESIS 49:10)

Many have wondered at this mysterious ancient prophecy. Great French commentators offered the solution that the verse alludes to the ongoing competition between Joseph and Judah, later embodied in the establishment of the Northern Kingdom by Jeroboam I upon the death of King Solomon. The establishment of the kingdom of Jeroboam (an Ephraimite, thus a descendant of Joseph) put an end to the hegemony of Judahite rule. Furthermore, that kingdom of Jeroboam was prophesied by Ahijah the Shilonite. Thus, it was precisely at the time of the arrival of the Shilonite (from Shiloh) that the royal scepter departed from Judah, which is to say, that the undivided rule of the Davidic dynasty ceased.[48]

The excesses of King Solomon, an early experiment with the model of cosmocracy, demanded that the pendulum swing in the opposite direction. Israel would once again toil in the vineyard of nationalism, except this time the "nationalism within nationalism" of a divided kingdom. The tribal consciousness of King Jeroboam I was subject to extreme pride. There are those who view the two golden calves of Jeroboam, the one erected in Dan, the other in Bethel, as symbolic of Menasseh and Ephraim, Joseph's two sons.[49] (Earlier, the Golden Calf in the Desert was linked in rabbinic tradition to Joseph himself.)[50]

There would seem to be a dialectic at work here. As far as the genius of Messiah Son of David advances in the direction of unification and synthesis, so must the talent of Messiah Son of Joseph achieve in the opposite direction of breakdown and fragmentation.

A quaint *aggadah* or legend of the Talmud bears out this point:

The Holy One, blessed be He, grabbed Jeroboam by his garment and said to him: "Repent, and I and you and [David] the son of Jesse will stroll together in the Garden of Eden."
Jeroboam asked Him: "Who shall lead?"
"The son of Jesse shall lead."
"If so, I am not interested."[51]

True to character to the bitter end, even to the point of sounding ludicrous, Jeroboam will not be enticed by the promise of a utopian confederation with David at its helm. Jeroboam had been divinely appointed to be the instrument of dismantling David's kingdom. He is forever nitpicking at the details of the proposed structure. "Who shall lead?"

CROSSCURRENTS

The winds of unification and fragmentation blow to and fro. At times, all the valiant efforts and campaigns of Messiah Son of Joseph are but a preparation for an advanced, elevated consciousness that will flourish in the Days of Messiah Son of David. "Therefore it shall be said in the Book of the Wars of the Lord—love (*vahev*) in the end."[52] And the opposite scenario exists as well. There are times in history when the work of unification, the superb governmental architecture of David and Solomon paves the way for the fault-finding and fissuring of Jeroboam. "The scepter shall not depart from Judah, nor the ruler's staff from between his feet, until Shiloh comes, and to him an assembly of peoples."⁵³ And, "Who shall lead?"

CONCLUSION

[Jacob] had a dream, and behold, a ladder was set on the earth and its top was reaching to the heavens, and behold, the angels of God were ascending and descending on it (*bo*). (Genesis 28:12)

According to the Midrash, the angels of the Land of Israel were ascending and the angels of Beyond the Land were descending.⁵⁴ It is possible that the final word of the verse *"bo"* refers not to Jacob's ladder but to Jacob himself. The angels were ascending and descending within him (*bo*)!⁵⁵ Within each of us there are these ascending and descending angels (the Greek word *angelos*, as the original Hebrew word *mal'akh*, conveys the sense of "messenger"), angels of the Land, and angels of Beyond the Land.

When Jacob later reenters the land, the process reverses itself: "And Jacob went on his way, and angels of God encountered him. Jacob said when he saw them, 'This is the camp of God.' So he called the name of that place *Mahanayim* [Two Camps]."⁵⁶ Once again, the Midrash explains that the angels of the Land of Israel came out to greet him and to accompany him to the Land. The two camps refer to the two groups of angels: the angels of Beyond the Land who escorted him up to this point, and the angels of the Land of Israel who came to receive him.⁵⁷

Each spiritual process is unique. There are those, such as Herzl and Joseph, Viceroy of Egypt, whose focus (like that of Jacob reentering the Land) shifts from the cosmopolitan to the ancestral.

At a certain point in their career, the angels of Beyond the Land take leave of them and they are embraced by the angels of the Land of Israel.

And then there are those, such as Rav Kook and the Biblical Judah, whose spiritual evolution takes them beyond the confines of the ghetto to encompass the globe. In a portentous dream, like our Father Jacob, they witness a changing of the guard: angels of the Land of Israel ascending and angels of Beyond the Land descending. Within themselves they experience a shift of consciousness, a change of perception. Ultimately, their calling, their mission broadens.

And finally, there are the hybrids among us who, as *Mordechai ha-Yehudi*, attempt to fuse the two aspirations of nationalism and cosmocracy.

---

[1] Adapted by the author from *"Du-Partsufin shel ha-Meshihiyut,"* which first appeared in Bezalel Naor, *Avirin* (Jerusalem, 5740/1980), pp. 16-24.
[2] Rabbi Abraham Isaac HaKohen Kook, *Orot Yisrael* (Jerusalem, 1942), 6:6; reprinted in *Orot* (Jerusalem, 1950), p. 160.
    Cf. Rabbi Zadok Hakohen Rabinowitz of Lublin, *Mahshevot Haruts* (Piotrków, 1912); 35c-36b; idem, *Dover Tsedek* (Piotrków, 1911), 40d-41c.
[3] In one of his journals Rav Kook recorded this confession:
> I love all. I am incapable of not loving people, all the peoples. In all the depths of my heart I want the glory of all, the mending of all. My love for Israel is more ardent, more profound, but the inner desire extends with its mighty love to all, literally. I have no need to force this feeling of love; it flows straight from the holy depth of the wisdom of the godly soul."
> (*Shemonah Kevatsim* 2:76)

    This *pensée* first appeared in *'Arpilei Tohar* (Jerusalem, 1914).
[4] The writer Alexander Ziskind Rabinowitz (AZaR), a great admirer of Rav Kook during his days as Rabbi of Jaffa, recollected Rav Kook confiding:
> Whoever said about me that my soul is torn, expressed it well. Certainly it is torn. A human whose soul is not torn is inconceivable. Only the mineral is whole. But a human possesses opposite aspirations; a

constant war is waged in his midst. The entire work of man is to unify the oppositions in his soul through a universal idea, by whose greatness and loftiness all is encompassed and arrives at total harmony. Understandably, this is but an ideal to which we aspire; no mortal can ever achieve it. Yet by our striving, we can come ever closer. It is this that the kabbalists refer to as *"yihudim"* ("unifications").

(Quoted in Elhanan Kalmanson, *Ha-Mahshavah ha-Yisraelit* [Jerusalem, 1920; photo offset Jerusalem, 1967], p. 13)

[5] This ability is visualized in the short film *Cosmic Zoom* (1968) directed by Eva Szasz.

Rav Kook wrote that our amazement at the minuscule should in no way lag behind our amazement at the magnitude of the universe. He paralleled the Psalmist's exclamation, "How great are Your works, O LORD" (Psalms 92:6) with "How tiny are Your works, O LORD!" See *Orot ha-Torah* 3:8, and *'Eyn AYaH*, vol. 4, ed. Rabbi Ya'akov Filber (Jerusalem: Makhon RZYH, 2000), *Shabbat* 54b (chap. 5, par. 12), p. 23.

[6] See our essay "Rav Kook's Shattered Vessels and Their Repair."

[7] Numbers 1:52.

[8] Genesis 44:5.

[9] Rabbi Hayyim Joseph David Azulai, *Devash le-Fi* (Livorno, 1801), s.v. *gavi'a*, quoting the kabbalist Rabbi Nathan Shapira Yerushalmi.

[10] Deuteronomy 10:22.

[11] Genesis 43:32.

[12] Genesis 46:34.

[13] Genesis 39:14.

[14] Exodus 2:19.

[15] *Deuteronomy Rabbah* 2:8.

[16] *Sifré, 'Ekev.*

[17] *b. Gittin* 8b, 47a; Maimonides, *MT, Hil. Terumot* 1:3; Nahmanides, Deuteronomy 11:24.

[18] As foreseen by Rabbi Moses Hayyim Luzzatto, in the future, the entire earth will enjoy the status of Syria, *"kibbush yahid,"* whereby the lands outside of Israel will be purified. Yet the sanctity of *"kibbush rabbim"* will still be restricted to *Erets Yisrael* proper. See Rabbi M.H. Luzzatto, *Ma'amar ha-Ge'ulah*, ed. H. Touitou (n.p., 2002), p. 37.

[19] For this latter understanding of the word *ehad* (one), the reader is referred to the vast Sufic literature concerning the practice of *tawhid*, and to the equally voluminous Hasidic literature concerning the meditative discipline of *yihud*. In both *tawhid* and *yihud* the adept arrives at the realization that all is God. As that great teacher of HaBaD Hasidism, Rabbi Eizik of Homel, unabashedly ejaculated in the Yiddish vernacular: *"Altz iz Gott!"* "All is God!" See Rabbi Yitzhak Eizik Halevi Epstein of Homel, *"Iggeret Kodesh"* (Holy Epistle), printed at the conclusion of *Hannah Ariel—Amarot Tehorot* (*Ma'amar ha-Shabbat*, etc.) (Berdichev: Sheftel, 1912), 4b.

[20] Maimonides, *Guide of the Perplexed* I, 63.

[21] Deuteronomy 33:5.

[22] *Exodus Rabbah* 2:6, 48:4; *Leviticus Rabbah* 31:4; Ibn Ezra, Hizkuni, Nahmanides (quoting "some *aggadot*") and Rabbeinu Behaye (Bahya ben Asher ibn Halawa) to Deuteronomy 33:5. See also Ibn Ezra and RaShBaM (Rabbi

Samuel ben Meir) to Genesis 36:31. And see Maimonides, *Commentary to the Mishnah, Shavu'ot* 2:2 (Kafah ed., p. 169).

23 *Seder 'Olam Rabbah*, chap. 7; *b. Zevahim* 102a.

24 Deuteronomy 34:6.

25 Deuteronomy 33:1; *Deuteronomy Rabbah* 11:4.

26 *b. Yevamot* 49b.

27 *b. Mo'ed Katan* 28a; *Bava Batra* 17a; Maimonides, *Guide of the Perplexed* III, 51.

28 In my perception of Moses as torn between universalism and nationalism, I seem to have been preceded by Rabbi Samuel Alexandrov of Bobruisk. See his *Mikhtevei Mehkar u-Bikoret*, vol. 3 (Jerusalem, 1932), pp. 18-21, 23. Alexandrov finds support for Moses' aloofness from Israel in the writings of MaHaRaL of Prague. See Rabbi Judah Löw, *Gevurot Hashem* (London: L. Honig & Sons, 1954), chap. 15 (75b): "In addition, when you know the level of Moses our Teacher, peace be unto him, inasmuch as he was set apart from *Kelal Yisrael* (the collective of Israel) by his level, and did not share the level of the rest of Israel, [Pharaoh's astrologers] could not know whether [Moses] was from Israel or from the nations, because according to his level, he had nothing in common with the rest of Israel. Understand this well."

29 Sa'adyah Gaon, *Emunot ve-De'ot* 8:5 (Kafah edition, p. 246).

30 See Yehudah Even-Shmuel, *Midreshei Ge'ulah* (Giv'atayim-Ramat Gan: Mossad Bialik, 1968), Introduction, p. 51, n. 67.

31 Obadiah 1:18; *b. Bava Batra* 123b.

32 "It is a tradition that Esau falls only by the hand of the children of Rachel" (*Genesis Rabbah* 73:7; 75:5). See also *Pesikta Rabbati*, ed. Meir Ish-Shalom (Vienna, 1880), chap. 13, "*Mini Ephraim Shoresham Amalek*" [Judges 5:14], 54a: "The seed of Amalek falls only by the hand of the children of Rachel." And see ibid. 54b.

33 *b. Sukkah* 52a.

34 See Rabbi Hayyim Vital, *Peri 'Ets Hayyim* (Dubrovna, 1804), *Sha'ar ha-'Amidah*, chap. 19, s.v. *ve-kissei David 'avdekha* (58c).The fervent wish that Messiah Son of Joseph not be killed was expressed earlier in *Zohar* III, 223a, 277b, and *Tikkunim me-Zohar Hadash* (Vilna, 1867), 27a.

35 Maimonides, *MT, Hil. Melakhim* 12:2.

36 *y. Berakhot* 1:1; *b. Berakhot* 4b, 9b, 42a; *Zohar* I, 132b, 205b (see commentary of *Sulam* there); Rabbi Hayyim Vital, *Peri 'Ets Hayyim* (Dubrovna, 1804), *Sha'ar Keri'at Shema'*, chap. 29 (50b), "*ge'ulah—Yesod; tefillah—Malkhut*"; Rabbi Levi Yitzhak Monson of Ozerna, *Bekha Yevarekh Yisrael* (Przemysl, 1905), Introduction and *Vayyeshev* (16c-d).

Rabbi Zadok Hakohen Rabinowitz of Lublin wrote: "Then David would have been Messiah, and Saul would have been worthy of being Messiah Son of Joseph, as Jonathan said [to David], 'And I shall be your second [in command] [1 Samuel 23:17]'" (*Peri Tsaddik*, vol. 2 [Lublin, 1907], Parashat Zakhor [bot. 91b]).

37 *b. Yevamot* 47b.

38 *b. Berakhot* 7b, *Bava Batra* 14b.

39 See Ezekiel 37.

40 *Esther Rabbah* 1:12.

41 *b. Yoma* 69a.

42 See Isaiah 45:1.

According to Buber, Rabbi Menahem Mendel of Rymanów viewed Napoleon favorably.

A descendant of Rabbi Shneur Zalman of Liadi recounted to the latter's biographer, Hayyim Meir Heilmann, that it was the Maggid of Kozienice (Rabbi Israel Hopstein) that locked horns with the Alter Rebbe concerning Napoleon. See H.M. Heilman, *Beit Rabbi* (Berdichev, 1902), Part One, chap. 22 (45b, note 1).

43 Ibid., chap. 22.
44 Esther 1:1.
45 Esther 1:22.
45* Esther 2:5. See commentary of Rabbi David Kimhi (RaDaK) to 2 Samuel 19:21 s.v. *le-khol Beit Yosef.*
46 *m. Shekalim* 5:1; *Menahot* 65a. And see *Tosafot, Menahot* 64b, s.v. *amar lehu Mordechai,* and *Bava Kamma* 82b, s.v. *ve-'al otah sha'ah.*
47 *Esther Rabbah* 6:2.
48 See Hizkuni, Rabbi Samuel ben Meir (RaShBaM) and *Da'at Zekenim mi-Ba'alei ha-Tosafot* to Genesis 49:10. (The verse quoted by Hizkuni in his first interpretation, "*Va-yavo'u Shiloh va-yamlikhu 'aleihem et Yarav'am*" ["They came to Shiloh and appointed as king over them Jeroboam"] is not to be found in the Bible.)
49 Abrabanel, 1 Kings 12:28.
50 Rashi, Exodus 32:4 quoting *Midrash Tanhuma, Ki Tissa* 19. See Deuteronomy 33:17 and Psalms 106:20.
51 *b. Sanhedrin* 102a.
52 Numbers 21:14; *b. Kiddushin* 30b.
53 Genesis 49:10.
54 Rashi, Genesis 28:12, quoting *Genesis Rabbah* 68:12.
55 In *Genesis Rabbah* (ibid.), Rabbi Hiyya and Rabbi Yannai disagreed whether the angels were ascending and descending on the ladder, or ascending and descending on Jacob.

Ibn Ezra (Genesis 28:12) quotes Rabbi Shelomo ha-Sepharadi as saying: "The ladder alludes to the supernal soul, and the angels of God—the thought of wisdom."

56 Genesis 32:2-3
57 Rashi ad locum, quoting *Midrash Tanhuma, Vayyishlah* 3.

"My Beloved is Like a Gazelle" (*Domeh Dodi li-Tsevi*): The Esthetic Messiah

An *Essai* in Rabbinic Surrealism, or Another Jewish Bestiary[1]

In the Song of Songs, King Solomon writes:

> My beloved is like a gazelle or a young hart; behold, he stands behind our wall, he looks in through the windows, he peers through the lattice.[2]

According to the Midrash, the verse describes the elusive character of the Redeemer: "Just as a deer appears and disappears and reappears, so the first Redeemer is revealed and occulted and revealed."[3] The commentators limn for us the timetable of the first Redeemer, Moses, who after an initial contact with the Children of Israel subjugated in Egypt, absented himself, only to reappear on the scene at a later time.[4] (Some make the astute observation that in the Bible code known as *ATBaSh*, the Hebrew word *tsevi* [deer] is permutated to *Moshe*.) And so too, we are told, the *future* process of redemption will be a symphony in three movements: revelation/occultation/revelation.[5]

Yet there is another sense in which the Beloved is compared to a deer. Besides its elusive behavior, the deer symbolizes the entire esthetic dimension. Part and parcel of the redemption of the soul of mankind is the redemption of the esthetic (perhaps erotic is the better word) dimension of being.

I will not commit the *faux pas* of writing that the Hebrew word for "deer," *tsevi*, has an additional meaning of "beauty." Though they look alike, these are actually two different words derived from separate proto-Semitic roots.

Be that as it may, the works of Solomon, Song of Songs and Proverbs (but especially the former) are replete with the image of the Beloved portrayed as a deer.

> Your two breasts are like two fawns that are twins of a gazelle, which feed among the lilies.[6]
>
> I adjure you, O daughters of Jerusalem, by the gazelles, and by the hinds of the field, that you awaken not, nor stir up love, until it please.[7]
>
> A lovely hind and a graceful doe, let her breasts satisfy you at all times; with her love be you ravished always."[8]

This fascination with the gazelle is common to both Hebrew and Arabic literature. Classical Arabic poetry abounds with the imagery of the graceful gazelle, a symbol of female pulchritude. (It has been theorized that *"ghazal,"* the word for love poetry in Arabic, is related to the word for gazelle.)

In medieval Arabic and Persian civilization the fawning (pun intended) on the graceful hind did not remain restricted to the realm of poetry (as in Hebraic civilization), but extended into the visual arts as well. In the Jewish world, the deer as visual image would be kept waiting in the woods for several centuries.

Belated as its arrival may have been, come the seventeenth century the icon of the deer exploded upon the Jewish world with full force. In 1666 ("the year of the beast" from the perspective of English Protestant millenarians),[9] a Turkish Jew by the name of "Tsevi" (first name "Shabbetai") captured the Messianic imagination of the Jewish People the world over. The symbolism of the deer was lost neither on Shabbetai Tsevi (he signed himself *"Tavya de-vei 'ila'ah,"* Aramaic for "celestial deer")[10] and his admirers, nor on his eventual critics (after the necessary sobering) who punned on his name *"tsevi shavur"* ("a broken deer," a Mishnaic reference).[11] Sabbatian iconography (the little that has survived in frontispieces of books) makes ample use of deer representation.[12]

The great visionary of Israel's rebirth, Rabbi Abraham Isaac Hakohen Kook (1865-1935), first Ashkenazic Chief Rabbi of Erets Israel, saw a similarity between Shabbetai Tsevi and Nietzsche.

> What Nietzsche is to humanity, Shabbetai Tsevi (may the name of the wicked rot) is to Judaism; and just as Nietzsche took leave of his senses, so Shabbetai Tsevi took leave of his religion. One shell (*kelipah*) related to the Footsteps of Messiah.[13]

Rav Kook's intriguing *pensée* has left many of us in suspense. Could he by some stretch be alluding to Nietzsche's triumphing of the Dionysian element over the Apollonian element?[14]

Messiah

Speaking of Rav Kook, in his seminal work, *Orot* (1920), Rav Kook would devote two crucial chapters to the "power of imagination" (*"ko'ah ha-medammeh"*) and the role it is destined to play in the redemptive process.

Initially, Rav Kook's survey of the contemporary scene assumes a rather pessimistic tone:

> All of contemporary culture is built on the foundation of the imaginative faculty. This is the pagan legacy of the civilized nations caught up in the imaginative faculty, from which developed physical beauty, both in action and in representation. The imaginative faculty progresses, and with it, the applied and empirical sciences, and in proportion to the ascendance of the imaginative faculty and its hold upon life, the light of intellect recedes, because the entire world supposes that all happiness depends on the development of the imaginative faculty. So things continue gradually, until the remains of reason in the spirit of secular wisdom are also converted to the imaginative faculty. The speakers and raconteurs, the dramaturges and all engaged in *les beaux arts*, assume prominence in society, while philosophy hobbles and totters because pure reason disappears. As much as reason recedes, so "impudence increases, and the wisdom of sages rots, the sin-fearing are reviled and truth is absent, and the face of the generation is as the

face of a dog."¹⁵ That inner gentleness, which comes from the spirit of wisdom, disappears. The longing for spirituality and transcendence; for divine communion; for the higher world; for the clarity of ethics in the apex of its purity; for the concepts of intellect in and of their eternal selves, become a rare spectacle. This global phenomenon is reflected proportionately in Israel *vis-à-vis* divine inspiration and love of Torah with an inner spirit and essential freshness of faithful Judaism. There rules in the world a material spirit. *Woe unto you, O land, when your king is a lad and your princes eat in the morning!*¹⁶

And then in an abrupt turnabout, we are treated to a glint of the brilliant ironic wit which is the signature of Kookian vision:

> But all of this is a far-reaching plan, the LORD's plan to perfect the imaginative faculty, for imagination is the healthy basis for the supernal spirit that will descend on it… the supreme divine spirit destined to come through King Messiah. Therefore, now the imaginative faculty is being firmly established. When it is completely finished, the seat will be ready and perfect for the supernal spirit of the LORD, fit to receive the light of the divine spirit, which is the spirit of the LORD, *a spirit of wisdom and understanding, a spirit of counsel and strength, a spirit of knowledge and awe of the LORD.*¹⁷

Not content with sociological study and survey of modern intellectual history, Rav Kook, a kabbalist of note, goes on to provide Lurianic underpinnings to his observations, whereby the harlotry first addressed by Joshua (or rather his spies) with only partial success, is later confronted by King Solomon, with complete (or near complete) success. In the Kookian interpretation of this Lurianic myth, Rahab the Harlot and the two harlots who appeared before King Solomon symbolize the unbridled power of imagination:[18]

> When the time had as yet not arrived for all the purity to appear at the final heights, there were sent by Joshua two spies to reconnoiter the land, and they came to the home of a harlot by the name of Rahab.[19] All is tied together with holiness and the highest good, but the attribute of judgment is aroused and true fear of punishment is required in proportion to the empowerment of the imagination and its deepening. But in the essence of the national will, the imaginative dimension—which entails the embodiment of knowledge on the one hand, and all description of beauty on the other—was still not completed at that time. This was brought to completion in the days of Solomon: *Then two harlots came* before the judgment of the King of Israel, who sits on the throne of the LORD.[20]

Rav Kook continues to trace the historic process of *"birur ko'ah ha-medammeh,"* the clarification of the power of imagination (to employ the terminology of Rabbi Nahman of Breslov),[21] through the idolatrous leanings of King Solomon in the First Temple period (attributed by the Bible to the influence of his foreign wives), which in turn prompted the hamstringing of imagination by the Men of the Great Assembly at the beginning of the Second Temple period, and finally culminating in the re-emergence and re-empowerment of imagination at the time of the national renascence in the Land of Israel:

> However, through the interference of the foreign women,[22] together with the inability to digest foreign things, there resulted the wickedness that caused the founding of the great city of Rome,[23] and the siftings of elements had to be stretched out for eons, until the imagination was disempowered in Israel. The drive for idolatry was captured in a "lead pot" and "slaughtered."[24] By the same token, *there is no more any prophet*,[25] and the flame of love for nation and land is not felt in the same profound way as in the good days. This is related to the pain of the entire world. Until at the End of Days, the traces of the power of imagination are revealed and the love of the Land is aroused. The thing appears with its dregs, but it is destined to be purified. *The smallest will become a thousand, and the youngest, a powerful nation, I am the LORD; in its time I will hasten it.*[26]

In Rav Kook's vision, a reactivation of the imagination is necessary for the return of prophecy to Israel. "*U-ve-yad ha-nevi'im adammeh.*" "By means of the prophets I have spoken in images."[27]

Rav Kook is indebted to Maimonides for placing the *ko'ah ha-medammeh*, the imaginative faculty, front and center, rendering it an essential component, perhaps even *the* essential component of prophecy.[28] While a dormant imagination may not pose an obstacle to the intellectual pursuit of Torah study, Israel's renewed quest for prophecy in its land makes the revival of the moribund *"medammeh"* an absolute necessity.

※※※

Rav Kook may not have been alone in the belief that the non-cerebral (or right-hemispheric) dimension, so long missing from Judaism, would play a vital part in the national renascence. There is an intriguing remark of the Rebbe of Sokhatchov that leads one to suspect that he too may have been thinking in such terms, that Israel in its struggle for final redemption must encompass a dimension hitherto almost alien to its being. His oral remarks (which fortunately, were preserved for posterity) take the form of commentary to the *Haftarah*, the reading from the Prophets for the Intermediate Sabbath of the Festival of *Sukkot* (Booths). According to Talmudic tradition, on that Sabbath morning we read *Be-Yom bo' Gog*,[29] Ezekiel's apocalyptic vision of the confrontation between the army of Gog and Magog on the one hand, and Jerusalem on the other.[30] Rav Hai Gaon, quoted in the *Tur*, explained that this occasion was deemed appropriate for that reading, because the War of Gog and Magog will take place on Sukkot.[31]

Rabbi Samuel Bornstein (1855-1926), the Rebbe of Sokhatchov (a school of Polish Hasidism known for its penetrating thought) could not leave matters at that. He probed for some intrinsic connection between the prophesied cosmic struggle and the observance of the commandment of *sukkot*, those booths or huts that serve as temporary residences throughout the festival.

But first, there arises the more basic question: Who are Gog and Magog? Some say that they symbolize the seventy nations of the world, all lined up against Israel. (The Hebrew words *"Gog u-Magog"* have the numerical value of 70.)[32] The Sokhatchover, drawing on a Midrash, traces Gog back to his ancestor Yephet, son of Noah. Likewise, Israel is traced back to Shem, son of Noah.[33] In the postdiluvian world, Yephet received the dimension of *"hitsoniyut"* ("outwardness"), and Shem, the dimension of *"penimiyut"* ("inwardness").[34] In the apocalyptic struggle of titans, Israel's eleventh-hour salvation will hinge on its ability to take hold of the outward dimension, symbolized by the commandment of the *sukkah* or booth, which may be fulfilled by the mere act of sleeping in the *sukkah*. In sleep, one is stripped of the cerebral and reduced to the external, bodily aspect of one's being.[35] (Though the Sokhatchover does not couch it in such terms, sleep is also a window of opportunity for unbridled imagination; for the soul to enter the imaginal world.)[36]

Rabbi Gershon Hanokh Leiner (1839-1890), the Rebbe of Radzyn, in *his* analysis of the confrontation between Gog and Israel, focuses specifically on the Greek connection. In this regard, the Radzyner quotes the Talmud: "Our rabbis permitted [to write a Torah scroll in] Greek."³⁷ As is well known, the civilization of *Yavan*, or Greece, excelled in the arts and appreciation of the esthetic dimension of being. The Talmud will justify the practice of writing a Torah scroll in Greek by invoking the verse, *"Yapht Elohim le-Yephet ve-yishkon be-'aholei Shem"* ("May God enlarge the boundaries of Yephet, and may he dwell in the tents of Shem"), which they paraphrased as, *"Yaphyuto shel Yephet yehé be-'aholei Shem"* ("The beauty of Yephet shall be in the tents of Shem").³⁸ To the Radzyner's thinking, implicit in Ezekiel's prophecy, "And it shall come to pass on that day that I will give unto Gog a place there for a grave in Israel,"³⁹ is the prediction that the good, positive element of Gog—or Greece—once extracted from the dross, will be incorporated within Israel's collective consciousness. Gog being buried in Israel, which is to say, the soil of Israel receiving into its midst the body of Gog, symbolizes the introjection of Greek civilization—or rather the salient, redeeming feature thereof—into the nation of Israel.⁴⁰ "And the precious, the good, found in this victory, will remain in Israel for eternity."⁴¹

✦

There is no denying that *HaZaL*, the Sages of blessed memory, were open to allowing the *'or hozer*, the reflected light of Hellenic (or Japhetic) civilization to shine upon Hebraic (or Semitic) civilization, but we find in the writings of the Rabbis another strain of thought whereby beauty shines upon Zion not as an *'or hozer*, a reflection of a foreign civilization, but as an *'or yashar*, a direct illumination from the source of Israel, whose rays extend to the entire world.

> The Sages say: "From Zion was created the world, for it is said, 'A psalm of Asaph. The God of gods, the LORD, spoke, and called earth, from the rising of the sun until its setting. Out of Zion, the perfection of beauty (*mi-Tsiyon mikhlal yophi*)'—from it is perfected the beauty of the world (*mimenu mukhlal yophyo shel 'olam*)."[42]
>
> Ten measures (*kabin*) of beauty (*yophi*) descended to the world; nine, Jerusalem took, and one, the rest of the world."[43]

In the mystical *Heikhalot* literature, we discover that the name of the "Prince of Torah" (*Sar ha-Torah*) is *Yophiel*, or in other texts *Yepheiphiyah*.[44] At first glance, this might strike us as a strange name for an angel: "The Beauty of *Yah*." However, as scholars have pointed out, the setting for the visionary experiences recorded in the *Heikhalot* is the Holy Temple in Jerusalem.[45] A student of the Talmud will recall that on the seventh day of Sukkot (or *Hoshana Rabba*) in the Temple, at the conclusion of the seven *hakafot* or circumambulations, they would bid farewell: *"Yophi lakh, mizbe'ah! Yophi lakh, mizbe'ah!"* ("Beauty to you, Altar! Beauty to you, Altar!"). According to the opinion of Rabbi Eliezer [ben Jacob], they would say: *"Yophi le-Yah ve-lakh, mizbe'ah! Yophi le-Yah ve-lakh, mizbe'ah!"* ("Beauty to *Yah*, and to you, Altar! Beauty to *Yah*, and to you, Altar!").[46] One speculates that the name of the angel

Yepheiphiyah derived from this salutation: *"Yophi le-Yah!"* Verily, the Temple in Jerusalem is the source of all beauty in the world.

❧❀❧

> Said Rav Hisda: "What is written, 'The LORD loves the gates of Zion more than all the dwellings of Jacob'?[47] The LORD loves gates distinguished by *Halakhah* more than synagogues and study-houses."
>
> This is what Rabbi Hiyya bar Ammi said in the name of 'Ulla: "From the day the Temple was destroyed, the Holy One, blessed be He, has naught in His world except the four ells of *Halakhah*."[48]

With the return of the lovely *Shekhinah* to Zion, all of the beauty and romance which are hers will reappear in the Gates of Zion. If, as the Sages say, the *Sha'arei Tsiyon* (Gates of Zion) are *"she'arim metsuyanim ba-halakhah"* ("gates distinguished by *Halakhah*"), then they are also *"she'arim metsuyanim"* ("decorative gates") without further modification.[49] With the destruction of the Temple, the Holy One's world was reduced to "four ells of *Halakhah*,"[50] but with the national rebirth, the Holy One's world broadens to encompass other dimensions as well. *"Ohev Hashem Sha'arei Tsiyon."* "The LORD loves the Gates of Zion."

And my Beloved, the Messiah, with his nose pressed up against the glass window like that of a fawn, is taking it all in.

1 In 2012, I published *The Kabbalah of Relation: "We Would Have Learned the 'Way of the Earth' From the Cock"* (A Jewish Bestiary), which dealt with the symbol of the cock in Talmud, Kabbalah and the surrealist art of Marc Chagall.
2 Song of Songs 2:9. Cf. ibid. 2:17.
3 *Numbers Rabbah* 11:2; *Song of Songs Rabbah*, Parashah 2.
4 See Rabbi Ze'ev Wolf Einhorn, *Peirush MaHaRZU* to *Exodus Rabbah* 5:19.
5 *Numbers Rabbah* and *Song of Songs Rabbah*, loc. cit.
6 Song of Songs 4:5.
 The recent shocking statement by author Melissa Mohr is an apt description of the contortions like verses are put through in various quarters: "Some of these euphemisms are obvious, as in the Song of Songs...It is almost painful to watch scholars insist that this passage has nothing at all to do with sex. No, it is truly and only about God's love for Israel ... or the soul's spiritual union with God" (Melissa Mohr, *Holy Sh*t: A Brief History of Swearing* [New York: Oxford University Press, 2013], pp. 83-84).
7 Song of Songs 2:7, 3:5. I am still undecided whether the comment by some that *"tseva'ot"* is a pun on the divine name *Tseva'ot* and *"ayelot ha-sadeh"* a pun on the divine cognomen *El Shaddai*, constitutes genuine Bible commentary or merely *leitsanut* (comedy).
8 Proverbs 5:19.
9 The reference is to the Book of Revelations by John of Patmos, wherein the number 666 is the mark of the beast, interpreted by Protestant millenarians to refer to the Antichrist. Recently, it has been speculated that the beast is actually a veiled reference to the Roman Emperor Nero.
10 b. *Hullin* 59b.
11 m. *Bava Metsi'a* 1:4.
12 See Bezalel Naor, *Post-Sabbatian Sabbatianism* (Spring Valley, NY: Orot, 1999), pp. 79-82, concerning the frontispiece to Rabbi Tsevi Chotsh, *Hemdat Tsevi* (Amsterdam, 1706).
13 Rabbi Abraham Isaac Hakohen Kook, *Kevatsim mi-Ketav Yad Kodsho*, vol. 1, ed. Boaz Ofen (Jerusalem, 5766/2006), *Pinkas "Aharon be-Boisk,"* par. 40 (p. 56).
14 See Friedrich Nietzsche, *The Birth of Tragedy* (1872).
15 m. *Sotah* 9:15.
16 Ecclesiastes 10:16.
17 Isaiah 11:2.
 Rabbi Abraham Isaac Hakohen Kook, *Orot* (1920), *Yisrael u-Tehiyato* (Israel and Its Renascence), chap. 17.
18 See Shlomo Katz, "Rahav and Yehoshua: Imagination and Intellect," *Orot: A Multidisciplinary Journal*, vol. 1 (5751/1991), pp. 49-64, and Editor's Apercu, pp. 65-67.
19 Joshua chap. 2.
20 1 Kings chap. 3. See Rabbi Hayyim Vital, *Sefer ha-Likkutim*, Joshua chap. 2; 1 Kings chap. 3; idem, *Likkutei Torah*, Joshua chap. 2; 1 Kings chap. 3.
21 *Likkutei MOHaRaN* II, 8:7. See further below note 28.
 Known as *"Tik'u Tokhahah,"* this was the last public discourse delivered by Rabbi Nahman before his passing. Rabbi David Sears speculates that it served as the template for Rabbi Nahman's one and only poem, *Shir Na'im*. See Rabbi Nachman of Breslov, *Shir Na'im/Song of Delight*, ed. Rabbi David

Sears (Spring Valley, NY: Orot, 2005).

On the other hand, in *Likkutei MOHaRaN* I, 26 (*"Ahavei lan mana"*), Rabbi Nahman takes an extremely dim view of the imaginative faculty, equating it with the *yetser ha-ra'*, or evil inclination. In that discourse, the key term is not *"birur ko'ah ha-medammeh"* ("clarification of the imaginative faculty") but *"shevirat ko'ah hamedammeh"* ("breaking of the imaginative faculty"), indicating its unredeemable character.

22 1 Kings 11:1-8.

23 *b. Shabbat* 56b, *Sanhedrin* 21b. However, a different version of the founding of Rome is recorded in Rashi, *Megillah* 6b.

24 *b. Yoma* 69b, *Sanhedrin* 64a, *'Avodah Zarah* 17.

25 Psalm 74:9. According to the *Sefer Hasidim*, Vilna Gaon and Rabbi Zadok Hakohen of Lublin, the cessation of prophecy was linked to the eradication of idolatry. See Bezalel Naor, *Lights of Prophecy/Orot ha-Nevu'ah* (1990).

26 Isaiah 60:22. *Orot, Yisrael u-Tehiyato*, chap. 18.

In *Shemonah Kevatsim* 5:190 the conclusion reads: "The smallest will become a thousand," "the thousand for you, Solomon" [Song of Songs 8:12]. This is actually the more logical conclusion. Logic would dictate that Solomon reappear in the conclusion to the *pensée*.

27 Hosea 12:11.

28 See Moses Maimonides, *Guide of the Perplexed* II, 36. Another latter-day visionary who pursued this line (while downplaying the indebtedness to Maimonides) was Rabbi Nahman of Breslov. Rabbi Nahman, as Rav Kook (who was very attached to and inspired by the writings of Breslov), is intent on the rectification and clarification of imagination as a means to reviving prophecy. See, e.g., *Likkutei Moharan* II, 8 (*Tik'u Tokhaha*), pars. 7-8. See now Zvi Mark, *Mistikah ve-Shiga'on bi-Yetsirat R. Nahman mi-Breslov* (*Mysticism and Madness in the Work of R. Nahman of Bratslav*) (Tel Aviv, 2003), chap. 5 (*"Dimyon, Nevu'ah ve-Emunah"*), especially pp. 86-95.

29 Ezekiel 38:18.

30 *b. Megillah* 31a.

31 Rabbi Jacob ben Asher, *Arba'ah Turim, Tur Orah Hayyim*, chap. 490.

32 *Midrash Tanhuma*, end *Korah*.

33 *Genesis Rabbah* 36:6. See Genesis 10:2: "The children of Yephet: Gomer and Magog and Media and Yavan and Tubal and Meshekh and Tiras." Cf. Ezekiel 39:1: "...Gog, chief prince of Meshekh and Tubal."

34 Rabbi Samuel Bornstein recorded this insight in the name of his father Rabbi Abraham Bornstein, author of the Responsa *Avnei Nezer*.

It would be apposite to point out that Noah's blessing to Yephet bespeaks the assignation of outwardness to Yephet and inwardness to Shem. "May God enlarge Yephet and may he dwell in the tents of Shem." In the Hebrew original it reads: *"Yapht Elohim le-Yephet ve-yishkon be-'aholei Shem"* (Genesis 9:27).

Yapht may, by a stretch, be related to the Hebrew word for "beauty," *yophi*. As the Rabbis paraphrased the verse: "The beauty (*yaphyuto*) of Yephet shall be in the tents of Shem" (*b. Megillah* 9b). The halakhic discussion there concerns the permissibility of writing Torah scrolls in the very esthetic Greek script. But this Rabbinic interpretation of the term is the stuff of *derash* or homily.

From a perspective of *peshuto shel mikra*, the simple sense of the verse, *yapht* as a verb (*p-t-h*) is an expression of width or spatial extension. (See Onkelos, Rashi and Ibn Ezra to Genesis 9:27; the last-mentioned in opposition to Sa'adya Gaon.) At the other extreme stand the "tents of Shem," archetypical domiciles symbolic of inwardness.

One notes that whereas in the Sokhatchover analysis Yephet and Shem in their new incarnations of Gog-and-Magog and Israel are pitted against one another, in the passage from the Talmud cited above there is expressed an ideal marriage of the two *Weltanschauungen*. Out of the confrontation of the two ideational continents of Yephet and Shem may yet come a synthesis, or better yet, a creative tension.

[35] Rabbi Samuel Bornstein, *Shem mi-Shemuel, Rosh Hashanah—Sukkot* (Jerusalem, 5734/1974), *Yom Shabbat Hol ha-Mo'ed Sukkot*, Year 5677 (191b-192a).

[36] The Arabic term *'alam al-mithal* (literally "the world of likeness"), rooted in Islamic philosophy (especially in the writings of Ibn Sina or Avicenna), was translated by Henri Corbin into Latin as *mundus imaginalis* or imaginal world. See Henri Corbin, "Mundus Imaginalis or, the imaginary and the imaginal," *Cahiers internationaux de symbolisme*, vol. 6 (1964), pp. 3-26.

[37] *b. Megillah* 9a.

[38] Genesis 9:27; *b. Megillah* 9b.

[39] Ezekiel 39:11.

[40] Rabbi Gershon Hanokh Leiner, *Sod Yesharim, Sukkot* (Warsaw, 1903), *Shalosh Se'udot shel Hol ha-Mo'ed Sukkot*, par. 39, s.v. *Ve-hayah ba-yom ha-hu be-yom bo' Gog 'al admat Yisrael* (63c-64a).

Historically speaking, Sokhatchov and Radzyn were on opposite sides of the barricades that went up after the Kotsk-Izhbitsa (Polish, Kock-Izbica) schism in 1839. Rabbi Abraham Bornstein of Sokhatchov (Polish, Sochaczew) was the son-in-law of the Kotsker Rebbe, Menahem Mendel Morgenstern. Rabbi Gershon Hanokh Leiner of Radzyn was the grandson of Rabbi Mordechai Joseph Leiner of Izbica, author of *Mei ha-Shilo'ah*. Both the Kotsker and the Izhbitser had studied under Rabbi Simha Bunem of Pshiskha (Polish, Przysucha). It was in Pshiskha that this uniquely intellectual form of Polish Hasidism was born.

[41] *Sod Yesharim, Sukkot*, end par. 39 (64a).

[42] Psalms 50:1-2; *b. Yoma* 54b. In Lurianic Kabbalah, the beauty of Zion is associated with Joseph, of whom it was said, "And Joseph was handsome in form and handsome in appearance (*yephé to'ar vi-yphé mar'eh*)" (Genesis 39:6). See Rabbi Hayyim Vital, *'Ets Hayyim* 32:5 (=*Sha'ar He'arat ha-Mohin*, chap. 5). There is Midrashic precedent for equating Zion with Joseph: "Whatever befell Joseph, befell Zion" (*Midrash Tanhuma, Vayyigash* 10). Astute commentators point out that both Joseph and Zion share the numerical value of 156.

An exploration of the esthetic dimension of the Biblical Joseph in Midrash and Kabbalah would make for a fascinating study. The famed Gaon of Rogatchov (1858-1936) dropped some tantalizing hints in this connection. See Rabbi Joseph Rosen, *Tsaphnat Pa'ne'ah, Bereshit* (Jerusalem, 1967), *Vayyeshev*, Genesis 39:2, 6 and *Haphtarat Vayyeshev* (pp. 143-147). In those spartan notes, the Rogatchover atypically references Lurianic Kabbalah, and sketches the features of an androgynous Joseph!

[43] *b. Kiddushin* 49b.
[44] See Reuben Margaliyot, *Mal'akhei 'Elyon* (Jerusalem, 1945), s.v. *Yophiel* (pp. 65-67) and s.v. *Yepheiphiyah* (p. 68); Gershom G. Scholem, *Jewish Gnosticism, Merkabah Mysticism and Talmudic Tradition* (New York, 1965), pp. 12-13. In Targum Pseudo-Jonathan to Deuteronomy 34:6, both Yophiel and Yepheiphiyah occur as *"rabbanei hokhmeta"* ("teachers of wisdom"). The enigmatic Galician kabbalist who perished in Siberian exile during the Second World War, Isaac Messer (1891-1942), lavished great attention on the Prince of Torah, Yophiel/Yepheiphiyah. See Isaac Messer, *U-Mi-Midbar Matanah*, ed. Moshe Hallamish (Jerusalem, 1985), pp. 40, 43-44. Concerning this mysterious student of Hillel Zeitlin, see Bezalel Naor, *Kabbalah and the Holocaust* (Spring Valley, NY, 2001), pp. 103-117.

The Lithuanian kabbalist, Rabbi Eizik Haver offered an explanation for the association of *yophi* or beauty with *"razin de-'oraita"* (mysteries of Torah). See Rabbi Yitzhak Eizik Haver (Wildman), *Afikei Yam*, vol. I (Jerusalem, 1994), *Kiddushin* 49b, s.v. *'Asarah kabin yophi* (p. 300). Note that his explanation differs from those of the Vilna Gaon (whom he quotes). See Elijah Gaon, *Yahel 'Or*, ed. Naphtali Herz Halevi [Weidenbaum] (Vilna, 1882), *Zohar* II, 247b (*Heikhalot*) (20d).

[45] See Michael D. Swartz, *Scholastic Magic: Ritual and Revelation in Early Jewish Mysticism* (Princeton, 1996), pp. 64-65; Elliot R. Wolfson, *Through A Speculum That Shines: Vision and Imagination in Medieval Jewish Mysticism* (Princeton, 1994), pp. 19-20; Moshe Idel, *Kabbalah: New Perspectives* (New Haven, 1988), p. 168.

Also Ithamar Gruenwald, *"Mekoman shel masorot kohaniyot bi-yetsiratah shel ha-mistikah shel ha-merkavah ve-shel shi'ur komah"* in *Early Jewish Mysticism*, ed. Joseph Dan (Jerusalem, 1987) [=*Jerusalem Studies in Jewish Thought*, vol. 6, nos. 1-2], pp. 65-120; Rachel Elior, *"Sifrut ha-heikhalot ve-ha-merkavah: zikatah la-mikdash, la-mikdash ha-shamaymi u-le-mikdash me'at,"* *Retsef u-Temurah* (2004), pp. 107-142; idem, "The priestly nature of the mystical heritage in *Heykalot* literature," *Expérience et écriture mystiques dans les religions du livre*, ed. Fenton and Goetschel (2000), pp. 41-54; idem, "The Merkavah tradition and the emergence of Jewish mysticism: from Temple to Merkavah, from Hekhal to Hekhalot, from priestly opposition to gazing upon the Merkavah," *Sino-Judaica* (1999), pp. 101-158; idem, *"Bein ha-heikhal ha-artsi la-heikhalot ha-shamaymiyim: ha-tefilah ve-shirat ha-kodesh be-sifrut ha-heikhalot ve-zikatan la-masorot ha-keshurot ba-mikdash,"* *Tarbiz* 64:3 (1995), pp. 341-380.

Inter alia, see Bezalel Naor, *The Limit of Intellectual Freedom: The Letters of Rav Kook* (Spring Valley, 2011), p. 109, concerning the focus of *Talmud Yerushalmi* on the Temple in Jerusalem.

[46] *t. Sukkah* 3:2; *b. Sukkah* 45b. Though this passage occurs in some versions of the *Mishnah, Sukkah* 4:5 (not Maimonides', to be sure), it is actually not a *mishnah* but a *beraita*. See *Hagahot B[ayit] H[adash]*; N.N. Rabbinowicz, *Dikdukei Soferim*; S. Lieberman, *Tosephta ki-Pheshutah*; Y. Kafah, *Peirush ha-Mishnah la-Rambam*. Though it should be obvious enough, my inclusion of the word *"Yophi"* in the opinion of Rabbi Eliezer [ben Jacob] is spelled out in Rabbeinu Menahem ha-Meiri, *Beit ha-Behirah, Sukkah*, ed. Liss (Jerusalem, 1966), p. 161 (col. a).

Rabbi Jacob Ettlinger was perplexed why Maimonides omitted this farewell salutation from his *Mishneh Torah, Hil. Lulav* 7:23. His proffered solution that Maimonides restricts his remarks to legal obligations, omitting mere custom, is less than satisfactory. (In that very *halakhah*, Maimonides mentions a *minhag Yisrael*!) See Rabbi J. Ettlinger, *'Arukh la-Ner, Sukkah* 45a.

My own suspicion is that Maimonides was squeamish about a formula that so readily lent itself to syncretistic interpretation. See the objection raised by the Talmud: *"Ve-ha ka meshattef shem shamayim ve-davar aher?"* "Is he not combining the name of Heaven and something else [i.e., combining *Yah* and the altar in a single salute]?" (*Sukkah* 45b). And though the Talmud reconciles the practice, Maimonides may have found the answer given to be forced, and being hypersensitive to any practices at all smacking of syncretism, saw fit to omit the custom from his code (for as *'Arukh la-Ner* pointed out, it was but a custom, not an obligation). In *Sefer ha-Mitsvot*, positive commandment 7, Maimonides quotes the *beraita* marshalled by the Talmud (ibid.): "Whoever combines the name of Heaven with something else, is uprooted from the world." (See further Maimonides, *Moreh Nevukhim*, ed. Michael Schwarz [2002], vol. I, pp. 142-143, n. 3.)

I surmise that deciding the *halakhah* in favor of the *tanna kamma* over Rabbi Eliezer ben Jacob was not an option for Maimonides, in view of the accepted principle of Talmudic jurisprudence that the *halakhah* is in accordance with Rabbi Eliezer ben Jacob, for "the Mishnah of Rabbi Eliezer ben Jacob is trim and clean (*kav ve-naki*)" (*b. Yevamot* 49b, *Gittin* 67a).

Postscript: I once heard from Rabbi J.B. Soloveitchik of Boston that his grandfather Rabbi Hayyim Soloveitchik of Brisk refused to utter the prayer *"Berikh Shemeh"* (a passage from *Zohar* II, 369a) before the open ark because he found syncretistic the passage *"sagidna kammeh u-mi-kamma di-ykar 'oraiteh"* ("I prostrate myself before Him and before the honor of His Torah"). Evidently, from the perspective of Halakhah, not only the altar, but the Torah too, is subject to syncretism.

(Recently Avishai Bar-Asher revealed that *"Berikh Shemeh"* is not integral to the text of the *Zohar* but is rather a printer's insertion. See A. Bar-Asher, "Berikh Shemeh," *Tarbiz*, vol. 86 [5779], pp. 147-198.)

For the same reason, Rabbi Hayyim Soloveitchik opposed singing on Simhat Torah the *piyyut "Ein Adir."* Rabbi Hayyim felt that its lumping together God, Moses, Torah and Yisrael smacks of syncretism. See Rabbi Mikhel Zalman Shurkin, *Harerei Kedem*, vol. 1 (Jerusalem, 2000), chap. 154 (p. 267).

[47] Psalms 87:2.

[48] *b. Berakhot* 8a.

[49] See Rashi, *Shabbat* 145b, s.v. *metsuyyanin—mekushatin*.

As Rabbi Nahman of Breslov expressed it in Yiddish: *"Ikh mein takeh dos Eretz Yisroel mit die shtieber, mit die heizer."* ("I mean literally this Land of Israel, with these homes, with these houses.")

[50] However, Rabbi Joseph Engel noted that both the anonymous author of the *Halakhot Gedolot* and Maimonides (Introduction to the *Commentary to the Mishnah*) do not have in their text of the Talmud the words *"Mi-yom she-harav beit ha-mikdash"* ("From the day the Temple was destroyed"). See Rabbi Joseph Engel, *Gilyonei ha-Shas, Berakhot* 8a.

The Philosopher King and the Poet Messiah: Hellenic and Hebrew Republics Compared

In Honor of Yom Yerushalayim 5777
Fiftieth Anniversary of the Reunification of Jerusalem 1967-2017

The Holy One, blessed be He, sought to make Hezekiah the Messiah, and Sennacherib—Gog and Magog.

The Attribute of Judgment remonstrated with the Holy One, blessed be He: "Master of the World, If You did not make David, King of Israel—who recited several songs and praises before You—the Messiah, then Hezekiah—for whom you performed all these miracles and he did not utter a single song before You—You shall make the Messiah?"

(Babylonian Talmud, *Sanhedrin* 94a)

In this legend of the Talmud we are told that King Hezekiah had all the makings of the Messiah but one—his failure to utter a song of thanksgiving. It would have been appropriate at the time of the miraculous deliverance of Jerusalem from the siege of Sennacherib, the King of Assyria, to compose a paean of praise to the Almighty in recognition of this momentous event. Failure to set the victory to song was deemed an offense so grievous that it disqualified the otherwise righteous king from a Messianic role. This is the simple interpretation of the passage in the Talmud. But might it tell us something deeper, more essential about the character of the long-awaited Messiah?

In Plato's *Republic*, the ruler of the ideal state will be a philosopher. In that tract, Plato takes advantage of the opportunity to express his utter disdain for poets:

> There is an old quarrel between philosophy and poetry. (*Republic*, 607b5-6)

The greatest Jewish philosopher of the medieval era, Moses Maimonides (1138-1204), was also dismissive of poets. In a response to Rabbi Jonathan Hakohen of Lunel, Maimonides wrote that "the way of 'the poets and the poetesses' (*ha-sharim ve-ha-sharot*) is not right in my eyes."[1] Maimonides' sensibilities were offended by the ambiguities ('the riddles and the parables") of poetry. His correspondent, Rabbi Jonathan, had written him a lengthy epistle gushing with the panegyric then in vogue in Provence. Maimonides was put on the spot. Mentioning the fact that his former colleagues back in *Sefarad* were wont to write in rhyme, and invoking the adage "When in Rome, do as the Romans do,"[2] Maimonides responded in kind, and one must say, his own verse does not lag behind.[3]

In his *Commentary to the Mishnah*, Maimonides grouped "books of poetry" (without differentiation) together with "those books found among the Arabs....that are devoid of wisdom or practical avail, just a waste of time." (The roster of trashy literature includes "chronicles, customs of the kings and genealogies of the Arab tribes.")[4]

Later in that same work, remarking upon the sage's advice, "All my days I grew up among the wise men and I found for the body no good but silence," Maimonides launches into a lengthy classification of the types of poetry:

> Know that the poems that are composed in any language are classified solely by their topics....I need to explain this—though it is simple—because I observed that if the great and pious of our nation are invited to a banquet or wedding or the like, and someone desires to sing in Arabic—even if that song be in praise of strength or willpower (which is desirable) or in praise of wine—then they put up a vocal protest and do not allow it to be heard. [On the other hand,] if the singer sings one of the Hebrew poems, none protests. They see nothing wrong with that, though the contents be forbidden or reprehensible. This is absolute folly, for what makes speech forbidden or permitted, desirable or repugnant, is not the language in which it is expressed, but the content. If the content of the song is exalted, then it is obligatory to say it in any language; and if it is inferior, then it should be avoided in any language.[5]

Maimonides goes on to explain his view that if there are two erotic poems, one in Hebrew, and the other in Arabic or Farsi, the Hebrew version is the more reprehensible in the Torah's opinion, precisely because of the sanctity of the tongue:

> It is not fitting to use it [i.e., Hebrew] for other than exalted matters. It is even more reprehensible if a verse of Torah or Song of Songs is used for that purpose [i.e., erotic poetry]. Then it is not merely reprehensible but forbidden, for the Torah forbade turning the prophetic language into lowly songs.[6]

Finally, in his philosophic work, *Guide of the Perplexed*, Maimonides took a jab at the poets who allow themselves unwarranted liberties by ascribing human attributes to the divinity.[7]

Given Maimonides' dim view of the poet, it is hardly surprising that what defines the Messiah in Maimonides' *Hilkhot Melakhim* (Laws of Kings) is first and foremost his study of Torah:

> If there should arise a king of the House of David *who studies the Torah* and performs the commandments as David his ancestor....[8]

Note that David's distinction as the "sweet-singer of Israel" has been dropped from the definition of Messiah. (In 2 Samuel 23:1 David is referred to as "Messiah of the God of Jacob and sweet-singer of Israel.")

In *Hilkhot Teshuvah* ("Laws of Return"), Maimonides fleshes out the personal attributes of King Messiah, endowing him with wisdom greater than that of Solomon, and prophecy approaching that of Moses:

> ....That king that shall arise from the seed of David, shall be a master of wisdom greater than Solomon, and a great prophet approaching Moses our Teacher, and therefore he shall teach the entire people and instruct them in the way of the Lord, and all the nations shall come to hearken to him, as it says: "And it shall be at the end of days, the mountain of the House of the LORD shall be established at the head of the mountains" [Isaiah 2:2].[9]

There is robust discussion in the secondary literature whether Maimonides subscribed to Plato's notion of the philosopher king. In the *Guide*, Maimonides cites but a single work of Plato: *Timaeus*.[10] If Maimonides was at all familiar with the drift of the *Republic*, it was only through the channeling of al-Farabi.[11] And while al-Farabi—whom Maimonides held in the highest esteem after Aristotle[12]—embraced the Platonic notion of placing the philosopher as ruler of the state, in Maimonides' own system, as laid out in the

Guide, it seems that the prophet has replaced the philosopher as ruler.[13] (Unable to find presence of the philosopher ideal in the *Guide*, both Shlomo Pines and Steven Harvey resorted to the *ad hominem* argument, finding Maimonides to have led the lifestyle of a philosopher-statesman.)[14]

It should not come as a shock that undoubtedly one of the most imaginative of charismatic teachers, the master storyteller Rabbi Nahman of Breslov, greatly enhanced Maimonides' depiction of the Messiah. In some respects their Messianic scenarios tally, but in other respects they diverge widely.

For two centuries, the contents of Rabbi Nahman's prophecy concerning the Messiah were kept secret within the confines of the Breslov community. In the recently released *Scroll of Secrets* (*Megillat Setarim*), wherein Rabbi Nahman paints a vivid picture of the future redeemer, we read that the Messiah "will be accepted as the halakhic authority throughout Israel" (starting at age twelve!).[15] Thus, the Messiah is well within Maimonides' framework of "studying Torah." Or, as Rabbi Nahman puts it: "He begins to scrutinize the Torah until he attains deep insights."[16]

Not all of the Messiah's day will be devoted to fielding *"she'elot u-teshuvot"* (questions of Jewish Law). "The daily schedule" will include "an hour in which...he will practice contemplative religious introspection (*hitbodedut*)."[17] Even that is not revolutionary from the Maimonidean perspective. Maimonides had prescribed solitude and contemplation as part of the daily regimen.[18]

However, beyond the scholarly and introspective side to Messiah's personality, Rabbi Nahman has restored his musical ability:

> And he will make new musical instruments and songs, for his genius in song will be very great. He will innovate in this art such that the souls of those who hear his songs will faint.[19]

The Sages may have been as contemptuous of Homer as Plato was (though for perhaps different reasons),[20] but that did not prevent them from envisioning the ruler of the future Hebrew republic as a poet in addition to Teacher of the Law.

As we have seen, Maimonides' role model for the Messiah was King David. The *Midrash Tehillim* has David praying "that men not read his words [i.e., the Psalms] as they read the books of Homer, but read them and study them so that they receive reward for them as they would for studying *Nega'im* and *Ohalot* (titles of two tractates of the Mishnah)."[21]

Let us return to King Hezekiah. Hezekiah is portrayed by the Sages as an unequalled disseminator of Torah:

He stuck a sword at the entrance to the study house and declared: "Whoever does not engage in study of Torah shall be stabbed by this sword!"

[Subsequently,] they inspected from Dan to Beer Sheba and found no ignoramus; from Gevat to Antipras and found no lad or lass, man or woman, who was unfamiliar with the laws of purity and impurity.[22]

Yet this truly amazing accomplishment, the phenomenal propagation of Torah study, was deemed insufficient when deciding Hezekiah's final status as Messiah. Though missing from Maimonides' *Laws of Kings* (*Hilkhot Melakhim*), a definite desideratum of King Messiah is that he be an accomplished *poet*.

---

[1] The Hebrew phrase, *"ha-sharim ve-ha-sharot,"* is a quote from 2 Chronicles 35:25.

[2] *Genesis Rabbah* 48:14; *Exodus Rabbah* 47:5. In the Midrash, Rabbi Meir quotes the maxim in Aramaic.

[3] See *Teshuvot ha-Rambam*, ed. Alfred Freimann (Jerusalem: Mekize Nirdamim, 1934), p. lix; quoted in Samuel K. Mirsky, *Commentary by R. Jonathan of Lunel on Mishnah and Alfasi Tractates Megillah and Mo'ed Katan* [Hebrew] (Jerusalem: Sura, n.d. [1956]), p. 12.

[4] Moses Maimonides, *Commentary to the Mishnah, Sanhedrin* 10:1 (Kafah edition, pp. 140-141). In his note, Rabbi Yosef Kafah writes that it is known that Maimonides was not an aficionado of "the poets and poetesses" (understatement) and refers the reader to *Pe'er ha-Dor*, no. 41. Published in Amsterdam in 1765, *Pe'er ha-Dor* is an early arrangement of Maimonides' responsa. Perhaps ironically, Rabbi Kafah would later impugn the ostensible exchange between the sages of Lunel and Maimonides. Thereupon, Rabbi Yitzhak Shilat took up the cudgels on behalf of the responsa to the sages of Lunel, defending their authenticity. See *Sefer Zikaron le-Harav Yitzhak Nissim*, ed. Meir Benayahu, vol. 2 (Jerusalem, 1985), pp. 235-252, 253-256.

For further reading on Maimonides' attitude toward poetry, see: H.

Schirmann, "Maimonides and Hebrew Poetry" (Hebrew), *Moznayim* 3 (1935):433-436; Yosef Tobi, *Between Hebrew and Arabic Poetry: Studies in Spanish Medieval Hebrew Poetry* (Leiden: Brill, 2010), pp. 422-466 ("Maimonides' Attitude Towards Secular Poetry, Secular Arab and Hebrew Literature, Liturgical Poetry, and Towards Their Cultural Environment").

[5] Moses Maimonides, *Commentary to the Mishnah, Avot* 1:16 (Kafah edition, pp. 273-274).

[6] Ibid. p. 274. See *b. Sanhedrin* 101a.

[7] Moses Maimonides, *Guide of the Perplexed* I, 59 (Pines translation, p. 141).

[8] *Mishneh Torah, Hil. Melakhim* 11:4.

[9] *Mishneh Torah, Hil. Teshuvah* 9:2.

It is possible that at this early stage of his writings, Maimonides had in mind to combine the Platonic ideal of the philosopher-king (assuming Solomon was a philosopher) and the ideal of the prophet-ruler that would later be espoused in the *Guide*. On Solomon in contradistinction to Moses, see *Guide* III, 54 (Pines translation, p. 633).

[10] Moses Maimonides, *Guide of the Perplexed* II, 13 (Pines translation, p. 283).

Inter alia, young Josef Solowiejczyk originally planned to write his doctoral dissertation at the Friedrich-Wilhelms-Universität of Berlin on the topic of "Maimonides and Plato," to demonstrate that Maimonides had been misconstrued as an Aristotelian, but unfortunately could find no *Doktorvater* to sponsor the project. See Aharon Lichtenstein, "R. Joseph Soloveitchik," in *Great Jewish Thinkers of the Twentieth Century*, ed. Simon Noveck (Clinton, Mass: B'nai B'rith, 1963), p. 285.

[11] See Leo Strauss, *Philosophie und Gesetz* (Berlin, 1935); idem, «Quelques remarques sur la science politique de Maimonide et de Farabi,» *Revue des Etudes Juives*, C (1936), pp. 1-37; Moses Maimonides, *Guide of the Perplexed*, transl. Shlomo Pines (Chicago: University of Chicago Press, 1964), Translator's Introduction, pp. lxxvi, lxxviii-xcii; Steven Harvey, "Maimonides in the Sultan's Palace" in *Perspectives on Maimonides: Philosophical and Historical Studies*, ed. Joel L. Kraemer (Oxford: Oxford University Press, 1991), p. 51, n. 16.

[12] Shlomo Pines, op. cit., p. lxxviii (referring to Maimonides' letter to Ibn Tibbon on p. lx).

[13] See Pines, op. cit., pp. lxxxviii-lxxxix.

[14] Pines, op. cit., p. lxxxix; Harvey, "Maimonides in the Sultan's Palace," pp. 47-75.

[15] Zvi Mark, *The Scroll of Secrets: The Hidden Messianic Vision of R. Nachman of Breslav* (Brighton, Mass.: Academic Studies Press, 2010), p. 55. Rabbi Nahman's vision of the Messiah as a *"moreh hora'ah"* (halakhic authority) may have been inspired by the portrayal of King David in rabbinic lore. See *b. Berakhot* 4a.

[16] Mark, pp. 55-56.

In an appendix to Rabbi David Sears' study of Rabbi Nahman's single poem, I explored how Rabbi Nahman interfaces with Maimonides. See Bezalel Naor, *"Shir Na'im* as a Reply to Maimonides," in Rabbi Nachman of Breslov, *Shir Na'im/Song of Delight*, transl. David Sears (Spring Valley, NY: Orot, 2005), pp. 123-126. (Available in the present collection on pp. 237-246.)

[17] Mark, p. 53.

[18] See *Guide of the Perplexed* III, 51; Harvey, "Maimonides in the Sultan's Palace," p. 68ff.

[19] Mark, p. 59.

Though Rabbi Nahman may have expressed reservations concerning the medium of poetry, he did bequeath to us a single magnificent poem, *Shir Na'im*. Rabbi David Sears viewed the poem as a summation of Rabbi Nahman's teachings over the course of a lifetime. See Rabbi Nachman of Breslov, *Shir Na'im/Song of Delight*, transl. David Sears, especially pp. 115-117 ("Rabbi Nachman and Poetry").

[20] See *m. Yadayim* 4:6; commentary of Hai Gaon *ad locum*; and discussion in Saul Lieberman, *Hellenism in Jewish Palestine* (New York, 1994), pp. 105-114. Unlike the Gaon who read in the Mishnah *"Homeros,"* Maimonides read *"Miram,"* for which he supposed a Hebrew derivation. (See Maimonides, *Commentary to the Mishnah*, Kafah ed., pp. 442-443.) This is less baffling than Maimonides' acceptance of an Aramaic provenance for "Epicurus" in the Mishnah, *Sanhedrin* 10:1 (Kafah ed., p. 140). Cf. Rashi, *Sanhedrin* 99b, s.v. *megalleh panim ba-Torah*.

[21] *Midrash Tehillim*, chap. 1 (Buber ed., 5a); quoted in Lieberman, op. cit., pp. 110-111.

[22] *b. Sanhedrin* 94b.

Messiah's Donkey of a Thousand Colors

TO THE STATE OF ISRAEL
ON ITS SEVENTIETH BIRTHDAY
1948-2018

In *Perek Helek*, the final chapter of Tractate *Sanhedrin* (98a), famous for its discussions of eschatological issues, we find a focus on the speed of Messiah's arrival (or lack thereof).

Rabbi Joshua ben Levi juggles two sets of seemingly opposite prophecies. In the first opposition, we have Isaiah prophesying: "In its time, I will hasten it."[1] Which is it? Will the redemption be on time or speeded up? Rabbi Joshua ben Levi reconciles the two by saying that this depends on the merits of Israel. If they merit, it will be accelerated; if they do not merit, it will be on schedule.

Next, the Rabbi is bothered by the discrepancy between Zechariah's vision and Daniel's vision. Daniel depicted the Messiah "coming with the clouds of heaven like a son of man."[2] The implication is, as Rashi put it succinctly: *"Bi-mehirut."* ("With speed.") Zechariah, on the other hand, pictured a plodding Messiah, "poor and riding on a donkey."[3] Rashi supplies the key word: *"Be-'atslut."* ("With lassitude.") Once again, Rabbi Joshua ben Levi judiciously mediates between the conflicting reports: "If they merit, 'with the clouds of heaven'; if they do not merit, 'a poor man, riding on a donkey.'"

Messiah

This segment of the Talmudic discussion is fairly well known. It is the third and final paragraph of this seminar on Messianism, which though less quoted in the literature, may prove most fascinating.

> Shabur Malka (King Shapur I) said to Samuel: "You say that Messiah comes on a donkey. I will send him a lightning-fast horse (*susa barqa*) that I have."
>
> Samuel replied to him: "Do you have one of a thousand colors?"

Rashi fleshes out Samuel's retort: "Do you have a horse of a hundred colors such as Messiah's donkey?"

(The discussion between the Persian king and the Babylonian sage took place in Farsi. Where Rashi has a hundred colors, we will adopt Rabbi Nathan ben Yehiel of Rome's more precise translation from the Farsi, *"khar hazar gawna"* ["a donkey of a thousand colors"]. Thus Samuel replied: "Do you have a donkey of a thousand colors?")[4]

Rashi sums up by saying that Samuel pushed back with any old response. In other words, Shapur was cynical about the Jews' belief in Messiah and, accordingly, received from Samuel an equally flippant reply. Evidently, Rashi did not attach much significance to the variegated donkey.

While Rashi left it at that, one of our greatest theologians, Maharal of Prague, took up the challenge: "And I say that [Samuel] returned to him *a very deep wisdom* by saying that it has a hundred colors."⁵ Emboldened by Maharal's example, let us re-examine the dialogue or religious disputation between Shapur and Samuel.

Shapur offers his lightning-fast steed (*susya barqa*). This is tantalizingly reminiscent of *Al-Buraq*, the flying horse of the Islamic hadiths.⁶ In Greek mythology, there was Pegasus. Scholars assume that Islamic tradition drew on older myths. Perhaps Shapur's *susya barqa* prefigures Muhammad's *Al-Buraq* (from the Arabic *barq* for "lightning"). Assuming the identification is correct, this Persian Pegasus travelled from Iran to the Arabian Peninsula where it became the vehicle for Muhammad's night journey and ascent to heaven. Later with the Islamic conquest, *Al-Buraq* returned to Iran, where it figures prominently in Persian iconography.

The Sasanid monarch was chiding the Jewish People for their Messiah dragging his feet, so to speak. Samuel revealed a dimension of the Messiah of which the king was totally unaware: The donkey of Messiah possesses a thousand colors.

What does the donkey of Messiah symbolize? Rav Kook, in his eulogy for Herzl the man (and Zionism the movement) explained that the *hamor* of Messiah is the *homer*, the raw material, the naturalistic setting which serves as the vehicle of the redemption.⁷ (Earlier, Maharal made the connection between *hamor* and *homer*.)⁸

There were sages who whimsically exclaimed: *"Yeitei ve-lo ahmineh!"* "May Messiah come and may I not see him!"⁹ The advent of Israel's redemption will be fraught with such trials and tribulations—*"hevlei Mashiah"* ("birth pangs of Messiah")—that more than one sage dreaded to see Messiah in the flesh.

Rav Yosef—the hero of Rav Kook's eulogy—shot back a stunning reply: "May Messiah come, and may I merit to sit in the shadow of the dung of his donkey!"[10] Rav Yosef was willing to descend three levels just to participate in the redemption. If the donkey is not lowly enough, then the droppings of the donkey; and if the droppings are not dark enough, then the shadow cast by those droppings.

For Rav Kook, secular Zionism, with its emphasis on the material aspect of nationhood, was the symbolic "Donkey of Messiah." And if Rav Kook's unpacking of the Messianic mythos is on the mark, then a "donkey of a thousand colors" is a State of Israel which is variegated.

Recently there was revealed to the outside world Rabbi Nahman of Breslov's *Scroll of Secrets* (*Megillat Setarim*). This is the great Hasidic master's prophecy concerning the Messiah. The document, heavily encrypted, was handed from generation to generation within the confines of the tight-knit Breslov community. Recently, Zvi Mark gained access to the *Scroll* and published it in book form.[11] Initially, the *Scroll* elicited disappointment. Readers expected that Rabbi Nahman, like Nostradamus before him, would assign dates or perhaps precise coordinates. Actually, Rabbi Nahman provided us with something more valuable: a glimpse into the "thousand colors" of the Messiah. Patterned after the paradigm of King Solomon and to an extent Rabbi Nahman's own personality—as Professor Mark observes—the Messiah envisioned by Rabbi Nahman exhibits genius in many different fields. He excels in realms as diverse as *Halakhah* and horticulture, medicine and music.

When we extrapolate to the collective "Donkey of Messiah," the modern State of Israel, we discover that it too is at the forefront of multiple fields of endeavor: agriculture, medicine, the military, music, and cyber-technology, to name a few.

Israel's redemption is no flying horse, no *susya barqa*. It is in Kookian terminology, a *tahalikh ha-go'el*, a redemptive process, slow and arduous. But it has something unknown to the King of Persia. Our redemption is a polychromatic phenomenon. "A donkey of a thousand colors."

---

[1] Isaiah 60:22.
[2] Daniel 7:13.
[3] Zechariah 9:9.
[4] See Rabbi Nathan ben Yehiel of Rome, *'Arukh*, s.v. *khar*; and Alexander Kohut, *Aruch Completum*, Part Four, (Vienna 1891), p. 178, s.v. *kar*.
[5] Rabbi Judah ben Bezalel Löw, *Hiddushei Aggadot* ad loc.
[6] The remarkable linguistic similarity was duly noted by the lexicographer Alexander Kohut. See his *Aruch Completum*, Part Two (Vienna 1878), p. 201, s.v. *barqa* 4.
[7] See "The Lamentation in Jerusalem," in Bezalel Naor, *When God Becomes History: Historical Essays of Rabbi Abraham Isaac Hakohen Kook* (New York, NY; Kodesh Press, 2016), p. 49.
[8] See Rabbi Judah ben Bezalel Löw, *Netsah Yisrael*, chap. 36; and idem, *Hiddushei Aggadot, Sanhedrin* 98.
[9] *b. Sanhedrin* 98b.
[10] Ibid.
[11] Zvi Mark, *The Scroll of Secrets: The Hidden Messianic Vision of R. Nachman of Breslav* (Brighton, Mass.: Academic Studies Press, 2010).

X

BOOK REVIEWS

The Maggid of Kozhnits

**Rabbi Israel ben Shabtai Hopstein. *'Avodat Yisrael*
(B'nei Berak: Pe'er mi-Kedoshim, 5773/2013)**

Rabbi Israel ben Shabtai Hopstein, the Maggid of Kozienice (or more commonly, the "Kozhnitser Maggid") (d. 1814) was a major figure in the third generation of East-European Hasidism founded by Rabbi Israel Ba'al Shem Tov, and specifically, a towering luminary within Polish Hasidism.

Like his contemporary, Rabbi Shneur Zalman of Liozhno (and later Liadi), Rabbi Israel studied under Rabbi Dov Baer, the Maggid of Mezritch (who led the Hasidic movement after the death of the founder, Ba'al Shem Tov). Interestingly enough, Rabbi Kalonymos Kalman Shapira of Piaseczna, who achieved immortality as the "Rebbe of the Warsaw Ghetto," viewed those two as leading expositors of Kabbalah, juxtaposing "the Kabbalah of the Rav [Shneur Zalman] and the Kabbalah of the Maggid of Kozienice."[1]

However, whereas Rabbi Shneur Zalman's most famous work, *Tanya*, has earned the sobriquet (at least among HaBaD Hasidim) "the Written Torah of Hasidism" (*"Torah she-bi-Ketav shel Hasidut"*), unfortunately, Rabbi Israel's magnum opus, *'Avodat Yisrael* (*Service of Israel*), a commentary on the Pentateuch, has suffered neglect. Until today, the book has been an example of poor typography. First published in 1842, *'Avodat Yisrael* has been reissued periodically with pitifully broken letters of "Rashi" script (today unfamiliar to Hebrew readers without rabbinic training). About now, the cognoscenti will chime in, *"Afilu Sefer Torah she-be-heikhal tsarikh mazal"* ("Even a Torah scroll in the ark requires luck") and *"Habent sua fata libelli"* ("Books have their fates").

Thankfully, this horrendous situation has now been remedied. Enter Pe'er mi-Kedoshim, a publishing concern headed by Rabbi Israel Menachem Alter of Gur. Pe'er mi-Kedoshim has committed itself to re-issuing the classic texts of Hasidic thought in deluxe, state-of-the-art editions. The Kozhnitser Maggid's *'Avodat Yisrael* is the premier volume in a series envisioned to include: *Degel Mahaneh Ephraim* by Ba'al Shem Tov's grandson, Rabbi Moshe Hayyim Ephraim of Sudilkov (next on the agenda); *No'am Elimelekh* by Rabbi Elimelekh of Lizhensk; *Zot Zikaron* by Rabbi Jacob Isaac Horowitz (the "Seer of Lublin"), et cetera.

The book displays all the benefits that the modern age of Hebrew printing has brought to the sacred realm. The cursive "Rashi" script has been replaced by the square characters familiar to every Hebrew reader, which have then been provided with vowel points and modern punctuation. Sidebars caption the highlights of the Maggid's comments. Footnotes reference sources in rabbinic and kabbalistic literature, as well as cross-referencing to parallel passages in the Maggid's own works. As is customary, the book is preceded by the *"Toledot"* (Biography) of the Author and followed by *"Maftehot"* (Indices). (At present these indices are purely topical. It is hoped that in the future there will be included an index of the works cited by the Maggid, which will allow students of his thought a glimpse of his library, and the horizon of his intellectual world.)

Quoting the Psalmist, "Who can understand errors?" (Psalms 19:12), the editors have encouraged readers to offer constructive criticism, including pointing out errata in the present printing. Let us take them up on their kind offer.

In *Parashat Bereshit*, end s.v. *vayyasem Hashem le-Kayin 'ot* (6a), the Maggid observes "that there are times when miracles are performed by the Other Side, as we find in the *Gemara*, and in the *Midrash, Parashat Toledot*, that through Arginiton miracles were performed for Rabbi Judah the Prince and his companions, and the Omnipresent has many emissaries." Where the Maggid alludes to an unspecified "*Gemara*," the editors have supplied within the text itself, within parentheses, "*Me'ilah* 17b." If one consults the text of that passage in the *Talmud Bavli*, one discovers that it concerns miracles wrought by Ben Temalyon (name of a demon) for Rabbi Shim'on ben Yohai during his mission to Rome. When offered the demon's help, rather than rebuffing him, Rabbi Shim'on resigned himself to accepting his intervention by saying: *"Yavo' ha-ness mi-kol makom."* ("Let the miracle come from any place.") This statement of Rabbi Shim'on is similar in tenor to the Maggid's conclusion: *"Harbeh sheluhim la-Makom."* ("The Omnipresent has many emissaries.") Clearly, the editors have read the text of *'Avodat Yisrael* in a disjointed fashion, interpreting that the *"Gemara"* and the *"Midrash, Parashat Toledot"* refer to two different stories.

My own reading of the situation is that the *"Gemara"* and the *"Midrash, Parashat Toledot"* refer to the identical story whereby

Rabbi Judah the Prince and his companions were spared the imperial wrath of Diocletian through the intervention of the demon Arginiton (or in the version of the *Yerushalmi*, "Antigris").[2] The "Gemara" of course is not the *Gemara Bavlit*, but the *Gemara Yerushalmit*, and the reference is to the *Talmud Yerushalmi* at the end of the eighth chapter of *Terumot*.[3]

In *Parashat Shemot*, beginning s.v. *ve-sham'u le-kolekha* (91a), the Maggid writes that Moses was confronted with a conundrum. On the one hand, he was pressing for some kind of divine assurance that his mission to Egypt be crowned with success and that the Hebrews indeed hearken to his voice. On the other hand, he was concerned that by its very nature a divine guarantee would rob the Hebrews of their free will, forcing them into belief. The assumption is that the Hebrews were redeemed from Egypt in the merit of their faith or *emunah*. (See *Exodus Rabbah, Beshallah* [*parashah* 23] playing on the words "*tashuri me-rosh Amanah*" [Song of Songs 4:8].) It is a tribute to the originality of the Kozhnitser Maggid that while most Biblical commentators busied themselves with the philosophic problem of God's hardening the heart of Pharaoh, thereby depriving him of the free will to respond affirmatively to the divine demands, the Maggid explored in the opposite direction the problem of preserving the Hebrews' free will to disbelieve. The Maggid's solution to the problem involves some rather esoteric doctrines of Kabbalah, namely "*hanhagat gadlut*" ("governance of greatness") versus "*hanhagat katnut*" ("governance of smallness"), best left for the adept in Jewish mysticism. I would just point out for the record that the editors missed a cue here. When the Maggid writes "'*Ve-hen' she-hu ahat*," he is clearly referencing the *Talmud*

Bavli, Shabbat 31b: *"She-ken bi-leshon yevani korin le-ahat 'hen.'"* (*"Hen* in Greek is one.")

In the section for the festival of *Shavu'ot*, s.v. *u-Moshe 'alah el ha-Elohim* (200a), the Maggid writes: "Since all Israel prepared themselves for the sanctity of the Lord, and a leader is commensurate to his generation, therefore Moses was able to ascend above." Now the crucial words, the key to understanding this thought, *"parnas lefi doro"* ("a leader is commensurate to his generation"), have been emended by the editors to: *"kol ehad le-fi koho"* ("each according to his ability"). Granted that in the old edition there was some fuzziness concerning these words (*"parush lefi doro"*), they could still be made out simply by correcting *"parush lefi doro"* to *"parnas lefi doro,"* a well-known Hebrew adage. In the present version, one is at a loss to glean the Maggid's meaning. (I see now that the wording *"kol ehad lefi koho"* does occur in the Warsaw 1878 edition of *'Avodat Yisrael.* Unfortunately, the edition I possess is without place or date. Unable to locate a copy of the *editio princeps* of 1842, I have no way of knowing which version occurs there.)

In *Parashat Mas'ei*, end s.v. *elleh mas'ei v'nei Yisrael* (240a), in regard to *Tish'ah be-Av*, the Maggid discusses the difference between the *"batei gava'ei"* ("inner chambers") and the *"batei bara'ei"* ("outer chambers"), alluded to by the Rabbis in *b. Hagigah* 5b. The Maggid's remarks in this passage are consonant with what he wrote elsewhere in *Ner Israel*, his commentary to the *Likkutim me-Rav Hai Gaon* (2a): "In the outer chambers there is sadness and mourning, but for one who is able to ascend to the inner chambers, to the will of the Creator, blessed be He, certainly there is happiness." (By the way, the kabbalists' reading of the passage in

Hagigah, while opposite Rashi's, coincides with the version of Rabbeinu Hananel. See Rabbi Shelomo Eliashov, *Hakdamot u-She'arim* [Piotrków, 1909], *sha'ar* 6, chap. 6, *"avnei milu'im"* [24b-27b].)

In *Parashat Devarim*, end s.v. *eleh ha-devarim* (246a) there is a quote from Rabbi Isaac Luria's commentary to the *Idra Zuta*. The Maggid supplies the exact page number: folio 120. The problem is that the passage does not occur there. The editors have left the reference in the text untouched. At least in a footnote we should be told that the quote may be found in Rabbi Jacob Zemah, *Kol ba-Ramah* (Korets, 1785), 122a.[4] See also Rabbi Hayyim Vital, *Sefer ha-Derushim* (Jerusalem, 5756 /1996), 214 (left column); and Rabbi Shalom Buzaglo, *Hadrat Melekh* (London, 5530/1770; photo offset B'nei Berak, 5734/1974), 139a.

In the section for *Tu be-Av*, s.v. *meyuhasot she-bahen* (256b-257a), the Maggid writes that there are times that *ki-ve-yakhol* (as it were), God so delights in Israel that He becomes as a young man (*bahur*). The Maggid writes that he has dealt with this in his commentary to the line in *Avot* (beginning chap. 6), "*Barukh she-bahar bahem u-ve-mishnatam.*" As the editors point out, the comment is not to be found in the Maggid's remarks on *Avot*. Instead, they refer us to a parallel passage in *Re'eh*, s.v. *ve-hinneh ha-Midrash* (270a). By the same token, they might have referred us to *Ner Israel* (commentary to *Likkutim me-Rav Hai Gaon*), 4b: "*Ve-nikra bahur ka-arazim....*"

In the section for Rosh Hashanah, there is a lengthy kabbalistic homily, the thrust of which is that on that day we ask the Holy One, blessed be He, to reinvest himself in the particular role of "*Elohei Yisrael*" ("God of Israel").

"The God of these [Jews] is asleep." Which is to say, [the nations] were not foolish enough to assert that the *Sibbat kol ha-Sibbot* (Cause of All Causes) is in a state of slumber, only "the God of these [Jews]," in other words, this particular *hanhagah* (governance) referred to as *"Elohei Yisrael"* (the God of Israel) is in a state of sleep…and unconsciousness, and He is but *"Elaha de-Elahaya"* (the God of Gods). Based on this, you will understand the *kavvanah* (mystical meditation) of Rabbi Isaac Luria for Rosh Hashanah, and we awaken Him by the *shofar* (ram's horn).[5]

The editors duly noted the reference to Rabbi Hayyim Vital, *Peri 'Ets Hayyim, Sha'ar ha-Shofar*, chap. 1. But what they should have noted is the following reference which would have been even more instructive:

> Now in the days of Mordechai was the mystery of the time of *dormita* of *Ze'ir Anpin*, and the mystery that Haman said, "There is (*yeshno*) one people spread and separated among the peoples" [Esther 3:8]. The Rabbis, of blessed memory, commented on the word *"yeshno,"* that Haman alleged "their God is asleep."
> (Rabbi Hayyim Vital, *Peri 'Ets Hayyim, Sha'ar ha-Purim*, beginning chap. 5)

The Holy Maggid loaded the *kavvanot* of Purim on to the *kavvanot* of Rosh Hashanah!

The Kozhnitser Maggid was a preeminent halakhist (specializing in *hetter 'agunot*, permitting wives of missing husbands to remarry), kabbalist, thinker (penning commentaries to the works of Maharal of Prague), and statesman. With all that, the following anecdote sent a shiver down my spine:

The Kozhnitser Maggid was on friendly terms with several prominent members of the Polish nobility. In the eighteenth century, Poland, dismembered and subjected to a tripartite division—whereby Prussia annexed the western portion of Poland; Austro-Hungary annexed Galicia in the south; and Russia annexed the east—simply ceased to exist. A certain Polish nobleman importuned the Maggid to intercede with Heaven on behalf of the Polish nation. The gentleman would not leave the Maggid's home until promised Polish independence. Finally, the Maggid foretold that at a time in the future Poland would once again be a sovereign nation—for a span of "three *shemitin*" (three sabbatical cycles or 21 years). When the Jews of Warsaw were being subjected to aerial bombardment by the Luftwaffe in September of 1939, they recalled the Maggid's prediction. In the aftermath of World War I, in 1918 to be precise, Poland once again declared its independence. Three *shemitin* had passed from 1918 until 1939. Warsaw capitulated to the Nazis on the eve of *Sukkot*, the *yahrzeit* of the Kozhnitser Maggid! This anecdote was told by a survivor of the Warsaw Ghetto, Joseph Friedenson, editor of *Dos Yiddishe Vort*, the Yiddish magazine of Agudath Israel of America (*"Toledot,"* p. 37).

The Maggid of Kozhnits

[1] Kalonymos Kalmish Shapira, *Hovat ha-Talmidim* (Jerusalem, 1990), p. 217. Besides being a descendant of the Kozhnitser Maggid, Rabbi Kalonymos Kalmish was the son-in-law of the Rebbe of Kozhnits of the day, Rabbi Yerahmiel Moshe Hopstein.

[2] See *Genesis Rabbah* 63:8. Rabbi Nathan of Rome, *'Arukh*, s.v. *Arganatin*, writes that this demon is a denizen of the bathhouse. Alexander Kohut's etymology, whereby the name is a compound of two Greek words, "argos nautis" (αργός ναύτης), or "swift sailor," is hardly convincing. (The same goes for the earlier suggestion of Benjamin Musafia.)

[3] In the biographical introduction to the book we are told that Rabbi Hayyim of Volozhin attested that the Kozhnitser Maggid was "familiar with *Talmud Yerushalmi*" (*"baki be-Shas Yerushalmi"*) (p. 30).

According to Rabbi El'azar Mordechai Kenig, a Kozhnitser Hasid, Rabbi Hayyim of Volozhin visited the Kozhnitser Maggid on several occasions. On one of those occasions, they exchanged views on the relative merits of the Hasidic leadership. See Rabbi Gedaliah Aaron Kenig, *Hayyei Nefesh* (Tel-Aviv, 1968), p. 89.

[4] I am indebted to Prof. Menachem Kallus for the correct address.

[5] *'Avodat Yisrael*, 290b.

Historians will have a field day trying to figure out how this element of Cardozan theology found its way into the writings of the Kozhnitser Maggid. The writings of Abraham Miguel Cardozo are forever offsetting the deistic notion of the other peoples ("philosophers and Ishmaelites") against the particularistic God of Israel (*Elohei Yisrael*), though the term Cardozo typically employs is the *"Sibbah Rishonah"* (First Cause), not the *"Sibbat kol ha-Sibbot"* (Cause of All Causes). See David J. Halperin, *Abraham Miguel Cardozo: Selected Writings* (Mahwah, NJ: Paulist Press, 2001), pp. 173-175. And when Cardozo does refer to the "Cause of all Causes," the Hebrew term he invariably employs is *"'Illat kol ha-'Illot,"* not *"Sibbat kol ha-Sibbot."*

An exception to this rule is found at the beginning of Cardozo's treatise, *Boker de-Avraham*. Discussing the belief system of "the second class, of the philosophers," he employs the term *"Sibbah le-khol ha-Sibbot"* for "Cause of all Causes." The treatise begins with the words, *"Bati le-faresh emunat avoteinu"* ("I have come to explain the faith of our fathers"). It is available in several manuscripts: See Library of the Hungarian Academy of Sciences, Budapest, Ms. Kaufmann A 232, p. 40; London Beth Din Ms. 124 = National Library of Israel Ms. Heb. 28°7405, f.1v.; Russian State Library, Moscow, Ms. Guenzburg 660, f.1v.; and Ms. Guenzburg 1109, f.2v.

(Scholem seems to equivocate whether the "Cause of all Causes" is identical in Cardozan theology with the "First Cause"; see Gershom Scholem, *Sabbatai Sevi: The Mystical Messiah* [Princeton, NJ: Princeton University Press, 1975], pp. 912-913.)

This opposition of the *Sibbah Rishonah* to *Elohei Yisrael* pervades the works later attributed (correctly or incorrectly) to Rabbi Jonathan Eybeschuetz, *Va-Avo ha-yom el ha-'ayin* and *Shem 'Olam*.

It may well be that the Kozhnitser Maggid was influenced in this respect by reading Pinhas Elijah Hurwitz of Vilna's *Sefer ha-Berit* (Brünn 1797), a work which enjoyed great popularity. (It appears that the Kozhnitser Maggid's contemporary, Rabbi Nahman of Breslov, delved into *Sefer ha-Berit*; see Mendel Piekarz, *Studies in Braslav Hasidism* [Hebrew] [Jerusalem: Mossad Bialik, 1995], pp. 249-252.)

Hurwitz devoted an entire chapter to the opposition of the philosophic notion of the *Sibbah Rishonah* to the particularist revelation of *Elohei Yisrael*, while, ironically enough, vilifying the man who promulgated this opposition: Abraham Cardozo! See *Sefer ha-Berit*, Part 1, *ma'amar* 20, chap. 15 (109a-111a).

Inter alia, Hurwitz speaks glowingly of Immanuel Hai Ricchi's *Yosher Levav*: "If you wish, beloved reader, to know who your Creator is, consult the aforementioned work, *Yosher Levav*" (ibid. 110b). (The quote from *Yosher Levav* which offsets the *Sibbah Rishonah* against *Ze'ir Anpin*, beginning with the words *"Ha-Kelal ha-'oleh,"* is to be found in the *editio princeps* of *Yosher Levav* [Amsterdam 1742] on 34a.) Elsewhere, I have dealt with crypto-Sabbatian passages in Ricchi's *oeuvre*; see Bezalel Naor, *Post-Sabbatian Sabbatianism* (Spring Valley, NY: Orot, 1999), pp. 53-57. For an original analysis of Cardozo's theology, see ibid. pp. 14-20.

I must confess that at the time I wrote *Post-Sabbatian Sabbatianism*, I mistakenly assumed that the reference to "philosophers and Ishmaelites" in *Sefer ha-Berit*, 110a, occurred in the quote from Rabbi Meir ibn Gabbai's *Derekh Emunah*. Upon inspection of *Derekh Emunah* (Padua, 1563), 4a, I see that those words in brackets were not in the original but issued from the pen of Pinhas Elijah Hurwitz. Thus, my statement at the conclusion of note 16 on page 159 of *Post-Sabbatian Sabbatianism* is erroneous. Again, "philosophers and Ishmaelites" (or in Halperin's rendition, "philosophers and Muslims") is a signature juxtaposition of Cardozo; see, e.g., chap. 7 of Cardozo's *Derush Zeh Eli ve-Anvehu*, transcribed in Gershom Scholem, "Two new theological texts by Abraham Cardozo" (Hebrew), *Sefunot*, vols. 3-4 (1960), pp. 281-282; translated to English by Halperin, op. cit., pp. 201-203.

In truth, Cardozo's fingerprints are all over the aforementioned chapter in *Sefer ha-Berit*, starting with Pharaoh's familiarity with the First Cause but ignorance of the God of Israel. Cf. *Derush Zeh Eli ve-Anvehu*, chaps. 13-14; in Scholem, pp. 292, 294; in Halperin, pp. 226, 229-230. It may be possible with further research to ascertain specifically which of Cardozo's sixty (!) manuscript works influenced Hurwitz.

"The Jackals" and "The Lion":
Animal Fables of Kafka and Rav Kook

In 1917, Franz Kafka (1883-1924), a surrealist writer living in Prague, published in Martin Buber's Zionist journal, *Der Jude*, a short story entitled "Jackals and Arabs." The plot of the story is rather simple; the meaning—like that of most of Kafka's works—continues to mystify readers to this day.

A European gentleman camped in the desert is approached by a pack of jackals who look to him as to the long-awaited savior. The oldest jackal explains that since time immemorial, generations upon generation of jackals have been waiting for his arrival. Momentarily, he presents the astonished guest "with a small pair of sewing scissors, covered with ancient rust," for the singular purpose of ridding the jackals of the Arabs, whom they detest, but whose yoke they are powerless to throw off. The interloper from the North politely demurs. In the next scene, an Arab chieftain arrives and proceeds to disabuse the European of the nonsense that the jackal blabbered to him. He explains that the Arabs keep jackals as pets, much as Europeans keep dogs. "They have the most lunatic hopes, these beasts; they're just fools, utter fools. That's why we like them; they are our dogs; finer dogs than any of yours." The Arab then cut up a camel carcass; the carrion was immediately snatched up by the jackals. "They had forgotten the Arabs, forgotten their hatred, the all-obliterating immediate presence of the stinking carrion bewitched them."

What is one to make of Kafka's parable? Given its context, it seems reasonable to assume that the Arabs are truly Arabs and the jackals—Jews. The Jews look to Europe to free them from Arab oppression in *Erets Yisrael*. The tool of their deliverance is sewing scissors, an unlikely choice of arms. Why scissors? Is Kafka poking fun at the Jews as being a nation of tailors?

(In a "contrapuntal" interpretation, Edward Said appropriated Kafka's parable for the cause of Palestinian liberation, whereby the "Arabs" become Jews, and the jackals—Palestinians. But then wouldn't Kafka have been guilty of mixing metaphors? Palestinians brandish a knife, not scissors. As they say in Yiddish: *"Nu, a kashya auf a mayseh!"* "A question on a tale!")

Some view Kafka's piece as uncannily prescient. Shortly thereafter in 1917, His Majesty's Government promised in the Balfour Declaration, "the establishment in Palestine of a national home for the Jewish people." Famous words. Unfortunately, the Balfour Declaration was a valueless paper. It would take another three decades for "Perfidious Albion" to lower the Union Jack and for General Sir Alan Cunningham, British High Commissioner for Palestine, to set sail from Haifa harbor for England. Kafka was right. Europe would not liberate the Jews of *Erets Yisrael*. How then, would the liberation be accomplished? That brings us to our next animal fable, by Abraham Isaac Hakohen Kook (1865-1935).

Not nearly as famous as Kafka's "Jackals and Arabs," Rav Kook's *"Ha-Aryeh ba-Sugar"* ("The Lion in the Cage") first appeared in print in Rabbi Moshe Zuriel's collection *Otserot ha-RAYaH* circa 1990. "The Lion in the Cage" is the story of an ancient lion, broken in spirit, living out his days within the confines of a cage. His cubs, who were born in captivity, know no better, and find their surroundings most comfortable, if not outright enjoyable. In fact, they are at a loss to understand what it is exactly that oppresses the spirit of the old lion. And then one day, the leonine patriarch reveals to them his secret:

> *There is a world full of light,*
> *Freedom and liberty prevail.*
> *There is a vast forest tall with trees*
> *And stately with mighty cedars.*
> *The fragrance is refreshing*
> *And free animals abound.*
> *When I was your age, my children,*
> *I ruled the forest with pride and might*
> *And all bowed before me.*
> *If not for my pursuers*
> *who broke my bones,*
> *and this cramped cage—*
> *I would still rule the forest,*
> *And you too would be free and proud.*

Learning the lie of their "gilded cage" existence, the lion cubs now look with deep dissatisfaction upon their environs. Eventually, this dissatisfaction will lead to a prison break:

The words of the Old One
strengthened the cubs' heart,
and with the might of lions
they began to break down the cramped cage.
With claws and jaws and the roar of lions
they frightened away their smug captors.
With a mighty spirit
imbued with the delight of the forest
they shattered the walls of the cramped cage.

And with that, lo and behold, the ancient lion was rejuvenated:

The Old One was suddenly alive,
his broken bones healed with joy.
Rebuking his enemies, he and his cubs returned
and established the kingdom of the forest.

Who is the ancient lion? Who are the lion cubs?

While lacking the haunting quality of a Kafkaesque story, neither is Rav Kook's tale totally transparent. Treading uncertain ground, we might say that the ancient lion represents the sages of Israel, who in exile preserved the memory of the homeland. The ancient sages were, alas, weak when it came to establishing facts on the ground. Yet they were able to communicate to the young an odium for exile, and to fan the spark of the longing for Zion. It was the youth of Israel, impudent, brazen Zionists, who, once their conscience, their Jewish identity had been pricked, threw off the yoke of the oppressor.

As for Kafka, today the *literati* debate whether this tormented genius was a Zionist or anti-Zionist. Perhaps it would be fair to say that Kafka lived in the elusive shadow of the legendary Golem of Prague, created by *Der Hohe Rabbi Loew* to act as a Jewish savior. When the Golem proved unruly, his creator was forced to pull the plug on him. A sleeping giant lying amid the *sheimos* ("sacred trash") up in the attic of the Altneuschul, the Golem is the stuff of which dreams are made.

Bridging the Kabbalistic Gap

Avinoam Fraenkel. *Nefesh HaTzimtzum* (2015)

Volume 1: Rabbi Chaim Volozhin's *Nefesh HaChaim* with Translation and Commentary
Volume 2: Understanding *Nefesh HaChaim* through the Key Concept of *Tzimtzum* and Related Writings

Recently there has been a spate of English translations of the classic of Mitnagdic philosophy, *Nefesh ha-Hayyim* by Rabbi Hayyim of Volozhin (1749-1821), eminent disciple of the Vilna Gaon. This is perhaps the most glorious—certainly the lengthiest—of the translations, one that attempts to rewrite the debate between Hasidim and *Mitnagdim*.

The present edition, the most extensive to date, is divided in two volumes. Volume One consists of a Hebrew-English edition of the entire book with the exception of the famous note by the author's son, Rabbi Isaac (Itzeleh) of Volozhin, known as *"Ma'amar Be-Tzelem."* That note and other related writings of Rabbi Hayyim have been translated in Volume Two. In a unique typesetting innovation, the translator divides the complex Hebrew sentences into phrases, easing the English reading.

In the lengthy introduction to Volume Two, entitled *"Tzimtzum—The Key to Nefesh HaChaim,"* Avinoam Fraenkel has carved out for himself a most ambitious goal: to tackle the perennial problem of latter-day Kabbalah, namely the Lurianic doctrine of *Tzimtzum* or divine self-contraction. Traditionally, there have been two schools of thought on the matter: those who hold *"Tzimtzum ki-peshuto,"* i.e., the doctrine is to be taken literally; and those convinced that *"Tzimtzum she-lo ki-peshuto,"* i.e., *Tzimtzum* is not to be taken literally. As Fraenkel points out, this terminology first gained currency in the debate between two Italian kabbalists, Rabbi Joseph Ergas (author of *Shomer Emunim*) and Rabbi Immanuel Hai Ricchi (author of *Yosher Levav*) back in 1736-7.[1]

Fraenkel's thesis is that even when things are *"pashut"* (simple), they truly are not so *"pashut"* (simple). Even when a kabbalist such as Rabbi Shelomo Eliashov (author of *Leshem Shevo ve-Ahlamah*) writes boldly that he understands the doctrine literally as did the author of *Yosher Levav*—that requires complexification.

You might ask: Of what concern is this rarefied debate to the masses of Jews living in the twenty-first century? Ah! It just so happens that many, if not most, historians have assumed that this debate, which translates into transcendentalist versus immanentist theology, was at the heart of the terrible controversy between the *Mitnagdim* and Hasidim that tore apart East European Jewry in the late eighteenth century. At that time, the Vilna Gaon issued a *herem*, an official rabbinic ban excommunicating the followers of the Ba'al Shem Tov.

If it can be proven that there is essentially no difference of theology between the *Tanya* (the "Bible" of Hasidism), written by Rabbi Shneur Zalman of Liadi, founder of the HaBaD school of

Hasidism, and the *Nefesh ha-Hayyim* (the *"Shulhan 'Arukh"* of Mitnagdic ideology), then we will have dissolved any continuing animus between Hasidim and *Mitnagdim*, and *"Shalom 'al Yisrael"* (Peace to Israel). This is the fondest wish of the author.

The truth is—as the author makes us aware—this is not the first attempt to smooth over theological differences between the *Tanya* and *Nefesh ha-Hayyim*. On the eve of World War Two, Rabbi Eliyahu Eliezer Dessler—a preeminent master of the Mussar school, *Mashgi'ah Ruhani* of Gateshead and later of the Ponevezh Yeshivah in B'nei Berak—then residing in London, wished to issue a proclamation to the effect that there is essentially no *mahloket*, no difference of opinion between Rabbi Shneur Zalman and Rabbi Hayyim regarding the correct interpretation of *Tzimtzum*. Rabbi Dessler's distinguished houseguest at the time was Rabbi Yitzhak Horowitz (known in Lubavitch as "Reb Itche Der Masmid," on account of his legendary *"hatmadah,"* or devotion to learning), who acted as fundraiser on behalf of the Lubavitcher Rebbe, Joseph Isaac Schneersohn. Rabbi Dessler asked Rabbi Horowitz to sign on the proclamation.

To make a long story short, eventually Rabbi Dessler's overtures were forwarded to the son-in-law of the Rebbe, Rabbi Menachem Mendel Schneerson (eventual successor to his father-in-law as Rebbe of Lubavitch), who penned a formal reply. For the life of him, Rabbi M.M. Schneerson could not fathom how someone with competence in Kabbalah (which Rabbi Dessler certainly did possess) could fail to see the obvious differences between the HaBaD and Volozhin understandings of *Tzimtzum*. (Rabbi Schneerson further outlined that there was a difference between the Vilna Gaon and his student Rabbi Hayyim of Volozhin regarding *Tzimtzum*, a point in the letter which continues to rile *Mitnagdim* to this day. In fact, Rabbi Yosef Zussman of Jerusalem, eminent disciple of Rabbi Ya'akov Moshe Harlap, wrote several unanswered letters to the Lubavitcher Rebbe, remonstrating how absurd it is to entertain the notion that Rabbi Hayyim, who adored his master the Gaon, disagreed with him on so basic an issue.)

Left without a "partner in peace" of the opposite camp, Rabbi Dessler's proclamation was buried. Where titans such as Rabbis Dessler and Schneerson could not see eye to eye, Avinoam Fraenkel certainly has his work cut out for him. Before we proceed further to the "nuts and bolts" of the *Tanya—Nefesh ha-Hayyim* debate, the reader may wish to listen to some music pleasing to the ear:

- When Rabbi Abraham Mordechai Alter, Rebbe of Gur ("*Imrei Emet*") asked Rav Kook how he knew so much *Hasidut*, Rav Kook responded that he had studied *Nefesh ha-Hayyim*.
- Rabbi Michael Eliezer Forshlager of Baltimore, a foremost student of Rabbi Avraham Bornstein, Rebbe of Sokhatchov (author of Responsa *Avnei Nezer*) carried in his *tallit* bag a volume which consisted of *Tanya* and *Nefesh ha-Hayyim* bound together at Rabbi Forshlager's special request.
- Once around the family table in Brooklyn, Rabbi Menachem Mendel Schneerson (by then Lubavitcher Rebbe) spoke so enthusiastically of *Nefesh ha-Hayyim* that his brother-in-law, Rabbi Shemariah Gurary, said in jest:

"Then perhaps we Hasidim should take to studying *Nefesh ha-Hayyim.*"

Back to the *mahloket*. What are the cold facts concerning the debate?

It is incontrovertible that Rabbi Hayyim has stood the *Zohar*'s terms *"memalé kol 'almin"* ("filling all worlds") and *"sovev kol 'almin"* ("surrounding all worlds") on their heads. What for the *Tanya* is *"memalé kol 'almin,"* is for *Nefesh ha-Hayyim, "sovev kol 'almin,"* and vice versa. Rabbi Shelomo Fisher of Jerusalem has written that this is merely semantics.[2] Others read into the shift of terminology a substantive controversy as to *Weltanschauung*. What for Hasidism is common experience, namely the immanence, the immediate presence of God, is for Mitnagdism a recondite mystery reserved for the elite.

In the words of Rabbi Eizik of Homel, a major disciple of Rabbi Shneur Zalman of Liadi and of his son, Rabbi Dov Baer of Lubavitch (*Mitteler Rebbe*):

> This belief is possessed by all the Hasidim, but the *Mitnagdim*, even those who are not etc. [the word etc. occurs in the original], do not have this faith, only in a very, very concealed manner, as Israel were in Egypt....They have no room for this faith that *Altz iz Gott* (All is God).[3]

Fraenkel observes that much of the "poisoning of the waters" was brought about by the publication of a spurious letter attributed to the *"Alter Rebbe,"* Rabbi Shneur Zalman, in the anonymous

Matzref ha-'Avodah (Koenigsberg, 1858). Later the letter was incorporated in Heilman's more responsible *Beit Rebbi* (Berdichev, 1902). In the forged epistle, Rabbi Shneur Zalman writes that it has come to his awareness that the Vilna Gaon understands *Tzimtzum* literally.

This letter contributed to Rabbi Menachem Mendel Schneerson's formulation concerning the Vilna Gaon's view of *Tzimtzum*. One might mistakenly assume that once the letter is exposed as a forgery, HaBaD should have no problem accepting that there truly was no disagreement between the two rival camps concerning *Tzimtzum*. But Fraenkel knows that this is not the end of his troubles.

There is the matter of the passage in the second part of *Tanya* (titled *Sha'ar ha-Yihud ve-ha-Emunah*) which reserves some pretty harsh language for the literalists:

> ...the error of some wise men in their own eyes, may the Lord forgive them, who erred and were mistaken in their study of the writings of the ARI [i.e., Rabbi Isaac Luria], of blessed memory, and understood the doctrine of *Tzimtzum* mentioned there literally, that the Holy One, blessed be He, withdrew Himself and His essence, God forbid, from this world, only that He supervises from above.[4]

Who are the unnamed villains of this passage? To endeavor to answer this question, we would do well to research the printing history of the *Tanya*. The passage in question was missing from all editions of the *Tanya* printed before the year 1900. In that year, the passage surfaced in the Romm edition printed in Vilna at the behest of Rabbi Shalom Dov Baer Schneersohn of Lubavitch. Until that time, it had been preserved in manuscript in the keeping of the heirs of the *Ba'al ha-Tanya*. That means that for over a century since the *Tanya* was first printed in Slavuta in 1796, this sensitive piece—a sort of *J'accuse*, if you will—was suppressed. Why was it ever suppressed to begin with, and why was it finally revealed in 1900?

An obvious solution would be that the passage obliquely lambasted the Vilna Gaon, and it was not until a century later that a direct descendant of the author felt that times had changed and that the sociological "climate" had warmed sufficiently to allow for an unexpurgated version of the *Tanya* to appear in print. This time, no *herem* would be issued in Vilna.

And for the record, Rabbi Menachem Mendel was not the first Schneerson to assume that the Gaon understood *Tzimtzum* literally. Earlier, the Rebbe of Kopyst, Rabbi Shelomo Zalman Schneerson (1830-1900), author of *Magen Avot*, wrote in a letter to Rabbi Don Tumarkin: "This is the entire subject of *Tzimtzum*, and this is the Hasidism of the Ba'al Shem Tov and the Maggid, may they rest in peace, that the *Tzimtzum* is not to be taken literally, as opposed to the opinion of the *Mishnat Hasidim* [i.e., Rabbi Immanuel Hai Ricchi] and the Gaon Rabbi Elijah, of blessed memory."[5]

Fraenkel is not willing to accept that the passage in *Tanya* is directed at the Vilna Gaon or earlier Rabbi Immanuel Hai Ricchi. He stands in good company. Upon receipt of Hayyim Yitzhak

Bunin's *Mishneh HaBaD* II (Warsaw, 1933), Rav Kook wrote back to the author requesting that he retract his statement that the pejorative "wise men in their own eyes" refers to the author of *Mishnat Hasidim* and the Gaon of Vilna.[6]

But then the question remains. Who are the "bad guys" of the *Tanya*? Fraenkel would have us believe that the reference is to the likes of the crypto-Sabbatian Nehemiah Hiyya Hayyon, against whom Ergas inveighed in his polemical works *Tokhahat Megulah* and *Ha-Tzad Nahash* (London, 1715).[7]

If that were the case, the language of the *Tanya* is too mild and reserved. Sabbatians (believers in the pseudo-Messiah Shabtai Tzevi) are usually treated to much more invective, such as "blasted be their bones." There is a parallel passage in the work of Rabbi Aaron Halevi Horowitz of Staroshelye, *Sha'arei ha-Yihud ve-ha-Emunah*. There the language is even more compassionate and conciliatory. It is hard to imagine that the *Ba'al ha-Tanya* and his prime pupil Rabbi Aaron Halevi Horowitz would show such empathy towards a Sabbatian heresiarch. With very few exceptions, members of the rabbinate were not *"melamed zekhut"* when it came to deviants of the Sabbatian persuasion. The passage reads:

> ...As it occurred to some latter-day kabbalists who attempt to be wise (*mithakmim*)...to understand *Tzimtzum* literally, as if He contracted Himself, and this is a crime, and their sin is too great to forbear, but their merit is that they have not spoken all these things with premeditation, God forbid, but from lack of understanding. May the LORD

forgive them, "for in respect of all the people it was done in error" [Numbers 15:26].[8]

Tzimtzum-literalism is not a characteristically Sabbatian posture, nor is it the exclusive domain of Sabbatians. Rabbi Jacob Emden, the arch-nemesis of the Sabbatians, took *Tzimtzum* literally, drawing an analogy to the vacuum created by a pump.[9] In fact, Emden excoriated Ricchi for belaboring the point, when "certainly, absolutely, it is not to be construed other than literally, and it is one of the *a priori* assumptions for the believer in our holy religion, if not for anti-religious *apikorsim* who do not concede the creation of the world."[10]

There is another problem with deflecting the *Tanya*'s critique away from the Gaon of Vilna toward Sabbatian kabbalists. If Sabbatians were being targeted, then why did the passage need to be suppressed at all? The Vilna Gaon and his disciples were certainly condemnatory of Sabbatianism in all its guises, so there would have been nothing in the passage to give offense to the *Mitnagdim*, the opponents of Hasidism.

Fraenkel's work is much more difficult than that of Rabbi Dessler, for Fraenkel has tasked himself with harmonizing the view of Rabbi Shelomo Eliashov (1841-1926), author of the *Leshem*, as well. Rabbi Shelomo Eliashov wrote—both in his *Helek ha-Be'urim* and in his recently published correspondence with fellow Mitnagdic kabbalist Rabbi Naftali Herz Halevi Weidenbaum—that he subscribes to the literalist interpretation of *Tzimtzum* as described in Ricchi's *Yosher Levav*.[11] The *Leshem* went so far as to cast aspersions on the *Likkutim* printed at the conclusion of *Be'ur ha-Gra* to *Sifra di-Tzeni'uta*, which present a non-literal reading of *Tzimtzum*.[12]

Professor Mordechai Pachter was struck by the most incongruous dovetailing of the perspectives of Lubavitch and the *Leshem* concerning the Vilna Gaon's interpretation of *Tzimtzum*. Both ascribe to the Gaon a literalist interpretation.[13]

"To cut to the chase," Fraenkel's strategy for reconciling what appear glaring differences of opinion, involves invoking the kabbalistic theory of relativity, namely the distinction between the divine perspective and the human perspective. The Aramaic expressions that convey this thought are *"le-gabei dideh"* versus *"le-gabei didan."*[14] (In *Nefesh ha-Hayyim*, the Hebrew terms *"mi-tsido"/"mi-tsideinu"* serve the same purpose.)[15] This distinction is certainly a valuable tool but it should not be overused. It strikes this reader as overly simplistic to assume that all writers (with the exception of Sabbatians) who grasp *Tzimtzum* literally are necessarily writing from the human perspective, while writers who understand *Tzimtzum* non-literally are necessarily writing from the divine perspective. And if the distinction should not be overused, *a fortiori* it should not be misused. To ascribe the human perspective (as opposed to divine perspective) to Rabbi Immanuel Hai Ricchi when he clearly writes the opposite, is to do violence to his words. A key passage in his *Yosher Levav* (quoted in fact by Fraenkel) reads:

Therefore relative to us (*le-gabei didan*), it is as if there was no *Tzimtzum* and we can say that the *Tzimtzum* is not literal. However, relative to the *Ein Sof* (*le-gabei ha-Ein Sof*) itself, it is literal.[16]

How it is then possible to flip around the author's mindset and reverse his stated position, is beyond me.

At day's end, the warring factions within *Knesset Yisrael* may have to make peace with their differences of opinion intact, even in the matter of *Tzimtzum*.

---

[1] Prof. Menachem Kallus confided to the writer (BN) that in his estimation the earliest discussion whether *Tzimtzum* was intended literally or not, is to be found in the notes to Rabbi Hayyim Vital's *'Ets Hayyim* penned by Rabbi Meir Poppers (ca. 1624-1662). Poppers writes that it sounds to him as if Luria's disciples Rabbi Hayyim Vital and Rabbi Yosef ibn Tabul understood from the Rav (i.e., Isaac Luria) that "the *Tzimtzum* is literal" (*"ha-tzimtzum ke-mishma'o"*). See Rabbi Meir Poppers, *'Or Zaru'a*, ed. Safrin and Sofer (Jerusalem: Hevrat Ahavat Shalom, 1986), *Sha'ar ha-'Iggulim ve-ha-Yosher*, chap. 2 (p. 29).
[2] See *"Derush ha-Tefillin"* in Rabbi Shelomo Fisher, *Beit Yishai—Derashot* (Jerusalem, 2004), p. 355.
[3] Rabbi Eizik of Homel, *"Iggeret Kodesh"* (Holy Epistle) printed at the conclusion of *Hannah Ariel—Amarot Tehorot* (*Ma'amar ha-Shabbat*, etc.) (Berdichev: Sheftel, 1912), 4b.
[4] *Tanya* II, 7 (83a).
[5] Published in M.M. Laufer, *Ha-Melekh bi-Mesibo*, vol. 2 (Kefar Habad: Kehot, 1993), p. 286.
   Rabbi Shelomo Zalman's younger brother, Rabbi Shemariah Noah of Bobruisk, discusses the literalist interpretation of *Yosher Levav* (by Rabbi Immanuel Hai Ricchi, author of *Mishnat Hasidim*). See Rabbi Shemariah Noah Schneerson, *Shemen la-Ma'or*, vol. 1 (Kefar Habad, 1964), Bo, s.v. *ve-kakhah tokhlu 'oto*, par. 2 (f. 130).
[6] Rav Kook's manuscript, dated 3 Tamuz 5693 (i.e., 1933), was published in *Haskamot ha-RAYaH* (Jerusalem: Makhon RZYH Kook, 1988), no. 85 (pp. 104-105). In his letter to Bunin, Rav Kook insisted that at the earliest opportunity Bunin make amends for having slighted the honor of the authors of

Mishnat Hasidim and *Sha'arei Gan 'Eden* (and the Vilna Gaon).

Ironically, Rav Kook's maternal grandfather Raphael Felman was a *hasid* of the Rebbe of Kopyst.

Fraenkel dismisses out of hand the notion that the *Tanya* pilloried Ricchi because of the fact that references to Ricchi's *Mishnat Hasidim* figure prominently in the *Tanya*. See *Nefesh HaTzimtzum*, vol. 2, p. 79, n. 89. This argument is unconvincing. It is quite conceivable that the *Ba'al ha-Tanya* was fond of *Mishnat Hasidim*, a popular digest of Lurianic Kabbalah, while viewing Ricchi's other work *Yosher Levav* as being beyond the pale. And for the very reason that such a venerable kabbalist erred in his judgment concerning *Tzimtzum*, he was worthy of compassion. Cf. Rabbi Zadok Hakohen of Lublin:

> There were already found many great men, authors among the *mekubbalim* (kabbalists), who stumbled in this [i.e., *hagshamah*, or corporealization], including the author of *Yosher Levav*, who explained the matter of *Tzimtzum* and similarly many matters of Kabbalah in [terms of] total corporealization, as the understanding will recognize. I have spelled out his name, for some authors who came after him already publicized him in print, in order to clarify his errors in this respect. Behold he was a great and holy man, as is known, and erred only in his faith. Though this too is a great error and requires atonement (as explained above), nonetheless, it is not such a grievous sin, as explained in the words of the RABaD [i.e., Rabbi Abraham ben David of Posquières]...."
>
> (Rabbi Zadok Hakohen Rabinowitz, *Sefer ha-Zikhronot* in *Divrei Soferim* [Lublin, 1913], 32d)

The reference is to RABaD's animadversion to Maimonides' statement in *MT*, *Hil. Teshuvah* 3:7 that one who professes belief in a corporeal deity has the halakhic status of a *"min,"* or heretic. See *Hasagot ha-RABaD le-Mishneh Torah*, ed. Bezalel Naor (Jerusalem, 1985), pp. 56-58, 141-142.

*

In deference to *"Ha-Ga'on he-Hasid"* Rav Kook, in the second edition of *Mishneh HaBaD*, when explicating the *Tanya*'s oblique mention of "some wise men in their own eyes," Bunin omitted his previous reference to *Mishnat Hasidim* of Rabbi Immanuel Hai Ricchi and *Sha'arei Gan 'Eden* of Rabbi Jacob Koppel of Mezritch, while retaining the reference to the Vilna Gaon. Bunin explained that he felt justified in retaining the reference to the Vilna Gaon on the basis of the letter addressed by the *Ba'al ha-Tanya* to his Hasidim in Vilna, wherein we read that the Vilna Gaon understood *"Tzimtzum"* in the literal sense. Obviously, Bunin was unaware that the letter was a forgery. See Hayyim Yitzhak Bunin, *Mishneh HaBaD*, vol. 1, book 1, part 1 (Warsaw, 1936), pp. 68-69, note 5.

On the *Gnazim* website there is accessible Bunin's response to the letter of Rav Kook published in *Haskamot ha-RAYaH*. Bunin's letter is datelined "16 Marheshvan 5694 [i.e., 1933], Warsaw." Addressed to *"Ha-Rav ha-Ga'on he-Hasid"* Rav Kook, Bunin apologizes for not having responded sooner. Rav Kook's letter reached him only in Tishri and since then, "mighty burdens" prevented his responding.

Bunin respectfully differs with Rav Kook's opinion. In his work *Yosher*

Levav, Rabbi Immanuel Hai Ricchi (the author of *Mishnat Hasidim*) repeatedly reiterates that *Tzimtzum* must be taken literally. It is inconceivable that such a *ga'on* and *tsaddik* (as Ricchi) would dissemble. As for the author of *Sha'arei Gan 'Eden*, though his language is opaque, a straightforward assessment will turn up that he too was of the opinion that *Tzimtzum* is to be construed literally. Bunin then quotes verbatim several phrases from *Sha'arei Gan 'Eden* to prove his point.

Rav Kook made reference in his letter to Rabbi Meir Popper's gloss at the beginning of *'Ets Hayyim* concerning *Tzimtzum*: "Said Meir: The *Rav* [Luria] said this in relation to us *(be-'erkeinu).*" Bunin responded that the gloss represented an earlier understanding; this would not prevent those who came later (such as the Vilna Gaon) from understanding *Tzimtzum* differently. (Oddly enough, Rav Kook was under the mistaken impression that the gloss was written by Rabbi Meir Asch [Eisenstadt], author of *Panim Me'irot*. Bunin followed suit. This same blunder of Rav Kook occurs in a letter written two years earlier on 26 Tevet, 5691 [i.e., 1931] to Rabbi Yahya al-Kafah; see *Ma'amrei ha-RAYaH*, vol. 2, ed. Elisha Aviner [Langenauer] [Jerusalem, 1984], p. 521.)

Finally, against his better judgment, in deference to Rav Kook, Bunin promises in a future edition to publish a retraction.

See: http://gnazimorg.startlogic.com/1935-1865-אברהם-יצחק-הכהן-קוק

[7] Fraenkel's "Shabbetian *Tzimtzum Kipshuto*" (as opposed to the "Acceptable *Tzimtzum Kipshuto*") strikes this writer as a "straw man" contrived for purposes of *pilpul*.

[8] Rabbi Aaron Halevi, *Sha'arei ha-Yihud ve-ha-Emunah* (Shklov, 1820), Part 1, Gate 1, chap. 21, note (f.51).

[9] Rabbi Jacob Emden, *Mitpahat Sefarim* (Altona, 1768), 35b-36a (i.e., 45b-46a).

[10] *Mitpahat Sefarim* 35b (i.e., 45b).

To the question of whether Ricchi himself was a crypto-Sabbatian, I devoted an entire chapter of my book *Post-Sabbatian Sabbatianism* (1999): "Immanuel Hai Ricchi—Literalist among Kabbalists." See now Tzvi Luboshitz, "An Early Version of the *Simsum* Debate in Immanuel Hay Ricchi's *Yosher Levav*," *Kabbalah*, 42 (2018), pp. 267-320.

[11] Rabbi Shelomo Eliashov, *Helek ha-Bi'urim* (Jerusalem, 1935), 3a-b. The letters of Rabbi Eliashov to Rabbi N.H. Halevi Weidenbaum were published in Rabbi Moshe Schatz, *Ma'ayan Moshe* (Jerusalem, 2011).

[12] *Helek ha-Bi'urim*, 5b. However, recently Yosef Avivi vouched for the authenticity of the manuscript; see Yosef Avivi, *Kabbalat ha-GRA* (Jerusalem, 5753 [i.e., 1993]), p. 27.

[13] Mordechi Pachter, "The Gaon's Kabbalah from the Perspective of Two Traditions" (Hebrew), in *The Vilna Gaon and his Disciples* (Ramat-Gan: Bar-Ilan University Press, 2003), pp. 119-136.

[14] See Rabbi Menahem Azariah da Fano, *Ma'amar ha-Nefesh*, Part 2, chap. 4 in *Ma'amrei ha-RaMA' mi-Fano* (Jerusalem: Yismah Lev, 1997), p. 339; Rabbi Immanuel Hai Ricchi, *Yosher Levav* (Amsterdam, 1737), chap. 15 (10a); Rabbi Moshe Hayyim Luzzatto (i.e., attributed to—), *KaLaH Pithei Hokhmah* (Koretz, 1785), *petah* 27 (31b); idem, *Peirush Arimat Yadai* in *Adir ba-Marom* II, ed. Spinner (Jerusalem, 1988), p. 74; Rabbi Aaron Halevi Horowitz, *Sha'arei ha-Yihud ve-ha-Emunah* (Shklov, 1820), Part 1, Gate 1, note to

chap. 21 (43b-44a); Rabbi Isaac of Volozhin, *"Ma'amar Be-Tzelem"* (note to *Nefesh ha-Hayyim*, Gate 1, chap. 1) in Avinoam Fraenkel, *Nefesh HaTzimtzum*, vol. 2, p. 397; Rabbi Abraham Isaac Hakohen Kook, *Shemonah Kevatsim* (Jerusalem, 2004), 2:120 (vol. 1, p. 284).

[15] *Nefesh ha-Hayyim* III, 6.

[16] Rabbi Immanuel Hai Ricchi, *Yosher Levav* (Amsterdam, 1737), chap. 15 (10a). Quoted in *Nefesh ha-Tzimtzum*, vol. 2, pp. 260-261. See also Fraenkel's discussion of Ricchi's position on pp. 63-71.

Maimonides:
Between Philosophy and Halakhah

Rabbi Joseph B. Soloveitchik's Lectures on the Guide of the Perplexed.
Edited with an Introduction by Lawrence J. Kaplan (2016)

In the late 1970s, Rabbi Joseph B. Soloveitchik entrusted Lawrence Kaplan with the formidable task of translating his classic Hebrew monograph *Ish ha-Halakhah* into English. It was published in 1983 under the title *Halakhic Man.* Now Professor Kaplan has stewarded this project: A student's notes of a course on the *Guide of the Perplexed* that Rabbi Soloveitchik offered in Yeshiva University's Bernard Revel Graduate School in the academic year 1950-1951.

Kaplan is much more than a translator or even editor of Rabbi Soloveitchik's works. Over the years, he has emerged as a leading interpreter of Soloveitchik's thought, as well as a gifted thinker in his own right. He is at once reverential towards and critical of his *Rav*'s thought. In the words of Dov Schwartz, in his Foreword to the book: "His admiration of R. Soloveitchik has not detracted from his critical sense. As a student, he transcends the scholar in him, and as a scholar, he transcends the student in him." I would go one step further in defining the role of Lawrence Kaplan. To employ the by now famous imagery of Rabbi Hutner, Kaplan is that "singular student who has the unique ability to grasp the thought of the *Rav* when he is silent; when he passes from speech to silence."[1]

⁂

Rabbi Soloveitchik opened the course with this salvo:

> There are two aspects to creativity in the realm of philosophy. The first is philosophical creativity, whereby one brings new thoughts to the totality of man's historical treasures. The second is creativity in the realm of philosophical style. Philosophical style refers to one's philosophical formulae and terminology, the choice of one's words, the literary categories one employs. If a philosopher is both philosophically creative and, as well, creates a new philosophical style, he will revolutionize philosophy.
>
> Sometimes, however, a philosophical genius is handicapped by the routine philosophical jargon that prevails in a particular climate. Literary categories are always needed as tools enabling one to express subjective ideas. Each epoch has its own jargon and categories....Not every creative genius will be able to fashion new tools. Some may be exceedingly creative in the area of philosophical analysis, but lack creativity in the field of literary inventiveness. They are unable to find a new medium or instrumentality to present their thought.

Maimonides was such a genius. He was a great genius in the realm of philosophical analysis and imagination. Indeed, in the *Mishneh Torah*, in the realm of *Halakhah*, he was able to mint new terms, to fashion new philosophic categories. There he was creative in all senses. But in the *Guide* there is sterility as to the form of presentation. He used the old, routine, Aristotelian philosophical jargon. Perhaps his use of Arabic hampered him; perhaps he was so overawed by Aristotle that he adopted his tools and took on his tradition.[2]

One can imagine students sitting on edge in shock and awe upon delivery of this candid appraisal of the book widely held to be the pinnacle of Jewish Philosophy! I will leave it to others more conversant with the Judeo-Arabic literary tradition to opine on the correctness of Rabbi Soloveitchik's assessment. It is not difficult to glean where Rabbi Soloveitchik was coming from and where he was going to with this bold, perhaps even brash statement. His grandfather Rabbi Hayyim Soloveitchik (known in the *yeshivah* world as "Reb Hayyim Brisker") was a genius in both senses. He excelled in originality of thought and expression. The *"Brisker Derekh,"* the revolutionary method of conceptualization that he bequeathed to coming generations of Talmudists, came equipped with an equally exciting lexicon: *heftsa/gavra, hiyyuv/kiyyum, shnei denim, din mesuyyam*. And Rabbi Soloveitchik himself would prove a master at coining neologisms, of which the present volume has its fair share: "ethical-intellectual," "metaphysical-transcendental" (p. 82).

While the modern reader might find these hyphenated terms a bit old-fashioned or outlandish, in context they do serve their purpose.

Rabbi Joseph B. Soloveitchik was renowned for having inherited his grandfather's consuming passion for Maimonides' *Mishneh Torah*. It is public knowledge that in the realm of *Halakhah*, the Rabbi of Boston perpetuated Rabbi Hayyim's razor-sharp method of analyzing that *magnum opus*. What remains a little known fact is that Rabbi Hayyim Soloveitchik was an avid student of the *Guide* as well. In Volozhin, Rabbi Hayyim confided to a visitor, Rabbi Yosef Alexander—Rabbi of Darbian (today Darbenai, Lithuania) and author of a commentary to the prayer book, *Porat Yosef* (Warsaw, 1898)—that it had taken him two years to study the *Guide*.[3] Rabbi J.B. Soloveitchik shared with his students that not only was his grandfather Rabbi Hayyim expert in the *Guide* but that he wished to pen a commentary thereto—a wish that unfortunately remained unfulfilled due to the exigencies of time. On that occasion, Rabbi Soloveitchik related that he received directly from his grandfather guidance how to deal with contradictions between the *Guide* and *Mishneh Torah*.[4] It seems that at one point in time Rabbi Hayyim's study partner in the *Guide* was an enigmatic HaBaD Hasid by the name of Rabbi Hayyim Abraham Dov Baer Hakohen Levine (known in Hasidic circles as "the *Mal'akh*," "the Angel").[5]

Rabbi Hayyim Soloveitchik's enthusiasm for the *Guide* was shared by his contemporaries, Rabbi Meir Simhah Cohen and

Rabbi Joseph Rosen. These two, who served respectively as the Mitnagdic and Hasidic Rabbis of Dvinsk, produced monumental commentaries of their own on *Mishneh Torah*. While Rabbi Hayyim had no recourse to the *Guide* in his *Hiddushei Rabbenu Hayyim Halevi*, the *Tsaphnat Pa'ne'ah* of Rabbi Joseph Rosen (known as the "Rogatchover" after his birthplace in Belarus) and the *'Or Same'ah* of Rabbi Meir Simhah Cohen abound with references to the *Guide*.

There is a simple explanation why Rabbi Hayyim Soloveitchik's *Hiddushei Rabbenu Hayyim Ha-Levi* has no truck with the *Guide* while *'Or Same'ah* is replete with references to the *Guide*. The former deals only with the halakhic portions of *Mishneh Torah*, while the latter takes up with the philosophic sections of *Sefer ha-Madda'* as well.

In the case of *Tsafnat Pa'ne'ah*, the involvement with the *Guide* is much more complex. For starters, unlike Reb Hayyim Brisker who was prevented from writing a commentary to the *Guide*, Rabbi Joseph Rosen (or as he was referred to colloquially, "Reb Yoshe Denaburger," after Denaburg, the former name of Dvinsk, today Daugavpils, Latvia) penned notes to that philosophic work. While he rails time and time again against the heresies of Moses Narboni (Moses of Narbonne),[6] he has no problem with the *Giv'at ha-Moreh* of Solomon Maimon, whom he refers to simply as *"Ha-Mefaresh"* ("the Commentator"). It is conceivable that this HaBaD Hasid was simply unaware who authored the anonymous commentary to the *Guide*.[7]

But the relation of *Tsafnat Pa'ne'ah* to the *Guide* does not end there. Those same Aristotelian categories which Rabbi J.B. Soloveitchik found to be time-worn, routine, and hackneyed—*homer/tsurah, harkavah mizgit/harkavah shekhenit, 'etsem/mikreh, he'eder/metsi'ut*—were now introduced into Talmudic analysis! (Tail end of the story: The Rogatchover's method of analysis, plucked from the *Guide*, found one disciple in Rabbi J.B. Soloveitchik's long-standing friend, Rabbi Menahem Schneerson, the Lubavitcher Rebbe.)

Whereas numerous scholars perceive two distinct Maimonides—one, the halakhist of *Mishneh Torah*; the other, the phlosopher of the *Guide*—these three *Litvishe gedolim* (Lithuanian titans) saw no discontinuity, no disconnect, no split in personality.[8] Rabbi Meir Simhah concluded: "The words of *Rabbeinu* [i.e., Maimonides] in all of his books—the *Yad*, the *Guide*, and the *Commentary to the Mishnah*—one *Geist* runs through them."[9]

Rabbi Yehiel Ya'akov Weinberg had the audacity to tell Rabbi Moshe Soloveichik that though his father, Rabbi Hayyim Soloveitchik's interpretations of Maimonides' *Mishneh Torah* are certainly not what Maimonides intended, nonetheless Rabbi Hayyim's novellae are of interest in their own right. "Reb Hayyim was a new Maimonides in his own right."[10] We might be tempted to say something similar concerning Rabbi Joseph B. Soloveitchik's interpretation of Maimonides' *Guide*. While in places it leaves the reader far from convinced that this was Maimonides' original intention, it is fascinating in its own right. "Reb Yoshe Baer was a new Maimonides in his own right."[11]

Maimonides Between Philosophy and Halakhah

In his thorough Introduction, Professor Kaplan mentions *en passant* a *Yahrzeit Shi'ur* of Rabbi Soloveitchik, "*Be-'Inyan Mehikat Hashem*," "devoted to an analysis of Maimonides' theory of divine attributes and the resulting obligation of imitating God" (p. 23). While Kaplan is certainly correct when he writes that it "takes the form of a commentary on the opening paragraphs of *Laws of the Foundations of the Torah*, Chapter 6," upon internal inspection we discover that the *shi'ur* is infused with the spirit and substance of the *Guide*. This is a summation from the *shi'ur*:

> A new light is shed, if so, upon all the twenty-four books of the *TaNaKh*. I always had difficulty with the role of the prophets of Israel. On the one hand, we hold that a prophet is not permitted to innovate, to add or detract by even an iota; on the other hand, the word of the LORD came to the prophets, they prophesied and their prophecy was written down for eternity. What is the purpose of their prophecy, since they cannot innovate any *halakhah*? True, they rebuked Israel, and exhortation was one of the purposes for which our prophets were sent. But I still find it difficult to say that in their prophecy they did not relate to Israel the word of the LORD in a halakhic sense. But now all is crystal clear. An entire teaching is contained in the Prophets—the teaching of the ways of the Holy One, blessed be He; the teaching of the attributes that obligates

man in *imitatio Dei*. Therefore Maimonides included the chapter dealing with erasing the Name—which essentially is the chapter of the proper names and attributes—in the *Laws of the Foundations of the Torah* before the explanation of the foundation of prophecy, because in the teaching of the names of the Holy One, blessed be He—"I will make all My goodness pass before you, and will proclaim the name of the LORD before you; and I will be gracious to whom I will be gracious, and will show mercy on whom I will show mercy."—is hidden the foundation of prophecy and its purpose. In brief, prophecy comes to teach man how to participate in the attributes of the Holy One, blessed be He, and merit to be called by the same.[12]

The Biblical quote is from Exodus 33:19. This verse is discussed by Maimonides in the *Guide*, Part I, Chapter 54. That chapter concludes:

> For the utmost virtue of man is to become like unto Him, may He be exalted, as far as he is able; which means that we should make our actions like unto His, as the Sages made clear when interpreting the verse, *You shall be holy*. They said: *He is gracious, so be you also gracious; He is merciful, so be you also merciful.*[13]

Rabbi Soloveitchik's discussion in *"Mehikat Hashem"* of the role that prophecy plays and of the two forms of *imitatio Dei* (behavioral versus characteriological) is seminal. It might be interesting to contrast that Maimonidean interpretation to Abraham Joshua Heschel's perception of the prophets, who express the word of an anthropopathic deity—a notion in direct contravention of the strictures set up by Maimonides in the *Guide*. For Rabbi Soloveitchik (as for Maimonides), God engages in activities designed to evoke and inculcate in man various character traits. In Rabbi Heschel's reading of the prophets, God goes so far as to share in the pathos, the emotion described so vividly by the *nevi'im*.[14]

In his Preface, Prof. Kaplan apprises us that the present volume takes us through the student's notes of the First Course, but there yet awaits "Course Two." This reviewer was privileged to hear Rabbi Soloveitchik hold forth on the *Guide of the Perplexed* one Saturday night in the Maimonides School that he founded in Boston. (On that memorable occasion, the Philosopher of Boston explored Maimonides' solution to the problem of evil in the *Guide*, Part III, Chapter 12.) Is there any chance that there exists a record of *that* series of lectures?

---

[1] Rabbi Isaac Hutner, *Pahad Yitzhak: Hanukkah* (New York, NY, 1989), 8:5 (pp. 64-65).
[2] *Rabbi Joseph B. Soloveitchik's Lectures on the* Guide of the Perplexed, pp. 75-76.
[3] Rabbi Uri Moinester, *Karnei Re'em* (New York, 1951), p. 104, note 1.
[4] Rabbi Hershel Reichman, *Reshimot Shi'urei Maran ha-GRID Ha-Levi: Sukkah*

(New York, 1990), p. 258.

[5] Rabbi Yisroel Besser, *Mishpacha*, no. 191 (2 Shevat, 5768/2008), p. 41. Rabbi Baruch Baer Leibowitz, eminent disciple of Rabbi Hayyim Soloveitchik, referred to Rabbi Levine as *"a mensch vos hot geshushket mit mein rebbe in Moreh."* Although the Yiddish is idiomatic and well-nigh untranslatable, the gist is "someone who whispered with my rabbi [i.e., Hayyim Soloveitchik] in the *Guide.*"

See also the testimony of the *Mal'akh*'s son, Rabbi Raphael Zalman Levine, quoting Rabbi Baruch Baer Leibowitz: "[Rabbi Hayyim Soloveitchik] *flegt zikh shushkenen mit ihm* [i.e., Mal'akh] *gantze teg nokhanand."* The idiomatic Yiddish translates as, "[Rabbi Hayyim Soloveitchik] would whisper with him [i.e., the *Mal'akh*] for days on end." Rabbi Baruch Baer concluded by saying that no one knew what they discussed. See Rabbi C.S. Glickman, *Mi-Pihem u-mi-Pi Ketavam* (Brooklyn, NY, 2008), p. 145. The sense is that the two men (Rabbi Hayyim Soloveitchik and the *Mal'akh*) were sequestered, studying in private.

[6] The expressions that Rabbi Joseph Rosen reserves for Narboni are so vituperative that rather than print them in the commentary of *Tsafnat Pa'ne'ah*, the editor, Rabbi Kasher, saw fit to relegate them to an appendix to the work. See Rabbi Joseph Rosen, *Tsaphnat Pa'ne'ah*, Deuteronomy, Part Two/*Moreh Nevukhim*, ed. Rabbi Menahem Mendel Kasher (Jerusalem, 1965), p. 422.

[7] In the Sulzbach 1828 edition of *Moreh Nevukhim* in which Rabbi Joseph Rosen penned his notes, the commentary *Giv'at ha-Moreh* was printed without the author's name. Thus, Rabbi Rosen would have been unaware that the commentary was written by Solomon Maimon, a notorious renegade. See Rabbi Menahem M. Kasher's introduction to Rabbi Joseph Rosen, *Tsaphnat Pa'ne'ah, Moreh Nevukhim.*

[8] The three shared in common exposure to Rabbi Hayyim's father, Rabbi Joseph Baer Soloveitchik of Brisk (author of *Beit ha-Levi*). As a youth, Joseph Rosen of Rogatchov studied with the *Beit ha-Levi* when he served as Rabbi of Slutsk. As for Rabbi Meir Simhah Cohen, when he was a young man in Bialystok, his talent was duly noted by Rabbi Joseph Baer Soloveitchik, who recommended him for the (Mitnagdic) rabbinate of Dvinsk.

[9] Rabbi Meir Simhah Cohen, *Meshekh Hokhmah* (Riga, 1927), *Yitro*, s.v. *lo yiheyeh lekha* (44a).

[10] In letters to Dr. Gavriel Cohen written in the year 1965, Rabbi Weinberg recollected a conversation he had years earlier with Rabbi Moshe Soloveitchik concerning his father Rabbi Hayyim Soloveitchik's exegesis of Maimonides. See *Kitvei ha-Gaon Rabbi Yehiel Ya'akov Weinberg*, ed. Melekh Shapiro, vol. 2 (Scranton, 2003), p. 219, note 4. See also Marc B. Shapiro, *Studies in Maimonides and His Interpreters* (Scranton, PA: University of Scranton Press, 2008), Hebrew Section, pp. 30-31.

[11] In *yeshivah* circles, Rabbi Joseph Baer Soloveitchik of Boston was referred to colloquially as "Reb Yoshe Baer."

[12] Rabbi Joseph Dov Halevi Soloveitchik, *Shi'urim le-Zekher Abba Mari* (Jerusalem: Mossad Harav Kook, 2002), vol. 2, pp. 188-189.

[13] Maimonides, *Guide of the Perplexed*, transl. Shlomo Pines (Chicago: University of Chicago Press, 1964), p. 128.

[14] See Abraham Joshua Heschel, *The Prophets* (1962).

Hallel from Heaven and *Hallel* from Hell

The Post-Holocaust Responses of Paul Celan, Aharon Appelfeld and Meshulam Rath

> *"Just as the praise of the Holy One ascends to Him from Heaven, so it ascends from Hell." (Midrash)*

What do the poet Paul Celan, the novelist Aharon Appelfeld, and the religious legalist Meshulam Rath share in common? Two things.

First, they all emerged from Tchernowitz (today Chernivtsi, Ukraine), capital of Bukovina, a relic of the Habsburg era, located at the eastern extreme of the defunct Austro-Hungarian Empire. Tchernowitz, whose Jewish population was estimated at 50,000 in the interbellum (roughly half the total population). Tchernowitz, where Jews spoke German while their gentile neighbors spoke Ruthenian or Ukrainian, or maybe Romanian.

Second, these three men bequeathed a literary legacy of Holocaust response that deserves our careful attention.

※

Paul Celan (1920-1970), whose last name is an anagram of his original patronym Ancel (Antschel), would after the war reinvent himself in Paris as a German poet of distinction, hailed by many as the greatest of the postwar German poets. His existence was riddled with contradictions. A Jew living in France, writing in German, no less. He could not extricate himself from the tongue. The language of the murderers was also the language of his mother—a mother whose loss haunts his poetry. We may say that Celan was a survivor who did not survive. A quarter of a century later the Holocaust would catch up to him, plunging his body into the Seine, drowning out a voice that had been slowly drowning for half its life. As Katharine Washburn, one of Celan's many translators, wrote: "Celan described the trajectory of his own poetic career as *'still geworden,'* becoming silent."

Celan's poem *Todesfuge* (Death Fugue), written while the war yet raged, created a sensation when it was published in Germany in 1952 and established the poet's career. It captures the eerie incongruity of Jewish violinists being forced to perform concert music in the death camps. One of the most haunting images is the following:

> *Er ruft streicht dunkler die Geigen*
> *Dann steigt ihr als Rauch in die Luft*
> *Dann habt ihr ein Grab in den Wolken*
> *Da liegt man nicht eng.*

> He shouts strike the fiddles darker
> Then you'll rise as smoke in the air
> Then you'll have a grave in the clouds
> There you won't lie cramped.

As the years went by, Celan's poems became sparser. Begrudgingly few words and their meanings obtuse beyond comprehension. There was set in motion a total breakdown of language (running a course parallel to Celan's mental breakdown). Celan was being overtaken by silence, his voice being choked as a rehearsal for its final "stilling" in the Seine.

But before the total strangulation of sense, Celan's eye would light on the King within the Nothing.

> *Im Nichts—wer steht da? Der König.*
> *Da steht der König, der König.*
> *Da steht er und steht.*
> *Judenlocke, wirst nicht grau.*

> In Nothing—what dwells there? The King.
> There the King dwells, the King.
> There he dwells and dwells.
> Jew's curl, you'll turn not grey.[1]

Had Celan read Rabbi Nahman of Breslov?[2] Or had their minds' eyes shared a common vision of a King who reposes in the Void? And might Celan's cranium have yet retained the verses of Judah the Pious of Regensburg's *Hymn of Glory* sung in synagogue on the Sabbath:

> The tresses of His head are like His youthful days;
> His locks are black curls.

And maybe the two mystical visions of Nahman of Breslov and Judah the Pious collided in Celan's imagination, yielding a marriage of Heaven and Hell; the destruction of Jewry and its immortality.

Aharon Appelfeld (1932-) was a boy at the time of the Holocaust. Like Celan, he is eternally orphaned of his mother. Unlike Celan, he traded his maternal language of German for Hebrew. Since settling in Israel after the War in 1946, he has produced novel after novel in the "sacred tongue." In those novels, he returns time and again to Tchernowitz. The guises change from narrative to narrative; through the diaphanous veil we easily make out the features of the boy orphaned of his mother. (Both Celan and Appelfeld are openly Oedipal.) Appelfeld and his readers are forced to forever revisit the scene of the trauma; to reopen a wound that never heals.

Appelfeld was spared Celan's agony of taking German's infamously long words and dissecting them until they dissolve into nothingness. Instead, Appelfeld opted for a Hebrew language that is trim and laconic, a quality that persists in English translation. To quote the New York Times Book Review of *All Whom I Have Loved*, "he has an artfully spare writing style."

Though Appelfeld's silence is not as invasive as Celan's, it should not be underestimated:

> But in his heart Hugo knows that what had been would never be again. The time in the ghetto and in hiding is

already embossed on his flesh, and the power of the words he would use has faded. Now it isn't words that speak to him, but silence. This is a difficult language, but as soon as one adopts it, no other language will ever be as effective.[3]

A theme that runs through Appelfeld's novels is the sociological observation, usually made by devout Ukrainian peasants, that the Old Jews believed in God and prayed in the synagogue but the New Jews no longer believe and have no use of synagogues.

Finally, we come to Meshulam Rath (1875-1962), the elder Rabbi of Tchernowitz. He survived the inferno that engulfed Europe and settled in Israel in 1944, where he was frequently consulted by the Chief Rabbinate. (Since youth, Rath had been identified with the Religious Zionist movement.)

Even those who could not abide Meshulam Rath's Zionist sympathies dared not impugn his credentials as a world-class halakhic authority. Rabbi Meshulam Rath's most famous—and controversial—legal decision concerns reciting *Hallel* (Psalms of thanksgiving) on Israel's Independence Day. In 1952, at the behest of Rabbi Judah Leib Maimon, he penned a formal responsum wherein he expressed his bold opinion that it behooves Jews to recite *Hallel* with a blessing on *Yom Ha-'Atsma'ut*.

Rabbi Rath entitled his collection of responsa *Kol Mevaser* (*Voice of the Herald*):

I pray that just as I merited after the terrible Holocaust to see the beginning of the redemption, so may the LORD grant me the privilege to hear the voice heralding our complete redemption, speedily in our days.[4]

The poet who emerged from the Holocaust a young man, lapsed into silence, and eventually madness and suicide. The novelist who emerged from the vanished world an adolescent, also succumbed to silence. It was the old rabbi, the septuagenarian sage, who saw a world destroyed and rebuilt, that summoned the strings of King David's harp. And these strings would not establish for the Jews a space in the sky—as in Celan's *Death Fugue*—but a space on Earth.

Celan's cryptic remark proved true:

Judenlocke, wirst nicht grau.

Jew lock you'll turn not gray.

---

[1] *"Mandorla"* from *Die Niemandsrose* (1963); in *Paul Celan: Poems*, translated by M. Hamburger (New York: Persea Books, 1980), pp. 156-157.
[2] See *Likkutei MOHaRaN* I, 64 ("Bo el Par'oh").
[3] Aharon Appelfeld, *Blooms of Darkness*, translated by Jeffrey M. Green (New York: Schocken, 2010), p. 53.
[4] From the Introduction to *Kol Mevaser*, datelined B'nei Berak, 23 Menahem-Av 5715 (i.e., 1955).

When Elijah's Mantle Fell:
The Judaism of Leonard Cohen

Now that the dust has begun to settle on the freshly dug grave of Leonard Cohen (1934-2016), and we are hopefully past the hullabaloo, past the media circus which witnessed (in Leonard's own words) "all the lousy little poets coming round," we may begin to examine with some sobriety the literary legacy of this celebrated bard.

No, Leonard Cohen did not receive the coveted Nobel Prize for Literature. Instead, it was awarded to another Jewish poet, Bob Dylan (*né* Robert Zimmerman). But, about the same time that Dylan was announced a Nobel laureate, Cohen bequeathed to us what would become his farewell song, his *Kaddish*, "You Want It Darker." With that, the prodigal son returned home and was clutched to the bosom of his people. Complete with the Biblical Hebrew refrain *"Hineni"* ("I'm ready") and backed up by the cantorial rendition of the *hazan* of historic Congregation Shaar Hashomayim in Montreal, the synagogue Leonard grew up in as a boy, "this last song he left us is the most Jewish he ever wrote" (Rabbi Lord Jonathan Sacks). Indeed, as the Talmud put it, "There is one who acquires eternity in a single hour."[1]

Cohen's identity as a priest descended from Aaron, was not lost on him. Time and again, he invoked his priestly powers. At the conclusion of one memorable concert in Israel, Cohen actually extended his hands in priestly benediction, pronouncing—in the outlandish Ashkenazic pronunciation of his forebears—the three verses of the ancient formula.

Besides bestowing blessing, the High Priest in days of yore also acted as an oracle. In his prophetic imagination, the letters engraved in the precious and semi-precious stones on his breastplate would light up like a console, delivering a Delphic message to the nation. Cohen preserved this tradition as well in his literary *oeuvre*, referring to it self-deprecatingly as "entertainment for cryptologists."

Having properly vetted him as an authentic Jewish voice, one asks where exactly in the pantheon of Judaism does Leonard Cohen's God belong? Certainly Cohen's God is not the Lithuanian Mitnagdic God of his maternal grandfather, Rabbi Solomon Klonitzky-Kline, author of *Otsar Ta'amei Hazal*, a thesaurus of aggadic interpretations of the Pentateuch. Unlike classical rabbinic Judaism, with its transcendental vision of the deity, Cohen's faith is decidedly pantheistic. His God is embodied and incarnate. (Stated succinctly, Leonard's credo reduces to the belief that the divinity is splendid as a woman but pathetic as a god.) But neither is his the faith of the Hasidim. From the very beginning, the *Tanya* (referred to in HaBaD circles as "the Bible of Hasidism"), drives a wedge between the "animal soul" (*nefesh ha-behemit*) and the "divine soul" (*nefesh ha-elohit*). If there is a Judaism that can accommodate the enigmatic soul of Leonard Cohen, it is, Heaven shudder—Sabbateanism. In the wake of the appearance of the Messiah of Izmir, seventeenth-century Shabbetai Tsevi, there was constructed—and deconstructed—a kabbalistic universe in which lust, passion and sensuality interplay with the divine.

One of the vestments of the priest was the *avnet*, the belt or girdle. The Talmudic sages disagreed what fabric it consisted of, whether it was pure white linen (the garb of the angels on high) or mixed with multi-variegated wool, embracing all the sensual colors of life: crimson, blue and purple.[2] In fact, the great codifier Maimonides adopted the latter approach.[3] And the *avnet* was extremely long, which required it to be wrapped around the *cohen*'s frame several times. Thirty-two cubits in length, no less![4] Thirty-two (*Lamed Bet*) being the Hebrew word for "heart." It may have been richly colored, and it certainly was hearty, but a divide it was nonetheless, a barrier between the upper and lower parts of man.

In Leonard Cohen's art, we have a priestly wardrobe *sans* girdle. All the divine poetry of man's higher self and all the graphic detail of man's lower self, come together. No one is more aware of this ongoing battle, this war waged between the physical nature and the spiritual nature, than Leonard Cohen himself.

In *My Life in Art*, which contains an unpublished memoir of the time he spent in Israel during and in the aftermath of the Yom Kippur War, Cohen recorded the contents of a letter he received from "Asher," an all too sincere convert to Judaism, whose fundamental belief assaulted, challenged, disturbed, and provoked Leonard on so many levels of his being. One thing is certain. Cohen was unable to ignore the gauntlet thrown down by this unlikely acquaintance.

Just shy of his fortieth birthday, Cohen left behind his partner Suzanne Elrod and their infant son Adam on the idyllic Greek isle of Hydra, in order to be with his people in this dark hour of their history. In Athens airport, as he was about to board the plane bound for Tel-Aviv, Cohen met this strange man, Asher, who was himself leaving behind the comforts of California to show his solidarity with his new nation of Israel. Cohen would eventually head for the front to perform a concert for the Israeli soldiers. The troops begged him to sing "Suzanne" encore after encore. Cohen's appearance outside Ismailia, on the Egyptian side of the Suez Canal, has been preserved for posterity in the iconic photograph shot together with General Ariel Sharon. The mysterious gentleman's gravitation to the Holy Land, however, remains unrecorded. Asher vanishes —except in the annals of Cohen's memoir.

From Jerusalem, Asher addresses a letter to Leonard. The letter is oracular, but speaks in no uncertain terms. By some neat trick of ventriloquism, Asher becomes the voice of Cohen's conscience. In so many words, he imparts to Cohen this uncommon wisdom:

> *Now is the time to seize the opportunity and become the real Cohen you were always intended to be. Grab on to the cape of the Prophet Elijah thrown to you.*
>
> *The Law requires that the High Priest be married. "'He shall atone for himself and for his house.' 'His house.' This is his wife."*[5]

> *Having joined together physical and spiritual natures, the High Priest may then go on to serve in the rebuilt Temple of physical and spiritual Jerusalem.*

The letter resounds with a definite tone of celestial authority though at no point is it as brutal as the dictation of Joseph Caro's *maggid*.

Implicit in the letter is the rabbinic tradition whereby Elijah was a Cohen.[6] As much as Cohen may have reached for it, he was simply incapable of grasping the symbolic mantle of Elijah. It would continue to elude him. The singer decided to leave the Land of Israel.

Another Cohen, who earned the sobriquet "the High Priest of Rebirth," Rabbi Abraham Isaac HaCohen Kook (1865-1935), recorded *his* vision of Elijah heralding the Messianic Age:

> *Behold, I see with my eyes the light of Elijah's life rising. His power for his God is increasingly revealed. The holiness in nature breaks down fences. It proceeds to be united with the holiness that is above coarse nature; with the holiness that fights nature.*[7]

Rav Kook envisioned Elijah, "the Angel of the Covenant," the genius of holiness in the flesh, as holding the key to unlock the secrets of the flesh and of the divine seal inscribed in the Israelite body.[8] As Abraham Isaac HaCohen Kook was preparing to leave this world so fraught with contradictions, another Cohen was preparing to enter the fray of earthly existence and unravel—or perhaps complexify—its mysteries.

> *They said to him: "He is a hairy man, with a girdle of skin girded about his loins."*
> *And he said: "It is Elijah the Tishbite."*[9]
> *He lifted up the mantle of Elijah that had fallen from him.*[10]

The mantle of Elijah still waits to be lifted.
The loins have yet to be girded.

---

[1] *b. 'Avodah Zarah* 10b, 17a, 18a.
[2] *b. Yoma* 12b.
[3] Maimonides, *MT, Hil. Klei ha-Mikdash* 8:1.
[4] Ibid. 8:19.
[5] *m. Yoma* 1:1.
[6] *b. Bava Metsi'a* 114b.
[7] Rabbi Abraham Isaac HaKohen Kook, *Orot*, Lights of Renascence, chap. 30.
[8] *Orot*, Israel and Its Renascence, chap. 29.
[9] 2 Kings 1:8.
[10] 2 Kings 2:13.

The Religious-Zionist Manifesto of Rabbi Yehudah Leib Don Yahya

In 1901 there appeared in Vilna a 32-page booklet entitled, *Ha-Tsiyoniyut mi-nekudat hashkafat ha-dat* (*Zionism from the Viewpoint of Religion*). The author was Yehudah Don Yahya.[1] The final eight pages of the work contain a supplement (*Millu'im*) by one Ben-Zion Vilner, criticizing the anti-Zionism of the Rebbe of Lubavitch. (One ventures that "Ben-Zion Vilner" is a pseudonym.)

What is remarkable about this manifesto that argues that Zionism is totally compatible with traditional Judaism, is that the author, Rabbi Yehudah Leib Don Yahya, was an intimate student of Rabbi Hayyim Soloveitchik, a most outspoken opponent of the Zionist movement.[2]

To add to the intrigue, Don Yahya's grandfather, Rabbi Shabtai Don Yahya of Drissa, had been an ardent Hasid of Rabbi Menahem Mendel of Lubavitch (known by his work of Halakhic responsa as "*Tsemah Tsedek*").[3] Yehudah himself would go on to serve as rabbi of the HaBaD Hasidic community of Shklov.[4] Although, as we shall see, within the HaBaD community, there were differing responses to Zionism along the fault line of the Kopyst—Lubavitch dispute.

Today, students who immerse themselves in the Torah novellae of Rabbi Hayyim Soloveitchik may come across the name of Rabbi Yehudah Leib Don Yahya, but they have no idea who this disciple was. Appended to *Hiddushei ha-GRaH he-Hadash 'al ha-Shas* (issued upon the ninetieth anniversary of Rabbi Hayyim's passing in 2008) are Don Yahya's memoirs of his beloved mentor in the Volozhin Yeshivah. In 2018 (coincidentally a century since Rabbi Hayyim's passing) there appeared in print a *Tagbuch* or diary, in which Rabbi Hayyim jotted down his insights on Talmud and Maimonides' code.[5] In his introduction to the volume, the editor, Rabbi Yitzhak Abba Lichtenstein, notes that Rabbi Hayyim would allow some scholars to copy down entries from the journal. Indeed, one such scholar was Rabbi Yehudah Leib Don Yahya. Two novellae that appear in the *Tagbuch* were previously published in Don Yahya's *Bikkurei Yehudah* (1939).[6]

One asks: What would prompt such a devoted disciple to break from his master's ideology concerning Zionism?

To understand how such a phenomenon as Yehudah Don Yahya was possible, one needs to trace his membership in Nes Ziyonah, the underground proto-Zionist movement that existed in the Volozhin Yeshivah from 1885 until its disbandment in 1890.

This was the era of Hovevei Zion (Lovers of Zion), a Russian Jewish movement to settle the Land of Israel that predated Herzlian political Zionism. Nes Ziyonah, which blossomed independently within the ranks of the student body of the famed Volozhin Yeshivah, interfaced with Hovevei Zion, presided over by Rabbi Samuel Mohilever of Bialystok. Members of Nes Ziyonah were sworn to secrecy. The membership included such illustrious scholars as Moshe Mordechai Epstein of Bakst,[7] Menahem Krakovsky,[8] and Isser Zalman Meltzer. Moshe Mordechai Epstein would eventually become Rosh Yeshivah of Slabodka. Menahem Krakowsky would one day assume the position of *"Shtodt Maggid"* of Vilna. Finally, Isser Zalman Meltzer would become Rosh Yeshivah of Slutzk and later 'Ets Hayyim of Jerusalem.[9] It was through the last-mentioned disciple, who was especially close to Rabbi Hayyim Soloveitchik, that Rabbi Hayyim was able to discover the identities of the students who belonged to Nes Ziyonah.[10]

Nes Ziyonah had sprung up without the knowledge of the elder dean of the Yeshivah, Rabbi Naftali Tsevi Yehudah Berlin (NeTsIV). In fact, according to Israel Kausner, who wrote a history of Nes Ziyonah, the members of the secret society prided themselves that they had been able to prevail upon Rabbi Berlin to join the greater Hovevei Zion movement and to assume a role of leadership alongside Rabbis Samuel Mohilever and Mordechai Eliasberg of Bausk.[11] In 1890, somehow Nes Ziyonah came to the attention of the Russian government authorities. One of its leaders (Yosef Rothstein) was arrested but subsequently released. When Rabbi Berlin learned that such a society had sprung up in the Yeshivah under his very nose, he was aghast. He feared that Nes Ziyonah might jeopardize the existence of the Yeshivah, which was under constant government scrutiny.[12] Leaving aside pragmatic considerations, in principle, Volozhin had always been a bastion of pure Torah learning; there was no room in it for Zionist activism.[13] Nes Ziyonah ceased to exist. (Hovevei Zion, with its office in Odessa, was legalized by the Tsarist government in 1890.)[14]

The idealistic young men who had formed Nes Ziyonah were not ones to easily give up. Nes Ziyonah morphed into Netsah Yisrael, whose express goal was to advocate on behalf of Zionism and religion. (Nes Ziyonah had restricted its activities to settling the Land of Israel.) Most prominent in this reincarnation of Netsah Yisrael was—Yehudah Leib Don Yahya.[15]

It is against this backdrop—the publicistic activity of Netsah Yisrael—that one must view Don Yahya's tract, *Zionism from the Viewpoint of Religion*.

Let us briefly sum up some of the more salient points of Don Yahya's booklet.

The author begins by clarifying that the return of the nation to its land can in no way be viewed as the *complete* redemption prophesied in Scripture. The prophets' vision, while including the ingathering of exiles, extends beyond that to global mankind's acknowledging God and embracing His Torah.[16]

On the other hand, Don Yahya is flummoxed by various rabbis who adopt an all-or-nothing attitude to the Zionist organization's striving to secure from the Ottomans a safe haven for Jews in the Holy Land. Just because the Zionist dream does not encompass the comprehensive vision of our prophets of old, is no reason to reject Zionism. Granted that the Zionist goals are much more modest in scope; that still does not justify opposing the movement. Don Yahya's own reading of the sources—Biblical and Rabbinic—is gradualist. He anticipates a phased redemption. The Jews' return to the Land is certainly the beginning, the first installment in a protracted process which will eventually—upon completion of "the full and encompassing redemption" (*"ha-ge'ulah ha-sheleimah ve-ha-kelalit"*)—culminate in the restoration of the Davidic dynasty in the person of King Messiah and the rebuilding of the Temple.[17]

The author adopts as his paradigm the Second Temple period. Taking issue with those who construe the return from Babylonian captivity as a "temporary remembrance" (*"pekidah li-zeman mugbal"*), Don Yahya maintains that the Second Commonwealth had the potential to develop into full-blown redemption. With that model in mind, he writes that return from exile and settling the Land can evolve beyond that to greater spiritual dimensions.[18]

After having made his case for the compatibility of the nascent Zionist movement and Judaism, Don Yahya tackles the painful question why some of the great Torah geniuses oppose Zionism.[19]

Don Yahya has a couple of explanations. First, knowledge of Torah is divided into *Halakhah* and *pilpul*, on the one hand, and matters of belief and opinion, on the other. Contemporary *ge'onim* (unlike their medieval predecessors Maimonides and Nahmanides) have devoted their lives to *Halakhah*, to the exclusion of *emunot ve-de'ot* (beliefs and opinions). "In regard to the portion of Torah which is beliefs and opinions, their view does not exceed the view of an average Jew."[20]

Rather conveniently, Don Yahya holds up as examples of recent Torah authorities who plumbed the depths of the beliefs contained in the *Aggadah*, and who concluded that the redemption shall begin with the Jews receiving permission to settle the Land of Israel—Rabbis Naftali Tsevi Yehudah Berlin and Mordechai Eliasberg—two rabbis who stood at the helm of Hovevei Zion.[21]

A second reason for the opposition of some *ge'onim* to Zionism is that they have been fed misinformation (or disinformation) by those of lesser stature who surround them. As the great men eschew reading newspapers, they must rely for information on extremists (*kana'im*) who skew their perception. They are told that the leaders of the Zionist movement are men who are not simply unobservant in their private lives, but furthermore, intent on uprooting Judaism.[22]

According to Don Yahya, the Zionist leaders profess no proficiency in matters of religion and are amenable to working with the great rabbis in matters pertaining to religion. He cites the example of a responsum from one of the great halakhic decisors of the generation to accommodate the Colonial Bank so that the prohibition of charging interest (*ribbit*) be not transgressed. Don Yahya personally witnessed both the question from Zionist officialdom and the responsum issued by the elderly *ga'on*.[23] (Undoubtedly, "the elderly *ga'on*" [*"ha-ga'on ha-yashish"*] was Don Yahya's own father-in-law, Rabbi Shelomo Hakohen, the *dayyan* or chief justice of Vilna.)[24]

Don Yahya points out the democratic character of the Zionist congresses. If more religious Jews would join the ranks of the Zionist movement, they would be able to turn the tide and steer the movement in a more religious direction.[25]

The author chides those religious elements opposed to Zionism not to gloat and say, "We told you so." In the event that Zionism deviates from Judaism, this will be a self-fulfilling prophecy of doom; the anti-Zionist agitators will then be held responsible for bringing about that outcome by instructing observant Jews to stay clear of the movement.[26]

II.

As stated above, the *Millu'im* or Excursus of the pamphlet is a harshly worded rejoinder to the Rebbe of Lubavitch, Rabbi Shalom Dov Baer Schneersohn (1860-1920), who had made public his vehement opposition to Zionism on religious grounds.[27]

Again, one asks: How is possible that a staunch HaBaD Hasid such as Rabbi Yehudah Leib Don Yahya appended such an excursus to his work? From a remove of more than a century this seems inconceivable.

We need once more to place this pamphlet within the context of the times. Today, HaBaD has assumed a monolithic character, but at the turn of the twentieth century there existed a great divide between two competing "courts" within HaBaD Hasidism: Kopyst and Lubavitch.[28] When Rabbi Menahem Mendel Schneersohn of Lubavitch (author of the responsa *Tsemah Tsedek*) passed in 1866, a dispute erupted over succession to the throne. The youngest son, Shmuel (MaHaRaSh), remained in Lubavitch and inherited control of that city. An older son, Yehudah Leib (MaHaRIL), moved to the city of Kopyst, taking some of the Hasidim with him.[29] When within a year of the *Tsemah Tsedek*'s passing, Yehudah Leib passed, his son Shelomo Zalman (author of the Hasidic work *Magen Avot*) became the Kopyster Rebbe. And when in 1900 the Kopyster Rebbe passed, he was succeeded by his younger brother Rabbi Shemaryah Noah Schneerson (author of the Hasidic work *Shemen la-Ma'or*). Though there was a brief attempt on the part of Rabbi Shemaryah Noah Schneerson to establish himself in the city of Kopyst, eventually he returned to his rabbinate in Bobruisk, which then became the center of this branch of HaBaD Hasidism.[30] With the passing of the Rebbe of Bobruisk in 1923, this branch ceased to exist, leaving only the Lubavitch faction. At that point, remnants of the Bobruisker Hasidim transferred their allegiance to the Lubavitcher Rebbe.

In the early years of the twentieth century there erupted a major financial dispute between Bobruisk and Lubavitch regarding control of the purse strings of Kollel HaBaD in Erets Yisrael. (One may find evidence of the dispute in letters of Rav Kook from this period, when as Rabbi of Jaffa, he offered guidance how to come to a compromise.)[31] The tension arose because each Rebbe wanted his representative in Erets Yisrael to be responsible for disbursement of the funds raised by the Hasidim in Russia for the support of their brethren in the Holy Land.

Thus, there are historians who would explain the tension between Bobruisk and Lubavitch as being purely financial.[32] Truth be known, there were ideological issues dividing the two cousins, Rabbi Shemariah Noah of Bobruisk and Rabbi Shalom Dov Baer of Lubavitch. In general, it may be said that the Bobruisker was more progressive, more forward-looking. The Lubavitcher was more old-school, more conservative in outlook. These different *Weltanschauungen* found expression on many fronts.

When the Russian government sought to demand of the rabbis proficiency in the Russian language, the Bobruisker (as Rabbi Meir Simhah Cohen of Dvinsk) found this a reasonable demand; the Lubavitcher (as Rabbi Hayyim Soloveitchik of Brisk and Rabbi

Israel Meir Kagan [a.k.a. *Hafets Hayyim*]) fought against this proposal tooth and nail.[33]

When it came to deciding which city should serve as the center of HaBaD Hasidism in Erets Yisrael—Hebron or Jerusalem—Rabbi Shalom Dov Baer militated to retain the center in the provincial town of Hebron rather than allow the center to shift to Jerusalem.[34] In this way, the Lubavitcher Rebbe believed he could shield the Hasidim from the distractions of urban civilization. The Bobruisker did not think it realistic to keep the Hasidim "down on the farm." Willy-nilly, establishment of a *"bibliotek"* in Hebron would bring secular literature to the curious eyes of Hasidic youth.[35]

And finally, we arrive at the issue with which we began: Zionism. While Lubavitch would have no truck with Zionism, out of the *"Kibbutz"* (study-hall for advanced rabbinic students) of Bobruisk there would emerge prominent rabbis of the Mizrahi or Religious Zionist movement.[36]

The answer to the question how Rabbi Yehudah Leib Don Yahya, a fervent HaBaD Hasid, could oppose the Rebbe of Lubavitch is simple: Don Yahya was a Kopyster Hasid,[37] not a Lubavitcher Hasid.

---

[1] Yehudah Leib Don Yahya was born in Drissa (today Verkhnyadzvinsk, Belarus) in 1869 and passed in Tel-Aviv in 1941. Besides this Zionist manifesto, Rabbi Don Yahya published two volumes of *Halakhah* and essays and sermons: *Bikkurei Yehudah*, vol. 1 (Lutzin, 1930); vol. 2 (Tel-Aviv, 1939).

Volume One of *Bikkurei Yehudah* was published in Lutzin (Ludza) by the author's cousin, Rabbi Benzion Don Yahya, Rabbi of Lutzin. At that time,

Rabbi Yehudah Leib served as Rabbi of Chernigov, Soviet Russia. In his preface to the work, Benzion Don Yahya explains that the manuscript was sent to him for publication because there is no longer a Hebrew press in Russia. On pages 36-38, the editor traces the lineage of the Don Yahya family. We learn that his paternal grandfather was Rabbi Shabtai Don Yahya, Rabbi of Drissa for sixty years until his death at approximately age 90 in 1907. One of Rabbi Shabtai's sons, Rabbi Eliezer, became Rabbi of Lutzin (Ludza), a rabbinate inherited by his son, the editor (Rabbi Benzion). In 1840, there were born to Rabbi Shabtai twins: Menahem Mendel and Hayyim. Menahem Mendel served as Rabbi of Kopyst for some years, passing there in 1920. Hayyim served as Rabbi of Shklov, and after his father Shabtai's passing, as Rabbi of Drissa, until his own passing in 1913. Hayyim's son, Yehuda Leib, served as Rabbi in Shklov and Vietka, until he inherited from his father the Rabbinate of Drissa in 1913. (In *Bikkurei Yehudah*, vol. 2, f. 159, there is a letter dated 5673 [i.e., 1913] from Rabbi Meir Simhah of Dvinsk to Rabbi Don Yahya congratulating him on assuming the rabbinate of his father and grandfather in Drissa.) In 1925, Yehudah Leib was accepted as Rabbi of Chernigov.

In Shklov, Rabbi Yehudah Leib Don Yahya ministered to the *"Kehal Hasidim"* (exclusive of the Mitnagdim, who would have had their own *Rav*). (See below note 4.) However, it should be mentioned that the communities of Vietka and Chernigov as well figure prominently in the annals of HaBaD Hasidism.

The Rabbi of Vietka, Rabbi Dov Baer Lifshitz, author of an important commentary on Tractate *Mikva'ot*, *Golot 'Iliyot* (Warsaw, 1887), refers to Rabbi Shneur Zalman of Liadi as *"dodi zekeini"* ("my great uncle"). See ibid., Addendum to Introduction, and 7c. Rabbi Lifshitz's mentor and predecessor in the rabbinate of Vietka was Rabbi Nathan Gur-Aryeh, a premier disciple of Rabbi Shneur Zalman.

The man who immediately preceded Rabbi Don Yahya as Rabbi of Chernigov, Rabbi David Tsevi (Hirsch) Hen (referred to by the Hasidim as "RaDaTs") was acknowledged as one of the greatest of HaBaD Halakhists in his day. In 1925, through the intervention of Chief Rabbi Kook, he was able to emigrate from the Soviet Union to Erets Yisrael together with his daughter Rahel, son-in-law Rabbi Shalom Shelomo Schneerson (brother of Rabbi Levi Isaac Schneerson, Rabbi of Yekaterinaslav, today Dnieperpetrovsk, and uncle of Rabbi Menahem Mendel Schneerson, Lubavitcher Rebbe of Brooklyn), and granddaughter Zelda, who would later achieve fame as a Hebrew poet. See *Iggerot ha-RAYaH*, vol. 4 (Jerusalem, 1984), Letter 1330 (p. 251), in which Rav Kook attempts to install the recently arrived Rabbi S.S. Schneerson as Rav of Haderah. Rav Kook's involvement in bringing RaDaTs and family to Erets Israel is discussed in the recently published annals of the Hen Family, *Avnei Hen*, ed. Eliezer Laine and S.Z. Berger (Brooklyn, NY: Kehot, 2015).

Reviewing the second volume of *Bikkurei Yehudah*, Rabbi Zevin wrote an especially insightful appreciation of Rabbi Yehudah Leib Don Yahya. Rabbi Zevin, himself a HaBaD Hasid, noted how rare it was to find in the twentieth century a HaBaD Hasid who combined both persona of the *maskil* (intellectual) and the *'oved* (master of contemplative prayer). (In the latter connection, Rabbi Zevin observed that Rabbi Don Yahya wore daily three pairs of *tefillin*: Rashi, Rabbenu Tam, and *Shimusha Rabbah*.) Beyond HaBaD Hasidism, Don

Yahya mastered Rabbi Hayyim Soloveitchik's method of Talmudic analysis and the process of *pesikah* (halakhic decision) of Don Yahya's father-in-law, Rabbi Shleimeleh Hakohen, the Dayyan of Vilna. See Rabbi Shelomo Yosef Zevin, *Soferim u-Sefarim* (Tel-Aviv: Abraham Ziyoni, 1959), pp. 296-300.

It is noteworthy that the volume contains a responsum to Rabbi Mordechai Shmuel Kroll, the Rav of Kefar Hasidim in Erets Yisrael, and halakhic novellae of Rabbi Kroll. See *Bikkurei Yehudah*, vol. 2, ff. 121-129, 160-162. Rabbi Kroll was the eminent disciple of Rabbi Don Yahya.

[2] Rabbi Hayyim Soloveitchik's opposition to Zionism is well known. One particular statement should illustrate how extreme was Rabbi Hayyim's opposition to the new movement. The following incident took place in Minsk in 1915 (when many Jews were forced to flee their homes before the German invasion and seek refuge in the large city located farther east).

> Young Raphael Zalman Levine was walking down the street with his father, Rabbi Abraham Dov Baer Levine (known as the *"Mal'akh,"* the "Angel"). Pinned to the adolescent's lapel was an insignia of the *Keren Kayemet le-Yisrael* (Jewish National Fund), to which he had recently donated. The elder Levine was adamantly opposed to the Zionist enterprise and demanded that his son remove the pin, which he found offensive. Father and son were in the midst of an intense argument when, lo and behold, they saw approaching them from the opposite direction none other than the great Rabbi Hayyim Soloveitchik.
> Rabbi Levine said to Rabbi Soloveitchik: "My son wants to ask you a *she'elah* (question)."
> Rabbi Soloveitchik turned to Raphael Zalman: "You can ask your father." (Rabbi Levine and Rabbi Soloveitchik were friends.)
> Rabbi Levine persisted: "My son wants to ask you a *she'elah* in *emunah* (a matter of faith)."
> *"Emunah?"* Rabbi Soloveitchik's face now assumed a serious expression. Young Raphael Zalman was put on the spot and forced to ask Rabbi Hayyim what he thought of his donation to the Jewish National Fund. It just so happened that across the street was a church.
> Rabbi Hayyim responded to his young questioner: "If you have a few spare kopecks in your pocket, you can place them there rather than in the *pushke* of the *Keren Kayemes.*"
> (Reported by Rabbi Yochanan Lefkowitz and by Prof. Richard Sugarman, who heard this anecdote on two separate occasions from the mouth of Rabbi Raphael Zalman Levine of Albany, NY)

The episode is also reported in Rabbi Raphael Zalman Levine's name in Rabbi C.S. Glickman, *Mi-Pihem u-mi-Pi Ketavam* (Brooklyn, NY, 2008), pp. 119-120.

Though the sharpness of Rabbi Hayyim Soloveitchik's statement is shocking, halakhic opposition to donating to the Zionist cause was shared by several East European rabbinic leaders. A decade later in 1925, four distinguished leaders of Polish Jewry, the Hasidic Rebbes of Gur, Ostrovtsa, Radzyn, and Novominsk, addressed a letter to Rav Kook adjuring him to curtail his support of *Keren Kayemet le-Yisrael* and *Keren ha-Yesod*. See *Iggerot la-RAYaH*, ed. B.Z. Shapira (Jerusalem, 1990), Letter 199 (pp. 303-304); facsimile on p. 590.

Rav Kook, unlike the Polish Rebbes, differentiated between the two funds, lending his support to *Keren Kayemet le-Yisrael*, which directed funds to the physical reclamation of the land, but not to *Keren ha-Yesod*, which funded secular (and perhaps anti-religious) culture. See Rabbi Tsevi Yehudah Hakohen Kook, *Li-Sheloshah be-Ellul*, vol. 1 (1938), par. 44 (p. 22); *Iggerot ha-RAYaH*, vol. 5: 5682, ed. Ze'ev Neuman (Jerusalem, 2019), pp. 407-413.

[3] According to his namesake and great-grandson, journalist Shabtai Don Yahya (who wrote under the pen name of "Sh. Daniel"), the Rabbi of Drissa was known in Lubavitch as "Reb Shebsel Drisser." Sh. Don Yahya wrote that it was said that the Rabbi of Drissa might have become one of the great men of the generation in terms of Talmudic learning, but his Hasidic exuberance stunted his academic growth. See Shabtai Don Yahya, *Rabbi Eliezer Don Yahya* (Jerusalem, 1932), pp. 10-11.

(The title-page makes the point that the book bears the encomium of Chief Rabbi Kook. Shabtai Don Yahya was one of the first students of Merkaz Harav and a devoted disciple of Rav Kook. *Rabbi Eliezer Don Yahya* is a biography of the author's paternal grandfather, the Rabbi of Lutzin, son of Rabbi Shabtai Don Yahya. As a youth, Avraham Yitzhak Hakohen Kook studied under Rabbi Eliezer Don Yahya in Lutzin. Rabbi Eliezer Don Yahya was born 4 Tammuz 5598 [i.e., 1838] and passed on his birthday, 4 Tammuz 5686 [i.e., 1926]. A photograph of the funeral of Rabbi Eliezer Don Yahya in Lutzin in 1926 may be found in Rabbi Yitzhak Zilber's autobiography, *To Remain a Jew*. Zilber's original surname was "Ziyoni." Rabbi Eliezer Don Yahya inherited the rabbinate of Lutzin from his illustrious father-in-law Rabbi Aharon Zelig Ziyoni.)

Rabbi Yehudah Leib Don Yahya often quotes the *Tsemah Tsedek* in his halakhic responsa.

[4] In the biography of Rabbi Yehudah Leib Don Yahya in Shmuel Noah Gottlieb's *Ohalei Shem* (Pinsk, 1912), p. 207, s.v. *Shklov*, it states that Don Yahya assumed the rabbinate of Shklov in 1906. However, as early as Friday, 17 Menahem Av [5]664," i.e., 1904, Rabbi Shelomo Hakohen addressed his son-in-law as *"Rav Av-Beit-Din* of the congregation of Hasidim of Shklov." See *Bikkurei Yehudah*, vol. 2 (Tel-Aviv, 1939), 145a.

In *Shklover Yidden* (1929) and *Feter Zhoma* (1930), the Yiddish and Hebrew poet and writer Zalman Shneur portrayed the Hasidim of his birthplace, Shklov.

Earlier, Rabbi Yehudah Leib's father, Rabbi Hayyim Don Yahya, had served as Rabbi of Shklov. A halakhic responsum of Rabbi Hayyim Don Yahya (datelined "5653 [i.e., 1893], Shklov") was published in the journal of the Skvere Kollel, *Zera' Ya'akov* 26 (Shevat 5766 [i.e., 2006]), pp. 17-21. On p. 20, Rabbi Hayyim mentions the learned opinion of his (twin) brother from Kopyst [i.e., Rabbi Menahem Mendel Don Yahya].

[5] Rabbi Yitzhak Lichtenstein writes in the introduction to the volume that there were many such *Tagbikher* that were lost to posterity. This particular journal was inherited by Rabbi Hayyim's son, Rabbi Moshe Soloveichik. (Behind the scenes, the *Tagbuch* was made available to Rabbi Lichtenstein by his maternal uncle, Prof. Haym Soloveitchik of Riverdale, son of Rabbi J.B. Soloveitchik of Boston, son of Rabbi Moshe Soloveichik.)

[6] See *Bikkurei Yehudah*, vol. 2 (Tel-Aviv, 1939), 142a-144b. The volume was edited by the author's son-in-law Rabbi Yitzhak Neiman. Rabbi Zevin explains

that though the volume was submitted for publication in 1939, it was not issued until 1941, a few weeks before the author's passing. See S.Y. Zevin, *Soferim u-Sefarim* (Tel-Aviv: Abraham Ziyoni, 1959), p. 297. The two novellae of Rabbi Hayyim Soloveitchik (to *Bava Kamma* 13a and *Ketubot* 21a) were reprinted in the memorial volume for Rabbi Neiman, *Zikhron Yitzhak* (Jerusalem, 1999), along with several novellae of his father-in-law, Rabbi Don Yahya.

[7] See Israel Klausner, *Toledot "Nes Ziyonah" be-Volozhin* (Jerusalem: Mossad Harav Kook, 1954), pp. 25, 65, 113. A young Moshe Mordechai Epstein appears in a group photo on p. 26.

[8] Ibid. p. 24.

[9] Rabbis Epstein and Meltzer would eventually become brothers-in-law by their marriage to two sisters, daughters of the Maecenas, Shraga Feivel Frank of Kovno.

[10] Heard from Rabbi Yosef Soloveichik of Jerusalem (son of Rabbi Ahron Soloveichik of Chicago), a great-grandson of Rabbi Hayyim Soloveitchik. Rabbi Yosef Soloveichik explained the exact halakhic reasoning whereby his ancestor was able to release young Isser Zalman Meltzer from his solemn oath.

Despite Rabbi Hayyim's disapproval of Nes Ziyonah, he rejoiced at the release of the ringleader Rothstein subsequent to the latter's arrest by the Russian police:

> Also the Gaon Rabbi Hayyim of Brisk, of blessed memory, greatly rejoiced over me. He received me with joy and brought me before the NeTsIV, of blessed memory, who was pleased by my return, though he did say to me that this is not the place [for activism]. "A *mitsvah* that can be performed by others, we do not cancel for it the study of Torah" [*MT, Hil. Talmud Torah* 3:4]....Evidently, the NeTsIV too was content but had to act as if he disapproved....
> (Yosef Rothstein, in Israel Klausner, *Toledot "Nes Ziyonah" be-Volozhin*, p. 123)

See earlier on p. 13, NeTsIV's opposition to students taking time out from their Torah study for activism—even on behalf of a cause as dear to NeTsIV's heart as *Yishuv Erets Yisrael*.

[11] Ibid. p. 14.

[12] Ibid. p. 19.

[13] See above note 10.

[14] Klausner, *Toledot "Nes Ziyonah" be-Volozhin*, p. 21.

[15] Ibid. pp. 22-24. The members of Netsah Yisrael were also sworn to secrecy. Netsah Yisrael lasted until the closing of the Volozhin Yeshivah by the Russian authorities in 1892.

[16] *Ha-Tsiyoniyut mi-nekudat hashkafat ha-dat*, pp. 5-6.

[17] Ibid. pp. 6-7.

[18] Ibid. pp. 7-10.

[19] Ibid. p. 15.

[20] Ibid.

[21] Ibid. p. 16.

[22] Ibid.

[23] Ibid. pp. 16-17. Don Yahya does not go into Halakhic details. The way to circumvent the problem of *ribbit* (interest) is by drafting a *"heter 'iska."*

Rabbi Tsevi Yehudah Hakohen Kook relates that when the Zionist Colonial Bank was founded, his father, Rabbi Avraham Yitzhak Hakohen Kook, entered into negotiations with the Zionist officials and rabbis, which resulted in a *"shtar heter 'iska."* See Rabbi Tsevi Yehudah Hakohen Kook, *Li-Sheloshah be-Ellul*, vol. 1 (1938), par. 17 (pp. 11-12).

[24] The elderly *Dayyan* of Vilna, Rabbi Shelomo Hakohen (author of *Heshek Shelomo*) was exceptionally respectful of Theodor Herzl when the latter visited Vilna, extending to him the priestly benediction at a reception in Herzl's honor. See Israel Cohen, *History of Jews in Vilna* (Philadelphia: Jewish Publication Society of America, 1943), p. 350; and Israel Klausner, *Vilna: "Jerusalem of Vilna," 1881-1939*, vol. 2 (Hebrew) (Israel: Ghetto Fighters' House, 1983), p. 339.

Another son-in-law of Rabbi Shelomo Hakohen, Rabbi Nahum Greenhaus of Trok (Lithuanian, Trakai), a suburb of Vilna, was, like Don Yahya, an outspoken advocate of Zionism. Because of their support of the movement, both Rabbi Shelomo Hakohen and Rabbi Nahum Greenhaus suffered persecution by anti-Zionist elements in Lithuanian Jewry. See Klausner, ibid. pp. 330-333.

Rabbi Nahum Greenhaus' namesake was Rabbi Nahum Partzovitz (known in his youth as "Nahum Troker"), who would one day become the illustrious Rosh Yeshivah of the Mirrer Yeshiva in Jerusalem. Rabbi Nahum Partzovitz's father, Rabbi Aryeh Tsevi Partzovitz, inherited the rabbinate of Trok from his father-in-law, Rabbi Nahum Greenhaus.

A third son-in-law of Rabbi Shelomo Hakohen of Vilna was Rabbi Meir Karelitz, the older brother of Rabbi Abraham Isaiah Karelitz (author of *Hazon Ish*). Rabbi Meir Karelitz was prominent in Agudah circles, both in Vilna and later in Erets Yisrael.

[25] *Ha-Tsiyoniyut mi-nekudat hashkafat ha-dat*, p. 17.
[26] Ibid.

This modern disagreement sounds vaguely reminiscent of the disagreement between Resh Lakish and Rabbi Yohanan in *Talmud Bavli, Yoma* 9b-10a. Resh Lakish said of Babylonian Jewry: "God hates you. If you had gone up to the Land of Israel *en masse* in the days of Ezra, the divine presence would have rested in the Second Temple and there would have been a resumption of full-blown prophecy. Now that you have gone up in pitifully small numbers (*dalei dalot*), but a remnant of prophecy remains, the *bat kol* (heavenly voice)." Rabbi Yohanan responded: "Even if all of Babylonian Jewry would have gone up to the Land in the days of Ezra, the divine presence would not have rested in the Second Temple, for it is written: 'God will broaden Japheth and dwell in the tents of Shem' [Genesis 9:27]. Though God will broaden Japheth, the divine presence rests only in the tents of Shem." Rashi explains that the divine presence was prevented from resting in the Second Temple because it was built by the Persians; the divine presence rested only in the First Temple which was built by Solomon of the seed of Shem.

(Interestingly enough, the great halakhist Rabbi Moses Schreiber extends Rabbi Yohanan's thinking by attributing the fragmentation of Torah and the proliferation of controversy between the House of Shammai and the House of Hillel — to Herod's construction of the Temple. See *Torat Moshe*, ed. Shim'on Sofer [Pressburg, 1906], *Vayyikra*, s.v. *Asham hu ashom asham la-*

Hashem [Lev. 5:19], 6c.)

Evidently, Rabbi Don Yahya (like Resh Lakish) was convinced that what was crucial to effecting a spiritual revolution in Erets Yisrael was a critical mass. His opponents (like Rabbi Yohanan) could not be swayed that it was merely a matter of numbers. To their thinking, non-Jewish influence at the very inception of the Zionist movement would preclude it from bringing about the hoped for spiritual renascence so woefully lacking in the Jewish collective.

[27] See *'Or la-Yesharim* (Warsaw, 1900), pp. 57-61. For other (later) recordings of Rabbi Shalom Baer Schneersohn's anti-Zionist stance, see Bezalel Naor, *When God Becomes History: Historical Essays of Rabbi Abraham Isaac Hakohen Kook* (New York, NY: Kodesh Press, 2016), p. 168, n. 10.

[28] Actually, there was another "court" contending for the legacy of HaBaD, that of Liadi. The Rebbe of Liadi, Rabbi Hayyim Shneur Zalman Schneerson, was a third son of the *Tsemah Tsedek*. After Rabbi Hayyim Shneur Zalman's passing, his son, Rabbi Yitzhak Dov Baer Schneerson (author of the commentary to the *Siddur, Peirush MaHaRID*), succeeded him as Rebbe of Liadi.

For the sake of simplification, I have restricted my remarks to the competition between Kopyst and Lubavitch.

[29] In his autobiography, Chaim Tchernowitz ("*Rav Tsa'ir*") revealed some of the intrigue in the aftermath of the *Tsemah Tsedek*'s passing that led to the Kopyst-Lubavitch schism. See Ch. Tchernowitz, *Pirkei Hayyim* (New York, 1954), pp. 104-106.

[30] See Hayyim Meir Heilman, *Beit Rabbi* (Berdichev, 1902), vol. 3, chap. 9.

[31] See *Iggerot ha-RAYaH*, vol. 1 (1962), Letter 39, to Rav Kook's maternal uncle, Rabbi Yehudah Leib Felman of Riga, a Kopyster Hasid (pp. 34-36). The letter is datelined, "Jaffa, 3 Marheshvan, [5]667," i.e., 1906. At that time, the financial dispute was between the three competing "courts" of Bobruisk, Liadi, and Lubavitch. See ibid. p. 36.

In 1920, Rav Kook once again acted as an arbiter in the financial dispute between the *kollelim* of Bobruisk and Lubavitch. See *Iggerot ha-RAYaH*, vol. 4, ed. Rabbi Ya'akov Filber (Jerusalem: Makhon RZYH, 1984), Letter 1080 (p. 90). See also Letter 1165 (p. 154) of 22 Shevat, 5683 [i.e., 1923], addressed to HaBaD Hasidim in America, upholding the sterling reputation of Kollel Bobruisk, which had been maliciously besmirched. The administrator of Kollel Bobruisk was Rabbi Hayyim Eliezer Hakohen Bichovsky. See Rav Kook's letter to him in *Iggerot ha-RAYaH*, vol. 1, ed. Rabbi Tsevi Yehudah Kook (Jerusalem: Mossad Harav Kook, 1962), pp. 160-161 (Letter 132). (Eliezer has been misspelled "El'azar.")

[32] Roughly thirty years ago, I heard this monetary explanation from Rabbi Chaim Liberman, who had served as personal secretary and librarian of Rabbi Joseph Isaac Schneersohn of Lubavitch.

Interestingly enough, in the 1880s there emerged a theological dispute between the Rebbes of Kopyst and Lubavitch. The way it came about was in the following manner. After the passing of Rabbi Samuel (MaHaRaSh) of Lubavitch in 1882, his sons published an edition of their ancestor Rabbi Shneur Zalman of Liadi's *Torah 'Or* on the first three *parshiyot* or pericopes of the Torah (*Bereshit, Noah, Lekh Lekha*). Entitled *Likkutei Torah*, it was brought out in Vilna in 1884. The publishers took the liberty of incorporating into the text comments of the recently deceased Rabbi Samuel Schneersohn. The Kopyster Rebbe, Rabbi Shelomo Zalman Schneerson (author of *Magen Avot*), was outraged and penned a public letter of protest.

One comment of his uncle Rabbi Samuel (to *Parashat Noah*) in particular provoked the Kopyster Rebbe, this touching on the proper way to understand Rabbi Isaac Luria's metaphor of *Tsimtsum*. In three letters to Rabbi Dan Tumarkin of Rogatchov (a Lubavitcher Hasid), the Kopyster Rebbe clarified his position on *Tsimtsum* and how it differed from that of Rabbi Samuel Schneersohn. The correspondence is briefly alluded to in H.M. Heilman, *Beit Rabbi*, vol. 3, chap. 10, s.v. *Rabbi Dan Tumarkin*. The entire exchange is available in Rabbi Mordechai Menashe Laufer, *Ha-Melekh bi-Mesibo*, vol. 2 [Kefar Habad, 1993], pp. 283-293. (This truly fascinating correspondence was brought to my attention a generation ago by Baruch Thaler.)

Regarding the publication of *Likkutei Torah* (Vilna, 1884), see further Hayyim Meir Heilman, *Beit Rabbi*, vol. 1, 87a; vol. 3, 16a, 28a; Rabbi Yehoshua Mondshine, "'*Likkutei Torah*' *le-Shalosh Parshiyot*," *Kefar Habad*, nos. 931, 933. Available online at:

http://www.shturem.net/index.php?section=blog_new&article_id=29

[33] This issue was raised at the rabbinical conference held in St. Petersburg in 1910. The decisions reached by the delegates were relayed to Stolypin, Minister of the Interior. Some of the heated exchange between the Bobruisker and the Lubavitcher behind closed doors has been preserved in the memoirs of Isaac Schneersohn, one of the delegates to the conference; see I. Schneersohn, *Leben un Kamf fun Yiden in Tsarishen Rusland 1905-1917* (Paris, 1968). The chapters concerning the 1910 conference were translated from Yiddish into Hebrew by Rabbi Yehoshua Mondshine, *"Asifat ha-Rabbanim be-Rusya bi-Shenat 'Atar," Kefar Habad*, no. 898. Available online at: http://www.shturem.net/index.php?section=blog_new&article_id=24

According to Isaac Schneersohn, it was none other than he (Crown Rabbi of Chernigov) who proposed abolishing the position of *Kazyonny Ravin* (in Hebrew, *"Rav mi-Ta'am,"* or Crown Rabbi), thus wresting authority from the secular-trained, modern *"Rabbiner"* and consolidating communal power in the hands of the Talmudically-trained traditional *Rav*—provided he be proficient in the Russian language.

[34] Historically, the HaBaD community in Hebron preceded that of Jerusalem. In 1823, Rabbi Dov Baer Shneuri of Lubavitch (*"Mitteler Rebbe"*), the second-generation leader of the HaBaD movement, founded a HaBaD community in Hebron. Later, in 1847, a group of HaBaD families from Hebron relocated to Jerusalem.

[35] See *Kuntres me-Admo"r shelit"a mi-Bobruisk: Teshuvot nitshiyot va-amitiyot 'al Kuntres Admo"r shelit"a de-Libavitz* (1907), pp. 18-19. I described the contents of the booklet in Kestenbaum Catalogue, Auction Sale 38 (Thursday, November 29th, 2007), Lot 85, p. 28. Available at: https://www.kestenbaum.net/media/catalog/product/pdfs/Auction_38.pdf

[36] Two names come to mind: Rabbi Nissan Telushkin in the United States and Rabbi Shelomo Yosef Zevin in Erets Yisrael. Both studied in the *"Kibbutz"* of the Bobruisker Rebbe and received ordination from him. Eventually, with the extinction of Bobruisker Hasidism, both Telushkin and Zevin would transfer their allegiance to Lubavitch. However, their affiliation with the Religious

Zionist movement could at times place them in an unenviable position. Particularly Rabbi Zevin oftentimes found himself between a rock and a hard place. Rabbi Menachem Mendel Schneerson, the Lubavitcher Rebbe residing in Brooklyn, would on occasion expect of Rabbi Zevin to promote positions at variance with his Mizrahi colleagues in Erets Yisrael (such as Chief Rabbi Isaac Halevi Herzog). See Marc B. Shapiro, *Changing the Immutable: How Orthodox Judaism Rewrites Its History* (Oxford: Littman, 2015), pp. 235; 238, n. 87.

A brief autobiographical sketch of Rabbi Telushkin (a native of Bobruisk) is found at the conclusion of his halakhic work on *mikva'ot* (ritual baths), *Tahorat Mayim* (Brooklyn, NY: Kehot, 1990), pp. 355-356 (*"Le-Zikaron"*).

[37] In Rabbi Don Yahya's letter to Rabbi Shelomo Yosef Zevin concerning the counterintuitive thought process that informed Rabbi Hayyim Soloveitchik's halakhic decisions, Rabbi Don Yahya refers to himself as a "Hasid [of] Kopyst." The context is Rabbi Hayyim's desire to procure a *"Yanover esrog"* (citron from Genoa, Italy) to fulfill the commandment, in compliance with the tradition of HaBaD, and earlier the *HaTaM Sofer, Orah Hayyim*, no. 207. See *Hiddushei ha-GRaH he-Hadash 'al ha-Shas* (B'nei Berak: Mishor, 2008), p. 586.

However, in *Zikhron Yitzhak* (Memorial Volume for Rabbi Yitzhak Neiman) (Jerusalem, 1999), p. 141 (which is the source of *Hiddushei ha-GRaH*), Rabbi Don Yahya refers to himself as a "Hasid (HaBaD)." It would be interesting to see the original of the letter, which may yet be in the hands of the heirs of Rabbi Zevin. From the fact that the word "HaBaD" is placed in parentheses, one is inclined to assume that this is an addition on the part of an editor (Rabbi Zevin?). According to the Introduction (*"Petah Davar"*) to *Zikhron Yitzhak*, this is the first publication of the letter from Rabbi Don Yahya to Rabbi Zevin.

(Inter alia, elsewhere Rabbi Zevin quoted Rabbi Don Yahya concerning Rabbi Hayyim Soloveitchik's leniency in regard to fasting on Yom Kippur, which Rabbi Zevin followed up with a more comprehensive explanation by Rabbi Isaac Ze'ev Soloveitchik, the son of Rabbi Hayyim. See Rabbi Shelomo Yosef Zevin, *Ha-Mo'adim ba-Halakhah* [Tel-Aviv: A. Zioni, n.d.], *"Yom ha-Kippurim,"* p. 82.)

Klausner, *Toledot "Nes Ziyonah" be-Volozhin*, p. 17, records that in 1889, the members of Nes Ziyonah were able to elicit letters of support for the conception of *Yishuv Erets Yisrael* from the Hasidic Rebbes of Kopyst and Bohush (a branch of Ruzhin).

*

Postscript: By the time Rabbi Joseph Isaac Schneersohn of Lubavitch relocated to Riga, Latvia, old animosities between the remnants of Kopyster hasidim and the rival Lubavitch court were set aside. See Rabbi Eliyahu Hayyim Althaus' letter describing *Shemini 'Atseret* 1929 in Riga, when "even the critics, the *Kamats Kufin*" were overwhelmed. Facsimile in Rabbi Chaim Rapoport, *The Afterlife of Scholarship: A Critical Review of 'The Rebbe' by Samuel Heilman and Menachem Friedman* (2011), p. 208. "Komats Kuf" was Lubavitch code for "Kopyst."

See also Rabbi Shaul Shimon Deutsch, *Larger than Life* (New York, NY, 1997), p. 45 concerning Rabbi Ben-Zion Don-Yahya. In the document on p. 35 the Rabbi of Lutzin's name appears as "Ben-Zion Donhin."

Of Priests and Prophets: The Way of Knowing and the Way of Not-Knowing

Shnayor Z. Burton. *Mishnat Ya'akov: Derushim Nivharim be-Mo'adei ha-Shanah* (5779/2019)

Rabbi Shnayor Burton is a distinguished Talmudic scholar who resides in the Flatbush section of Brooklyn. This is his second work of Jewish Thought.

In 2017 he published *Orot Ya'akov: Derushim Nivharim be-Ma'asei Avot*. That volume focuses on the lives of the patriarchs of our nation, Abraham, Isaac and Jacob, whose sagas are recorded in the Book of Genesis.

The present sequel volume contains *derushim* (homilies) on the cycle of the year, the Sabbath and festivals.

In the introduction to the work, the author calls our attention to the first *derush*, "Torat Moshe ve-Derekh ha-Nevi'im" ("The Torah of Moses and the Way of the Prophets"). It is to this seminal thought that I shall devote my remarks.

The three outstanding Jewish theologians of twentieth-century America—Abraham Joshua Heschel, Isaac Hutner and Joseph Baer Soloveitchik (in alphabetical order of their last names)—in one context or another, all dwelled on the phenomenon of the prophets of Israel.

In the case of Rabbi Soloveitchik, it was the spartan yet incisive observation that the entire project of the prophets consists of a divulgence of the divine attributes, to the end of *imatatio dei*. Rabbi Soloveitchik's remarks are predicated on Maimonides, *Hil. De'ot* 1:6: "Thus too, the prophets described God by all the various attributes, 'long-suffering' and 'abounding in kindness,' 'righteous' and 'upright,' 'perfect,' 'mighty' and 'powerful,' and so forth, to teach us that these qualities are good and right, and that a human being should cultivate them, and imitate [God], as much as one can."[1]

Rabbi Hutner's perception of the prophets took the form of an intriguing exploration of their silence when confronted with the problem of theodicy. For the *Pahad Yitzhak* (as for Rashi earlier), the essence of the prophet is speech (*navi* from *niv*)[2] and the ability to describe the divine attributes. With the destruction of the Temple there occurred a cosmic breakdown and a muting of the prophetic voice.[3]

Finally, as a young man, Abraham Joshua Heschel wrote his doctoral dissertation on the subject. *The Prophets* is a massive work that attempts to arrive at the essence of Israelite prophecy. Painstakingly, we are introduced to a God who is—to employ Heschel's term—"anthropopathic." God commiserates with man and shares in man's suffering. This is a reversal of Maimonides' teaching.[4] The divine attributes are not virtual realities designed for human imitation. They are reality!

Priests and Prophets

Our author, whether consciously or not, continues the conversation. He sets up the opposition of the Torah of Moses and the Way of the Prophets. Some of the ideas are already familiar to us, but there is something fresh, something new here, specifically the value assigned to the *korbanot*, the sacrifices in the Temple. For Rabbi Shnayor Burton, the sacrificial cult is not just one aspect of the Torah, but its essence. And it is the sacrifices which are the escarpment between the two surfaces of the Torah and the Prophets.

The prophets—Isaiah, Jeremiah—rail time and time again against the sacrificial cult. Why? Simply, theirs is a critique not so much of the institution itself, but of the corruption and the moral turpitude that came to be associated with it.

In Rabbi Burton's presentation we wake up to the realization that the way of the priests and the way of the prophets are in a sense antithetical to one another. If the prophets bestowed upon us knowledge of God's ways, the sacrifice takes us beyond that to the unfamiliar and ultimately unknowable. The act of bringing a sacrifice is an act of surrender, an admission of ignorance. The way of the prophets is the way of knowing. The way of the sacrifices is the way of not-knowing.[5]

The prophets allow us to know God's goodness.[6] The Torah takes us beyond human ken, beyond earthbound notions of "God,"[7] beyond "good."[8] Torah is the Absolute, the Prophets are the attributes.

Perhaps this is the secret of Maimonides' downgrading of the sacrifices in his philosophic work, the *Guide*. Whereas in his halakhic work, *Mishneh Torah*, the sacrifices enjoy a robust life (something unseen in the several centuries intervening between the completion of the Talmud and Maimonides' own day), in the *Guide* the sacrifices suffer immensely, as they are held up to the scrutiny of comparative religion and reduced to the primitive state of Near Eastern civilization. Many over the centuries, including Maimonides' greatest admirers, have been perplexed how the same author could so abruptly shift gears.

I would suggest that in *Mishneh Torah* Maimonides writes from the perspective of Moses the legislator. In the *Guide*, which according to scholarly consensus is (or at least, contains) Maimonides' promised *Book of Prophecy*,[9] he writes from the perspective of the prophetic—not the Mosaic—tradition. And that tradition, which constitutes the way of knowing God, carries with it, *eo ipso*, an adversarial attitude to the very institution of sacrifice.

Unbeknown to our author, some of the themes that he addresses were encapsulated by Rav Kook in an enigmatic code.

The verse in Exodus 22:1 reads: "If the thief is discovered while tunneling in...." The Hebrew word for the underground (or tunnel) is *"mahteret."* Rav Kook envisioned this as two words: *mah torat*. *Mah* (*mem, het*) is the number forty-eight, symbolizing the forty-eight prophets.[10] *Torat* is Torah in the *nismakh* (construct) form. The thief is an allusion to Jesus, who was depicted in the old work *Toledot Yeshu* as a *"gonev shem shamayim,"* someone who absconds with the divine name.[11]

What appeared to Rav Kook in a kabbalistic reverie was that the "theft," the misappropriation perpetrated by Christianity, consisted in the prioritization of the Prophets over the Torah. In mainstream Judaism, the Torah is primary and the Prophets secondary. Christianity reversed the order, making the Torah secondary (*"nismakh"*) to the Prophets. Christianity latched onto the compassion of the prophets while obsoleting the laws of the Torah.[12]

(As a student of students of Rav Kook, I might add a postscript that in Catholicism, the singular divine "I" of *Anokhi*, the undefinable, indescribable Giver of the Torah, was fractured into a trinity of attributes.)

The saintly *"Hafets Hayyim,"* as he was known, Rabbi Israel Meir Kagan, pushed young Talmudists, especially *kohanim* such as himself, to become conversant with the fifth order of the Talmud, *Kodashim*, which deals with sacrifices. To this end, he himself authored the digest *Likkutei Halakhot*, accomplishing for the exotic order of *Kodashim* what Rabbi Isaac Alfasi in his *Halakhot* had accomplished for the other, actual orders of the Talmud.

The *Hafets Hayyim* explained that the rebuilding of the Temple is imminent and therefore, the teachers of Torah must be competent to rule in matters pertaining to the Temple service.

That the sacrifices have seized the imagination of a young, talented thinker with such force, may be indicative of our proximity to the Temple. The *Beit ha-Mikdash* will require not only *poskei halakhot* (decisors) to adjudicate thorny matters of ritual law, but also *hogei de'ot* (thinkers) to breathe life into an otherwise moribund service, and to make peace between the way of knowing and the way of not-knowing.[13]

---

[1] See Rabbi J.D. Halevi Soloveitchik, *Shi'urim le-Zekher Abba Mari*, vol. 2 (Jerusalem: Mossad Harav Kook, 2002), "*Mehikat Hashem*" (pp. 188-189).

Cf. Rabbi Nahman of Breslov, *Likkutei MOHaRaN* I, 212. (Elsewhere, we have discussed Rabbi Nahman's use of Maimonides' *Sefer ha-Madda'*. Although in this instance, Rabbi Nahman's remarks might also have been inspired by the *Shir ha-Kavod* ["*An'im Zemirot*"] attributed to the *Hasidei Ashkenaz*.)

[2] Rashi, Exodus 7:1.

[3] See Rabbi Isaac Hutner, *Pahad Yitzhak: Kuntres ve-Zot Hanukkah* (New York, NY, 1989), *ma'amar* 8 (pp. 63-75).

Textual problems arise in regard to this *ma'amar*. The key phrase *"ro'eh ve-shotek"* ("He sees and is silent") does not occur in the *Bavli* version of the crisis (*Yoma* 69b), rather in the *Yerushalmi* version (*Berakhot* 7:3, *Megillah* 3:7). And in the *Yerushalmi*, God's silence does not result in the muting of prophecy. On the contrary, "It is fitting to call this [God] '*gibbor*' ('mighty'), for He sees the destruction of His house and is silent!" By fusing *Bavli* and *Yerushalmi*, Rabbi Hutner has in effect created his own narrative.

[4] For Maimonides, the belief that God is anthropopathic is just as grievous as the belief that God is anthropomorphic. See *Guide of the Perplexed* I, beginning chap. 53.

[5] The thought occurs to this writer that perhaps this is implicit in the *halakhah*, "Any priest who does not admit to the service [of the sacrifices] has no portion in the priesthood" ("*Kol kohen she-eino modeh ba-'avodah, ein lo helek ba-kehunah*") (*Hullin* 132b; *Menahot* 18b). The statement is problematic because such a *kohen* should be disqualified on grounds of heresy (*apikorsut*). See RaShI, RITBA, and other *rishonim* cited in Rabbi Yitzhak Goldstoff, *Mikdash ha-Kodesh*, vol. 2 (Jerusalem, 1999), 35:2 (118b-119b). Beyond the belief system of any Jew, there may be required of the priest a special belief in the sacrifices, involving *bittul*, or surrender, to that which is unknowable.

[6] One ventures that this is the significance of the term *"nevi'im tovim"* ("good prophets") in the blessing preceding the *haftarah*, the reading from the Prophets. The *raison d'être*, the entire project of the prophets, is to manifest the

goodness of God.

See also Rabbi Nehemiah's interpretation of the verse in Exodus 2:2: "'*Tov*' (good)—*hagun li-nevi'ut* (worthy of prophecy)" (*b. Sotah* 12a).

[7] See Exodus 6:3.

[8] See Maimonides, *Guide of the Perplexed* I, 2.

[9] See *Shemonah Perakim* (Maimonides' introduction to *Avot*), chap. 7 (Kafah ed., p. 260, col. a); the introduction to the *Commentary to the Mishnah*, Kafah ed., p. 5, col. a; and the introduction to *The Guide of the Perplexed*, transl. Shlomo Pines (Chicago: University of Chicago Press, 1964), pp. 9-10.

[10] *b. Megillah* 14a.

[11] In the legend recorded in *Toledot Yeshu*, Jesus made off with the secret divine name (*shem ha-meforash*) that was recorded in the Temple in Jerusalem, and subsequently employed the name for magical purposes.

This legend runs parallel to the Geonic tradition concerning Parvah Amgusha of the Talmud. In the tradition recorded by Rabbeinu Hananel, Parvah Magus tunneled under the Temple in order to observe the High Priest's behavior on the Day of Atonement, but was discovered in the process. See *b. Yoma* 35a, Rabbeinu Hananel ad loc. (quoted in Rabbi Nathan of Rome, *'Arukh*, s.v. *Parvah*, which in turn is quoted in *Tosafot, Yoma*, s.v. *Parvah Amgusha*); and Maimonides, *Commentary to the Mishnah, Middot* 4:8 (Kafah ed., p. 300). Though unstated, it is possible that Parvah sought to learn the *shem ha-meforash*, which would have been pronounced by the High Priest on the Day of Atonement.

The divine name was to remain a secret tradition zealously guarded by the priests in the Temple. See *b. Kiddushin* 71a. According to Rashi, *'Avodah Zarah* 17b, s.v. *'alav li-sereifah*, pronunciation of the name of forty-two letters enabled one to "do with it as one desires." See Ephraim Kanarfogel, "Rashi's Awareness of Jewish Mystical Literature and Traditions," in *Raschi und Seine Erbe*, ed. Krochmalnik, Liss and Reichman (Heidelberg: Hochschule für Jüdische Studien, 2007), pp. 29-30.

Concerning the name of forty-two letters, see Rashi, *Kiddushin* 71a, s.v. *shem ben shteim 'esreh; Sanhedrin* 60a, s.v. *shem ben arba' otiyot; Sanhedrin* 101b, s.v. *u-bi-leshon 'agah*, and *Margaliyot ha-Yam* ad loc.

[12] See Rabbi Abraham Isaac Hakohen Kook, *Kevatsim mi-Ketav Yad Kodsho*, vol. 1, ed. Boaz Ofen (Jerusalem, 2006), *Pinkas Rishon le-Yaffo*, para. 43 (pp. 98-99); Rabbi Hayyim Avihu Shvarts, *Mi-Tokh ha-Torah ha-Go'elet*, vol. 3 (Jerusalem, 1989), p. 225; Rabbi Tsevi Yehudah Hakohen Kook, *Li-Netivot Yisrael*, vol. 2 (Jerusalem, 1979), "*Ha-Pesha' be-Yisrael*" (pp. 60-61).

This same thought is conveyed in *Shemonah Kevatsim* 5:127, where the opposition is also between Halakhah and Aggadah.

[13] See Rabbi Nahman of Breslov, *Likkutei Moharan* I, 6:4, 7; II, 7:7.

The Two Luminaries:
Rabbi Nahman of Breslov and Rav Kook

Moshe Nahmani. *Shnei ha-Me'orot* (5779/2019)

Moshe Nahmani has distinguished himself as a foremost independent researcher of the annals of Rav Kook. Like Rav Kook, he has an affinity for Breslov Hasidism (something which alienates him from some disciples of Rav Kook, who would wish to distance and disentangle the Rav from Hasidism). The past several years, he has emerged as a most vocal and outspoken defender of animal welfare. (Again, this causes some friction between Nahmani and some representatives of Kookian tradition who regard the Rav's writings on vegetarianism as a *"hilkheta li-Meshiha,"* something that awaits the Messianic Era.)

We are all indebted to Moshe Nahmani for his latest work, a carefully documented presentation of the overlap and spiritual affinity between the elder Rav Avraham Yitzhak Hakohen Kook (and his son Rav Tsevi Yehudah Hakohen Kook) on the one hand, and Rabbi Nahman of Breslov, on the other. Besides invaluable anecdotes provided by disciples,[1] there are at least two great finds in terms of archival material. First and foremost are Rav Tsevi Yehudah's notes in the marginalia of his copy of *Likkutei MoHaRaN*, Rabbi Nahman's magnum opus. Second, is the lengthy letter Rabbi Avraham Sternhartz addressed to Rav Kook in the summer of

1934, seeking the Chief Rabbi's assistance in easing his immigration from Soviet Russia to Erets Yisrael.

Rabbi Avraham Sternhartz was the grandson of Rabbi Nathan Sternhartz of Nemirov and Breslov, who acted as Rabbi Nahman's *sofer* (scribe). But Rabbi Nathan was much more than just an amanuensis. Rabbi Nahman believed that the soul-connection between the two, Nahman and Nathan, extended back in time. Rabbi Nathan would become Rabbi Nahman's chief disciple and interpreter. After Rabbi Nahman's passing, Rabbi Nathan became the leader of the Breslover Hasidim.

After Rabbi Avraham Sternhartz's arrival in Erets Yisrael in 1936,[2] he transmitted the Breslov tradition to disciples, most notably Rabbi Gedaliah Kenig, who before his passing in 1980, initiated the establishment of the now thriving Breslov community in Tsefat.

What is most curious about Rabbi Sternhartz's letter of introduction to Rav Kook (on pages 69-72) is that he presents himself as a grandson, on his father's side, of the great Rabbi David Tsevi, *Av Beit Din* of several communities, and on his mother's side, of Rabbi [Nahman] of Tcherin, author of *Parpera'ot la-Hokhmah* [a commentary on *Likkutei MOHaRaN*]. It is definitely true that Rabbi Nathan's father-in-law was the esteemed halakhist Rabbi David Tsevi Auerbach of Sharigrad, Kremnitz, and Mohilev, but why not state the most obvious claim to fame, namely descent from Rabbi Nathan Sternhartz himself?

Rabbi Nahman and Rav Kook

I turn now to Rav Tsevi Yehudah's notes to *Likkutei MOHaRaN*.[3] Perhaps the most important contribution is Rav Tsevi Yehudah's finding that an important passage in *Likkutei MOHaRaN* I, 6:3 has its antecedent in the classic ethical work by Bahya ibn Pakuda, *Hovot ha-Levavot* (*Duties of the Heart*).

Rabbi Nahman writes:

> Even if one knows in oneself that one did complete *teshuvah* (repentance), nonetheless, one must repent of the first repentance, because in the beginning, when one did *teshuvah*, one did [so] according to one's understanding, and afterward, when one does *teshuvah*, one certainly recognizes and understands more *Hashem*, blessed be He. We find that according to one's present understanding, certainly the first understanding was a corporealization. We find that one must repent of one's first understanding for having corporealized the sublimity of the divinity.

Rav Tsevi Yehudah jotted down:

> See *Ho[vot] ha-L[evavot], Sha'ar 'Avoda[t] H[ashem]*, chap. 3, fifth advantage of arousal of reason: "they renew repentance" ("*mehaddeshim teshuvah*").

Nahmani unpacks Rav Tsevi Yehudah's shorthand notation. In the aforementioned paragraph, Bahya recorded the practice of "some devotees[4] that spent their lifetimes doing repentance. Every day they used to find a new way of repentance,[5] as they increased their understanding of God's greatness and their neglect of their obligation to obey Him in the past."[6]

It is of course edifying to learn that Rabbi Nahman was preceded in his conception of ongoing repentance (perhaps "return" is the better translation of *"teshuvah"*) by the eleventh-century Spanish *dayyan*, Bahya ibn Pakuda. But it seems to me that there is an essential element in Rabbi Nahman's teaching lacking in the earlier *Hovot ha-Levavot*. That is the element of *"hagshamat Elohut"* (corporealization of divinity). This is the revolutionary thought of Rabbi Nahman of Braslav. And it is this same daring that we will encounter in the writings of Rav Kook (the elder).

In *Zer'onim*, one of the earliest collections of Rav Kook's *pensées*, published in the literary journal *Ha-Tarbut ha-Yisraelit* in Jaffa in 1913,[7] we find this striking statement:

> From epoch to epoch, the mixture of pure belief in the Unity [of the deity] with the darkness of corporealization (*hagshamah*) is increasingly clarified....[8]

What Rav Kook has done in few words is to apply the method of Rabbi Nahman, previously reserved for the individual, to mankind as a whole. For Rabbi Nahman, spiritual growth consists of shedding puerile conceptions of the divinity for more advanced, more rarefied notions. And for Rav Kook, this evolution of consciousness is written not just on the tablet of the individual heart but on the tablet of the heart of collective mankind.[9] And then, it is not just the individual Jew who is involved in an ongoing process of *teshuvah*, but *Knesset Yisrael*, and beyond that, the human race as a whole. In the writings of the two spiritual luminaries, Rabbi Nahman and Rav Kook, *teshuvah* achieves epic proportions.

In 1978, newlywed and newly arrived in Jerusalem (we made *'aliyah* upon completion of our *"Sheva' Berakhot"*), I was privileged to meet several times with Rav Tsevi Yehudah Kook in the privacy of his home at 30 Ovadyah Street in the Ge'ulah section of town. On one of these occasions, the octogenarian sage shared with me impromptu some of his reflections on Breslov.

Rav Tsevi Yehudah recounted in a humorous vein his experience with a certain unnamed rabbi from America who would daily stroll with him. This regimen of the daily walk went on for some time. Then one day during their outing together, Rabbi Tsevi Yehudah mentioned Rabbi Nahman of Breslov. The next day, the man did not arrive for the walk. So ended this *"havruta."* (Nahmani has the story on page 112 *sans* the "American" identity of the mystery man.)

The elder Rav Kook wrote a by now famous letter to his adolescent son Tsevi Yehudah,[10] advising some caution when studying the works of the "great man," Rabbi Nahman. Basically, the father communicated to his son that there is required "a healthy soul in a healthy body." Rav Kook also recommended that the study of Rabbi Nahman be balanced by studying opposed views.[11]

Perhaps it was for the sake of providing balance that Rav Tsevi Yehudah dropped on me that the wondrous *Sippurei Ma'asiyot*, the tales of Rabbi Nahman, were looked at askance both in Gur and HaBaD.

I later fact-checked this with Breslover Hasidim who informed me that indeed the *Hiddushei ha-RIM* (Rabbi Yitzhak Meir Rotenberg-Alter, the founder of Gerrer Hasidism) had made a study of the stories of Rabbi Nahman. The RIM was able to follow the storyline as far as it was based on the Kabbalah of the ARI (Rabbi Isaac Luria). But it seems that at a certain point Rabbi Nahman left the ARI behind and ventured out on his own, and there the RIM was lost.

As for HaBaD's rejection of Rabbi Nahman's stories, to this day I have no idea to what Rav Tsevi Yehudah, *zt"l*, was alluding.

Again for the sake of balance, when asked by a student as to the nature of Rabbi Nahman's *Stories*, Rav Tsevi Yehudah responded that contained within them are moral lessons (*divrei mussar*).[12]

Moshe Nahmani has put together a wonderful collection of anecdotes and documents (including, on page 16, a facsimile of Rav Kook's own copy of *Likkutei MOHaRaN*). Much maligned during their lifetimes and even after, these two great luminaries, Rabbi Nahman and Rav Kook, are now shining brightly. And we can rest assured that their lights will glow ever brighter with the passage of time.

[1] I wish to correct a slight imprecision of language in one of these quotes. Nahmani quotes Rav Kook's disciple, Rabbi Israel Porath. The latter's testimony is of paramount importance for the reason that Rabbi Israel Porath was one of three major Torah scholars who would journey from Jerusalem to study under Rav Kook in Jaffa, the other two being Rabbi Tsevi Pesah Frank and Rabbi Ya'akov Moshe Harlap. Eventually, Rabbi Porath went on to become Rabbi of Cleveland, Ohio, where he was esteemed by all members of the Jewish community, regardless of their affiliation. He also authored a multivolume work on the Talmud, *Mavo ha-Talmud* (*The Outline of the Talmud*), whose peculiar methodology was inspired by Rav Kook.

In *Shnei ha-Me'orot* (p. 14) we read:

> According to what [Rav Kook] communicated to me in private....his heart was drawn to the ways of [spiritual] service of Hasidism, and he especially devoted himself to the mysticism of Rabbi Nahman of Breslov. He read and studied much his books *and conversations*, and delved deeply into his thoughts.

The quote is taken from *Hayyei ha-RAYaH*, a biography of Rav Kook by a later disciple, Rabbi Moshe Tsevi Neriyah.

However in Rabbi Porath's original appreciation, which appeared in *Sefer ha-Do'ar*, there is a slightly different wording:

> According to what [Rav Kook] communicated to me in private....his heart was drawn to the ways of [spiritual] service of Hasidism. He especially devoted himself to the mysticism of Rabbi Nahman of Breslov. He read and studied much his books, and delved deeply into his thoughts *and conversations*.
> (Rabbi Israel Porath, "*Harav A.Y. Kook z"l,*" in *Sefer ha-Do'ar: Mivhar ma'amarim la-yovel ha-shishim 5682-5742*, ed. Miklishanski and Kabakoff [New York: Histadrut ha-'Ivrit ba-Amerika, 1982], p. 199, col. 1)

[2] For more details of Rabbi Avraham Sternhartz's narrow escape from Soviet Russia, see Bezalel Friedman's biography of Rabbi Levi Yitzhak Bender, *Ish Hasidekha* (Jerusalem, 1993), pp. 178-179. (It includes a photo of Rebbetzin Sternhartz's Soviet passport of December 1935.)

[3] I should add that not only did Rav Tsevi Yehudah annotate his copy of *Likkutei MOHaRaN*, but in the marginalia of his copy of *Orot ha-Kodesh*, on two occasions found sources for his father's statements in *Likkutei MOHaRaN*. See Rav Tsevi Yehudah's notes to *Orot ha-Kodesh*, appended to vol. 4 of *Orot ha-Kodesh* (Jerusalem: Mossad Harav Kook, 1990), p. 595. These notes pertaining to *Likkutei MOHaRaN* appear (in somewhat abridged form) in *Shnei ha-Me'orot*, pp. 115-116.

[4] Judah ibn Tibbon translated into Hebrew as *"perushim"* (ascetics). The reference is probably to Sufi ascetics.

[5] In Ibn Tibbons' Hebrew translation (as that of Kafah): *"mehaddeshim teshuvah."*

[6] Bahya ben Joseph ibn Pakuda, *The Book of Direction to the Duties of the Heart* (*Al-Hidaya ila Fara'id Al-Qulub*), transl. Menahem Mansoor (London: Routledge & Kegan Paul, 1973), p. 184 (the fifth reason).

[7] The editors were Alexander Ziskind Rabinowitz (*AZaR*) and Tsevi Yehudah Hakohen Kook.

[8] Reprinted in *Orot* (Jerusalem, 1950), p. 127.
  In the continuation of that paragraph, Rav Kook writes:

> In the last days of the human spirit's return to the sphere of pure belief, the final, fine shell (*kelipah*) of corporealization falls away, which is the attribution of general being to the divinity. (Ibid., p. 127)

Cf. Rabbi Mordechai Gimpel Barg's notes of Rav Kook's lectures on the *Book of Kuzari*, where we encounter the startling neologism *"kelipat nogah di-kedushah"* ("translucent shell of sanctity"):

> During the time that the world exists, the coarse, thick shells (*kelipot*) have already fallen off faith. Our work now is to remove the fine shells, which at first glance are imperceptible: the translucent shell of sanctity (*kelipat nogah di-kedushah*).
> (*Ma'amrei ha-RAYaH*, vol. 2, ed. Elisha Aviner [Langenauer] [Jerusalem, 1984], p. 490, end chap. 4)

Rav Kook's contradistinction of *"kelipot gasot"* ("coarse shells") versus *"kelipot dakot"* ("fine shells") may very well have been influenced by chapter four of Rabbi Shneur Zalman's *Iggeret ha-Kodesh*. See *Tanya* IV, chap. 4 (105b-106a). According to the author of the *Tanya*, man has the ability to remove the coarse shells, but the fine shell, which only the LORD can remove, remains until the coming of the Messiah. (The context is the "circumcision of the heart" and the distinction between *"milah"* and *"peri'ah."*)

For further clarification of Rav Kook's project of de-corporealization, see (on page 242) our remarks concerning the Maimonidean term *"mehuyyav ha-metsi'ut"* and Rabbi Nahman of Breslov's adoption of that term.

[9] The following poetic piece does seem geared to the individual and to one's daily trials and tribulations in regard to *"hagshamah"* (corporealization):

> **Let us escape**
> Let us escape from the depth of corporealization.
> Corporealization shadows us
> day in and day out,
> hour by hour,
> moment by moment.
> Give us ethics free of unworldliness,
> belief free of corporealization!
> Give light!
> Give light!
> Air and life for the soul!
> Not suffocation of the breath.
>
> (Rabbi Abraham Isaac Hakohen Kook, *Hadarav*, ed. Ron Sarid [3rd edition, 2008], p. 44)

This striking *pensée*, composed in Jerusalem between the years 1921-1924, comes from a transcript of Rabbi Tsevi Yehudah Hakohen Kook; see ibid., p. 249.

[10] On page 25, Nahmani writes that the letter was sent in 1906. As Tsevi Yehudah was born in 1891, he would have been aged fifteen when he received the letter.

[11] Nahmani bemoans the fact that the manuscript of the letter has gone missing. See *Shnei ha-Me'orot*, p. 94.

On at least one occasion we find young Tsevi Yehudah seeking his father's explanation of a certain passage in *Likkutei MOHaRaN* (I, 4). See *Tsemah Tsevi* (Jerusalem, 1991), Letter 21 (datelined "Halberstadt, *Motsa'ei Shabbat ha-Gadol*, 5674 [i.e., 1914]"), p. 63; *Shnei ha-Me'orot*, pp. 95-96.

Another passage in *Tsemah Tsevi* understood by Nahmani as a query to the elder Rav Kook, was actually misinterpreted. In Letter 15, datelined "Jaffa, 22 Sivan 5673 [i.e., 1913]" (p. 45), Tsevi Yehudah requested Rabbi Ya'akov Moshe Harlap's assistance in obtaining a copy of Rabbi Nathan Sternhartz's *Likkutei Tefillot*. The three titles requested of Rabbi Harlap were: *Likkutei Tefillot, Shev Shma'teta*, and *Kuntres ha-Hitpa'alut*. *Shev Shma'teta* by Rabbi Aryh Leib Hakohen (author of *Ketsot ha-Hoshen* and *Avnei Milu'im*) is a work immensely popular in yeshivah circles. *Kuntres ha-Hitpa'alut* is a Hasidic work on meditation by Rabbi Dov Baer Shneuri of Lubavitch (*"Mitteler Rebbe"*). Rabbi Harlap's response is found in *Hed Harim*, p. 51. He felt confident that *Shev Shma'teta* and *Likkutei Tefillot* were readily obtainable in Jerusalem. He was in doubt as to *Kuntres ha-Hitpa'alut*.

[12] *Shnei ha-Me'orot*, p. 111.

Rabbi Nahman himself said upon concluding his thirteenth and final story, "The Seven Beggars" (which by all standards is his masterpiece), "This story... has in it much *mussar*."

Etatism and Halakhah:
Family Feud and Political Theory

Rabbi Yitzhak Goldstoff. *Mikdash ha-Kodesh*. 2 volumes: *Hilkhot Beit ha-Behirah; Hilkhot Klei ha-Mikdash*. Jerusalem 5754-5759 [1994-1999].

In what proved a controversial eulogy for his uncle, Rabbi Yitzhak Ze'ev Soloveitchik of Brisk and Jerusalem (1886-1959),[1] Rabbi Joseph Baer Soloveitchik of Boston attempted to provide explanation why the "Brisker Rov" refused to receive Israeli Prime Minister David Ben-Gurion in his home, when his counterpart in Bnei Berak, Rabbi Abraham Isaiah Karelitz ("*Hazon Ish*") did receive the Prime Minister. According to the younger Soloveitchik, the reason was simple: *Medinat Yisrael* (the State of Israel) does not appear in Maimonides' Code of Law![2]

At the time that Rabbi Soloveitchik delivered the eulogy, a youthful Rabbi Dovid Cohen (a disciple of Rabbi Isaac Hutner, *Rosh Yeshivah* of Yeshivah Rabbi Chaim Berlin in Brooklyn) vocally protested to defend the honor of the *Hazon Ish*, and was bodily removed from the premises. (The next day in private phone conversation to his disciple, Rabbi Hutner told him to stand strong and "not be ashamed because of people who ridicule him [in the service of the LORD]."[3]

The nephew, Rabbi J.B. Soloveitchik, who figured as the ideologist of the *Mizrachi* (Religious Zionist) movement, on another occasion clearly defined his own position and that of the movement he represented: "The *Agudah* draw the line between *Erets Yisrael* (the Land of Israel) and *Medinat Yisrael* (the State of Israel). We draw the line between *Medinat Yisrael* (the State of Israel) and *Memshelet Yisrael* (the Government of Israel)." In other words, Rabbi J.B. Soloveitchik recognized the State of Israel; whatever qualms he had were not with the State *per se*, rather with the policies of the particular government at its helm.

What has all this to do with the book under review?

On the one hand, the work bears the formal *haskamah* (endorsement) of Rabbi Yehiel Mikhel Feinstein, the highly esteemed son-in-law of Rabbi Isaac Ze'ev Soloveitchik (the "Brisker Rov"). And indeed, the work excels in the so-called *"Brisker derekh"* ("Brisk methodology") of *diyyukim ba-Rambam*,[4] what a layman might describe as micro-managerial attention to the text of Maimonides (parenthetically, a method the *Hazon Ish* objected to). On the other hand, we find in this breathtakingly erudite work a new diagnostic tool not to be found in the traditional Brisker toolkit, namely the collective concept of *"malkhut"* (kingdom), as opposed to the individual *melekh*, or king.

Thus does the author explain the difference between the anointment of high priests and that of kings. Whereas each successive generation of high priest must be anointed anew, only the first king of the dynasty requires anointment; his heirs need not be anointed (except in the case of contention, or *mahloket*). The

Etatism and Halakhah

author explains that in the case of the priests, it is the individual priest who must be anointed. In the case of kings, at the other extreme, it is the institution of the kingdom that is anointed. This is an innovative understanding of Maimonides. The abstract concept of *malkhut* rather than the concrete person of the *melekh* is anointed.[5]

The author will implement this collectivizing tool in yet another regard: the difference between the institution of *kehunah*, or priesthood, and the individual priest. In *Hilkhot Klei ha-Mikdash*, Maimonides speaks about the establishment of the priesthood in general, abstract terms, not specifying who is to bestow honor upon the priesthood. In the following *halakhah*, Maimonides articulates the specific honors to be bestowed upon the priest. For Rabbi Goldstoff, the introductory *halakhah* demands respect for the institution of *kehunah* (collective *"ve-kidashto"*); the second *halakhah* addresses the respect to be shown the individual *kohen*. There is a practical outcome: Respect for the institution of *kehunah* must be accorded even by the priests themselves; respect for the individual *kohen* (individual *"ve-kidashto"*) comes from a Yisrael (Israelite; non-priest), not from a fellow priest.[6]

As stated above, this novel differential (which arguably may be inherent in Maimonides himself) is not the bequest of Brisk. Where, then, does it come from? Perhaps it is the influence of a thinker taboo in today's ultra-Orthodox world—Rav Kook, who famously differentiated between *kelal* (collective) and *perat* (individual). Or perhaps it is simply the *reshimu* (to employ a kabbalistic term), the residuum of the reality of the State and the etatism against which the Brisker Rov fought tooth and nail.[7]

---

[1] The *hesped* (eulogy) in Yiddish was delivered in Yeshiva University's Lamport Auditorium in the aftermath of the Brisker Rov's passing in Jerusalem on the Eve of Yom Kippur, 9 Tishri 5720 (i.e., 1959). A redacted Hebrew version of the eulogy, entitled *"Mah Dodekh mi-Dod,"* was published on the Brisker Rov's fourth *Yahrzeit*, 9 Tishri 5724 (i.e., 1963), in *Ha-Do'ar* (New York), pp. 752-759. Later, it was included in a collection of Rabbi Yosef Dov Soloveitchik's essays, *Divrei Hagut ve-Ha'arakhah* (Jerusalem, 1982), pp. 57-97.

[2] The version of *Ha-Do'ar* (p. 757) reads:
> They said of him [i.e., Rabbi Yitzhak Ze'ev Soloveitchik] that he was opposed to the State of Israel. This statement is not correct. Opposition to a State expresses adopting a position regarding a political body, which is itself a political act. My uncle was completely removed from all socio-political thought or response. What might be said of him, is that the State found no place within his halakhic thought system nor on his halakhic value scale. He was unable to "translate" the idea of a sovereign, secular State to halakhic properties and values.

I have utilized the English translation of Rabbi Jeffrey Saks with slight modifications. See Jeffrey Saks, "Rabbi Joseph B. Soloveitchik and the Israeli Chief Rabbinate: Biographical Notes (1959-60)," *B.D.D.* 17, September 2006, pp. 48-49.

Rabbi Sacks sums up: "It is not that Reb Velvel was an anti-Zionist, *per se*, but that, as a Halakhic Man and "Man of Pure Halakhic Truth," the secular State of Israel did not register on his radar screen" (ibid., p. 49).

*

In Maimonides' code, appointment of a king requires a *beit din* (court of law) of seventy sages and a prophet; see *Hil. Melakhim* 1:3.

In a by now famous responsum, Rav Kook argued that in the absence of monarchy, those powers revert to the nation of Israel as a whole. This responsum paved the way for viewing the eventual State of Israel, elected by the people, as invested with the powers of kingship. The operative principle is *"haskamat ha-'ummah"* ("consensus of the nation"). See Rabbi Abraham Isaac Hakohen Kook, *Mishpat Kohen*, 144:15:1 (336b-338a).

Remarkably, Rav Kook was preceded in this line of thinking by Rabbi Abraham Weinberg of Slonim; see *Hesed le-Avraham* to the Prophets (Jerusalem, 1986), 1 Samuel, chap. 8 (pp. 52-53).

Rabbi Shelomo Yosef Zevin brought support for Rav Kook's position from the wording of Nahmanides ("a commandment upon the king, or the judge, or whoever has authority over the people"). See Rabbi S.Y. Zevin, *Le-'Or Ha-Halakhah* (Jerusalem, n.d.), p. 16; *Sefer ha-Mitsvot 'im Hasagot ha-Ramban*, ed. C.B. Chavel (Jerusalem: Mossad Harav Kook, 1981), p. 409.

Etatism and Halakhah

[3] A quote from Rabbi Moses Isserles' gloss to *Shulhan 'Arukh, Orah Hayyim* 1:1.

[4] This method with its hypercritical analysis of Maimonides' code was founded by Rabbi Hayyim Soloveitchik of Brisk (Brest-Litovsk) (1853-1918). In the United States, it was promulgated by his grandson, Rabbi Joseph Baer Soloveitchik of Boston (1903-1993). For a while, Rabbi Soloveitchik maintained in Boston an institute of higher learning, Heikhal Rabbeinu Hayyim Halevi (named after his grandfather). In 1941, Rabbi Soloveitchik invited the refugee Rabbi Mikhel Feinstein to teach there. (These two were second cousins. Rabbi Soloveitchik's mother, Pesha, and Rabbi Feinstein's father, Avraham Yitzhak, were first cousins. Later in Erets Yisrael in 1946, Rabbi Mikhel Feinstein would wed Lifsha, the daughter of the *Brisker Rov*, making him Rabbi Soloveitchik's first cousin by marriage.) That same year of 1941, Rabbi Soloveitchik succeeded his recently deceased father, Rabbi Moshe Soloveichik, as *Rosh Yeshivah* at Yeshivah Rabbi Yitzhak Elhanan in New York.

[5] The pertinent texts read as follows:

> ... Even a [high] priest, the son of a [high] priest, we anoint, as it says: "And the anointed priest that shall be in his stead from among his sons" [Leviticus 6:15].
> (*Hilkhot Klei ha-Mikdash* 1:7)

> ... And we do not anoint a king, son of a king, for the kingdom is the inheritance of the king forever, as it says: "He and his sons in the midst of Israel" [Deuteronomy 17:20].
> (*Hilkhot Klei ha-Mikdash* 1:11)

See *Mikdash ha-Kodesh*, vol. 2, chap. 8 (f.23).

[6] The pertinent texts read as follows:

> It is a positive commandment to set the priests apart and to sanctify them and prepare them for sacrifice, as it says: "And you shall sanctify him for he sacrifices the bread of your God" [Leviticus 21:8].
> (*Hilkhot Klei ha-Mikdash* 4:1)

> And every man of Israel must treat them with much respect and give them precedence for everything holy: to be the first to open the Torah [reading]; to bless first [after meals]; and to take the choice portion first.
> (*Hilkhot Klei ha-Mikdash* 4:2)

See *Mikdash ha-Kodesh*, vol. 2, chap. 55 (f.187 ff.)

[7] Although not his coinage, "etatism" was certainly the *bête noire* of Yeshayahu Leibowitz, who gave the term currency in Israeli discourse.

Rav Yosef Dov Soloveitchik zt"l
on the *Seder ha-'Avodah* of *Yom ha-Kippurim*
A Synopsis of
The Rav's Yiddish *Teshuvah Derashah* 5736 (1975)
by Bezalel Naor

The thrust of Rav Soloveitchik's lecture is a fascinating exploration of our custom of reciting (and reliving) the ritual of the Day of Atonement in the Second Temple. The Rav described the *Seder ha-'Avodah* as "the climax of the sanctity of the day" (*"der hoikh-punkt fun kedushas ha-yom"*). It was the Rav's distinct impression that Jews were so "spellbound" (*"baki-shuft"*) by the recitation, that they found it difficult to take leave of it. This is borne out by the practice in Baghdad of old. The *Seder ha-'Avodah* was so beloved to the Jews of Baghdad that they recited *Seder ha-'Avodah* not only at *Mussaf* (the Additional Service), as is our custom, but at *Shaharit* (the Morning Service) and *Minhah* (the Afternoon Service) as well. Despite the efforts of several generations of Ge'onim to uproot this custom, they were unsuccessful in doing so.[1] This was also the impression conveyed to the young Soloveitchik growing up, by his grandfather, Rabbi Hayyim Soloveitchik, and father, Rabbi Moshe Soloveichik. The recitation of the *Seder ha-'Avodah* was so beloved to them, that it was only with the greatest difficulty that they were able to bid it farewell.

(At this point in his delivery, the Rav digressed, recalling nostalgically how the Modzhitser Hasidim in Warsaw prolonged the third

Sabbath meal well into the night. Evidently, it was very hard for them to take leave of the Sabbath Queen. One of the unforgettable scenes from this *derashah* is the Rav's vivid portrayal of one of the poverty-stricken Hasidim that he encountered in the Modzhitser *shtiebel* at *Shalosh Se'udot, Yankel der Treiger* [Yankel the Porter]. During the week, Yankel wore an outfit that was "more holes than material" ["*mehr lekher vie materiel*"]. Like his fellow porters in Warsaw, he was a human beast of burden. The Rav comically described how one would see a commode or other heavy furniture walking down the street with two little feet under it. But on Shabbat, at the Third Meal in the Modzhitser *shtiebel*, the same *Yankel der Treiger* was unrecognizable. He appeared a prince with a *shtreimel* on his head and a *kapote*.

The Rav's point was that once upon a time, Jews could not get enough of the Sabbath. They simply could not let go of her. Whereas today, we modern Jews say to her coolly, "Goodbye, I'll see you next week.")

Why was the *Seder ha-'Avodah* so extremely important? What is its significance? The Rav presented three *"ta'amim,"* or reasons for the custom. One is readily available in Rashi; the other two are original.

1. Rashi attributes the *sheli'ah tsibbur*'s (prayer leader's) recitation of the *Seder ha-'Avodah* to the principle of *"U-Neshalmah pharim sefateinu,"* "Our lips will pay bulls" (Hosea 14:3).[2] After the destruction of the Temple in Jerusalem, we compensate for our inability to offer physical sacrifices by reciting the Torah reading thereof.

Rav Soloveitchik's Seder ha-'Avodah

The Rav found a difficulty with Rashi's explanation. If that were the reason for reciting the *Seder ha-'Avodah* in *Mussaf*, it should be incumbent upon each and every individual, just as *Mussaf* is incumbent upon the individual. In the controversy between Rabbi El'azar ben Azariah and the Sages in the Mishnah, the *halakhah* is in accordance with the opinion of the Sages. (Rabbi El'azar ben Azariah held that *Mussaf* is recited only *"be-haver 'ir"*; the Sages disagreed and held that the obligation of *Mussaf* devolves upon each individual.)[3] Just as *Mussaf* is recited by each individual and not delegated to the *sheli'ah tsibbur* (prayer leader), so the recitation of the *Seder ha-'Avodah* should be the obligation of each individual. Why then is it recited by the *sheli'ah tsibbur*?

2. In the Temple, besides the offerings of the various sacrifices, there was also a Torah reading by the *kohen gadol* (high priest). This reading took place after the scapegoat had been dispatched to the wilderness to Azazel. The reading was considered of such paramount importance that the ruling is *"Keri'ah me'akevet."* The Torah reading is indispensable to the sacrifices.[4]

The Rav wondered aloud whether in the Second Temple the *kohen gadol*'s reading was accompanied by Targum, Aramaic translation. The practice of Targum was instituted at the very beginning of the Second Temple by Ezra the Scribe.[5]

The Rav reasoned that especially in the Second Temple when there were controversies between the Pharisees and the Sadducees as to the exact sequence of the high priest's actions on the Day of Atonement, it would have been imperative that his reading be supplemented by explanatory Targum, so that the common folk not suspect him of having deviated from the order of the Torah.[6]

The Rav proposed that the *sheli'ah tsibbur*'s recitation of the *Seder ha-'Avodah* is a commemoration of the *kohen gadol*'s Torah reading on *Yom ha-Kippurim*. But here a difficulty arises. The *kohen gadol*'s reading is from the Written Torah (*Torah she-bi-khetav*), whereas the *sheli'ah tsibbur*'s reading is from the Oral Torah (*Torah she-be-'al peh*).

At this point, the Rav relied on *derush sefarim* (homiletic literature), most notably *Beit Halevi* of his great-grandfather and namesake, Rabbi Yosef Dov Baer Halevi Soloveitchik,[7] to the effect that Yom Kippur is the manifestation of the Oral Torah; the celebration, the *"Yom Tov of Torah she-be-'al peh."*

This contention is constructed of many sources. First, there is the Mishnah, end *Ta'anit*: "There were never such festivals (*yamim tovim*) for Israel as the fifteenth of Av and Yom Kippur." The *Gemara* explains that the distinction of Yom Kippur is due to the fact that it is "the day the second tablets were given."[8] And yet, we celebrate *Shavu'ot* as the time of the giving of the Torah. What was the difference between the first and second tablets? The first tablets contained not only the Written Law but the Oral Law as well.[9] In fact, the letters that flew off the tablets, causing Moses to drop them and shatter them,[10] were not the letters of the Written Law but those of the Oral Law.[11] Subsequently, the second tablets contained only the Written Law.[12] So what was unique about the giving of the second tablets on Yom Kippur was that for the first time the *Torah she-be-'al peh* came into its own and emerged as a distinct entity.¹³ And it is the Torah *she-be-'al peh* that the *kohen gadol* manifests by his Torah reading on Yom Kippur. His concluding remarks, "More than I read before you is written here,"¹⁴ may allude to the Oral Law. And it is this same manifestation of *Torah she-be-'al peh* that the *sheli'ah tsibbur* accomplishes with his recitation of the *Seder ha-'Avodah*. (As opposed to *Amits Ko'ah*, the medieval *piyyut* by Rabbi Meshullam ben Kalonymos, recited in Ashkenazic congregations, the antique *Atah Konanta*, recited in Sephardic congregations, goes back to the Tannaitic era, and is attributed by some to a priest. Thus, it eminently qualifies as *Torah she-be-'al peh*.)¹⁵

The Rav anticipated that one might counter that *Sukkot*, not Yom Kippur, should rightly be termed the *Yom Tov* of *Torah she-be-'al peh*. The Rambam begins the laws of *Sukkah* with its physical dimensions, which are surely *Torah she-be-'al peh*. As we say, "*Shi'urin, hatsitsin u-mehitsin, halakhah le-Moshe mi-Sinai.*" ("Measurements... are oral tradition to Moses from Sinai.")¹⁶ And in regard to various observances of *Sukkot* there were controversies between the Pharisees and the Sadducees: *nisukh ha-mayim* (the water libation) and *'aravah* (the willow branch).¹⁷

The Rav's response was that, in truth, *Sukkot* is but the continuation, the extension of Yom Kippur. The Midrash comments on the verse in regard to the four species: "'And you shall take for you on the first day'—the first day of reckoning sins."¹⁸ The Jew emerges from Yom Kippur spiritually cleansed: "Before the LORD you shall be purified."¹⁹ And as Rabbi Akiva said: "*Ashreikhem Yisrael!* Happy are you, Israel! Before whom are you purified, and who purifies you? Your Father in heaven."[20] And it is this joy, this *simhah* that comes from having received from heaven the greatest gift, a gratuitous gift (*matnat hinam*), a sense of spiritual purity (*taharat ha-nefesh*), that pervades the ensuing Yom Tov of Sukkot.

3. Finally, quoting the Talmud Yerushalmi, the Rav offers a third "*ta'am*" for the speciality of the *Seder ha-'Avodah* on Yom Kippur. The Yerushalmi states: "Any generation in which the Temple is not rebuilt in its days, it is as if it is destroyed in its days."[21]

The Rav ventured that on Yom Kippur we must atone not only for our individual sins but for the historic, collective sin of not having rebuilt the Temple. *"Aval anahnu va-'avoteinu hatanu."* "We and our fathers have sinned."[22] This refers to the ongoing historic sin that nineteen hundred years later we are still bereft of the Temple in Jerusalem. Our recitation of the *Seder ha-'Avodah* followed by the *kinot*, the elegy of the Ten Martyrs (*'Asarah Harugei Malkhut*), is our way of expiating this historic sin.

If the Rav's portrayal of *Yankel der Treiger* is comedic, his depiction of the transition from the *Seder ha-'Avodah* is pathos-laden and starkly, brutally tragic. The abrupt transition from "*Mar'eh Kohen*"—the face of the high priest, when he emerged from the Holy of Holies, radiating the splendor of the divine presence (*ziv ha-Shekhinah*)—to the present reality, a world without Temple, without sacrifices, without Kohen, Levite and Israelite—was likened by the Rav to a rude awakening from a beautiful dream. For a brief, too brief moment, we were transported to the Temple in Jerusalem with all of its glorious splendor and pageantry. And then suddenly, with a clap, we find ourselves back in our spiritually impoverished waking life. *"Me-'igra ramah le-bira 'amikta!"* "From a mighty mountain to a profound pit!"

"Es iz geven, yeh. Ober es iz nit mehr."

"It was, yes. But it is no more."

"Dos iz geven azei, ober nisht itzter."

"This was so, but not now."

In order for us to appreciate the enormity of the loss, it would be necessary to recount the past glory. The Rav juxtaposed the verse in Lamentations 1:7: "Jerusalem remembered [in] the days of her affliction and of her anguish all her treasures that she had from the days of old."[23]

"All this occurred when the Temple was on its foundation and the Holy Sanctuary was on its site, and the *Kohen Gadol* stood and ministered—his generation (*doro*) watched and rejoiced."[24]

The Rav commented ruefully: "'His generation'—not ours."

"Ashrei 'ayin ra'atah kol eleh." "Fortunate is the eye that saw all these."[25]

"But our forefathers' iniquities destroyed the Temple, and our sins delayed the Final Redemption." (*"Aval 'avonot avoteinu heherivu naveh, ve-hat'oteinu he'erikhu kitso."*)[26]

"Any generation in which the Temple is not rebuilt in its days, it is as if it is destroyed in its days."

※

The Rav offered historical insight into Rabbi Akiva's proverb that concludes the Mishnah, Tractate *Yoma*. In the generation that followed the destruction of the Temple, the Jewish People could not imagine how it would be possible to celebrate Yom Kippur, a day which pivots on the service in the Temple. Rabbi Akiva appeared to us then as a great consoler, driving home the message that as important as the Temple ritual was, in the final analysis, it is the LORD who purifies Israel of all its sins, and the LORD we have not lost.

"*Ashreikhem Yisrael!*
Happy are you, Israel!
Before whom are you purified, and who purifies you?
Your Father in heaven."

---

[1] See the responsum of Hai Gaon in B.M. Lewin, *Otsar ha-Ge'onim*, *Yoma* (Jerusalem, 1934), no. 121 (p. 41); Natronai Gaon, quoted in *Seder Rav Amram Gaon*, ed. Daniel Goldschmidt (Jerusalem: Mossad Harav Kook, 2004), p. 169; and Rabbi Yosef Dov Halevi Soloveitchik, *Kuntres be-'Inyan 'Avodat Yom ha-Kippurim*, ed. Rabbi Aharon Lichtenstein (Jerusalem, 1986), *Yoma* 36b, s.v. *ha-hu de-nahit* (pp. 30-31).
[2] Rashi, *Yoma* 36b, s.v. *ha-hu de-nahit*.
[3] *m. Berakhot* 4:7.
[4] See *b. Yoma* 5b, "*Mikra parashah me'akev*," and Rashi, *Yoma* 68b, s.v. *ba' likrot*. This is one of two opinions in Rabbeinu Menahem ha-Me'iri, *Beit ha-Behirah*, *Yoma*, beginning chap. 7.
[5] Maimonides, *Hil. Tefillah* 12:10.
[6] The Pharisees upheld the oral tradition of "*Hamesh tevilot va-'asarah kiddushin*" ("Five ritual immersions and ten washings of the hands and the feet"), whereby *ipso facto* the verse in the Torah portion is out of sequence. See *b. Yoma* 71a. The Sadducees, on the other hand, maintained the order spelled out in the Torah.

In the Rav's opinion, this Pharisaic practice would have appeared to the public much more egregious than the more famous controversy between the Pharisees and the Sadducees as to where the incense should be lit. According to the Sadducees, the high priest "*matkin mi-ba-huts*," "lights outside" the *kodesh kodashim*, or Holy of Holies; the Pharisees, on the other hand, held that the high priest "*matkin mi-bifnim*," "lights inside" the Holy of Holies. See *b.*

Yoma 19b, 53a.
7 See Rabbi Yosef Dov Baer Halevi Soloveitchik (of Brisk), *She'elot u-Teshuvot Beit Halevi*, Part Two, *derush* 18
8 *b. Ta'anit* 30b.
9 *y. Shekalim* 6:1, quoted in *Beit Halevi*.
10 *y. Ta'anit* 4:5.
11 This is the novel idea of *Beit Halevi*.
12 *Beit Halevi* relied on the *Yerushalmi, Shekalim*. However, according to *Exodus Rabbah* 46:1 it was the exact opposite: The first tablets contained only the Ten Commandments and the second tablets contained also "*halakhot, midrash,* and *aggadot.*" See *Yefeh To'ar* ad loc. (This Midrash was brought to my attention by the indefatigable Torah scholar Rabbi Moshe Zuriel *shelit"a*.)
13 According to the *Beit Halevi*, since the Oral Law was not included in the second tablets, it was now to be written in the heart of Moses and the hearts of the Jewish People. Thereby, Israel ascended to a greater level. No longer would the Torah and Israel be two but one. ("*Ha-Torah ve-Yisrael kula had hu.*")
14 *m. Yoma* 7:1; *b. Yoma* 68b.
15 See Rabbi Yom Tov ben Abraham Asevilli, *Hiddushei ha-RITBA, Yoma* 56b, s.v. *Ha-hu de-nahit kameh de-Rava*, quoting '*Ittur*: "We hear from this that [the *sheli'ah tsibbur*] recites it in the language of the Mishnah (*leshon ha-Mishnah*), such as *'Atah Konanta'* of Yosé ben Yosé."
16 *b. Sukkah* 5b.
17 *m. Sukkah* 4:9; *b. Sukkah* 43b-44a.
18 Leviticus 23:40; *Midrash Tanhuma, Emor*, 22.
19 Leviticus 16:30.
20 *m. Yoma* 8:9.
21 *y. Yoma* 1:1.
22 Preface to *Vidui* (Confession of sins).
23 The Rav directed us to Ibn Ezra's commentary ad locum.
24 Afterword to *Seder ha-'Avodah*.
25 Ibid.
26 Ibid.

A King's Palace

Aharon Hayyim Zimmerman. *Agra la-Yesharim*. Jerusalem, 1983.

Rabbi Aharon Hayyim Zimmerman (1915-1995) served as *Rosh Yeshivah* of Beit Midrash le-Torah (Hebrew Theological College) in Chicago. He was famed for his genius in both Talmud and mathematics. In his youth, he studied in his uncle Rabbi Baruch Dov Leibowitz's *yeshivah* in Kamenitz. (Rabbi Leibowitz was married to Rabbi Zimmerman's father's sister. Sister and brother were the children of Avraham Yitzhak Halevi Zimmerman, Rabbi of Kremenchug, Ukraine.)

Rabbi Zimmerman's first work, *Binyan Halakhah* (New York, 1942), on Maimonides' *Mishneh Torah*, bore the *haskamot* (endorsements) of Rabbi Baruch Dov Leibowitz and Rabbi Isaac Herzog, Chief Rabbi of Erets Israel, who was visiting the United States at the time. In his letter of recommendation, Rabbi Herzog implored Chicago Jewry to appreciate the young prodigy in their midst.

Later, Rabbi Zimmerman produced a massive work entitled *Agan ha-Sahar* (New York, 1955), which dealt with the halakhic problems associated with the international date line. In this ambitious undertaking, the author upheld the ruling of the sage of B'nei Berak, Rabbi Abraham Isaiah Karelitz (*"Hazon Ish"*), while lambasting his theoretical opponent, Rabbi Menahem Mendel Kasher (author of *Torah Sheleimah*).

The dilemma arose during the brief sojourn of the Mirrer Yeshivah in Kobe, Japan in 1941. From Japan, queries were sent to Erets Israel, both to Chief Rabbi Herzog and to the *Hazon Ish*. The majority of *posekim* (halakhic decisors) in Erets Yisrael, at a special session convened by Chief Rabbi Herzog, ruled that the Sabbath should be observed in Japan on Saturday by the local reckoning. The *Hazon Ish*, on the other hand, held that the new day begins in China (not at an imaginary line drawn in the Pacific Ocean), which means that the Sabbath should be observed on Sunday by Japanese standards. Eventually, the *Hazon Ish* penned a comprehensive study, *Kuntres Shmoneh 'Esreh Sha'ot* ("Eighteen Hours") explaining his reasoning (based on Rabbi Yehudah Halevi's *Kuzari*) that the day begins in the East in China six hours before Erets Israel, and ends in the West eighteen hours after Erets Israel.[1]

The present *sefer*, *Agra la-Yesharim*, advocates for reviving the *mitsvah* of *shemirat ha-mikdash*, guarding the Temple Mount. (Rabbi Zimmerman, a Levi, may have felt a personal connection to this particular commandment as it devolves upon the Levites.) In his code, Maimonides writes:

> Guarding the Temple is a positive commandment, and though there be no fear of enemies or brigands, for its

guarding is only for its honor; there is no comparison between a palace that has guards and a palace that has no guards.[2]

In truth, Rabbi Zimmerman was not the first to raise the issue of reviving this ancient practice of stationing guards outside the Temple. A century earlier, Rabbi Hillel Moshe Meshel Gelbstein (1833-1907), a Kotzker and later Lubavitcher Hasid, published a work *Mishkenot le-Abir Ya'akov* (Jerusalem, 1881), advocating for this lost commandment (what we would refer to as a *"mitsvah yetomah,"* or "orphan commandment"). Rabbi Gelbstein sent his work to the great authority Rabbi Abraham Bornstein of Sochaczew (1839-1910), son-in-law of the Kotzker Rebbe, Rabbi Menahem Mendel Morgenstern. The Sochaczewer's response to Rabbi Gelbstein (published in his collected responsa, *Avnei Nezer*) was negative. For various reasons, the Sochaczewer concluded that the commandment is not applicable at this time. The responsum in *Avnei Nezer* begins with a demurral:

> Regarding his honor's discussion whether it is obligatory at this time to station guards for the Temple. I shall answer him according to my limited intellect but not as a matter of practical halakhah (*halakhah le-ma'aseh*) for it is not my place to decide a matter that affects *Kelal Yisrael* (the Jewish People). Thank God, Israel is not a widower. [I.e., there are others more qualified to decide.] I write in a purely theoretical manner.[3]

Rabbi Zimmerman takes up the cudgels once again. A typical chapter (chap. 9) discusses whether a pedigreed Levite (*"Levi meyuhas"*) is required to guard the Temple.

At the present time, when guardianship over the Temple Mount is entrusted to the Jordanian *wakf*, it seems improbable that guard duty will be assigned to the Levites.

I should like to share with the reader the gist of the final chapter of *Agra la-Yesharim* (chap. 42). The paradoxical nature of the thought, which by the author's own assessment contains "very deep matters" (*"devarim 'amukim me'od"*),[4] goes to the heart of the philosophical problem of divine dictate versus free will.

Rabbi Zimmerman makes a strong case that ultimately the building of the Holy Temple must be "in the hands of heaven" (*"bi-yedei shamayim"*). Rashi and *Tosafot* adduced in this regard the verse in Exodus 15:17: "The Temple of the LORD Your hands established." However, Rashi and *Tosafot* referred to the future Third Temple which "will come from heaven."[5] Rabbi Zimmerman, based on the verse in 1 Chronicles 29:1, extends the definition to *all* Temples, including the First Temple built by Solomon, and the second built (or rather enlarged) by Herod. The verse in Chronicles reads: "... for the palace (*birah*) is not for man, but for the LORD God."

In regard to King Herod, we find the statement in the Talmud: "Without a king, the Temple cannot be built."[6] This might seem a prosaic statement of fact. However, the legendary *gaon*, Rabbi David Friedman of Karlin, interpreted the statement halakhically.[7] For Rabbi Zimmerman, this Talmudic statement is not only of halakhic significance, but theological significance as well. Since ultimately the construction of the Temple is accomplished by the Almighty, how is it possible that it be brought about by a human? The solution, according to our author, lies in the words of Proverbs 21:1: "The heart of a king is in the hand of the LORD." Only a king, who is stripped of the common man's free will, and is wholly subservient to the divine will, is uniquely suited to build the LORD's Temple, a task definitionally not "in the hands of man" (*"bi-yedei adam"*) but "in the hands of heaven" (*"bi-yedei shamayim"*).

In my humble opinion, the thought may betray Izhbitser-Radzyner influence. After leaving Chicago, and before his '*aliyah* to Erets Israel, Rabbi Zimmerman dwelled in the Boro Park section of Brooklyn and prayed in the *beit midrash* of the Rebbe of Radzyn. On the other hand, Rabbi Zimmerman writes that he presented the kernel of the idea (that a king is stripped of free will) to his *rebbe*, Rabbi Baruch Dov [Leibowitz], who concurred that this is the true interpretation (*"ha-peshat ha-amiti"*).[8] Rabbi Zimmerman also found support for this concept in the work of the famous Sephardic *gaon*, Rabbi Hayyim Palache, *Re'eh Hayyim*.[9]

---

[1] The *Kuntres Shemoneh 'Esreh Sha'ot* was published in *Hazon Ish, Orah Hayyim/Mo'ed*, ed. Rabbi Samuel Greineman (3rd edition, B'nei Berak, 1967), chap. 64 (ff. 93-96). The *Hazon Ish*'s study was written as a direct response to Rabbi Yehiel Mikhel Tukachinsky's work *Ha-Yomam be-Kadur ha-'Arets* (Jerusalem, 1943). Rabbi Tukachinsky, one of the sages of Jerusalem, was married to the granddaughter of Rabbi Samuel Salant, revered Ashkenazic Chief Rabbi of

Jerusalem for almost seventy years until his passing in 1909.
2 Maimonides, *MT, Hil. Beit ha-Behirah* 8:1.
3 Rabbi Abraham Bornstein, *Avnei Nezer, Yoreh De'ah* (Piotrków, 1913), no. 449.
4 *Agra la-Yesharim*, 271a.
5 See Rashi and *Tosafot, Rosh Hashanah* 30a; *Sukkah* 41a; and *Shavu'ot* 15b.

However, see the Vilna Gaon's interpretation of the verse "The Temple of the LORD Your hands established," in *Aderet Eliyahu* (Warsaw, 1887), Deuteronomy 1:10: "It appeared that they were making [the Temple] but they were not making [it] at all ... And so in the Temple... They were lifting the stone, but it was not they who were lifting, but the LORD gave strength and lifted their hand." The Gaon references the verse in 1 Kings 6:7 regarding the construction of Solomon's Temple. See *Numbers Rabbah* 14:3 and *Zohar* I, 74a.

6 *b. Bava Batra* 4a.
7 Rabbi David Friedman, Introduction to *Kuntres Derishat Zion vi-Yerushalayim*; published in idem, *She'elat David* (Piotrków, 1913), 14a. *Derishat Zion vi-Yerushalayim* is Rabbi Friedman's rebuttal of Rabbi Tsevi Hirsch Kalischer's *Derishat Zion* (Lyck, 1862).
8 *Agra la-Yesharim*, 270b.
9 Rabbi Hayyim Palache, *Re'eh Hayyim*, Part One (Saloniki, 1860), *Shemot*, 81a; quoted in *Agra la-Yesharim*, 270b-271a.

However, in the next paragraph, Rabbi Palache quotes from the works of Rabbi Hayyim Yosef David Azulai (HYDA) that the principle "The heart of a king is in the hand of the LORD" applies only to a righteous king; a wicked king remains a "master of free will" (*"ba'al behirah"*). This would throw a monkey wrench into Rabbi Zimmerman's remarks concerning King Herod, who most certainly was a wicked king.

Bibliography

Aaron Berechiah of Modena. *Ma'avar Yabok*. Mantua, 1626.

Abraham ben David of Posquières. *Hasagot ha-Rabad le-Mishneh Torah*. Ed. Bezalel Naor. Jerusalem: Zur-Ot, 1985.

Abraham ben Isaac of Narbonne. Sefer ha-Eshkol. Ed. Shalom and Hanokh Albeck. Jerusalem, 1935-1938.

Abraham Maimonides. *Birkat Avraham*. Responsa. Ed. Baer Goldberg. Lyck, 1859.

_____. *Ha-Maspik le-'Ovdei Hashem (Kitāb Kifāyah al-'Ābidīn)*. Transl. Yosef Dori. Jerusalem, 1973.

_____. *Peirush Rabbeinu Avraham ben ha-Rambam 'al Bereshit u-Shemot*. Ed. Efraim Yehudah Wiesenberg. London: L. Honig & Sons, 1958.

_____. *Peirush ha-Torah, Bereishit*. Ed. Moshe Maimon. Monsey, NY, 2020.

Abraham son of Vilna Gaon. Commentary to Psalms. *Sefer Tehillim 'im peirush...Be'er Avraham*. Ed. Samuel Luria. Warsaw, 1887.

_____. *Tirgem Avraham*. Commentary on *Targum Onkelos*. Jerusalem 1896; photo-offset Tel-Aviv: Ya'akov A. Landa, n.d.

Abrams, Daniel. *The Book Bahir: An Edition Based on the Earliest Manuscripts*. Los Angeles: Cherub, 1994.

_____. *R. Asher ben David: His Complete Works and Studies in His Kabbalistic Thought*. Ed. Daniel Abrams. Los Angeles: Cherub, 1996.

Abulafia, Abraham. *Sefer ha-Heshek*. Ed. Matithyahu Safrin.

Jerusalem, 1999.

Adler, Shemariah Menashe. *'Emek ha-Bakha*. Keidan, 1935.

———. *Mar'eh Kohen*. London, 1919. *Mahadura Tinyana*. London, 1928. *Mahadura Telita'ah*, vol. 1. Piotrków, 1931. *Mahadura Telita'ah*, vol. 2. Warsaw, 1933. *Mahadura Hamisha'ah*. London, 1945. Concerning the *Herem de-Rabbeinu Gershom*. London, 1953.

———. *Maror de-Rabbanan*. Appended to *Mar'eh Kohen Tinyana*. London, 1928.

———. *Zikhron Elhanan*. London, 1920.

Agus, Jacob. *Banner of Jerusalem*. Biography of Rav Kook. New York: Bloch, 1946. Later retitled, *High Priest of Rebirth*. New York: Bloch, 1972.

Alexander, Yosef, of Darbian (Darbenai, Lithuania). Commentary to prayer book. *Porat Yosef*. Warsaw, 1898.

Alexandrov, Samuel. *Mikhtevei Mehkar u-Bikoret*. vol. 1. Vilna, 1907. vol. 2. Cracow, 1910. vol. 3. Jerusalem, 1932.

Algaze, Yom Tov. *Tosefet de-Rabbanan*. In *Kehillat Ya'akov*. Saloniki, 1786.

Alkalai, Judah Hai. *Minhat Yehudah*. (Pressburg) 1843.

Alter, Abraham Mordechai, of Gur. *Mikhtevei Torah me-Admor mi-Gur*. Ed. Z.Y. Abramowitz and I.M. Alter. Tel Aviv, 1987.

Alter, Judah Aryeh Leib. *Sefat Emet*. On Pentateuch. 5 vols. Piotrków-Cracow, 1905-1908.

Alter, Robert. *The Hebrew Bible*. Transl. with commentary. 3 vols. New York: W.W. Norton, 2019.

Alter-Rotenburg, Isaac Meir, of Gur. *Hiddushei ha-RIM 'al ha-Torah*. Ed. Judah Leib Levin. Jerusalem, 2010.

Altmann, Alexander. "Moses Narboni's 'Epistle on *Shi'ur Qoma*.'" In *Jewish Medieval and Renaissance Studies*. Ed. Altmann. Cambridge, Mass: Harvard University Press, 1967.

Amram bar Sheshna. *Seder Rav Amram Gaon.* Ed. Daniel Goldschmidt. Jerusalem: Mossad Harav Kook, 2004.

Appelfeld, Aharon. *Blooms of Darkness.* Transl. Jeffrey M. Green. New York: Schocken, 2010.

Arieli, Yitzhak. *'Eynayim le-Mishpat.* Tractate *Makkot.* Jerusalem: Mossad Harav Kook, 1959.

____. *'Eynayim le-Mishpat. Bava Batra,* Part Two. Jerusalem, 1975.

Aristotle. *Nicomachean Ethics.*

Asher ben David. In *Otsar Nehmad* IV. Ed. Raphael Kirchheim. Vienna, 1864, pp. 37-43.

____. *R. Asher ben David: His Complete Works and Studies in His Kabbalistic Thought.* Ed. Daniel Abrams. Los Angeles: Cherub, 1996.

Asher ben Yehiel. *She'elot u-Teshuvot ha-ROSh.* Constantinople, 1517.

____. *Tosefot ha-ROSh 'al Masekhet Sotah.* Ed. Ya'akov Lifshitz. Jerusalem: Makhon Harry Fischel, 1968.

Ashkenazi, Hayyim Eliezer. "Heker ve-'Iyun be-Sifrei Rishonim (4)." *Yeshurun,* vol. 40 (Nisan 5779).

Ashkenazi, Tsevi. *She'elot u-Teshuvot Hakham Tsevi.* Amsterdam, 1712.

Auerbach, Benjamin Hirsch. *Sefer ha-Eshkol* with commentary *Nahal Eshkol.* Halberstadt, 1868-9.

Auerbach, Menahem Natan Nota. *Orah Ne'eman.* On *Shulhan 'Arukh, Orah Hayyim.* Jerusalem, 1924-1931.

Avivi, Yosef. *The Kabbalah of Rabbi A. I. Kook* (Hebrew). 4 vols. Jerusalem: Yad Ben-Zvi, 2018.

____. *Kabbalat ha-GRA.* Jerusalem, 1993.

____. *Zohar Ramhal.* Jerusalem, 1997.

Azriel of Gerona. *Be'ur 'Eser Sefirot 'al Derekh She'elah u-Teshuvah.* (Also known as *Sha'ar ha-Sho'el.*) Ed. Moshe Schatz.

Jerusalem, 1997.

_____. Commentary to *Sefer Yetsirah*. (Misattributed to Rabbi Azriel's disciple Nahmanides.) Mantua, 1562.

_____. *Commentary on Talmudic Aggadoth*. Ed. Isaiah Tishby. Jerusalem: Magnes, 1982.

_____. *Derekh ha-Emunah ve-Derekh ha-Kefirah*. Ms. Halberstam 444. In Azriel of Gerona, *Be'ur 'Eser Sefirot 'al Derekh She'elah u-Teshuvah*. Ed. Moshe Schatz.

_____. *She'elot u-Teshuvot*. In *Likkutim me-Rav Hai Gaon*. Warsaw, 1798.

Azulai, Abraham. *Hesed le-Avraham*. Amsterdam, 1685; Lvov, 1863, photo offset Jerusalem, 1968.

Azulai, Hayyim Joseph David (HYDA). *Birkei Yosef*. Commentary to *Shulhan 'Arukh*. 2 vols. Livorno, 1774-1776.

_____. *Devash le-Fi*. Livorno, 1801.

_____. *Hayyim Sha'al*. Responsa. 2 vols. Livorno, 1792-1795.

_____. *Mahazik Berakhah*. Commentary to *Shulhan 'Arukh, Orah Hayyim* and *Yoreh De'ah*. Livorno, 1785.

_____. *Shem ha-Gedolim*. Bibliography. 2 vols. Livorno, 1774, 1786.

Babad, Joseph. *Minhat Hinnukh*. Commentary to *Sefer ha-Hinukh*. Lvov, 1869.

Bachrach, Naftali. *'Emek ha-Melekh*. Amsterdam, 1648.

Bachrach, Ya'ir Hayyim. *Havot Ya'ir*. Responsa. Frankfurt am Main, 1699.

Baden, Joel S. *The Book of Exodus: A Biography*. Princeton, NJ: Princeton University Press, 2019.

Bahir. Attributed to Rabbi Nehunyah ben ha-Kanah. Amsterdam 1651. Facsimile edition in *The Book Bahir*. Ed. Daniel Abrams. Los Angeles: Cherub Press, 1994.

_____. "Hiddushei ha-Bahir." In Cremona 1558 edition of *Zohar*. Facsimile in Daniel Abram's edition of *Bahir*.

———. *Sefer ha-Bahir*. Ed. Reuven Margaliyot. With Commentary *'Or Bahir*. Jerusalem: Mossad Harav Kook, 1951.

Bahya ben Asher ibn Halawa. Commentary to Pentateuch. Ed. C.B. Chavel. 3 vols. Jerusalem: Mossad Harav Kook, 1966-1968.

Bahya ben Joseph ibn Pakuda. *The Book of Direction to the Duties of the Heart (Al-Hidaya ila Fara'id Al-Qulub)*. Transl. Menahem Mansoor. London: Routledge & Kegan Paul, 1973.

Bar-Asher, Avishai. "Berikh Shemeh." *Tarbiz*, vol. 86 (5779), pp. 147-198.

Barg, Mordechai Gimpel. Notes of Rav Kook's lectures on *Kuzari*. In *Ma'amrei ha-RAYaH*, vol. 2.

Baruch of Kosov. *'Ammud ha-'Avodah*. Czernowitz, 1863.

Batt, Avi. "*Lahashei ha-Havayah*." Available at: https://bmj.org.il/wp-content/uploads/2019/12/2.51.BAT_.pdf

Be'ery, Yehoshua B. *Ohev Yisrael bi-Kedushah*. 5 vols. Tel-Aviv, 1989.

Benjamin, Walter. "The Task of the Translator." In *Walter Benjamin: Selected Writings*, vol. 1 (1913-1926). Ed. Marcus Bullock and Michael W. Jennings. Cambridge, Mass.: Harvard University Press, 1996.

Benson, Michael. *Space Odyssey: Stanley Kubrick, Arthur C. Clarke, and the Making of a Masterpiece*. New York: Simon and Schuster, 2018.

Berger, Yisrael. *Simhat Yisrael*. Piotrków, 1910.

Berlin, Naftali Tsevi Yehudah. *'Emek ha-NeTSIV*. Commentary to Sifre. 3 vols. Jerusalem, 1959-1961.

Berlin, Saul. *Besamim Rosh*. Berlin, 1793.

Bernfeld, Shim'on. *Da'at Elohim*. Warsaw, 1897-1899.

Besser, Yisroel. In *Mishpacha*, no. 191 (2 Shevat, 5768/January 9, 2008).

Bodoff, Lippman. "Jewish Mysticism: Medieval Roots, Contemporary Dangers and Prospective Challenges." Available at: http://www.edah.org/backend/coldfusion/search/document.cfm?title=Jewish+Mysticism:+Medieval+Roots,+Contemporary+Dangers+and+Prospective+Challenges&hyperlink=Bodoff3_1.htm&type=JournalArticle&category=Orthodoxy+and+Modernity&authortitle&firstname=Lippman&lastname=Bodoff&pubsource=not+available&authorid=531&pdfattachment=Bodoff3_1.pdf

Bokser, Ben Zion. *Abraham Isaac Kook*. Mahwah, NJ: Paulist Press, 1978.

Bornstein, Abraham. *Avnei Nezer: Yoreh De'ah*. Piotrków, 1913.

Bornstein, Aharon Israel. *Ne'ot ha-Deshe*. 2 vols. Tel-Aviv, 1983.

Bornstein, Samuel, of Sochatchov. *Shem mi-Shmuel*. On Pentateuch and Festivals. 8 vols. Piotrków, 1927; photo offset Jerusalem, 1974.

Boyarin, Daniel. "Two Introductions to the Midrash on the Song of Songs" (Hebrew). *Tarbiz* 56:4 (1987), pp. 479-500.

Breuer, Mordechai. *'Ohalei Torah*. Jerusalem: Shazar Center, 2004.

Brill, Allan. "Auxiliary to *Hokhmah*: The Writings of the Vilna Gaon and Philosophical Terminology." In *The Vilna Gaon and His Disciples*. Ed. Hallamish, Rivlin, and Shuchat. Ramat Gan: Bar-Ilan University Press, 2003.

Brown, Benjamin. *The Hazon Ish: Halakhist, Believer and Leader of the Haredi Revolution*. Hebrew. Jerusalem, 2011.

Buber, Martin. *Bein 'Am le-Artso*. Jerusalem: Schocken, 1944. In English: *On Zion: The History of an Idea*. Syracuse, NY: Syracuse University Press, 1997.

_____. *Gog u-Magog*. Tel-Aviv, 1944. In English: *For the Sake of Heaven*. Philadelphia: Jewish Publication Society, 1945.

———. *Ich und Du*. Berlin: Schocken, 1922. In English: *I and Thou*. Edinburgh, 1937.

Bunin, Hayyim Yitzhak. Letter to Rav Kook. Available at: http://gnazimorg.startlogic.com/1935-1865-קוק-הכהן-יצחק-אברהם

———. *Mishneh HaBaD*, vol. 1, book 1, part 1. Warsaw, 1936.

Buzaglo, Shalom. *Hadrat Melekh*. On *Zohar*. London 1770; photo offset B'nei Berak, 1974.

Cardozo, Abraham, *Boker de-Avraham*. In manuscripts: Library of the Hungarian Academy of Sciences, Budapest, Ms. Kaufmann A 232; London Beth Din Ms. 124; Russian State Library, Moscow, Ms. Guenzburg 660; and Ms. Guenzburg 1109.

———. *Derush Zeh Eli ve-Anvehu*. Transcribed in Gershom Scholem. "Two new theological texts by Abraham Cardozo." Hebrew. *Sefunot*, vols. 3-4 (1960).

Celan, Paul. *Paul Celan: Poems*. Transl. M. Hamburger. New York: Persea Books, 1980.

Chajes, Tsevi Hirsch. *Hiddushei MaHaRaTs Hayyot*. Novellae to Talmud. Published in Vilna edition of Talmud.

———. *Torat Nevi'im*. Zolkiew, 1836.

Charitan, Levi Yitzhak. "*Sha'ar Simukhim le-Rabbeinu El'azar mi-Germaiza (Ha-Rokeah)*." In *Hitsei Giborim*, vol. 10 (Nissan, 5777/2017).

Charlop, Yehiel Mikhel. *Torat ha-Hof Yamim: Sefer ha-Zikaron*. New York, 1985.

Chotsh, Tsevi. *Hemdat Tsevi*. Amsterdam, 1706.

Cohen, Bezalel (*Dayyan* of Vilna). *Reshit Bikkurim*. Vilna, 1869; photo offset Jerusalem, 1969.

Cohen, David. *Kol ha-Nevu'ah*. Jerusalem: Mossad Harav Kook, 1979.

———. *Mishnat ha-Nazir*. Ed. Harel Cohen and Yedidyah Cohen. Jerusalem: Nezer David, 2005.

Cohen, Israel. *History of Jews in Vilna*. Philadelphia: Jewish Publication Society of America, 1943.

Cohen, Meir Simhah. *Meshekh Hokhmah*. Riga, 1927.

_____. *'Or Same'ah*. Commentary on *Mishneh Torah*.

Cohen, Solomon (Dayyan of Vilna). *Binyan Shelomo*. Vilna, 1889.

Copernicus, Nicolaus. *De Revolutionibus orbium coelestium (On the Revolutions of the Celestial Spheres)*. 1543.

Corbin, Henri. "Mundus Imaginalis or, the imaginary and the imaginal." *Cahiers internationaux de symbolism*, vol. 6 (1964).

Cordovero, Moses. *Elimah*. Lvov, 1881.

_____. *Pardes Rimonim*. Munkatch, 1906.

_____. *Shi'ur Komah*. Warsaw, 1883.

Dadon, Yitzhak. *Athalta Hi*. 2 vols. Jerusalem, 2006, 2008.

Dan, Joseph. "A Bow to Frumkinian Hasidism." *Modern Judaism*, May 1991, pp. 175-194.

_____. *History of Jewish Mysticism and Esotericism: The Middle Ages*. vol. 6. Jerusalem: Zalman Shazar Center for Jewish History, 2011.

Danzig, Abraham. *Hayyei Adam*. Vilna, 1810.

David ben Levi of Narbonne. *Sefer ha-Mikhtam*. In *Ginzei Rishonim / Berakhot*. Ed. Moshe Hershler. Jerusalem: Makhon ha-Talmud ha-Yisraeli, 1967.

David, Bruria Hutner. *The Dual Role of Rabbi Zvi Hirsch Chajes: Traditionalist and Maskil*. Ph.D. dissertation. Columbia University 1971.

Delmedigo, Yosef Shelomo (*YaShaR mi-Candia*). *Novelot Hokhmah*. Basel, 1631.

Deutsch, Shaul Shimon. *Larger than Life: The Life and Times of the Lubavitcher Rebbe Rabbi Menachem Mendel Schneerson*.

2 vols. New York, NY, 1995-1997.

Don-Yahya, Eliezer. *Even Shetiyah.* Vilna, 1893.

Don Yahya, Hayyim. Responsum datelined "5653 [i.e., 1893], Shklov." In journal of the Skvere Kollel, *Zera' Ya'akov* 26 (Shevat 5766 [i.e., 2006]), pp. 17-21.

Don Yahya, Shabtai. *Rabbi Eliezer Don Yahya.* Jerusalem, 1932.

Don Yahya, Yehudah Leib. *Bikkurei Yehudah.* vol. 1. Lutzin, 1930. vol. 2. Tel-Aviv, 1939.

Dov Baer of Mezritch. *'Or Torah.* Ed. Rabbi Isaiah Dinowitz. Korets, 1804.

Duran, Simeon ben Tsemah. *Magen Avot.* Livorno, 1785.

Duran, Solomon ben Simon. *She'elot u-Teshuvot ha-RaShBaSh.* Livorno, 1742.

Edels, Samuel Eliezer (MaHaRaShA). *Hiddushei Aggadot.* Commentary to legends of Talmud. 2 vols. Lublin-Cracow, 1627-1631.

Eisenstadt (Asch), Meir. *Panim Me'irot.* Responsa. Amsterdam, 1715.

El'azar of Worms (Roke'ah). "Sha'ar Simukhim le-Rabbeinu El'azar mi-Germaiza (Ha-Rokeah)." Ed. Levi Yitzhak Charitan. In *Hitsei Giborim*, vol. 10 (Nissan, 5777/2017).

_____. *Sodei Razayya* I-II. Ed. Aaron Eisenbach. Jerusalem, 2004.

Eliashov, Solomon. *Hakdamot u-She'arim.* Piotrków, 1909.

_____. *Helek ha-Be'urim.* Jerusalem, 1935.

_____. Letters to Naftali Herz Halevi Weidenbaum. In Moshe Schatz, *Ma'ayan Moshe.* Jerusalem, 2011.

_____. *Sefer ha-De'ah* (=Hu Derushei 'Olam ha-Tohu). Piotrków, 1912.

Eliezer ben Hyrcanus (attributed to—). *Pirke deRabbi Eliezer.* Translated and annotated Gerald Friedlander. New York: Sepher-Hermon, 1981.

Eliezer of Metz. *Yere'im*. Venice, 1566.

Elijah Gaon of Vilna. *Aderet Eliyahu*. Commentary to Pentateuch. Warsaw, 1887.

    ———. *Be'ur ha-GRA* to Proverbs. Ed. Menahem Mendel of Shklov. Shklov, 1798. Edited from manuscripts. Moshe Philip. Petah-Tikvah, 1985.

    ———. *Be'ur ha-GRA* to *Shulhan 'Arukh*.

    ———. *Be'ur ha-GRA* to *Sifra di-Tseni'uta*. Ed. Jacob Moses of Slonim. Vilna and Horadna, 1820. Ed. Samuel Luria. Vilna, 1882. Ed. Bezalel Naor. Jerusalem, 1997.

    ———. *Be'ur ha-GRA* to *Tikkunei Zohar*. Vilna, 1867.

    ———. *Yahel 'Or*. Commentary to *Zohar*. Ed. Naphtali Herz Halevi [Weidenbaum] of Bialystok. Vilna, 1882.

Elior, Rachel. "Bein ha-heikhal ha-artsi la-heikhalot ha-shamaymiyim: ha-tefilah ve-shirat ha-kodesh be-sifrut ha-heikhalot ve-zikatan la-masorot ha-keshurot ba-mikdash." *Tarbiz* 64:3 (1995), pp. 341-380.

    ———. "The Merkavah tradition and the emergence of Jewish mysticism: from Temple to Merkavah, from Hekhal to Hekhalot, from priestly opposition to gazing upon the Merkavah." *Sino-Judaica* (1999), pp. 101-158.

    ———. "The priestly nature of the mystical heritage in *Heykalot* literature." In *Expérience et écriture mystiques dans les religions du livre*. Ed. Paul B. Fenton and Roland Goetschel. Leiden: Brill, 2000. pp. 41-54.

    ———. "Sifrut ha-heikhalot ve-ha-merkavah: zikatah la-mikdash, la-mikdash ha-shamaymi u-le-mikdash me'at." In *Retsef u-Temurah: Yehudim ve-Yahadut be-Erets Yisrael ha-Bizantit-Notsrit* (Continuity and Renewal: Jews and Judaism in Byzantine-Christian Palestine). Ed. Yisrael L. Levin. Jerusalem: Yad Ben-Zvi, 2004. pp. 107-142.

_____. *The Theory of Divinity of Hasidut HaBaD.* Hebrew. Jerusalem: Magnes, 1982.

Emden, Jacob. *Mitpahat Sefarim.* Altona, 1768.

Emunat Hashem. Anonymous. Jerusalem, 1938.

Engel, Joseph. *Gilyonei ha-Shas.* 3 vols. Vienna, 1924-1937. 4th vol. Warsaw, 1938.

Entsiklopedia shel ha-Tziyonut ha-Datit. Ed. Yitzhak Raphael and Ge'ulah Bat-Yehudah. 6 vols. Jerusalem: Mossad Harav Kook, 1958-2000.

Epstein, Barukh. *Torah Temimah.* Commentary to Pentateuch. 5 vols. Vilna: Romm, 1902.

Epstein, Kalonymos Kalman. *Ma'or va-Shemesh.* Breslau, 1842.

Epstein, Pinhas. *Minhah Hareivah.* Commentary to Tractate *Sotah.* Jerusalem, 1923.

Epstein, Yitzhak Eizik, of Homel. *Hannah Ariel.* 3 vols. Berdichev: Sheftel, 1912.

_____. "Iggeret Kodesh" (Holy Epistle). Printed at conclusion of *Hannah Ariel,* Part 3: *Amarot Tehorot (Ma'amar ha-Shabbat,* etc.). Berdichev: Sheftel, 1912.

Ergas, Joseph. *Shomer Emunim.* Amsterdam, 1736.

Ettlinger, Jacob. *'Arukh la-Ner, Makkot.* Altona, 1855

_____. *'Arukh la-Ner, Sukkah.* Altona, 1858.

Even-Shmuel, Yehudah. *Midreshei Ge'ulah.* Givʻatayim-Ramat Gan: Mossad Bialik, 1968.

Eybeschuetz, Jonathan. *Kereiti u-Peleiti.* Commentary to *Shulhan 'Arukh, Yoreh De'ah.* Altona, 1763.

_____. (Attributed to—). *Shem 'Olam.* Pressburg, 1890-1.

_____. (Attributed to—). *Va-'Avo ha-yom el ha-'ayin.* Ed. Pawel Maciejko. Los Angeles, Cherub, 2014.

'Eyn Yaʻakov. Legends of the Talmud. Ed. Jacob ibn Habib. 2 vols. Salonika, 1515-1522.

Ezra of Gerona. Commentary to Song of Songs. In *Kitvei Ramban*. Ed. C.B. Chavel, vol. 2.

Ezrahi, Shulamit. *Ha-Mashgi'ah Rabbi Meir*. Biography of Rabbi Meir Hadash. Jerusalem: Feldheim, 2001.

Falk, Marcia. "The *Wasf*." In *The Song of Songs: Modern Critical Interpretations*. Ed. Harold Bloom. New York: Chelsea House Publishers, 1988.

Fano, Menahem Azariah da. *Ma'amar ha-Nefesh*. In *Ma'amrei ha-RaMA' mi-Fano*. Jerusalem: Yismah Lev, 1997.

Feldman, Tzvi. *Rav A.Y. Kook: Selected Letters*. Ma'aleh Adumim, 1986.

Ficino, Marsilio. *Commentarium in Convivium Platonis De Amore*. (Commentary on Plato's *Symposium on Love*.) Florence, 1484.

Filber, Ya'akov. *Le-'Oro*. Jerusalem, 1995.

Fisher, Shelomo Yehonathan Yehudah. *Beit Yishai: Derashot*. Jerusalem, 2003.

Forshlager, Michael Eliezer. *Torat Michael*. Ed. Dov Meir Krauser. Jerusalem, 1967.

Fox, Marvin. "Rav Kook: Neither Philosopher nor Kabbalist." In *Rabbi Abraham Isaac Kook and Jewish Spirituality*. Ed. David Shatz and Lawrence Kaplan. New York: NYU Press, 1995.

Fraenkel, Avinoam. *Nefesh HaTzimtzum*. 2 vols. Jerusalem: Urim, 2015.

Freimann, Avraham Hayyim. *Ha-ROSh ve-Tse'etsa'av*. Biography of Rabbi Asher ben Yehiel. Transl. Menahem Eldar. Jerusalem: Mossad Harav Kook, 1986.

Friedland-Ben Arza, Sarah. "*Shekhenut ve-korat gag—'al shnei 'ekronot darshanut tsuraniyim be-kitvei R' Zadok Hakohen mi-Lublin*." In *Me'at la-Zaddik*. Ed. Gershon Kitsis. Jerusalem, 2000.

Friedman, Bezalel. *Ish Hasidekha*. Biography of Rabbi Levi Yitzhak Bender. Jerusalem, 1993.

Friedman, David, of Karlin. *She'elat David*. Piotrków, 1913.

Friedman, Shamma Yehudah. "Ha-Rambam ve-ha-Talmud." *Dinei Yisrael*, 26-27 (5769-5770).

Frumer, Aryeh Tsevi, of Kozhiglov. *Erets Tsevi*. Lublin, 1938.

Gabbai, Meir ibn. *'Avodat ha-Kodesh*. Venice, 1567; Warsaw, 1891, photo offset Jerusalem 1973.

_____. *Derekh Emunah*. Padua, 1563.

Gelbstein, Hillel Moshe Meshel. *Mishkenot le-Abir Ya'akov*. Jerusalem, 1881.

Gellman, Jerome. "Buber's Blunder: Buber's Replies to Scholem and Schatz-Uffenheimer." *Modern Judaism*, February 2000, pp. 20-40.

Gershuni, Yehudah. "Be-'Inyan Keri'at Bikkurim." In *Kovets Ma'amarim*, included in *Shitah Mekubetset 'al Masekhet Pesahim*. Ed. Yehudah Gershuni. New York, 1966.

Gikatilla (Chiquitilla), Joseph. *Gates of Light*. Transl. Avi Weinstein. San Francisco, CA: HarperCollins, 1994.

_____. *Ginat Egoz*. Ed. Mordechai Attiyah. Jerusalem: Yeshivat Ha-Hayyim ve-ha-Shalom, 1989.

_____. *Sha'arei Orah*. Ed. Joseph Ben-Shlomo. 2 vols. Jerusalem: Bialik Institute, 1970.

Ginsburg, Aryeh Leib. "Hiddushei Sha'agat Aryeh 'al ha-Torah." *Arazim* 5 (Jerusalem, 2019), pp. 14-125.

_____. *Turei Even*. Metz, 1781.

Glickman, C.S. *Mi-Pihem u-mi-Pi Ketavam*. Brooklyn, NY, 2008.

Goldberg, Mayer. *Margaliyot shel Torah*. Jerusalem, 1990.

Goldfeld, Lea Naomi. "Hilkhot Melakhim u-Milhamot u-Melekh ha-Mashiah." *Sinai* 96 (1985), pp. 67-79.

Goldman, Eliezer. *"Zikato shel ha-Rav Kook la-Mahshavah ha-Eropit."* In *Yovel Orot.* Ed. Binyamin Ish-Shalom and Shalom Rosenberg. Jerusalem: WZO, 1988.

Goldstoff, Yitzhak. *Mikdash ha-Kodesh.* 2 vols. *Hilkhot Beit ha-Behirah; Hilkhot Klei ha-Mikdash.* Jerusalem, 1994-1999.

Gottlieb, Efraim (Ed.). *The Hebrew Writings of the Author of* Tiqqunei Zohar *and* Ra'aya Mehemna. Hebrew. Jerusalem: The Israel Academy of Sciences and Humanities, 2003.

———. *Mehkarim be-Sifrut ha-Kabbalah.* Ed. Joseph Hecker. Tel-Aviv, 1976.

Gottlieb, Shmuel Noah. *Ohalei Shem.* Pinsk, 1912.

Graetz, Heinrich. *Geschichte der Juden von den ältesten Zeiten bis auf die Gegenwart.* 11 vols. Leipzig: Leiner, 1853-1875.

———. *History of the Jews from the Earliest Times to the Present Day.* Transl. Bella Löwy. London, 1891-1892.

Green, Arthur. "The Song of Songs in Early Jewish Mysticism." In *The Song of Songs: Modern Critical Interpretations.* Ed. Harold Bloom. New York: Chelsea House Publishers, 1988.

Grossman, Avraham. *Rashi: Religious Beliefs and Social Views.* Hebrew. Alon Shevut, 2016.

Gruenwald, Ithamar. "Mekoman shel masorot kohaniyot bi-yetsiratah shel ha-mistikah shel ha-merkavah ve-shel Shi'ur Komah." In *Early Jewish Mysticism.* Ed. Joseph Dan. Jerusalem, 1987. [=*Jerusalem Studies in Jewish Thought*, vol. 6, nos. 1-2, pp. 65-120.]

Habermann, Abraham M. "Shirat Harav." In *Sinai* 17 (5705/1945).

Halperin, David J. *Abraham Miguel Cardozo: Selected Writings.* Mahwah, NJ: Paulist Press, 2001.

Hariton, Moshe. "Ma'amar Rabbeinu ha-Zaken, 'Mi li ba-shamayim...'" Letter to Editor. *Heikhal ha-Besht*, no. 4, year 3 (Tishri 5766), pp. 167-168.

Harlap, Jacob Moses. *Beit Zevul*. Part Six. Jerusalem: Beit Zevul and Harry Fischel Institute, 1966.

_____. *Hed Harim*. Letters to Abraham Isaac Kook. Ed. Tsevi Yehudah Kook. Jerusalem, 1953.

_____. *Hed ha-Hayyim ha-Yisraeliyim*. Jerusalem, 1912

_____. Letter to Hayyim Ya'akov Levene. In *Yeshurun* 30 (Nissan, 5774/2014), p. 501 (facsimile).

_____. Letter to Hizkiyahu Yosef Mishkovksi. In *Zeved Tov* (*Festschrift* for Rabbi Zevulun Charlop). Ed. Ari S. Zahtz. New York: Yeshiva University Press, 2008. Letter 7 (p. 103).

_____. Letter to Yehudah Klein (Amital). In *'Alon Shevut*, Year 5, no. 20 (Adar 5734), pp. 18-21. Included in 64-page brochure on Rabbi Harlap issued by the Israeli Ministry of Education. Ed. Aryeh Strikovsky, no. 271 (Tishri 5767), pp. 45-46. The brochure is available online: http://meyda.education.gov.il/files/tarbut/pirsumeagaf/kitveet/271pdf.pdf?fbclid=IwAR2uIdw9XhInuL_bW8LyHDq77j9J-QGkNxBgG4WorTDjbXHulQKlgLL5l1KU

_____. *Mei Marom*, vol. 1: Commentary to Maimonides' *Shemonah Perakim*. Jerusalem, 1945; photo offset Jerusalem: Beit Zevul, 1982.

_____. *Mei Marom*. vol. 5: Nimmukei ha-Mikra'ot. Jerusalem, 1981.

_____. *Mei Marom*. vol. 10: Leviticus. Jerusalem, 1997.

Haronian, Emanuel. *The Attitude to Human Self in the Teaching of Rav Kook and Rav Harlap*. Hebrew. MA Thesis. Ben-Gurion University, February 2020. Available at: www.academia.edu

Harvey, Steven. "Maimonides in the Sultan's Palace." In *Perspectives on Maimonides: Philosophical and Historical Studies*. Ed. Joel L. Kraemer. Oxford: Oxford University Press, 1991.

Harvey, Warren Zev. "Leibowitz's Anti-Greek Concept of the Messiah." Hebrew. *Iyyun*, vol. 42 (October 1993), pp. 517-520.

_____. Video of dialogue between Professors Yeshayahu Leibowitz and Zev (Warren) Harvey of 30/5/1993. Available at: https://www.youtube.com/watch?v=wkcnXAsFUgA

Haver (Wildman), Yitzhak Eizik. *Afikei Yam*. 2 vols. Jerusalem, 1994.

_____. *Pithei She'arim*. 2 parts. Warsaw, 1888; photo offset Tel-Aviv: Sinai, 1964.

Havlin, David. *Ve-Nitsdak Kodesh*. Jerusalem, 1981.

Havlin, Shelomo Zalman. *Ha-Mashpi'a*. Biography of Rabbi Shelomo Zalman Havlin. Jerusalem, 1982.

Hayes, Yitzhak. *Si'ah Yitzhak* to Tractate *Makkot*. Podgorze, 1900.

Hayyim ben Isaac, of Volozhin. *Nefesh ha-Hayyim*. Ed. Yissachar Dov Rubin. B'nei Berak, 1989.

Hazan, Abraham ben Nahman, of Tulchin. *Yemei ha-Tela'ot*. Jerusalem, 1933.

Heilman, Hayyim Meir. *Beit Rabbi*. 3 parts. Berdichev, 1902.

Heilprin, Menahem Menkhin. *Hagahot u-Be'urim* to Rabbi Hayyim Vital, *'Ets Hayyim*. Warsaw, 1891.

Heinemann, Isaak. *Ta'amei ha-Mitsvot be-Sifrut Yisrael*. Jerusalem, 1966.

Heller, Yom Tov Lipmann. *Tosefot Yom Tov*. Commentary to Mishnah. 6 vols. Prague, 1614-1617.

Henkin, Eitam. "Ki hekhin beit haroshet lehatir 'agunot." Study of Rabbi Joseph Shapotshnick. *Asif* 2 (2015).

_____. *Ta'arokh Lefanai Shulhan*. Biography of Rabbi Yehiel Mikhel Epstein, author of *'Arukh ha-Shulhan*. Israel: Maggid, 2018.

Herczeg, Yisrael. *Keren David, Makkot.* Jerusalem, 1982.

Herrera, Abraham Cohen de. *Casa de la Divinidad / Beit Elohim.* Translated from Spanish to Hebrew by Isaac Aboab da Fonseca. Amsterdam, 1655. Jerusalem, 2006.

_____. *Puerta del Cielo / Sha'ar ha-Shamayim.* Translated from Spanish to Hebrew by Isaac Aboab da Fonseca. Amsterdam, 1655. Jerusalem, 2006.

Heschel, Abraham Joshua. "Did Maimonides Believe That He Attained Prophecy?" Hebrew. In *Louis Ginzberg Jubilee Volume.* Ed. Saul Lieberman et al. New York, 1945.

_____. *The Prophets.* New York: Jewish Publication Society of America, 1962.

Hitchens, Christopher. *God Is Not Great.* (United Kingdom) Atlantic Books, 2007.

Hoffman, David Zvi. *Midrash Tanna'im* to the Book of Deuteronomy. Berlin, 1908.

Hoffman, Joshua. "Rav Kook's Mission to America." *Orot: A Multidisciplinary Journal of Judaism,* vol. 1 (5751/1991), pp. 78-99.

Hopstein, Israel ben Shabtai, of Kozhnits. *'Avodat Yisrael.* B'nei Berak: Pe'er mi-Kedoshim, 2013.

_____. *Ner Israel.* Commentary to *Likkutim me-Rav Hai Gaon.* Piotrków, 1913.

Horowitz, Isaiah Halevi. *Shnei Luhot ha-Berit.* Amsterdam, 1648.

_____. *Siddur ha-SheLaH.* Amsterdam, 1717. 2 vols. Jerusalem: Ahavat Shalom, 1998.

Hoshke, Reuben (Sofer) of Prague. *Yalkut Re'uveni.* Wilmersdorf, 1681.

Hoter ben Shelomo. *She'elot R. Hoter ben Shelomo.* Ed. Yosef Kafah. Jerusalem, 2001.

Hurwitz, Aharon Halevi, of Staroshelye. *'Avodat ha-Levi.* Commentary on Pentateuch. Lemberg, 1861-1862.

———. *Sha'arei 'Avodah*. Shklov, 1821.

———. *Sha'arei ha-Yihud ve-ha-Emunah*. Shklov, 1820.

Hurwitz, Pinhas Elijah, of Vilna. *Sefer ha-Berit*. Part 1. Brünn, 1797.

Hutner, Isaac. "'Holocaust'—A study of the term and the epoch it is meant to describe." *Jewish Observer*, October 1977.

———. Letter to M.M. Schneerson. Datelined, "Monday, *Va-Yakhel—Pekudei*, 5737." In *Heikhal ha-Besht*, Year 11, no. 35 (Tishri 5774/2014), pp. 75-77.

———. Letter to Tsevi Yehudah Hakohen Kook. Datelined, "28 Ellul 5722." In *Iggerot la-RAYaH*. Ed. Ben-Zion Shapira. 2nd edition, Jerusalem, 1990. Appendix, Letter 47 (p. 585).

———. *Ma'amrei Pahad Yitzhak: Pesah*. Brooklyn, NY, 2017.

———. *Ma'amrei Pahad Yitzhak: Sukkot*. New York, NY, 2002.

———. *Pahad Yitzhak: Hanukkah*. New York, NY, 1989.

———. *Pahad Yitzhak: Iggerot u-Ketavim*. Ed. Yonatan David. Brooklyn, NY, 2016.

———. *Pahad Yitzhak: Rosh Hashanah*. New York, NY, 2003.

———. *Reshimot Lev*. See *Rutta, Leibel*.

———. *Sefer ha-Zikaron le-Maran Ba'al Pahad Yitzhak*. Ed. Yonatan David. Brooklyn, NY, 2014.

Ibn Ezra, Abraham. *Commentary to Pentateuch*. Ed. Asher Weiser. Jerusalem: Mossad Harav Kook, 1977.

———. *Yesod Mora ve-Sod Torah*. Ed. Joseph Cohen and Uriel Simon. Ramat Gan: Bar-Ilan University Press, 2002.

Ibn Kaspi, Joseph. *'Ammudei Kesef u-Maskiyot Kesef*. Ed. Salomo Werbluner. Frankfurt am Main, 1848.

———. *Mishneh Kesef* I. Ed. Isaac Last. Pressburg, 1905; photo offset Jerusalem, 1970.

———. *Sefer ha-Mussar/Yoreh De'ah*. In Eliezer Ashkenazi of

Tunis, *Ta'am Zekenim*. Frankfurt am Main, 1854. In Isaac Last, *'Asarah Klei Kesef.* Pressburg, 1903.

———. *Shulhan Kesef.* Ed. Hannah Kasher. Jerusalem: Ben-Zvi Institute, 1996.

Ibn Sahula, Isaac. *Meshal ha-Kadmoni.* Venice, 1546.

Ibn Waqar, Joseph ben Abraham. *Shorashei ha-Kabbalah (Principles of the Qabbalah)*. Ed. Paul B. Fenton. Los Angeles: Cherub Press, 2004.

Idel, Moshe. *The Angelic World: Apotheosis and Theophany.* Hebrew. Tel-Aviv: Yedioth Ahronoth, 2008.

———. "The Kabbalah in Byzantium—Preliminary Remarks." In *Jews in Byzantium: Dialectics of Minority and Majority Cultures*. Ed. Robert Bonfil. Leiden: Brill, 2012.

———. *Kabbalah: New Perspectives.* New Haven: Yale University Press, 1988.

———. "Maimonides' *Guide of the Perplexed* and the Kabbalah." *Jewish History* 18 (2004).

———. *R. Menahem Recanati ha-Mekubal.* vol. 1. Jerusalem and Tel-Aviv: Schocken, 1998.

Ilan, Aharon. *'Eynei Yitzhak.* Biography of Rabbi Yitzhak Arieli. Jerusalem, 2018.

Ilan, Mordechai. *Torat ha-Kodesh.* 2 vols. B'nei Berak, 2006.

Isaac ben Abba Mari of Marseille. *'Ittur.* Venice, 1608.

Isaac ben Sheshet Perfet. *She'elot u-Teshuvot RIVaSh.* Constantinople, 1546-1547.

Isaac 'Or Zaru'a of Vienna. *'Or Zaru'a.* 2 vols. Zhitomir, 1862.

'Iyyun (Sefer ha-). Attributed to Rabbi Hammai. In *Likkutim me-Rav Hai Gaon.* Warsaw, 1798.

Jacob ben Asher. *Arba'ah Turim.* Piove di Sacco, 1475.

Jaffe, Mordechai Gimpel and Nathan Nota Luria. *Elef ha-Magen.* Commentary to Tractate *Horayot.* Warsaw, 1912.

James, William. *The Varieties of Religious Experience*. New York: Longmans, Green, & Co., 1902.

Jonathan ben David of Lunel. *Commentary by R. Jonathan of Lunel on Mishnah and Alfasi Tractates Megillah and Mo'ed Katan*. Hebrew. Ed. Samuel K. Mirsky. Jerusalem: Sura, n.d. (1956).

Judah ben Samuel of Regensburg. *Sefer Hasidim*. Ed. Jehuda Wistinetzki. Berlin: Mekitsei Nirdamim, 1893. With commentary *Mishnat Avraham* by Abraham Aaron Price. 2 vols. Toronto, 1955; New York, 1960.

_____. *Sefer Hasidim*. Ed. Reuven Margaliyot. Jerusalem: Mossad Harav Kook, 1957.

Judah Halevi. *Book of Kuzari*. Transl. Hartwig Hirschfeld. New York: Pardes, 1946.

_____. *Kuzari*. Transl. Yehudah Even-Shmuel. Tel-Aviv: Dvir, 1972.

Justman, Pinhas Menahem. *Siftei Tsaddik*. Piotrków-Bilgoraj, 1924-1935.

Kafah, Yahya ben Shelomo (Sliman). *'Amal u-Re'ut Ru'ah va-Haramot u-Teshuvatam*. Tel-Aviv, 1914; limited facsimile edition Jerusalem 1976.

Kafah, Yosef. "She'elot hakhmei Lunel u-teshuvot 'ha-Rambam' kelum mekoriyot hen?" In *Sefer Zikaron le-Harav Yitzhak Nissim*. Ed. Meir Benayahu. vol. 2. Jerusalem, 1985.

Kafka, Franz. "Jackals and Arabs." In *Der Jude*. Ed. Martin Buber. 1917.

Kagan, Israel Meir. *Mishnah Berurah*. Commentary to *Shulhan 'Arukh, Orah Hayyim*. 6 vols. Warsaw, 1884-1907.

Kahan, Moshe. "Joseph ibn Kaspi—From Arles to Majorca." *Iberia Judaica* VIII (2016), pp. 181-192.

Kalischer, Tsevi Hirsch. *Derishat Zion*. Lyck, 1862.

Kalmanson, Elhanan. *Ha-Mahshavah ha-Yisraelit*. Jerusalem,

1920; photo offset Jerusalem, 1967.

Kalmin, Richard. *Jewish Babylonia between Persia and Roman Palestine*. Oxford: Oxford University Press, 2006.

Kanarfogel, Ephraim. "Rashi's Awareness of Jewish Mystical Literature and Traditions." *Raschi und Seine Erbe*. Ed. Daniel Krochmalnik, Hanna Liss and Ronen Reichman. Heidelberg: Hochschule für Jüdische Studien, 2007. pp. 23-34.

Kanievsky, Hayyim. *Kiryat Melekh*. Commentary to *Mishneh Torah*. Bnei Berak, 1983.

Kaplan, Aryeh. *Meditation and Kabbalah*. York Beach, Maine: Samuel Weiser, 1985.

Kaplan, Lawrence J. *Maimonides—Between Philosophy and Halakhah: Rabbi Joseph B. Soloveitchik's Lectures on* The Guide of the Perplexed. Jerusalem: Urim, 2016.

Karelitz, Abraham Isaiah. *Hazon Ish, Orah Hayyim / Moʻed*. Ed. Samuel Greineman. 3rd edition. B'nei Berak, 1967.

_____. *Hazon Ish, Yoreh De'ah*. Ed. Samuel Greineman. B'nei Berak, 1962.

Karo, Joseph. *Beit Yosef*. Commentary on *Arbaʻah Turim*. 4 vols. Venice-Sabbioneta, 1550-1559.

_____. *Shulhan ʻArukh*. Venice: Bragadin, 1565.

Kasher, Menahem Mendel. *Mefʻaneʻah Tsefunot*. New York, 1959.

_____. *Torah Shelemah*. Talmudic-Midrashic encyclopedia on the Pentateuch. 42 vols. Jerusalem-New York, 1927-1992.

Kasher, Moshe Shelomo. *Ha-Gaʻon ha-Rogatchovi ve-Talmudo*. Jerusalem, 1958.

Katz, Shlomo. "Rahav and Yehoshua: Imagination and Intellect." *Orot: A Multidisciplinary Journal*, vol. 1 (5751/1991).

(Keidaner, Yaʻakov). *Matzref ha-ʻAvodah*. Koenigsberg, 1858.

Kenig, Gedaliah Aaron. *Hayyei Nefesh*. Tel-Aviv, 1968.

Kiener, Ronald C. "Jewish Mysticism in the Lands of the Ishmaelites: A Re-Orientation." In *The Convergence of Judaism and Islam: Religious, Scientific, and Cultural Dimensions*. Ed. Michael M. Laskier and Yaacov Lev. Gainesville: University Press of Florida, 2011.

Kitsis, Gershon. *"Mi-Peri Tsaddik."* Bibliography of Rabbi Zadok Hakohen. In *Me'at la-Zaddik*. Ed. Gershon Kitsis. Jerusalem, 2000.

Klausner, Israel. *Toledot "Nes Ziyonah" be-Volozhin*. Jerusalem: Mossad Harav Kook, 1954.

———. *Vilna: "Jerusalem of Vilna," 1881-1939*. Hebrew. vol. 2. Israel: Ghetto Fighters' House, 1983.

Klonitzky-Kline, Solomon. *Otsar Ta'amei Hazal*. New York: Shulsinger, 1939.

Kohut, Alexander. *Aruch Completum*. 8 vols. Vienna, 1878-1892.

Kook, Abraham Isaac. *"Afikim ba-Negev."* In *Ha-Peless*. Berlin, 1903-1904. Photo offset in Moshe Zuriel. *Otserot ha-RAYaH*. Old series, vol. 2. Tel-Aviv, 1988, pp. 733-779.

———. *'Arpilei Tohar*. Jerusalem, 1914. Jerusalem: Makhon RZYH Kook, 1983. Ed. Yitzhak Shilat (Greenspan).

———. *"Ha-Aryeh ba-Sugar"* ("The Lion in the Cage"). Poem. In Moshe Zuriel. *Otserot ha-RAYaH*. Old series. vol. 3. n.p., n.d. [circa 1990], pp. 1281-1282.

———. Commentary to *The Legends of Rabbah bar Bar Hannah*. Ed. Bezalel Naor. Monsey, NY: Orot/Kodesh, 2019.

———. *'Ets Hadar ha-Shalem*. Ed. Judah Zoldan. Jerusalem, 1986.

———. *'Eyn Ayah*. Commentary to *'Eyn Ya'akov* Legends of the Tamud. Ed. Ya'akov Filber. 4 vols. Jerusalem: Makhon RZYH, 1987-2000.

———. *Hadarav*. Ed. Ron Sarid. Third edition. 2008

———. *Haskamot ha-RAYaH*. Ed. Y.M. Yismah and B.Z Kahana. Jerusalem: Makhon RZYH, 1988.

_____. *Haskamot ha-RAYaH* (1897-1928). Ed. Ari Yitzhak Shvat, Zuriel Hallamish, and Yohanan Fried. Jerusalem: Beit Harav, 2017.

_____. *Hevesh Pe'er*. Ed. Yitzhak Arieli and Uri Segal Hamburger. Jerusalem, 1925.

_____. *Iggerot ha-RAYaH*. Ed. Tsevi Yehudah Kook. vol. 1 (1888-1910). Second edition corrected. Jerusalem: Mossad Harav Kook, 1962.

_____. *Iggerot ha-RAYaH*. Ed. Tsevi Yehudah Kook. vol. 2 (1911-1915). Second edition corrected. Jerusalem: Mossad Harav Kook 1961.

_____. *Iggerot ha-RAYaH*. Ed. Tsevi Yehudah Kook. vol. 3 (1916-1919). Jerusalem: Mossad Harav Kook, 1965.

_____. *Iggerot ha-RAYaH*. vol. 4 (1920-1925). Ed. Ya'akov Filber. Jerusalem: Makhon RZYH Kook, 1984.

_____. *Iggerot ha-RAYaH*. vol. 5 (1922). Ed. Ze'ev Neuman. Jerusalem: Makhon RZYH Kook, 2019.

_____. *Iggerot la-RAYaH*. Ed. Ben-Zion Shapira. Second edition expanded. Jerusalem: Makhon RZYH, 1990.

_____. *'Ittur Soferim*. 2 vols. Vilna, 1888. In 1 vol. photo offset Jerusalem, 1974. With notes of Tsevi Yehudah Kook.

_____. "*Kelil Tif'eret.*" Rejoinder to Rabbi Turbowitz. In *Torah mi-Zion*. Jerusalem, 1900. Reprinted in *Hevesh Pe'er*. Ed. Yitzhak Arieli and Uri Segal Hamburger.

_____. *Kevatsim mi-Ketav Yad Kodsho*. Ed. Boaz Ofen. 3 vols. Jerusalem, 2006, 2008, 2018.

_____. *Kitsur Mesillat Yesharim*. Appended to Tsevi Yehudah Kook. *Li-Sheloshah be-Elul*. vol. 2. Jerusalem, 1947, pp. 23-31; reprinted in *Ma'amrei ha-RAYaH*. vol. 2. Jerusalem, 1984, pp. 273-276; and in Moshe Zuriel. *Otserot ha-RAYaH*. New series. vol. 2, pp. 297-300.

_____. *The Koren Rav Kook Siddur*. Ed. Bezalel Naor. Jerusalem: Koren, 2017.

_____. Letter to Yehudah Newman. Datelined "London, 21 Tevet, 5679" [i.e., December 24, 1918]. Available at: http://orot.com/newly-acquired-manuscript-rav-kook/

_____. *Ma'amrei ha-RAYaH*. 2 vols. vol. 1. Ed. Elisha Langenauer and David Landau. Jerusalem, 1980. vol. 2. Ed. Elisha Aviner (Langenauer). Jerusalem, 1984.

_____. *Metsi'ot Katan*. Ed. Harel Cohen. Israel: Maggid, 2018.

_____. *Mishpat Kohen*. Jerusalem, 1937.

_____. "*Ha-Misped bi-Yerushalayim*" ("The Lamentation in Jerusalem"). Eulogy for Theodor Herzl. In Bezalel Naor. *When God Becomes History: Historical Essays of Rabbi Abraham Isaac Hakohen Kook*, pp. 38-56.

_____. *Mitsvat ha-RAYaH*. On *Shulhan 'Arukh, Orah Hayyim*. First published as appendix to Menahem Natan Nota Auerbach. *Orah Ne'eman*. Jerusalem, 1924-1931. Published separately in expanded edition. Ed. Tsevi Yehudah Kook. Jerusalem: Mossad Harav Kook, 1970.

_____. *Orot*. Ed. Tsevi Yehudah Kook. Jerusalem, 1920. Enlarged Jerusalem, 1950.

_____. *Orot*. Original 1920 edition. Transl. Bezalel Naor. Jerusalem: Maggid, 2015.

_____. *Orot ha-Kodesh*. Ed. David Cohen. 3 vols. Jerusalem: 1938-1950. vol. 4. Ed. David Cohen and Yohanan Fried. Jerusalem: Mossad Harav Kook, 1990.

_____. *Orot ha-Mitsvot*. In Moshe Zuriel. *Otserot ha-RAYaH*. Old Series, vol. 4. Tel-Aviv, 1992, pp. 28-47. Reprinted from *Be-Shemen Ra'anan* (Rabbi Natan Ra'anan-Kook Memorial Volume), vol. 1.

_____. *Orot ha-Torah*. Ed. Tsevi Yehudah Kook. Jerusalem, 1940.

_____. *Orot Yisrael*. Ed. Tsevi Yehudah Kook. Jerusalem, 1942.

_____. *Otserot ha-Rayah*. Ed. Moshe Zuriel. Old series. 4 vols. Tel-Aviv, 1988-1992. New Series. 5 vols. Rishon le-Zion, 2002. vols. 6-7. Ed. Moshe Zuriel, Shai Hirsch, and Ari Shvat. Rishon le-Zion, 2016.

_____. *Pinkas Yod Gimel*. (Also *Pinkas Rishon le-Yaffo*.) Ed. Ben-Zion Shapira. Jerusalem: Makhon RZYH Kook, 2004. Reprinted in *Pinkesei ha-Rayah*, vol. 1, and in *Kevatsim mi-Ketav Yad Kodsho*, vol. 1.

_____. *Pinkesei ha-RAYaH*. 4 vols. Jerusalem: Makhon RZYH Kook, 2008-2017. vol. 1. Ed. Ben-Zion Shapira and Ze'ev Neuman. vol. 2. Ed. Ben-Zion Shapira and Levi Yitzhaki. vol. 3. Levi Yitzhaki. vol. 4. Tsevi Mikhel Levin and Ben-Zion Shapira.

_____. *Reish Millin*. London, 1917.

_____. *Reish Millin*. Part Two (*Ha-Shorashim*). Jerusalem: Makhon RZYH Kook, 2003.

_____. *Shabbat ha-Arets*. Jerusalem, 1910.

_____. *Shemonah Kevatsim*. 2 vols. Second Edition. Jerusalem, 2004.

_____. *Shemu'ot RAYaH: Bereshit/Shemot*. Ed. Kalman Eliezer Frankel and Hayyim Yeshayahu Hadari. 2nd edition. Jerusalem: WZO, 2015.

_____. *Siddur 'Olat Re'iyah*. Ed. Tsevi Yehudah Kook. 2 vols. Jerusalem, 1939, 1949.

_____. "Talelei Orot." In *Tahkemoni*. Bern, 1910. Reprinted in *Ma'amrei ha-RAYaH*, vol. 1. Jerusalem, 1980, pp. 18-28.

_____. *When God Becomes History: Historical Essays of Rabbi Abraham Isaac Hakohen Kook*. Ed. Bezalel Naor. New York, NY: Kodesh Press, 2016.

_____. *Ha-Yeshivah ha-Merkazit ha-'Olamit bi-Yerushalayim*. 12 pp. Jerusalem: Y.A. Weiss [1924].

_____. "Zer'onim." In *Ha-Tarbut ha-Yisraelit*. Ed. Alexander Ziskind Rabinowitz (*AZaR*) and Tsevi Yehudah Kook.

Jaffa, 1913. Reprinted in 1950 edition of *Orot*.

Kook, Tsevi Yehudah. *Li-Netivot Yisrael*. vol. 1. Tel-Aviv, 1967. vol. 2. Jerusalem, 1979.

———. *Li-Sheloshah be-Ellul*. Biography of Rabbi Abraham Isaac Kook. vol. 1. Jerusalem, 1938. vol. 2. Jerusalem, 1947.

———. *Mi-Tokh ha-Torah ha-Go'elet*. See *Schwartz, Hayyim Avihu*.

———. *Tsemah Tsevi: Iggerot Harav Tsevi Yehudah Hakohen Kook*. vol. 1 (1907-1919). Ed. Landau, Neuman, and Rahmani. Jerusalem, 1991.

Lachter, Hartley. "Spreading Secrets: Kabbalah and Esotericism in Isaac ibn Sahula's *Meshal ha-Kadmoni*." *Jewish Quarterly Review*, Vol. 100, No. 1 (Winter 2010), pp. 111-138.

Laine, Eliezer and S.Z. Berger. *Avnei Hen*. Annals of the Hen Family. Brooklyn, NY: Kehot, 2015.

Landau, Ezekiel. *Doresh le-Zion*. Ed. Samuel Landau. Prague, 1827.

Landes, Rachel. "My Father, Mayer Goldberg." October 15, 2009. Unpublished memoir.

Langermann, Y. Tzvi. "On Some Passages Attributed to Maimonides." Hebrew. In *Me'ah She'arim: Studies in Medieval Jewish Spiritual Life in Memory of Isadore Twersky*. Ed. Fleischer, Blidstein, Horowitz, and Septimus. Jerusalem: Hebrew University Magnes Press, 2001.

Laniado, Samuel. *Keli Yakar*. Commentary on Early Prophets. Venice, 1603.

Laufer, Mordechai Menashe. *Ha-Melekh bi-Mesibo*. 2 vols. Kefar Habad: Kehot, 1993.

Leiner, Gerson Hanokh. *'Eyn ha-Tekhelet*. Warsaw, 1891; photo offset New York, 1954.

———. Introduction to his father, Rabbi Ya'akov Leiner's *Beit*

Ya'akov, Bereishit. Warsaw, 1890. Also published separately as *Ha-Hakdamah ve-ha-Petihah.*
———. *Sod Yesharim, Rosh Hashanah.* Warsaw, 1902.
———. *Sod Yesharim, Sukkot.* Warsaw, 1903.
———. *Sod Yesharim 'al ha-Torah.* Brooklyn, NY, 1971.

Leiner, Mordechai Yosef of Izbica. *Mei ha-Shilo'ah.* vol. 1. Vienna, 1860. vol. 2. Lublin, 1922.

Leiner, Mordechai Yosef El'azar. *Tif'eret Yosef.* Jerusalem, 1961.

Leiner, Ya'akov. *Beit Ya'akov.* 3 vols. Genesis. Warsaw, 1890. Exodus. Lublin, 1903. Leviticus. Warsaw. 1937.
———. *Seder Haggadah shel Pesah 'im Sefer ha-Zemanim.* Jerusalem, 2010.

Leiner, Yeruham. *Tif'eret Yeruham.* Brooklyn, NY, 1967.

Lessing, Gotthold Ephraim. *Nathan der Weise (Nathan the Wise).* Berlin: C.F. Voss, 1779.

Levi, Gedaliah. "Kibbuts Derushei ha-Melakhim de-Mitu." In Jacob Tsemah, *Kol be-Ramah.* Ed. Eliyahu Attiah. Jerusalem: Makhon B'nei Yissachar, 2001.

Levin, Joshua Heschel. *'Aliyot Eliyahu.* Biography of Vilna Gaon. Jerusalem, 1989.

Levin, Sholom Dov Baer. *Mi-Beit ha-Genazim.* Brooklyn: Kehot, 2009.

Levinas, Emmanuel. *Difficile liberté: Essais sur le Judaïsme.* Paris, 1963.
———. *Du sacré au saint : Cinq nouvelles lectures talmudiques.* Paris, 1977.
———. *L'Au-delà du verset : Lectures et discours talmudiques.* Paris, 1982.
———. *Quatre lectures talmudiques.* Paris, 1968.

Levinger, Jacob. *Maimonides' Techniques of Codification: A Study in the Method of* Mishneh Torah. Hebrew. Jerusalem: Magnes, 1965.

Lewin, Benjamin Menashe. *Otsar ha-Ge'onim*. 12 vols. Haifa-Jerusalem, 1928-1943.

Lichtenstein, Aharon. "R. Joseph Soloveitchik." In *Great Jewish Thinkers of the Twentieth Century*. Ed. Simon Noveck. Clinton, Mass: B'nai B'rith, 1963.

Lieberman, Saul. *Hellenism in Jewish Palestine*. New York, 1994.

———. Letter to Louis Ginzberg. In Marc B. Shapiro, *Saul Lieberman and the Orthodox*.

———. *Midreshei Teiman*. Jerusalem, 1940.

———. *Mishnat Shir ha-Shirim*. Appendix to Gershom Scholem. *Jewish Gnosticism, Merkabah Mysticism and Talmudic Tradition*, pp. 118-126.

———. *Sheki'in*. Jerusalem, 1939.

———. *Tosefta ki-Fshutah*. Commentary to *Tosefta*. 10 vols. New York, 1955-1988.

Liebes, Yehuda. *Studies in the Zohar*. Albany: State University of New York Press, 1993.

Lifschitz, Hayyim. *Shivhei ha-RAYaH*. Jerusalem, 1995.

Lifshitz, Dov Baer. *Golot 'Iliyot*. On Tractate *Mikva'ot*. Warsaw, 1887.

Lifshitz, Jacob Koppel, of Mezritch. *Sha'ar Gan 'Eden*. Koretz, 1803.

Lintop, Pinhas. *Binyan ha-'Ummah*. Piotrków, 1907.

———. *Kana'uteh de-Pinhas*. Ed. Bezalel Naor. Spring Valley, NY: Orot, 2013.

———. *Yalkut Avnei Emunat Yisrael*. Warsaw, 1895.

Lobel, Diana. *A Sufi-Jewish Dialogue: Philosophy and Mysticism in Bahya Ibn Paquda's* Duties of the Heart. Philadelphia: University of Pennsylvania Press, 2007.

Löw, Judah ben Bezalel (MaHaRaL) of Prague. *Gevurot Hashem*. Cracow, 1582. London: L. Honig & Sons, 1954.

_____. *Hiddushei Aggadot*. 4 vols. London: L. Honig & Sons, 1960.

_____. *Netsah Yisrael*. Prague, 1599. London: L. Honig & Sons, 1957.

_____. *Tif'eret Yisrael*. Venice: Daniel Zanetti, 1599. London: L. Honig & Sons, 1955.

Luboshitz, Tzvi. "An Early Version of the *Simsum* Debate in Immanuel Hay Ricchi's *Yosher Levav*." *Kabbalah*, 42 (2018), pp. 267-320.

Luria, David. *Be'ur ha-RaDaL*. Commentary to *Pirkei de-Rabbi Eliezer*. Warsaw, 1852.

Luzzatto, Moses Hayyim. *Adir ba-Marom* II. Ed. Yosef Spinner. Jerusalem, 1988.

_____ (attributed to—). *KaLaH Pithei Hokhmah*. Koretz, 1785. Ed. Yosef Spinner. Jerusalem, 1987.

_____. *Ma'amar ha-Ge'ulah*. Ed. H. Touitou. n.p., 2002.

_____. *Mesillat Yesharim* (Dialogue Version from Ms. Günzburg 1206, Russian State Library, Moscow; and Thematic Version from first edition, Amsterdam, 1740). Ed. Avraham Shoshana. Jerusalem: Ofeq, 1994.

Ma'arekhet ha-Elohut. Mantua, 1558.

Maccoby, Hayyim Zundel. *Imrei Hayyim*. Ed. Max Mansky. Tel-Aviv, 1929.

Maimon, Solomon. *Giv'at ha-Moreh*. Commentary to *Moreh Nevukhim*. Sulzbach, 1828.

Malbim (Wisser), Meir Leibush. *Mikra'ei Kodesh*. Commentary on the Prophets and Hagiographa. Warsaw, 1874.

Malka, Solomon. *Monsieur Chouchani: L'énigme d'un maitre du XXème siècle*. Paris, 1994.

Margaliyot, Abraham Tsevi. *Keren 'Orah*. Commentary to Pentateuch. Jerusalem, 1986.

Margaliyot, Hayyim Mordechai. *Sha'arei Teshuvah*. Commentary to *Shulhan 'Arukh*. Dubno: Press of Hayyim Mordechai Margaliyot, 1820 (completed 1825).

Margaliyot, Reuven. *Mal'akhei 'Elyon*. Jerusalem: Mossad Harav Kook, 1988.

⎯⎯⎯. *Margaliyot ha-Yam*. On Tractate *Sanhedrin*. Jerusalem: Mossad Harav Kook, 1958.

⎯⎯⎯. *Nitsutsei 'Or*. Notes to *Zohar*. In *Zohar*. Ed. Reuven Margaliyot. Jerusalem: Mossad Harav Kook, 2002.

⎯⎯⎯. *Shem 'Olam*. Jerusalem: Mossad Harav Kook, 1989.

⎯⎯⎯. *Yesod ha-Mishnah va-'Arikhatah*. Lwów, 1933.

Mark, Zvi. *Mistikah ve-Shiga'on bi-Yetsirat R. Nahman mi-Breslov* (*Mysticism and Madness in the Work of R. Nahman of Bratslav*). Tel Aviv, 2003.

⎯⎯⎯. *The Scroll of Secrets: The Hidden Messianic Vision of R. Nachman of Breslav*. Brighton, Mass.: Academic Studies Press, 2010.

Marx, Karl. *The Portable Karl Marx*. Ed. Eugene Kamenka. New York: Penguin, 1983.

Mayse, Ariel Evan. "Tree of Life, Tree of Knowledge: Halakha and Theology in *Ma'or va-Shamesh*." *Tradition* 51:1 (2019).

Meir, Jonatan. "Hillel Zeitlin, William James and Hasidism." Lecture delivered March 7, 2016 at "Life as a Dialogue," International Conference in Honor of Ephraim Meir, Bar Ilan University. Available at youtube:

https://www.youtube.com/watch?v=h2TKkSbwcsA

Menahem ben Solomon ha-Me'iri. *Beit ha-Behirah, Berakhot*. Ed. Shmuel Dikman. Jerusalem: Makhon ha-Talmud ha-Yisraeli, 1965.

⎯⎯⎯. *Beit ha-Behirah, Megillah*. Ed. Moshe Hershler. Jerusalem: Makhon ha-Talmud ha-Yisraeli, 1968.

⎯⎯⎯. *Beit ha-Behirah, Sukkah*. Ed. Avraham Liss. Jerusalem: Makhon ha-Talmud ha-Yisraeli, 1966.

⎯⎯⎯. *Beit ha-Behirah, Yoma*. Ed. Yosef Klein. Jerusalem:

Makhon ha-Talmud ha-Yisraeli, 1970.

Messer, Isaac. *U-Mi-Midbar Matanah*. Ed. Moshe Hallamish. Jerusalem, 1985.

Meyuhas ben Elijah. Commentary to Exodus. Ed. A.W. Greenup. Budapest, 1929.

Midrash Debarim Rabbah (from Oxford ms.). Ed. Saul Lieberman. Jerusalem, 1940.

Midrash Mishlei. Ed. Solomon Buber. Vilna: Romm, 1893.

Midrash Tehillim. Ed. Solomon Buber. Vilna: Romm, 1891.

Mirsky, Yehudah. *Rav Kook: Mystic in a Time of Revolution*. New Haven: Yale University Press, 2014.

Mohr, Melissa. *Holy Sh*t: A Brief History of Swearing*. Oxford: Oxford University Press, 2013.

Moinester, Uri. *Karnei Re'em*. New York, 1951.

Mondshine, Yehoshua. "Asifat ha-Rabbanim be-Rusya bi-Shenat 'Atar." *Kefar Habad*, no. 898. Available online at: http://www.shturem.net/index.php?section=blog_new&article_id=24

_____. "'Likkutei Torah' le-Shalosh Parshiyot." *Kefar Habad*, nos. 931, 933. Available online at: http://www.shturem.net/index.php?section=blog_new&article_id=29

Monson, Levi Yitzhak, of Ozerna. *Bekha Yevarekh Yisrael*. Przemysl, 1905.

Moses ben Hisdai Taku. *Ketav Tamim*. Ed. Raphael Kirchheim. In *Otsar Nehmad*, vol. 3. Vienna, 1860. Facsimile of manuscript of *Ketav Tamim*. Akademon, 1984.

Moses ben Maimon (Maimonides). *Commentary to the Mishnah*. Ed. Yosef Kafah. 3 vols. Jerusalem: Mossad Harav Kook, 1963-1968.

_____. *The Guide of the Perplexed*. Transl. Shlomo Pines. Chicago: University of Chicago Press, 1963.

_____. *Iggerot ha-Rambam*. Ed. Yitzhak Shilat (Greenspan).

2 vols. Ma'aleh Adumim, 1987-1988.

_____. *Iggerot ha-Rambam*. Ed. Yosef Kafah. Jerusalem: Mossad Harav Kook, 1972.

_____. *Mishneh Torah: The Book of Knowledge*. Transl. Moses Hyamson. Jerusalem: Feldheim, 1971.

_____. *Moreh ha-Nevukhim*. Transl. Judah al-Harizi. Ed. S. Scheier and S. Munk. 2 vols. Tel-Aviv: Mossad Harav Kook, circa 1965.

_____. *Moreh Nevukhim*. 2 vols. Transl. Michael Schwarz. Jerusalem: Tel-Aviv University Press, 2002.

_____. *Moreh Nevukhim*. Transl. Samuel ibn Tibbon. With commentary *Giv'at ha-Moreh* (by Solomon Maimon). Sulzbach, 1828.

_____. *Moreh ha-Nevukhim*. Transl. Yosef Kafah. 3 vols. Jerusalem: Mossad Harav Kook, 1972.

_____. *Pe'er ha-Dor*. Amsterdam, 1765.

_____. *Sefer ha-Mitsvot 'im Hasagot ha-Ramban*. Ed. C.B. Chavel. Jerusalem: Mossad Harav Kook, 1981.

_____. *Teshuvot ha-Rambam*. Ed. Alfred Freimann. Jerusalem: Mekize Nirdamim, 1934.

_____. *Teshuvot ha-Rambam*. Ed. Joshua Blau. 3 vols. Jerusalem: Mekitzei Nirdamim, 1958-1961.

Moses ben Nahman (Nahmanides). Commentary to Pentateuch. Ed. C.B. Chavel. 2 vols. Jerusalem: Mossad Harav Kook, 1959-1960.

_____. *Kitvei Rabbeinu Moshe ben Nahman*. Ed. C.B. Chavel. 2 vols. Jerusalem: Mossad Harav Kook, 1963-1964.

_____. *Sefer Iyov 'im Peirush ha-Ramban*. Commentary to Book of Job. Ed. Yehudah Leib Friedman. Israel: Feldheim, 2018.

_____. "Torat Hashem Temimah." In *Kitvei Rabbeinu Moshe ben Nahman*. vol. 1.

Moses of Coucy. *Sefer Mitsvot Gadol (SeMaG)*. Rome, before 1480.

Moshav Zekenim. Ed. Solomon David Sassoon. London, 1959.

Nahman ben Simhah, of Breslov. *Likkutei MOHaRaN*. Appended variants in Rabbi Nathan Sternhartz's manuscript. Ed. Nathan Tsevi Kenig. Jerusalem, 1985.

———. *Shir Na'im/Song of Delight*. Ed. David Sears and Bezalel Naor. Spring Valley, NY: Orot, 2005.

Nahmani, Moshe. "Mi Kan Hillel?" *Mussaf Shabbat, Makor Rishon*, 3 Ellul, 5771 (2.9.2011).

———. "She'areha Ne'ulim—Yeshivat Harav Kuk be-Yaffo." Available on the website www.shoresh.org.il. Dated 4/17/2012 or 25 Nissan, 5772.

———. *Shnei ha-Me'orot*. 2019

Naor, Bezalel. "Ascent and Descent in the Yom Kippur Rite: From the Hasidic Thought of Izbica-Radzyn." In *From A Kabbalist's Diary*. Spring Valley, NY: Orot, 2005.

———. *Avirin*. Jerusalem: Zur-Ot, 1980.

———. "The Curtains of the Tabernacle: R. Shelomo Zalman of Kopyst." In *Orot: A Multidisciplinary Journal of Judaism*, vol. 1 (5751/1991), pp. 33-41. Ed. Bezalel Naor.

———. *From A Kabbalist's Diary: Collected Essays*. Spring Valley, NY: Orot, 2005.

———. *Kabbalah and the Holocaust*. Spring Valley, NY: Orot, 2001.

———. *The Kabbalah of Relation: "We Would Have Learned the 'Way of the Earth' From the Cock"* (A Jewish Bestiary). Spring Valley, NY: Orot, 2012.

———. *Lev Atsal*. Commentary to Maimonides' *Sefer ha-Madda'*. n.p., 5733/1973.

———. *Lights of Prophecy/Orot ha-Nevu'ah*. New York: Union of Orthodox Jewish Congregations of America, 1990.

———. *The Limit of Intellectual Freedom: The Letters of Rav Kook*. Spring Valley, NY: Orot, 2011.

_____. *Mahol la-Tsaddikim*. Jerusalem and Monsey: Makhon RaMHaL/Orot, 2015.

_____. *Post-Sabbatian Sabbatianism*. Spring Valley, NY: Orot, 1999.

_____. "Rav Kook and Emmanuel Levinas on the 'Non-Existence' of God." In *Orot: A Multidisciplinary Journal of Judaism*, vol. 1 (5751/1991), pp. 1-11. Reprinted in Bezalel Naor, *From a Kabbalist's Diary: Collected Essays*.

_____. "*Reish Millin*—Mekorot ve-He'arot." In *Sinai* 97 (Nissan-Ellul 5745/1985), pp. 69-76. Also issued as *Zikhron RAYaH* (Memorial Volume on Rav Kook's Fiftieth *Yahrzeit*). Ed. Yitzhak Raphael. Jerusalem: Mossad Harav Kook, 1986.

_____. "*Shir Na'im* as a Reply to Maimonides." In Nachman of Breslov, *Shir Na'im/Song of Delight*. Ed. David Sears and Bezalel Naor. Spring Valley, NY: Orot, 2005, pp. 123-126.

_____. *Shod Melakhim*. Jerusalem: Makhon RaMHaL/Orot, 2017.

_____. *When God Becomes History: Historical Essays of Rabbi Abraham Isaac Hakohen Kook*. New York, NY: Kodesh, 2016.

_____. "'Zedonot na'asot ke-zakhuyot' be-mishnato shel Harav Kuk." In *'Ofer ha-Ayyalim: Sefer Zikaron le-ha-Kadosh 'Ofer Eliyahu Cohen*. Ed. Dani Kokhav (Koch). Jerusalem, 1994.

Nasr, Seyyed Hossein (Ed.).*The Study Quran: A New Translation and Commentary*. New York: HarperOne, 2015.

Nathan ben Yehiel of Rome. *'Arukh*. n.p. (Rome?), n.d. (circa 1477).

Nathan of Gaza. *Sefer ha-Beri'ah*. Ed. Leor Holzer. Jerusalem: Holzer, 2019.

Neiman, Yitzhak. *Zikhron Yitzhak*. Memorial volume. Jerusalem, 1999.

Neriyah, Moshe Tsevi. *Bi-Sdeh ha-RAYaH*. Tel-Aviv, 1991.

———. *Hayyei ha-RAYaH*. Tel-Aviv, 1983.

———. *Likkutei ha-Rayah*. Tel-Aviv, 1990.

———. *Mo'adei ha-Rayah*. 1st edition. Bnei Berak, 1991. 2nd edition. Jerusalem, 2015.

———. *Sihot ha-RAYaH*. 1st edition. Tel-Aviv, 1979. 2nd edition. Jerusalem, 2015.

———. *Tal ha-RAYaH*. Tel-Aviv, 1993.

Nietzsche, Friedrich. *Also Sprach Zarathustra*. Leipzig, 1883-1885. In English: *Thus Spoke Zarathustra*. In *Nietzsche*. Ed. Walter Kaufmann. New York: Viking Press, 1968.

———. *Die Geburt der Tragödie aus dem Geiste der Musik*. Leipzig, 1872. In English: *The Birth of Tragedy*. Edinburgh, 1909.

Nirenberg, David. *Anti-Judaism: The Western Tradition*. New York: W.W. Norton, 2013.

Nissim ben Reuben Gerondi. *Derashot ha-RaN*. Ed. Leon A. Feldman. Jerusalem: Shalem, 1973.

Offenberg, Sarah. "On Heresy and Polemics in Two Proverbs in *Meshal Haqadmoni*." Hebrew. *Jewish Thought* 1 (2019).

Otto, Rudolf. *Das Heilige*. Breslau, 1917. In English: *The Idea of the Holy*. [London]: Oxford University Press, 1923.

Ouaknin, Marc-Alain. *The Burnt Book: Reading the Talmud*. Transl. Llewelyn Brown. Princeton, 1995.

Pachter, Mordechai. "The Gaon's Kabbalah from the Perspective of Two Traditions." Hebrew. In *The Vilna Gaon and his Disciples*. Ed. M. Hallamish, Y. Rivlin and R. Shuchat. Ramat-Gan: Bar-Ilan University Press, 2003. pp. 119-136.

Palache, Hayyim. *Re'eh Hayyim*. On Pentateuch. Part One. Saloniki, 1860. Part Two. Izmir, 1865.

Pardo, David. *Maskil le-David*. Super-commentary to Rashi. Venice, 1760.

Pesikta Rabbati. Ed. Meir Ish-Shalom. Vienna, 1880.

Piekarz, Mendel. *Studies in Braslav Hasidism*. Hebrew. Jerusalem: Mossad Bialik, 1995.

Plato. *Republic*.

———.*Timaeus*

Plotski, Meir Dan. *Keli Hemdah*. Piotrków, 1906.

Pomeranchik, Aryeh. *Yehegeh ha-Aryeh*. Jerusalem, 1999.

Poppers, Meir. *Me'orei 'Or*. In *Me'orot Natan*. 1st edition. Frankfurt am Main, 1709. 2nd edition. Warsaw, 1867; photo offset in *Sifrei ha-'Arakhim be-Kabbalah*, Jerusalem, 1995.

———. *'Or Zaru'a*. Ed. Safrin and Sofer. Jerusalem: Hevrat Ahavat Shalom, 1986.

Porath, Israel. "*Harav A.Y. Kook z"l.*" In *Sefer ha-Do'ar: Mivhar ma'amarim la-yovel ha-shishim 5682-5742*. Ed. Miklishanski and Kabakoff. New York: Histadrut ha-[]Ivrit ba-Amerika, 1982.

———. *Mavo ha-Talmud* (*The Outline of the Talmud*). 7 vols. St. Louis, MO-New York, 1942-1960.

Price, Abraham Aaron. *Sefer Hasidim* with commentary *Mishnat Avraham*. 2 vols. Toronto, 1955; New York, 1960.

Ra'anan, Shalom Natan. *Be-Shemen Ra'anan*. Rabbi Natan Ra'anan-Kook Memorial Volume. Ed. Ben-Zion Shapira. 2 vols. Jerusalem: Makhon RZYH, 1990-1991.

Rabbinowicz, Raphael Nathan Nata. *Dikdukei Soferim*. Variae lectiones of Talmud. 16 vols. Munich, 1867-1886.

Rabinovitch, Nahum L. *Yad Peshutah*. Commentary to Maimonides' *Yad ha-Hazakah*. 21 vols. Jerusalem, 1984-2019.

Rabinowicz, Shelomo Hakohen, of Radomsk. *Tif'eret Shelomo*. 2 vols. Pentateuch; Festivals. Warsaw, 1867-1869. Reprinted

Jerusalem, 1992.

Rabinowitz, David Yitzhak Eizik, of Skolya-Vienna-Brooklyn. *Mekor ha-Berakhah*. On Tractate *Berakhot*. Brooklyn, 1967.

Rabinowitz, Zadok Hakohen, of Lublin. *Divrei Soferim*. Lublin, 1913; photo-offset B'nei Berak, 1967.

_____. *Dover Zedek*. Piotrków, 1911; photo-offset B'nei Berak, 1967.

_____. *Komets ha-Minhah*. Lublin, 1939; photo-offset B'nei Berak, 1967.

_____. *Mahshevot Haruts*. Piotrków, 1912; photo-offset Bnei Berak, 1967.

_____. *Peri Zaddik*. Commentary on Pentateuch. 5 vols. Lublin, 1901-1934; photo offset Jerusalem, 1972.

_____. *Poked 'Akarim*. Piotrków, 1922; photo-offset Bnei Berak, 1967.

_____. *Sefer ha-Zikhronot*. Appended to *Divrei Soferim*.

_____. *Sihat Mal'akhei ha-Sharet*. Lublin, 1927; photo offset B'nei Berak 1967.

_____. *Tsidkat ha-Tsaddik*. Lublin, 1902; Lublin, 1913, photo offset B'nei Berak 1967.

_____. *Yisrael Kedoshim*. Lublin, 1928; photo offset B'nei Berak 1967.

(Rabinowitz-Te'omim, Elijah David [ADeReT]). *Aharit ha-Shanim*. Warsaw, 1893.

Raccah, Mas'ud Hai. *Ma'aseh Rokah*. Commentary to *Mishneh Torah*. 3 vols. Venice-Livorno, 1742-1766. vol. 4. Tel-Aviv, 1964.

Rath, Meshulam. *She'elot u-Teshuvot Kol Mevaser*. Jerusalem: Mossad Harav Kook, 1955.

Rapoport, Chaim. *The Afterlife of Scholarship: A Critical Review of 'The Rebbe' by Samuel Heilman and Menachem Friedman*. 2011.

Raziel ha-Mal'akh. Amsterdam, 1701.

Ricchi, Immanuel Hai. *Yosher Levav*. Amsterdam, 1742.

Rivkin, Moshe Dov Baer. *Tif'eret Zion*. New York, 1975.

Roke'ah, El'azar. See *El'azar of Worms*.

Rosanes, Judah. *Mishneh le-Melekh*. Commentary to *Mishneh Torah*. Constantinople, 1731.

Rosen, Joseph, of Rogatchov and Dinaburg (Dvinsk). *Tsaphnat Pa'ne'ah*. Commentary to *Mishneh Torah*. Parts 1 and 2. Warsaw, 1902

———. *Tsafnat P'ane'ah*. Commentary to *Mishneh Torah*. Kuntres Hashlamah. Warsaw, 1909.

———. *Tsafnat P'ane'ah*. Commentary to *Mishneh Torah*. Mahadura Tinyana. Dvinsk, 1930.

———. *Tsafnat P'ane'ah*. Commentary to *Moreh Nevukhim*. Appended to Commentary to Pentateuch, vol. 6.

———. *Tsaphnat Pa'ne'ah*. Commentary to Pentateuch. Ed. Menahem Mendel Kasher. 6 vols. Jerusalem, 1960-1965.

———. *Tsaphnat P'ane'ah*. Tractate *Makkot*. Ed. Menahem Mendel Kasher. New York: Shulsinger Bros., 1959.

———. *She'elot u-Teshuvot Tsafnat Pa'ne'ah ha-Hadashot*. 3 vols. Modi'in 'Ilit, 2012.

Rosenberg, Shalom. *Darkhei Shalom* (Shalom Rosenberg Festschrift). Ed. Benjamin Ish-Shalom. Jerusalem, 2007.

Rosenfeld, Ben Zion. "*Yahaso shel ha-RAYaH Kook le-Hakhmei ha-Mizrah bi-Tekufat Yaffo 5664-5674 (1904-1914)*" ("Ha-Rav Avraham Isaac HaCohen Kook and his Attitude Regarding the Sephardi Sages During His Stay in Jaffa567–5664 1914–1904]4]"). *Libi ba-Mizrah* (*My Heart Is in the East*) 1 (2019), pp. 287-290.

Rosenwasser, Moshe Yehudah. "*Peirush ha-RaMBaN 'al ha-Torah le-'or ha-'imut 'im ha-Notsrut*." *HaMa'ayan* 47:2 (Tevet

5767), pp. 19-32.

Rotenberg, Moshe. *Bikkurei Aviv*. St. Louis, MO, 1942.

Rutta, Leibel. *Reshimot Lev*. Informal talks of Rabbi Isaac Hutner. 2 vols. softcover. Brooklyn, 1997. 2 vols. hardcover. Brooklyn, NY, 2000.

Sa'adyah ben Joseph al-Fayyumi. *Emunot ve-De'ot*. Ed. Yosef Kafah. Jerusalem: Sura/Yeshiva University, 1970.

Safran, Bezalel. "Maimonides on Free Will, Determinism and Esotericism." In *Porat Yosef: Studies Presented to Rabbi Dr. Joseph Safran*. Ed. Bezalel Safran and Eliyahu Safran. Hoboken, New Jersey: Ktav, 1992.

Saks, Jeffrey. "Rabbi Joseph B. Soloveitchik and the Israeli Chief Rabbinate: Biographical Notes (1959-60)." *B.D.D.* 17, September 2006, pp. 45-67.

Samson of Ostropolya. *Nitsutsei Shimshon*. Ed. Avraham Ya'akov Bombach. Jerusale, 2013.

Schäfer, Peter. *Synopse zur Hekhalot-Literatur*. Tübingen 1981.

Schirmann, Hayyim. "Maimonides and Hebrew Poetry." Hebrew. *Moznayim* 3 (1935):433-436.

Schneersohn, Isaac. *Leben un Kamf fun Yiden in Tsarishen Rusland 1905-1917*. Paris, 1968.

Schneersohn, Menahem Mendel, of Lubavitch ("*Tsemah Tsedek*"). *Derekh Mitsvotekha: Ta'amei ha-Mitsvot*. Poltava, 1911; photo offset Kefar Habad, 1973.

———. *'Or ha-Torah. Derush Kan Tsipor*. In *Tetse*, vol. 2, pp. 924-925.

———. *Reshimot 'al Shir ha-Shirim, Rut, Kohelet*. Brooklyn, NY: Kehot, 1960.

Schneersohn, Shalom Dov Baer. *Kuntres u-Ma'ayan mi-Beit Hashem*. Brooklyn: Kehot, 1958.

———. In *'Or la-Yesharim* (anti-Zionist collection). Warsaw, 1900.

Schneerson, Isaac Dov Baer, of Liadi. *Siddur 'im Peirush Ma-HaRID.* 2 vols. Berdichev, 1913; photo offset Kefar Habad, 1991.

Schneerson, Levi Isaac. *Likkutei Levi Yitzhak: Iggerot Kodesh.* Brooklyn: Kehot, 2004.

Schneerson, Menahem Mendel, of Brooklyn. *Likkutei Sihot,* vol. 10. Brooklyn: Kehot, 1981.

———. *Likkutei Sihot* (Yiddish). vol. 24. Israel, 2006.

Schneerson, Shelomo Zalman, of Kopyst. Letters to Don Tumarkin of Rogatchov. In Mordechai Menashe Laufer, *Ha-Melekh bi-Mesibo,* vol. 2.

Schneerson, Shemariah Noah, of Bobruisk. *Kuntres me-Admo"r shelit"a mi-Bobruisk: Teshuvot nitshiyot va-amitiyot 'al Kuntres Admo"r shelit"a de-Libavitz.* 1907.

———. *Shemen la-Ma'or.* 2 vols. Kefar Habad, 1964.

Scholem, Gershom (Gerhard). *Abraham Cohen Herrera: Leben, Werk und Wirkung.* 1978.

———. *Das Buch Bahir.* Leipzig, 1923.

———. *Jewish Gnosticism, Merkabah Mysticism and Talmudic Tradition.* New York, 1965.

———. *Major Trends in Jewish Mysticism.* New York: Schocken, 1971.

———. *On the Kabbalah and Its Symbolism.* New York: Schocken Books, 1970.

———. *On the Mystical Shape of the Godhead.* New York: Schocken Books, 1991.

———. *Origins of the Kabbalah.* Princeton University Press, 1990.

———. *Sabbatai Sevi: The Mystical Messiah.* Princeton, NJ: Princeton University Press, 1975.

———. "Two new theological texts by Abraham Cardozo." Hebrew. *Sefunot,* vols. 3-4 (1960).

Schreiber, Moses. *She'elot u-Teshuvot Hatam Sofer, Orah Hayy-*

im. Pressburg, 1855.

———. *Torat Moshe*. Commentary to Pentateuch. Ed. Shim'on Sofer. Pressburg, 1906. Photo-offset Brooklyn, NY, 1980.

Schwartz, Hayyim Avihu. *Mi-Tokh ha-Torah ha-Go'elet*. Teachings of Rabbi Tsevi Yehudah Kook. 4 vols. Jerusalem: Zur-Ot 1989.

Schwarzschild, Steven. "Isaac Hutner." In *Interpreters of Judaism in the Late Twentieth Century*. Ed. Steven T. Katz. Washington, D.C.: B'nai B'rith Books, 1993.

Schweid, Eliezer. "Prophetic Mysticism in Twentieth-Century Jewish Thought." *Modern Judaism*, May 1994.

Seder 'Olam Rabbah. Rabbi Yose ben Halafta. Ed. Moshe Ya'ir Weinstock. With commentary *"Seder Zemanim."* B'nei Berak, 1990.

Seeman, Don. "Evolutionary Ethics: The *Taamei Hamitzvot* of Rav Kook." *Hakirah* 26 (Spring 2019), pp. 13-55.

Sefer Yetzirah: The Book of Creation. Ed. Aryeh Kaplan. York Beach, Maine: Samuel Weiser, 1997.

Seidman, Naomi. *Faithful Renderings: Jewish-Christian Difference and the Politics of Translation*. Chicago: University of Chicago Press, 2006.

Shapira, Kalonymos Kalmish. *Hakhsharat ha-Avrekhim*. Jerusalem: Feldheim, 2001.

———. *Hovat ha-Talmidim*. Jerusalem, 1990.

Shapiro, Marc B. *Changing the Immutable: How Orthodox Judaism Rewrites Its History*. Oxford: Littman, 2015.

———. (Shapiro, Melekh.) *Iggerot Malkhei Rabbanan*. Scranton, 2019.

———. *Saul Lieberman and the Orthodox*. Scranton, PA: University of Scranton Press, 2006.

———. *Studies in Maimonides and His Interpreters*. Scranton,

PA: University of Scranton Press, 2008.

Sheleg, Yair. "Goodbye, Mr. Chouchani." *Haaretz*, Sept. 26, 2003.

Shilat, Yitzhak. *"Kelum teshuvot ha-Rambam le-hakhmei Lunel mezuyafot hen?"* In *Sefer Zikaron le-Harav Yitzhak Nissim*. Ed. Meir Benayahu. vol. 2. Jerusalem, 1985.

Shinawa (Sieniawa), Samuel. *Ramatayim Tsofim*. Commentary to *Tanna de-Vei Eliyahu*. Ed. Shmuel Tsevi Zinger. Jerusalem, 2016.

Shmalo, Gamliel. *"Radikaliyut filosofit be-'olam ha-yeshivot: Harav Yitzhak Hutner 'al ha-Sho'ah"* ("Philosophical Radicalism in the World of the *Yeshivot*: Rabbi Isaac Hutner on the Holocaust"). *Hakirah*, vol. 19.

Shneur Zalman ben Baruch, of Liadi. *Likkutei Torah*. Leviticus-Deuteronomy. Kehot: Kefar Habad, 1972.

⎯⎯⎯. *Likkutei Torah* (to first three portions of Genesis). Vilna, 1884.

⎯⎯⎯. *Ma'amrei Admor Hazaken—Et-halekh Liozhna*. Brooklyn, 2012.

⎯⎯⎯. *Siddur 'im DAH*. Ed. Dov Baer Shneuri of Lubavitch. New York, NY: Kehot, 1971.

⎯⎯⎯. *Tanya (Sefer shel Beinonim)*. Vilna, 1937.

⎯⎯⎯. *Torah 'Or*. Genesis-Exodus. Brooklyn: Kehot, 1972.

Shneur, Zalman (pen name of Shneur Zalkind). *Feter Zhoma*. Vilna: Kletzkin, 1930.

⎯⎯⎯. *Shklover Yidden*. Vilna: Kletzkin, 1929.

Shneuri, Dov Baer. *Be'urei ha-Zohar*. Brooklyn, NY: Kehot, 2015.

⎯⎯⎯. *Sha'arei Orah*. Johannisburg, n.d.; photo offset Brooklyn, NY: Kehot, 1979.

⎯⎯⎯. *Torat Hayyim, Bereshit*. Brooklyn: Kehot, 1993. *Shemot*. Facsimile of manuscript of R. Shmuel Sofer. 3rd printing. Brooklyn: Kehot, 1980.

Shurkin, Mikhel Zalman. *Harerei Kedem*. Teachings of Rabbi Yosef Dov Soloveitchik of Boston on Festivals. 2 vols. Jerusalem, 2000, 2004.

Shvat, Ari Yitzhak. "*Iggeret Harav Kook be-Nose' Talmud Torah le-Nashim*." In *Me'orot li-Yehudah* (Rabbi Yehudah Feliks Festschrift). Ed. M. Rehimi. Elkanah, 2012.

Siddur Eitz Chaim: The Complete Artscroll Siddur (Nusach Sefard). Transl. Nosson Scherman. Brooklyn, NY: Mesorah Publications, 1985.

Sklarevski, Paulina Sarah. "*Hiddush ha-Kedushah: Ha-RAYaH Kook bi-re'i tefisat ha-tsiyonut shel Buber be-sefer 'Bein 'Am le-Artso.'*" Term Paper. Jerusalem: Hebrew University, July 31, 2013. Available at www.academia.edu.

Solomon ben Abraham ibn Adret (RaShBA). *Ma'amar 'al Yishmael*. Ed. Bezalel Naor. Spring Valley, NY: Orot, 2008.

_____. *She'elot u-Teshuvot Rabbeinu Shelomo ben Adret*. Rome, circa 1470.

Soloveichik, Ahron. *Perah Mateh Aharon*. Novellae to Maimonides. 2 vols: *Sefer Madda'*; *Sefer Ahavah*. Jerusalem, 1997, 1999.

Soloveichik, Moses and Soloveitchik, Yosef Dov. *Hiddushei ha-GRaM ve-ha-GRYD: 'Inyenei Kodashim*. Jerusalem, 1993.

Soloveitchik, Haym. "Interview with Professor Haym Soloveitchik by Rabbi Yair Hoffman." *Five Towns Jewish Times*, Wednesday, January 8th, 2014. Available at: http://www.theyeshivaworld.com/news/headlines-breaking-stories/209453/interview-with-professor-haym-soloveitchik-by-rabbi-yair-hoffman.html

Soloveitchik, Hayyim, of Brisk. *Hiddushei ha-GRaH he-Hadash*. Vol. 3. Stencil. Jerusalem, 1967.

_____. *Hiddushei ha-GRaH he-Hadash 'al ha-Shas*. B'nei

Berak: Mishor, 2008.

———. *Hiddushei Rabbeinu Hayyim Halevi*. Novellae to *Mishneh Torah*. 1936.

———. *Kitvei Rabbeinu Hayyim Halevi mi-Ketav Yad Kodsho (Tagbuch)*. Ed. Yitzhak Abba Lichtenstein. Jerusalem, 2018.

Soloveitchik, Joseph Baer. *And From There You Shall Seek*. Translation of *"U-Vikkashtem mi-Sham*. Transl. Naomi Goldblum. Jersey City: Ktav, 2008.

———. *Halakhic Man*. Translation of *"Ish ha-Halakhah."* Transl. Lawrence J. Kaplan. Philadelphia: Jewish Publication Society of America, 1983.

———. *Maimonides between Philosophy and Halakhah: Rabbi Joseph B. Soloveitchik's Lectures on the* Guide of the Perplexed. Ed. Lawrence J. Kaplan. Brooklyn: Ktav; Jerusalem: Urim, 2016.

———. *"A Tribute to the Rebbetzin of Talne." Tradition* 17:2 (Spring 1978).

See also *Soloveitchik, Yosef Dov, of Boston*

Soloveitchik, Yitzhak Ze'ev, of Brisk and Jerusalem. *Hiddushei Maran RYZ ha-Levi 'al ha-RaMBaM*. Jerusalem, 1962.

———. *Hiddushei Maran RYZ Halevi 'al ha-Torah*. Jerusalem, 1962.

———. *Reshimot Talmidim me-Rabbi Yitzhak Ze'ev Halevi Soloveitchik 'al Seder ha-Torah*. Ed. Raphael Kook. Rehovot: Da'at Sofrim, 2016.

Soloveitchik, Yosef Dov, of Boston. *Harerei Kedem. See Shurkin, Mikhel Zalman.*

———. *Iggerot ha-GRYD Halevi*. Jerusalem, 2001.

———. *"Ish ha-Halakhah." Talpiyot* 1:3-4 (5704-5/1944).

———. *Kuntres be-'Inyan 'Avodat Yom ha-Kippurim*. Ed. Aharon Lichtenstein. Jerusalem, 1986.

———. *"Mah Dodekh mi-Dod?"* Eulogy of Rabbi Yitzhak

Ze'ev Soloveitchik. In *Ha-Do'ar* (1964), pp. 752-759; and in *Divrei Hagut ve-Ha'arakhah*. Jerusalem, 1982, pp. 57-97.

———. *Reshimot Shi'urei Maran ha-GRYD Ha-Levi: Shavu'ot—Nedarim*. 2 vols. Ed. Tsevi Yosef Reichman. Union City, NJ, 1993, 1996.

———. *Reshimot Shi'urei Maran ha-GRYD Ha-Levi: Sukkah*. Ed. Tsevi Yosef Reichman. New York, 1990.

———. *Shi'urim le-Zekher Abba Mari*. 2 vols. Jerusalem: Mossad Harav Kook, 2002.

———. "*U-Vikkashtem mi-Sham*." *Hadarom*, 1978.

See also *Soloveitchik, Joseph Baer*.

Soloveitchik, Yosef Dov Baer, of Brisk. *Beit Halevi*. On Genesis and Exodus. Warsaw, 1884.

———. *She'elot u-Teshuvot Beit Halevi*. 3 vols. Vilna, 1863; Warsaw, 1874-1891.

Spiegel, Ya'akov Shmuel. *'Ammudim be-Toledot ha-Sefer ha-'Ivri: Hagahot u-Magihim*. Ramat Gan: Bar-Ilan University Press, 2005

Spielman, Mordechai. *Tif'eret Tsevi*. On *Zohar*. 6 vols. Brooklyn, 1981-2003.

Spira, Hayyim El'azar, of Munkatch. *Sha'ar Yissakhar 'al Mo'adim*. Brooklyn, NY, 1992.

Spira, Tsevi Elimelech, of Dynów. *Igra de-Pirka*. Lvov, 1858.

Sternhartz, Nathan, of Nemirov and Breslov. *Hayyei MO-HaRaN*. Jerusalem: Keren R. Israel Dov Odesser, n.d.

——— (attributed to—). *Kin'at Hashem Tseva'ot*. Iasi or Lvov, 1852.

———. *Likkutei Halakhot*. On *Shulhan 'Arukh*. [Iasi]-Zolkiew, 1843-1849.

———. *Sihot ha-Ran*. B'nei Berak, 1976.

———. *Yemei ha-Tela'ot*. See Hazan, Abraham ben Nahman,

of Tulchin.

Strashun, Samuel. *Hiddushei RaShaSh*. Novellae to Talmud. Published in Vilna edition of Talmud.

Strauss, Leo. "How To Begin To Study *The Guide of the Perplexed*." In Moses Maimonides, *The Guide of the Perplexed*. Transl. Shlomo Pines. Chicago: University of Chicago Press, 1963.

———. "Notes on Maimonides' *Book of Knowledge*." In *Studies in Mysticism and Religion Presented to Gershom G. Scholem*. Ed. Urbach, Werblowsky, and Wirszubski. Jerusalem, 1967.

———. *Persecution and the Art of Writing*. Glencoe, Illinois: The Free Press, 1952.

———. *Philosophie und Gesetz*. Berlin, 1935.

———. "Quelques remarques sur la science politique de Maimonide et de Farabi." *Revue des Etudes Juives*, C (1936), pp. 1-37.

Swartz, Michael D. *Scholastic Magic: Ritual and Revelation in Early Jewish Mysticism*. Princeton: Princeton University Press, 1996.

Swift, Jonathan. *Gulliver's Travels*. London, 1726.

Ta-Shma, Israel. *Ha-Nigleh she-ba-Nistar*. Tel-Aviv, 1995.

———. *Rabbi Zerahyah Halevi (Ba'al ha-Ma'or) u-B'nei Hugo*. Jerusalem: Mossad Harav Kook, 1992.

Tchernichovsky, Shaul. "Before the Statue of Apollo." Poem. 1899.

Tchernowitz, Chaim. *Pirkei Hayyim*. New York, 1954.

Tchetchik, Ze'ev Dov. *Torat Ze'ev: Zevahim*. Zikhron Moshe, 1985.

Telushkin, Nissan. *Tahorat Mayim*. Brooklyn, NY: Kehot, 1990.

Tishby, Isaiah. *Mishnat ha-Zohar*. vol. 1. 2nd printing with corrections. Jerusalem: Mossad Bialik, 1949.

BIBLIOGRAPHY

Tobi, Yosef. *Between Hebrew and Arabic Poetry: Studies in Spanish Medieval Hebrew Poetry.* Leiden: Brill, 2010.

Tsemah, Jacob. *Kol be-Ramah.* Korets, 1785. Jerusalem: Makhon B'nei Yissachar, 2001. Ed. Eliyahu Attiah.

———. *Nagid u-Metsaveh.* Lublin, 1881.

———. *Zohar ha-Raki'a.* Korets, 1785.

Tukachinsky, Yehiel Mikhel. *Ha-Yomam be-Kadur ha-Arets.* Jerusalem, 1943.

Turbowitz, Ze'ev Wolf. *Tif'eret Ziv.* Brooklyn: Moinester Publishing Company, 1939.

———. *Tif'eret Ziv.* Warsaw, 1896.

———. *Ziv Mishneh.* Warsaw, 1904.

Urbach, Ephraim Elimelech. *Ba'alei ha-Tosafot.* 2 vols. Jerusalem: Bialik Institute, 1995.

Verman, Mark. *The Books of Contemplation: Medieval Jewish Mystical Sources.* Albany: State University of New York, 1992.

Vico, Giambattista. *Scienza Nuova.* 1725.

Vidas, Elijah de. *Reshit Hokhmah.* Munkatch, n.d. [1895].

Vital, Hayyim. *'Ets Hayyim.* Ed. Menahem Menkhin Heilprin. 3 vols. Warsaw, 1891; stereotype Jerusalem, 1910, photo offset Jerusalem, 1975.

———. *Likkutei Torah.* Vilna, 1880; photo offset Jerusalem, 1972.

———. *Peri 'Ets Hayyim.* Dubrovna, 1804.

———. *Sefer ha-Derushim.* Ed. Ya'akov Moshe Hillel. Jerusalem: Ahavat Shalom, 1996.

———. *Sefer ha-Likkutim.* Ed. Ze'ev Wolf Ashkenazi. Jerusalem, 1913.

———. *Sha'ar ha-Gilgulim.* Jerusalem: Keren Hotsa'at Sifrei Rabbanei Bavel, 1990.

———. *Sha'ar ha-Hakdamot.* Ed. Menahem Menkhin Heilprin. Jerusalem, 1909.

———. *Sha'ar ha-Kavvanot*. Ed. Menahem Menkhin Heilprin. Jerusalem, 1902.

———. *Sha'ar ha-Mitsvot*. Ed. Ze'ev Wolf Ashkenazi. Jerusalem, 1905.

Volkovski, Elijah Mordechai. *Hezyonei Amatsyahu*. (Additional title: *Shnei ha-Me'orot ha-Gedolim*.) Keidan: Movshovitz and Kagan, 1934. Photo offset in Moshe Yehiel Zuriel. *Otserot ha-RAYaH*. vol. 2. Tel-Aviv, 1988.

Wasserman, Abraham. *Koré ha-Degel*. 2020.

Wasserman, Elhanan Bunim. "*Divrei Aggadah*," appended to *Kovets He'arot le-Masekhet Yevamot*. Piotrków, 1932.

Waxman, Meyer. "*Ha-Gaon mi-Vilna*." In *Sefer ha-Shanah li-Yehudei Amerika*, vols. X-XI (1949).

Weinberg, Abraham, of Slonim. *Hesed le-Avraham*. Commentary to Prophets. Jerusalem, 1986.

Weinberg, Yehiel Ya'akov. *Kitvei ha-Ga'on Rabbi Yehiel Ya'akov Weinberg*. Ed. Melekh Shapiro. 2 vols. Scranton, 2003.

Weintraub, Israel Elijah. *Nefesh Eliyahu: Hakdamot u-She'arim*. n.p., 2002.

———. *Nefesh Eliyahu 'al Sifra di-Tseni'uta 'im Be'ur ha-GRA*. n.p., n.d.2012]].

Wengrover, Yedidyah. *R' Shem Tov Geffen*. Metula: Nezer David, 2017.

Wolberstein, Hilah. *Harav ha-Nazir: Ish ki yafli'*. Jerusalem: Makhon Nezer David, 2017.

Wolfson, Elliot R. *Through A Speculum That Shines: Vision and Imagination in Medieval Jewish Mysticism*. Princeton: Princeton University Press, 1994.

Yahuda, A.S. "A Contribution to Qur'an and Hadith Interpretation." *Ignace Goldziher Memorial Volume*, Part I. Ed. Samuel Löwinger and Joseph Somogyi. Budapest, 1948.

Yaron, Zevi. *Mishnato shel Harav Kook* (*The Philosophy of Rabbi Kook*). Jerusalem: W.Z.O., 1974.

Yom Tov ben Abraham Asevilli. *Hiddushei ha-RITBA*. Tractate *Yoma*. Constantinople, 1754; Berlin, 1860; Ed. Eliyahu Lichtenstein. Jerusalem: Mossad Harav Kook, 1976.

Yosef Hayyim of Baghdad (*"Ben Ish Hai"*). *Benayahu*. On Legends of Talmud. 3 vols. Jerusalem, 1998.

———. *Ben Yehoyada'*. On Legends of Talmud. 4 vols. Jerusalem, 1998.

Yosha, Nissim. *Myth and Metaphor: Abraham Cohen Herrera's Philosophic Interpretation of Lurianic Kabbalah* Hebrew. Jerusalem: Magnes, 1994.

Zeilberger, Benjamin. *Nahalat Binyamin: Bikkurim*. Jerusalem, 2016.

Zeitlin, Hillel. *Be-Hevyon ha-Neshamah* (*In the Hiding Place of the Soul*). In *Netivot*, vol. 1. Warsaw: Ahisefer, 1913, pp. 205-235.

———. *Hasidic Spirituality for a New Era: The Religious Writings of Hillel Zeitlin*. Ed. Arthur Green. Paulist Press: Mahwah, NJ, 2012.

———. *Rabbi Nahman of Bratslav: World Weariness and Longing for the Messiah: Two Essays by Hillel Zeitlin*. Hebrew. Introduction and notes Jonatan Meir. Jerusalem, 2006.

Zevin, Shelomo Yosef. *Ha-Mo'adim ba-Halakhah*. Tel-Aviv: A[braham] Zioni, 1953.

———. *Le-'Or ha-Halakhah*. 2nd edition. Jerusalem: Beit Hillel, n.d. [c.1980].

———. *Soferim u-Sefarim*. Tel-Aviv: A[braham] Ziyoni, 1959.

Ziemba, Menahem. *Tots'ot Hayyim*. Warsaw, 1921; photo offset Brooklyn, 1976.

Zilber, Yitzhak. *To Remain a Jew*. Transl. Sherry Dimarsky. New

York: Feldheim, c. 2010.

Zimler, Richard. *The Last Kabbalist of Lisbon*. Woodstock, NY: The Overlook Press, 1998.

Zimmer, Yitzhak (Eric). *"Tenuhot u-tenu'ot ha-guf bi-she'at Keri'at Shema'."* In *Asufot* 8 (1994).

Zimmerman, Abraham Isaac Halevi, of Krementchug. Novellae on Maimonides' *Mishneh Torah*. 2 vols. *Hiddushei ha-RAYaH*. Jerusalem, 1988.

Zimmerman, Chaim. *Agan ha-Sahar*. New York, 1955.

———. *Agra la-Yesharim*. Jerusalem, 1983.

———. *Binyan Halakhah*. Novellae on *Mishneh Torah*. New York, 1942.

Zinberg, Israel. *A History of Jewish Literature*. 12 vols. Transl. Bernard Martin. Cleveland: Case Western Reserve University, 1972-1978.

Zitrin, Mendel. *Shivhei Tsaddikim*. Warsaw, 1884.

Ziyoni, Menahem. *Sefer Ziyoni*. Cremona.

Zohar. Pritzker edition. 12 vols. vols. 1-9 ed. Daniel Matt. vol. 10 ed. Nathan Wolski. vol. 11 ed. Joel Hecker. vol. 12 ed. Nathan Wolski and Joel Hecker. Stanford, California: Stanford University Press, 2004-2017.

Zohar. Ed. Reuven Margaliyot. 3 vols. Jerusalem: Mossad Harav Kook, 1940-1946.

Zohar Hadash. Ed. Reuven Margaliyot. Jerusalem: Mossad Harav Kook, 1953.

www.ingramcontent.com/pod-product-compliance
Lightning Source LLC
Chambersburg PA
CBHW030106240426
43661CB00001B/31